Microeconomic Theory

Second Revised and Enlarged Edition

R.K. Mandal

ATLANTIC
PUBLISHERS & DISTRIBUTORS (P) LTD

Published by

ATLANTIC

PUBLISHERS & DISTRIBUTORS (P) LTD

7/22, Ansari Road, Darya Ganj, New Delhi-110002
Phones : +91-11-40775252, 40775214, 23273880, 23275880
Fax: +91-11-23285873
Web: www.atlanticbooks.com
E-mail: orders@atlanticbooks.com

First Edition 2007, 2018
Second Revised and Enlarged Edition 2022

Printed & bound in India by Atlantic Print Services

Dedicated to
my mother
Smt. Nandarani Mandal

Foreword

Microeconomics lays the basic foundation of the understanding of economics. A good grasp of microeconomics is vital for decision-making and understanding how a modern economy works. Microeconomics may become an exciting and dynamic subject for students if they can appreciate its relevance and usefulness.

Several books have been written on microeconomics by some outstanding authors who responded to these needs and these books are readily available in the market. However, these books differ widely in approaches, expositions, and analyses. Undergraduate students fail to make a synthesis of these approaches and analyses. Consequently, they often get confused and their love for microeconomics withers away.

Herein lies the relevance and usefulness of the book, *Microeconomic Theory*. This book is the outcome of long teaching experience of Dr. R.K. Mandal who has been experimenting on innovative teaching methods for the last two decades. The teaching excellence and experience that he has gained over time enabled him to bring out this book which may appear as a welcome relief for students of economics. This book is expected to give them an opportunity to gain in-depth understanding of the core of microeconomics.

The author has demonstrated his skill in presenting chapters on Consumption, Production, Markets, and Distribution. He deserves appreciation for his lucid but valuable presentation of chapters on 'General Equilibrium' and 'Input-Output Analysis'.

This book has been written in accordance with the undergraduate syllabus. However, graduate students of

Economics under different universities in India will find the book equally helpful.

Another unique feature of this book needs to be stressed upon. This book provides the service of both Text and Reference books at the same time. Thus, the author has rendered a valuable service for the cause of 'Teaching' and 'Taught' through the publication of this book. I wish him success in this endeavour which is his legitimate due.

Dr. Chandan K. Mukhopadhyay
Professor, Department of Economics
North Bengal University
Darjeeling, West Bengal

Preface to the Second Edition

The present edition is thoroughly revised and updated version incorporating the latest literature on the subject. Errors, if any, have been rectified and two new chapters (Chapter-1 and Chapter-2) have been incorporated with the thirteen chapters of the previous edition, making total fifteen chapters in this volume. Chapter-4 has also been updated and enlarged.

While I have spared no effort to improve the book both qualitatively and quantitatively, I believe that it is ultimate privilege of the readers to act as the judges. Basically, I believe that learning is a never-ending continuous process, the search must go without limit. In this case, the suggestions of the readers are very important and helpful. Consequently, these will always be appreciated and welcomed. I will be happy if the readers of the book are benefited.

Last but not the least, I express my deep gratefulness to Dr. K.R. Gupta, founder of Atlantic Publishers and Distributors Pvt. Ltd., who has inspired me to edit the book in time.

Ram Krishna Mandal

Preface to the First Edition

Primarily designed as a textbook for both graduate and undergraduate students, the present book provides an in-depth analysis of the essentials of microeconomics. It has a good balance in terms of conventional and modern topics. Beginning with an elucidation of fundamental concepts, the book deals in detail the varied theories under microeconomics in an easily accessible manner. Discussion is clear and accurate, employing diagrammatic presentations and mathematical tools and techniques wherever necessary so as to facilitate easy understanding of the topics. The use of engaging examples drawn on real world applications would further help students in grasping the ideas in no time. Besides, each unit contains model questions at its end for quick revision and self-assessment by the students. I have tried my best to keep this book as brief as possible. From my experience, I know that lengthy topics are less likely to be read. So, I have tried to give the clearest, most up-to-date, and most accessible course in the fewest possible words.

No book deals with all the topics prescribed by the Indian universities in a handy volume. This book has been designed primarily to meet the syllabi in a single handy volume of many universities in India in general and in North-East in particular. While writing this book, I have gone through the syllabi and examination papers of most of the universities where the subject is taught. The book is undoubtedly concise, comprehensible, and dependable, having a wide coverage of the syllabus. I hope that this book will find favour of undergraduate students of B.A. and B.Com. classes. It will ease the problems of the students. However, to enhance the utility of the book and make it more informative, the readers can send their comments and suggestions which will be incorporated in the subsequent editions of the book. Suggestions for improvement would be thankfully acknowledged.

I take this opportunity to convey my sincere gratitude to S. Ibomcha Meetei who worked hard to compose this book; without his help this book could not have been possible.

I acknowledge my sincere gratitude to Prof. Chandan K. Mukhopadhyay, Department of Economics, North Bengal University, Darjeeling District, West Bengal, who has written a valuable foreword for this book.

I am taking this opportunity to express my gratitude to my colleagues, especially Dr. S.D. Jha, Head, Department of Economics, Dera Natung Government College, Itanagar, Arunachal Pradesh, who has helped me immensely in accomplishing this great task.

Last but not least, I express my gratitude to Dr. K.R. Gupta, Chairman, M/s. Atlantic Publishers & Distributors (P) Ltd., who has taken keen interest in the publication of this book in time.

Ram Krishna Mandal

Contents

Chapter 1

Fundamental Concepts

UNLIMITED WANTS

In Economics, want means the desire to have a necessary or a luxury good. For survival or for comforts or for luxuries consumer needs some goods and services. By nature, human wants an endless number of things but there is a limited amount of resources to fulfill these wants. When a particular want is satisfied, another want arises. That is why, human wants are unlimited. Unlimited wants essentially mean that people never get enough, that there is always something else that they would like to have. When combined with limited resources, unlimited wants result in the fundamental problem of scarcity. A basic condition of human existence which means that people are never totally satisfied with the quantity and variety of goods and services, he consumes. It means that people never get enough, that there is always something else that they would want or need. People always want and need more than they have. Throughout history, there is no documented case of anyone ever becoming fully, completely, and absolutely satisfied.

Features of Wants

1. Due to the existence of unlimited human wants, all wants cannot be satisfied altogether. Hence, wants are to be classified into immediate necessities and postponables. Some wants are most urgent and have to be met first, while some wants are less urgent and hence can be postponed.

2. Certain wants are complement of each other. If one want is satisfied, another want is to be satisfied. For example, want of motor vehicle is satisfied, want of petrol is to be satisfied. In this case motor vehicle and petrol are complementary.
3. There are some wants, which compete with each other. These wants cannot be satisfied at a time due to scarcity of resources. Hence urgent wants are to be satisfied first and then less important wants are to be satisfied.
4. Differences in wants arise due to differences in space and time. It means that with change in place and time, wants are also changed. Suppose, in cold places, hot drinks are demanded and *vice versa*.
5. Due to demonstration effect, wants are to be created for many items.

RESOURCE SCARCITY

Resource Scarcity was the most controversial topic for respondents when considering which world issues are currently over or underestimated by the general public. This debate essentially encompasses the argument about whether or not political analysts are fear-mongering when they make dire resource predictions. As a trend, resource scarcity rose in importance from 7th to 4th place since 2011, with the bulk of concern coming from North American respondents. The pressures of population growth, economic growth and climate change are placing incredible stress on finite, non-renewable resources such as fossil fuels and minerals.

Therefore, Resource scarcity is the lack of availability of necessary supplies required to maintain life, or a specific quality of life, and is one of the fundamental ideas that economics is built on. Scarcity is the primary problem that comes about with economics due to the fact that human wants are unlimited in quantity, but the various resources we have available on our planet to fill human needs are limited and therefore must be rationed and careful choices must be made in distribution of resources.

In economics, the principles of scarcity and choice are important because without them economics would not exist. Scarcity and choice are what make economics an important skill to master. This is because in economics, a scarcity of resources means we must make wise choices as to how we distribute limited resources. This involves a tradeoff, or means we must give something up. So, ideally, we must choose to give resources to things which produce best results.

Scarcity refers to the limited availability of a commodity, which may be in demand in the market. It refers to a gap between limited resources and theoretically limitless wants. The notion of scarcity is that there is never enough of something to satisfy all conceivable human wants.

CHOICE

Choice means the act of choosing. But in Economics, it bears a significant meaning. Choice involves decision making. It can include judging the merits of multiple options and selecting one or more of them. Most people regard having choices as a good thing, though a severely limited or artificially restricted choice can lead to discomfort with choosing, and possibly an unsatisfactory outcome. In contrast, a choice with excessively numerous options may lead to confusion, and indifference in an unstructured existence and the illusion that choosing an object necessarily leads to the control of that object, can cause psychological problems.

OPPORTUNITY COST

Opportunity costs are fundamental costs in economics and are used in computing cost benefit analysis of a project. Such costs, however, are not recorded in the account books but are recognized in decision making by computing the cash outlays and their resulting profit or loss.

Opportunity cost refers to a benefit that a person could have received, but gave up to take another course of action. Stated differently, an opportunity cost represents an alternative given up when a decision is made. This cost is, therefore, most relevant for two mutually exclusive events. In investing, it is the difference in return between a chosen investment and one that is necessarily passed up.

Therefore, the concept of opportunity cost occupies a very important place in modern economic analysis. The opportunity cost of any good is in context of the next best alternative good which is sacrificed. The factors which are used for the manufacture of a car may also be used for the production of equipment for the military. The opportunity cost of production of a car is the output of the military equipment foregone or sacrificed, which could have been produced with the same amount of factors that have gone into the making of a car. It can be clearer from the following example.

A given set of productive resources can produce; say either commodity A or commodity B. If therefore, commodity A is produced, then commodity B is forgone. The opportunity of producing commodity B has, thus been lost. Therefore, the opportunity cost of producing one unit of commodity A is the amount of commodity B which could be produced by transferring the productive resources there. Similarly, opportunity cost of producing one unit of commodity B is the amount of commodity A which has been foregone and which could be produced by the same resources. As another example, a farmer who is producing wheat can also produce potatoes with the same factors. Therefore, the opportunity cost of one quintal of wheat is the amount of potatoes which could have been produced with the same factors.

In microeconomic theory, the opportunity cost, also known as **alternative cost,** is the value (not a benefit) of the choice of a best alternative cost while making a decision. A choice needs to be made between several mutually exclusive alternatives; assuming the best choice is made, it is the "cost" incurred by not enjoying the benefit that would have been had by taking the second best available choice.

In the words of Prof. Benham, "The opportunity cost of anything is the next-best alternative that could be produced instead by the same factors or by an equivalent group of factors costing the same amount of money". There are two important things in this definition:

(i) **Next-Best Alternative:** The opportunity cost of anything is the cost of next-best alternative and not the cost of other alternatives. Suppose, if costing the same amount of money, wheat worth ₹ 500, rice worth ₹ 400 or potatoes worth ₹ 300 can be produced on a same plot of land, the farmer will decide to produce wheat. On this plot of land in place of wheat, rice or potatoes can also be produced, hence both rice and potatoes are the alternatives to wheat. But the next best alternative to wheat is the rice and not the potatoes. The opportunity cost of wheat is, therefore, the rice worth ₹ 400 and not the potatoes worth ₹ 300. It is, therefore, said that the opportunity cost of anything is the values of its next-best alternative.

(ii) **By an Equivalent Group of Factors, Costing the same Amount of Money:** It has also been clarified by **Benham** in his definition that while producing the next-best alternative, cent per cent the same factors are not used which were used in the production of first commodity. For example, in the production of wheat and rice though land, workers, machines and fertilizers may be the same but there will be difference in seeds.

ECONOMIC PROBLEM OF A DEVELOPING COUNTRY

There are so many economic problems of developing country. Some of these are discussed below.

(i) **Low Income:** Low per capita income is one of the most defining economic problems of a developing country. Due to the shortage of capital, skilled labour and entrepreneurial ability, the per capita income is very low. On account of several constraints, an underdeveloped country has a poor rate of growth. This further shows the result in low gross national income and low per capita income in the economy. They suffer from low per capita income level, which results in low savings and low investments. It means the average person does not earn enough money to invest or save money. They spend whatever they make. Thus, it creates a cycle of poverty that most of the population struggles to escape. The percentage of people in absolute poverty (the minimum income level) is high in developing countries.

(ii) **Unutilized Resources:** Most of the developing countries are rich in natural resources. However, their exploration and exploitation is limited. Sometimes, foreign companies control them. Generally, raw products are exported at low prices. Therefore, developing countries that are well endowed with natural resources should use the revenues to increase wages and employment, boost private and public sector investment and so bring forward economic development. Many countries have made a mess of managing their natural resource revenues. The 'resource curse' is the term usually used to express the fact that countries that are well endowed with natural resources—particularly oil—have on average had worse economic performance than resource-poor countries.

One of the most unutilized or underutilized resources in developing countries today is not only the minerals and natural resources but also there are people who can help to utilize these to the maximum extent possible. This top position goes to the human resource-graduates from universities, colleges and technical institutes. This resource is known as the greatest asset to companies and businesses. But, it is currently not being utilised by the developing countries. Indeed, the developing countries would rather have a novice from the 'developed world' work with/for them than their own graduate professionals.

The extraction and utilization of natural resources, and the making of decisions concerning their use, are inhibited because technology, systems and procedures for extracting and utilizing resources are not equitably distributed nor does their development respond to need. This absence of a global sharing in technology and in the transfer and coordination of skills results in inefficient production and consequent waste of natural resources.

The constraints which impede sufficient utilization of local raw materials include: technological; markets and marketing (including commercial power and the response of industrialized economies); and external (such as infrastructure and long-term effects). The underdeveloped transport network has hampered the effective exploitation of the greater part of the natural resources in the least developed countries and thus set serious limitations to their use in the over-all development effort.

(iii) Low Level of Technology and Human and Physical Capital: In a developing country, the existing technology is old, backward and unproductive. It results in high cost of production. Since new technologies are expensive and require a considerable degree of skill for their application, the twin requirements for the absorption of new technology are the availability of capital and training of an adequate number of personnel. It is necessary to have a basic minimum level of education to adopt new technology. Further, deficiency of capital hinders the process of scrapping the old equipment.

Capital deficiency is another common problem of developing countries. Because the countries are poor, they save less which results in low capital formation. They possess less investment capital. It is also an important characteristic of developing countries that they have the shortage of human and physical capital. The capital is said to be the life blood of production. Accordingly, the countries having the dearth of capital will remain backward and poor. The shortage of capital in developing countries is attributed to Vicious Circle of Poverty (VCP). This VCP comes into being because of low incomes. The low incomes lead to low savings which lead to low investment and the low purchasing power which leads to low income again. Again the low income means the low purchasing power which leads to the emergence of limited market. The phenomenon of limited market leads to restrict the investment which would lead to reduce the level of income. In addition to VCP, the people of developing countries are highly influenced by "International Demonstration Effects", i.e., the people wish to attain same standard of living what it has been attained by the people of developed countries. This has promoted consumption in developing countries, particularly the imports of luxuries are widely encouraged. In this way, the savings in developing countries are wasted on the imported luxurious goods. The developing countries are not only furnished with low levels of living, but they are characterized by low levels of labor productivity. It is the production function which establishes a relation between inputs and outputs. Thus this concept is normally applied to know the productivity of labor. But this engineering concept must also be supplemented by the inputs like managerial competence, worker motivation and institutional flexibility. It has been observed that the productivity of labor in developing countries has been found very low as compared with developed countries.

According to principle of diminishing marginal productivity the Marginal Product (MP) goes on to fall along with increases in the units of labor. This happens because of the reason that amount of capital and state of management remains the same. Therefore, to escape law of diminishing marginal productivity need is to boost the savings and investment through domestic and-foreign investment. Again, investment in labour can be promoted through training and education. But the investment in physical stock and human resources will be least beneficial (as it is happening in developing countries) if the institutional changes are not brought in the economy. These changes may consist of reforming the land tenure system, taxation system, banking structure, educational system and creation of efficient and honest administration. Thus, the low productivity of labor in the developing countries is attributed to capital deficiency, reduced managerial qualities and obsolete and defective institutional structures. Moreover, the labor lack the quality of self-improvement, they are sluggish, they are least hardworking and ambitious, they do not believe in innovations and experiments and they are fond of work shirking.

(iv) Poverty and Inequality in the Distribution of Income

POVERTY

Developing countries are poor. By definition, GDP and Per Capita Income are at low level. General living standard of people in these countries is very slow. Poverty is visibly disturbing every aspect of life. General health services for people are insignificant. The life expectancy at birth does not exceed 60 years. There are two types of poverty:

(i) **Relative Poverty:** This is when income is a certain percentage less than the average income. For example, in the UK relative poverty is defined as income 50% less than average incomes. Therefore a rise in economic growth and average incomes will cause a change in what constitutes relative poverty.

Economic growth may or may not reduce relative poverty; it depends on the income distribution of the growth.

(ii) **Absolute Poverty:** This is an income below a certain level necessary to maintain a minimum standard of living (e.g. enough money to buy the basic necessities of food, shelter and fuel). Therefore, economic growth should be utilized to reduce absolute poverty, so long as the poorest can gain some increase in living standards from the nation's growth.

This absolute of poverty is in use in many countries, but it must be contrasted with relative poverty, where the poverty line is defined not in terms of some well defined basic needs, but as a fixed proportion of the mean income of the population. The European Union, for example, considers those people living under relative poverty whose economic resources are below 50 per cent of the mean income of country.

INEQUALITY IN THE DISTRIBUTION OF INCOME

Inequality in the distribution of income is the result of unequal distribution of household or individual income across the various participants in an economy. Income inequality is often presented as the percentage of income to a percentage of population.

Economic inequality is the difference found in various measures of economic well-being among individuals in a group, among groups in a population, or among countries. Economic inequality sometimes refers to income inequality, wealth inequality, or the wealth gap. Economists generally focus on economic disparity in three metrics: wealth, income, and consumption. The issue of economic inequality is relevant to notions of equity, equality of outcome, and equality of opportunity.

Economic inequality varies between societies, historical periods, economic structures and systems. The term can refer to cross-sectional distribution of income or wealth at any particular period, or to changes of income and wealth over longer periods of time. There are various numerical indices for measuring economic inequality. A widely used index is the Gini coefficient, but there are also many other methods.

Effects of Inequality in the Distribution of Income

(i) Research suggests that greater inequality hinders long term growth. Whereas globalization has reduced global inequality (between nations), it has increased inequality within nations.

(ii) High and rising inequality can slow and even stall progress towards the reduction in poverty, given the growth, inequality and poverty linkages in a country. Rising inequality is a key driver of domestic financial instability that is typically associated with adverse growth, poverty and distribution impacts. As the conditions of the poor deteriorate and inequalities worsen amidst depressed growth, budgetary outlays to sustain MDG investments may be difficult to maintain.

(iii) Income inequalities are linked to and can reinforce other inequalities. For countries with chronic and extensive poverty and long-term anemic growth, policies that address poverty reduction at the margins will be grossly inadequate. If growth is unable to generate domestic resources, the prospects for progress will be very uncertain.

(iv) High and rising inequality also reduce the possibilities that economic and social policies fostering inclusive growth and human development will be delivered and implemented. For instance, richer groups may secure economically inefficient advantages such as regressive taxes or an allocation of public funds for their own interest rather than for that of the country.

(v) Finally, in developing countries, where the institutions of government are often weak, inequality exacerbates the problem of creating and maintaining accountable government, thereby increasing the probability of the adoption of economic and social policies that inhibit growth and poverty reduction.

INCOME

The term, 'income' is used to denote a flow of money or goods accruing to an individual, group of individuals, a firm or the economy over a specified period of time. It is the earning in money or in kind for productive services over the specified period of time. It may be in money or in kind e.g. use of privilege enjoyed by a business executive. It may arise from the rendering of productive services or it may simply represent a gift or transfer payments.

For example, the income generated annually in a production unit, say a joint stock company engaged in textile milling, consists of wages and salaries paid over the year to labourers, clerks, office staff, etc. and of profits appropriable by the shareholders of the company or retained by the company for future use. The creditors of the company may as well earn interest-income on the funds lent by them. Again, the company may have to pay rent for the factory-site that would be income earned by landlords.

Income may be real income and money income. It follows that production gives rise to an annual flow of useful goods and services. This is the real income. It is divided among individuals on the basis of rendering productive services. Theses good and services bear money values. People are paid in money for their services. This money-income represents people's claims on real income.

Real income indicates the flow of goods and services earned by a person over a specified period and the money income refers to the sum of money earned by a person in a specific period. The real income content of a given money income depends on the purchasing power of money. The same volume of money income gives more real income when prices are low and less real income when prices are high. Payments for productive services are sometimes made partly in money and in kind (e.g. home town leave traveling concession free quarters facilities, etc.). In such cases, the calculation of real income should be including the benefits received in kind.

SAVING

Saving means refraining from current consumption and thereby making resources available for investment. Income which is not spent on consumption and which is not taxed is, by definition, saving. The implication of this definition is that saving represents money which, having been paid out by firms to household is not returned to them in the form of expenditure on goods and services. Thus, saving is that part of household income which is not spent on consumption. For example, a household plans to spend ₹ 10,000 out of his monthly income of ₹ 12,000, the remaining ₹ 2000 (12000-10000) he plans to save. Hence, saving is a residue.

If households save a part of their income, they must be spending less on goods and services than they receive as income. Saving is, thus, a withdrawal from the circular flow. Of course, some savings may return to the circular flow. Not only the households save, the firms may also save. Firms perform saving when they do not distribute all their profits. The undistributed part of the profits represents business savings. This money may also return to the circular flow, if the firms use it to build new factories. It may not also return to the circular flow it the firms keep it as reserves. Whatever subsequently happens to the money an act of saving is a withdrawal from the circular flow of income. Therefore, all savings are treated as withdrawals of money from consumption.

WEALTH AND WELFARE

Wealth is a stock of goods existing at a certain time period that confirms to the following requirements: (a) They must passes utility; (b) They must have a money value; (c) They must be limited in supply; and (d) It must be possible to transfer their ownership from one person to another. The terms, human wealth and non-human wealth are often used in order to distinguish between the tangible and intangible types of wealth. Capacity to generate income being a basic property of wealth, it follows that the value of a stock of wealth is given by the present value of the flow of income it generates non-human wealth are often used in order to distinguish between the tangible and intangible types of wealth. Capacity to generate income being a basic property of wealth, it follows that the value of a stock of wealth is given by the present value of the flow of income generates.

It indicates all material objects that are external to man, inherently useful, appropriable and relatively scarce. Akin to the concept of economic goods is in favour of an item of wealth is capable of satisfying wants and is scarce in relation to the want. Some economists include in wealth all material goods, as well as, non-material services. Goods covered by the category of wealth necessarily have money values. It means that such goods are marketable. These goods can be separated from their owners and sold in the market. Thus, contrary to the more literal usage, wealth as an economic category does not include the intrinsic attributes of men, such as, health, natural talent, etc. On other hand; marketability of goods does not necessarily mean that they are marketed. There is, for example, a great deal of property is collective ownership, e.g. road, bridges, parks, libraries, etc. in which there is no market. Such good do unmistakably constitute wealth.

Utilization of wealth would automatically promote the welfare of the community which receives the fruits of development. Where there is wealth there is high possibility of welfare. To achieve welfare we have to create first wealth. Proper utilization of wealth brings welfare very rapidly and thus, the country will develop. Wealth and welfare are very closely inter-related. Wealth is the means and welfare is the end. The idea of welfare may vary from place to place, man to man. But wealth has a definite meaning.

It a man is rich in having wealth he may lead not only likes a good live, he may also help others. Again a country with huge wealth bears a good possibility to be developed. Thus, wealth promote welfare, wealth can make people, happier and comfortable promoting mental, moral and physical well-being. A man cannot maintain himself without material goods like food, clothing, and shelter, i.e., he cannot live without wealth. A very little possession of wealth may not make him happy.

Again wealth and welfare—inter-related to each other is a matter of controversy. Welfare gives us always good sense i.e. a positive sense but wealth is not. Sometimes wealth gives us negative welfare. Because by definition, intoxicants such as alcoholic drink, opium, poisonous drug, tobacco etc. and also a bad book or like these are regarded as wealth, but their uses doe not promote human welfare. Increase in wealth does not necessarily mean an increase in welfare. We can say here that the number of economic goods has increased.

Thus, wealth and welfare are not synonymous under all circumstances. Wealth is for man and man is not for wealth. That is, wealth is a means while the end is human welfare. Wealth is nothing without its use. Wealth is a powerful means of promoting human welfare.

CAPITAL VALUE

Capital is regarded not only as central to the process of development but also as a strategic factor. By capital we mean the assets or resources which help to further production. This term has been defined by economist in a number of different ways but in general, it may be said to be the stock of goods which are used in production and which have themselves been produced. This term is also used in economics in various specialized connotations:

(i) Real capital: It is sometimes also called producer's capital such as machines, factories, railways, stock of raw materials, etc.

(ii) Fixed capital: It represents the commodities whose physical from do not change significantly in the course of their service, e.g., building, bridges, etc.

(iii) Circulating capital: Commodities which must be transformed physically when they can yield any service, e.g. raw materials of all kinds.

(iv) Specific capital: It is a special type of commodity which is not normally used. It is used for the purpose for which it is originally designed or constructed, e.g. a shipyard.

In the business world, the term capital is usually applied to the money subscribed by share or stockholders to companies and corporations, although the term is also used in the following connotations:

(i) Long-term capital: Money where is invested in shares, securities, bonds, etc.

(ii) Short-term capital: Money lent or invested only for short periods, such as bank advances.

(iii) Floating or working capital: Where money is in floating or liquid assets (cash, bank account, debts and bills receivable).

Two important aspects of capital are: (i) it involves sacrifice as in the production at of-consumable and consumable goods and (ii) it increases the productivity of other factors such as land and labour and this raises productivity of other factors such as land and labour. The increased productivity represents the reward for the sacrifice involved in creating capital.

The value of an asset on its current earnings is in relation to the prevailing rate of interest. For example if the prevailing rate of interest were 5% and the current annual earning of an asset were ₹ 100 its capital value would be twenty times its earnings i.e. ₹ 2000.

GRESHAM'S LAW

A number of debased, clipped and sweated coins of previous reins were in circulation during the reign of Queen Elizabeth. She thought to reform the currency system and thereby tried to replace bad coins by issuing new full weighted coins. But as soon as the new good coins were circulated in the market, they disappeared. That time Sir Thomas Gresham was her financial advisor. She consulted with him about the matter and told him to detect the reason behind it. Sir Thomas Gresham detected the reason behind it and explained why the good coins disappeared very soon from the market. The law evolved by him has since been named after him.

The law states that bad money tends to drive good money out of circulation. Bad money is the money which is inferior or cheaper in substance value. The explanations of this law may be given in the following ways:

1. In a country where there are circulations of good and bad coins of the same metal as legal tender, bad money tends to drive good money out of circulation. Bad money means old, worn out and light-weight coins.
2. The law operates under bimetallism. It let two cons made of silver and gold bearing same face value be

circulated in the market at the same time, silver coins will drive gold coins out of circulation. The reason is that the mint ratio being unchanged, one gold coin will exchange for sixteen silver coins i.e. gold is undervalued and silver is overvalued at the mint. In this silver coins are bad money while gold coins are good money. That is why, silver coins will drive gold coins out of circulation.

3. It is an inconvertible paper currency is issued in excess of the normal requirements of the economy, this excess supply of money in the market will tend to drive precious metals out of circulation.

Again if paper currency and metallic currency are circulated in the market, the paper currency, which is obviously bad money, tends to drive metallic currency, which is good money, out of circulation from the market.

Explanation: Good coins possess more intrinsic value than the bad ones. That is why, good coins are more preferred. Most of the people generally prefer to keep bright new rupees and spend dirty old rupees. Again coins in circulation get reduced in weight by general tendency for users to retain full weight coins and to spend light weight coins. Full weight coins are used in the following ways: (a) They are melted and used for the purpose of art, (b) They are hoarded, and (c) They are exported. Thus, full weight coins i.e., good money disappears from circulation in the market leaving behind only bad money.

EXERCISES

1. What do you mean by Unlimited Wants?
2. What is Resource Scarcity?
3. What is Scarcity?
4. What is Choice?
5. What is Opportunity Cost?
6. What are the main economic Problems of a developing country?
7. What is Human Capital?
8. Define Physical Capital.

9. Define Poverty.
10. What is Relative Poverty?
11. What is Absolute Poverty?
12. What is Acute Poverty?
13. What is Inequality in the Distribution of Income?
14. Define effects of Inequality in the Distribution of Income.
15. Define Income.
16. Define Saving.
17. Define Wealth and Welfare.
18. What is Capital Value?
19. Define Gresham's Law.

Chapter 2

Nature and Scope of Economics

VARIOUS DEFINITIONS OF ECONOMICS

The word, "Economics" has derived from the two Greek words viz. Oikos and Nemein. Oikos means house and Nemein means manage. It was believed in the early age that Economics was simply defined as "to manage house i.e., to satisfy selves'—wants in using natural resources." But in modern age, different economists in different times have wanted to define Economics from their own conceptions. Economics has such a large number of definitions. We can classify these definitions of Economics into four main groups:

(i) Wealth—Definitions i.e., early Definitions;

(ii) Welfare—Definition i.e., Marshallian Definition;

(iii) Scarcity—Definition i.e., Robbins' Definition; and

(iv) Growth-Oriented Definition i.e., Samuelson's Definition.

(i) **Wealth—Definitions i.e., Early Definitions: Adam smith, J.B. Say, J.S. Mill, J.E. Cairnes, F.A. Walker** and others have defined wealth—definitions of Economics. For the first time in 1776, Adam Smith wrote a book on Economics and provided it a status of a separate science. According to him, Economics is a science of wealth. The title of his book is, *An Inquiry into the Nature and Causes of Wealth of Nations*—itself clarifies his view regarding the nature of Economics. The French economist, **J.B. Say** said that Economics is the science which treats of wealth. **J.E. Cairnes** in his book, *The Character and Logical Method of*

Political Economy clearly said that "Economics deals with the phenomenon of wealth". The American economist, **F.A. Walker** called Economics as the body of knowledge which relates to wealth. So all the early economists of this group bear same opinion where wealth has been given central and prime place.

Criticism

Economics was defined in those days when religion was in a prime place and more important. Again some parts of Europe were experiencing industrial revolution. The industrialist started to accumulate wealth by fair and foul means. Poor labourers were exploited in many ways. Social reformers blamed these definitions. **Carlyle, Ruskin, William Morris** criticised Economics so badly on many grounds. Such that (1) Precious material goods were considered as wealth (2) Wealth was given too much importance. It ignored moral values and human welfare.

(ii) **Welfare—Definition i.e., Marshallian Definition:** People were not satisfied by the Wealth—Definitions. It was necessary to explain Economics properly. This group included **Prof. Marshall, Pigou, Cannon, Chapman, Fairchild, Beveridge** and others. These economists gave importance to the material welfare of human being in their definitions.

Marshall defines Economics in his first book, *Economics of Industry* in these words, "Political Economy or Economics is the study of man's actions in the ordinary business of life. It enquiries how he gets his income and how he spends it. .... Thus it is, on the one side, a study of wealth and on the other and more important side a part of the study of man". Further, in his second book, *Principles of Economics*, he defines "Economics is the study of mankind in the ordinary business of life; it examines that part of individual and social action which is most closely connected with the attainment and with the use of material requisites of wellbeing."

Beveridge said, "Economics is the study of the general methods by which men cooperate to meet their material needs."

According to **Cannon**, "The aim of Political Economy is the explanation of the general causes on which the material welfare of human beings depends."

In the words of **Pigou,** "The range of our inquiry becomes restricted to that part of social welfare that can be brought directly or indirectly into relation with the measuring rod of money."

According to these economists, the aim of Economics is to study human activities which are conducive to human welfare in its material aspect. Wealth furnishes man with material means of satisfying his wants and of promoting his welfare. Thus, Economics is a social science which studies material welfare of human being. Wealth is for man and man is not for wealth. That is, wealth is a means while the end is human welfare.

Criticism

Almost everybody accepted Marshall's definition and it created a good impression regarding the definition of Economics but it did not last for a long. **Prof. Robbins** attacked strongly on this definition in the following way.

(1) **Marshall**'s definition says that Economics studies only material goods. But it is not accepted. We do perform so many non-material services such as service of teacher, doctor, lawyer, etc. Though their services are non-material in character but these are part and parcel of Economics.

(2) **Prof. Lionel Robbins** has criticized the **Marshall**'s definition on the ground that 'welfare' economists tried to establish a connection between 'Economics' and 'Welfare'. He says that Economics studies several activities which are hardly conducive to welfare. Suppose the activities of the manufacturers of intoxicants, such as alcoholic drinks and opium, etc. are also economic activities. But the society is not benefited by these activities. These do not lead to human welfare though they can satisfy human wants.

(3) **Robbins** has clearly stated that material welfare cannot be accepted as an end of Economics. It is difficult to give value—judgement having no scale of measurement of human welfare. Money does not measure welfare satisfactorily because, two persons, one is rich and

another is poor, purchase a commodity paying the same price. Their derived utilities from the commodity are not identical. Obviously, the utility derived by the poor is higher than that by the rich. Thus, money cannot represent an equal utility or welfare for all persons.

(4) Economics would study man as a social being. But it would not study the problems of those individuals who are cut off or isolated from the rest of the society. As an example, we can say an Himalayan saint who is isolated from the society. But he is also subject to some of the fundamental laws of Economics as a regular member of a community.

(5) According to the 'Welfare' definition, Economics concerns itself with a certain group of activities rather than with a certain aspect of every activity. **Prof. Robbins** criticizes the 'welfare' definition on the ground that it is classificatory rather than analytical in character.

On account of these objections, **Prof. Robbins** rejects the 'Welfare' definition. To avoid these objections, he constructs a new definition entitled 'scarcity' definition which is free from all the above defects.

(iii) **Scarcity—Definition i.e., Robbins' Definition: Robbins** put forward a new and novel viewpoint in his definition of Economics in his book, *Nature and Significance of Economic Science* in 1931. He has taken the scarcity as a central point of his definition. That is why, his definition is known as Scarcity definition. **Stigler, Samuelson, Cairncross** and many other modern economists have also supported him. He defined Economics thus: "Economics is the science which studies human behaviour as a relationship between ends and scarce means which have alternative uses."

Robbins' definition was analytical rather than classificatory and free from the defects seen in the definition of **Marshall**. It concerned with the utilisation of scarce resources to achieve unlimited ends. We find that his definition lays down the following three fundamental propositions.

(a) **Ends:** 'Ends' refer to wants. Human beings have wants which are unlimited in number. If one want is satisfied, another crops up. Since human wants are unlimited, one is compelled to choose between the more urgent and the less urgent. That is why, Economics is also called a science of choice.

(b) **Scarcity:** The term, 'Scarcity' is used in a relative sense not in a absolute sense. It is scarcity in relation to requirements. A commodity may exist in a small quantity but if nobody has any use for it, we shall not call it scarce in the economic sense. On the other hand, there may be huge stocks for a commodity like coal, yet it is called scarce because the demand is even larger than the supply. It is demand in relation to supply of a commodity, which determines whether a commodity is scarce or not. Scarcity is thus a relative term.

(c) **Alternative uses:** Scarce means capable of alternative uses. The alternative uses are of varying degree of importance; some are more urgent and others less urgent. Choice comes again. So Economics is called a science of choice.

Superiority of Robbins' Definition

Robbins demolished the old structure of Economics based on material welfare and raised a new one with two foundation stones, viz. multiplicity of wants and scarcity of means. **Robbins'** definition is superior to the earlier definitions because of the following reasons.

(1) It is more scientific since it is not based on artificial classification of wants.

(2) It takes into account of all types of human wants, material or non-material, as well as all types of persons whether they are living in the society or not.

(3) **Robbins** greatly widened the scope of Economics.

(4) He raised Economics to the level of science whereas earlier economists regarded it as both a science and an art.

(5) He made Economics a positive science whereas earlier economists regarded it a normative science.

Criticism of Robbins' Definition

(1) Keynesian Economics, which explains the determination of national income and employment, is not covered by **Robbins'** definition.

(2) The theory of economic growth or economic development has recently become a very important branch of Economics. But **Robbins** definition does not cover it.

(3) **Robbins'** definition does not explain the problem of unemployment and hence gives no solution to the problems of underdeveloped countries.

(4) **Robbins'** conception of Economics is essentially a micro analysis. It is concerned with individual behaviour of economising ends with the limited means at its disposal. But Economics is not concerned with individualistic ends and means alone.

(5) **Prof. Robertson** regards **Robbins'** definition as "at once too narrow and too wide". It is too narrow since it does not include organisational defects which lead to idle resources. On the other hand, the problem of allocating scarce means among given ends is such that it may arise even in fields which lie outside the jurisdiction of Economics. Suppose, the captain of a team in a play ground or an army commander in battle field may be faced with the problem of scarce resources in the event of a member being injured. Thus **Robbins'** scarcity formulation is applicable even to non-economic problems thereby making the scope of Economics too wide.

(iv) **Growth-Oriented Definition Or Samuelson's Definition:** **Robbins** has exempted the problem of economic growth and simply taken the dynamic problem. **Prof. Samuelson** tries to remove the defect in Robbins' definition. He recognizes in his definition the dynamic changes both in the means as well as in the ends with the lapse of time. Therefore, his definition is called growth-oriented definition of Economics that is, defined as:

"Economics is the study of how men and society, choose with or without the use of money, to employ scarce productive resources which could have alternative uses, to produce various commodities over time, and distribute them for consumption now and in the future among various people and groups of society".

Implications of this definition

1. We see many similarities between Robbins' and Samuelson's definitions. Both of them have stressed the problem of scarcity of means in relation to unlimited ends.
2. Samuelson has included time factor in his definition but Robbins does not.
3. Samuelson's definition including the problem of growth shows its superiority over that of Robbins.
4. His definition is wider in scope in the sense that it is not only applicable to money economy but also equally applicable to barter economy.
5. His definition is dynamic in nature. This is the superiority of his definition. Human wants never remain fixed or static. They continually change with the lapse of time. Again the character of wants changes due to change in tastes, fashions, etc. To face the increasing wants of society, the resource, output, employment, income, etc. have to be adjusted on increasing basis.

   The growth-oriented definition appears to be the most satisfactory among all the definitions of Economics. It is applicable to all sorts of economies: past, present and future. It is also equally applicable to capitalist, mixed, socialist and communist economies. Thus, it is accepted as the most appropriate definition of Economics.

SCOPE OF ECONOMICS

'SCOPE' means the sphere of study, i.e., the field of study. In scope of economics we have to consider what economics studies and what lies beyond it. We have to examine whether it is a science or an art, a positive science or a normative science, pure on applied, static or dynamic. Now we discuss one by one.

ECONOMICS AS A SCIENCE

The term 'Science' indicates a systematized body of knowledge which traces the relationship between cause and effect. Coin care says, "Science is built up of facts as a house is built up of stones; but an accumulation of facts is no more a science than a heap of stones is a house". Thus, science is a systematized body of knowledge ascertainable by observation and experiment. It is a body of generalizations, principles, theories or laws which traces out a causal relationship between cause and effect. Economics is, in the sense, a science. It has generalizations which establish relationship between cause and effect. A definite result is expected to follow from a particular cause in economics like all other sciences. An example of a principle in chemistry is that all other things being equal, a combination of carbon (C) and oxygen (O_2) in the ratio of 1:2 will form carbon dioxide (CO_2). In physics, the law of gravitation states that things coming from a height must fall to the ground at an increasing rate of velocity, other things being equal. In Economics the law of demand tells us that other things remaining the same, a fall in price leads to extension in demand and a rise in price leads to contraction in demand. Here rise or fall in price is the cause and contraction or extension is its effect. Hence, Economics is a science like any other science, because it makes use of the scientific method in its research and investigation.

Another ground on which the status of science is sought to be denied to Economics is its so-called inability to predict the future course of events as accurate as the physical sciences like chemistry and physics can. But, for this failure, we cannot blame Economics. This is due to reason that it fails to predict accurately as it deals with the variables which are highly complex and changeable, again some of which are not amendable to correct prediction. Economics deals with men endowed with freedom of will, and there is no guarantee that they will act in a preconceived manner. As a result, exact quantitative prediction is not always possible in Economics. Suppose, a rise in price may not lead to contraction in demand rather it may expand demand if people fear a shortage in supply in anticipation of war. Even if demand contracts as a result of the rise in price, it is not possible to predict accurately how much the demand will contract. In this connection, **Marshall** says, "In Science that relates to man, exactness is less attainable".

Sometimes the meteorological forecasts also prove false. But it does not mean that meteorology is not a science. In fact, in certain respects, economic forecast is more reliable than meteorological forecast.

Today, Economics rightly deserves the little of science. Economists today are realizing more and more the need for practical application of Economics.

ECONOMICS AS AN ART

'Art' relates application but 'Science' relates principles. Art is the practical application of scientific principles. Science lays down certain principles while art puts these principles into practical use. An art is also a systematized body of knowledge, but unlike a science, it lays down precepts or specific solutions for specific problems. As **J.N. Keynes** has put it, "An art is a system of rules for the attainment of a given end". The object of art is the formulation of precepts immediately applicable to policy. The practical aspect of the art distinguishes it from science which may be merely theoretical. In this connection, **Cossa** says, "A science teaches us to know; an art teaches us to do. In a word, science explains and expounds; art directs; art imposes precepts, or proposes rules".

To analyze the causes and effects of poverty it falls within the purview of science and to lay down precepts for the removal of poverty it falls within the purview of art. There are several branches of Economics which offer us practical guidance in the solution of economic problems. The theory of consumption provides us with the well-known law of substitution, which tells a consumer how to maximize his satisfaction from his expenditure. Law of substitution goes in the purview of science while 'how to maximize his satisfaction' goes in the purview of art. Thus Economics is both a science and an art in this sense. So we treat Economics as a science and also as an art at the same time, because every science has an art or the practical side, while every art has a theoretical or the scientific side. It is fact what **Cossa** says, "Science requires art; art requires science, each being complementary to the other". Therefore, Economics is regarded as a science as well as an art.

ECONOMICS AS PURE OR APPLIED

As the world approaches towards modernization, most of the subjects are going to be based on division into pure and applied. This is same also in Economics. Today some economists, leaving the concept of Economics as a science or as an art, prefer to divide it into pure Economics and applied Economics. This is now more accepted than before. The distinction of Economics—Pure Economics and Applied Economics is more scientific, more popular, more dignified and conducive to better understanding to get proper solutions of economic problems. Pure Economics refers only to theoretical analysis and formulations. A pure economist is interested only in developing theoretical explanation for any phenomenon. Applied Economics, on the other hand, seeks to provide solutions to different problems that the society may be confronted with at any time. Applied economist searches intensively into these problems, studies the theoretical explanations, formulates policies and suggests remedies to overcome the problems. Pure economist furnishes the tools with which applied economist works. We see the same in the words of **Prof. Bye,** "Pure science furnishes the tools with which applied science works. The two go hand-in-hands, but the former must proceed, for without it the latter is without the proper means for the accomplishment of its task".

Nowadays, Applied Economics has received greater attention at the hands of economists, and there have been several publications on Applied Economics both in the U.K. and the U.S.A. Perhaps this is a reaction to the extremist positivism of Robbins who insists upon treating Economics as strictly a pure science. But, according to **Prof. Stigler**, at least ninety per cent of economists spend over half of their time on applied or empirical subjects, and, in fact only a small minority is interested in advanced theoretical discussions. Thus, it is clear that Applied Economics is more important than Pure Economics.

ECONOMICS AS A POSITIVE OR NORMATIVE SCIENCE

In discussing the scope of Economics, we have also to consider whether Economics is a positive or a normative science. In this connection, we see two groups: one group of economists believes that Economics is a positive subject of study, and while anther the other group of economists believes that Economics is a normative subject of study. Simply, it can be stated that 'positive' means 'what is' and 'normative' means 'what should be'. In another angle, positive science describes while the normative science evaluates. Suppose, the businessmen take profit maximization as their criterion, it is Positive Economics, but when we ask, 'Ought they to take this criterion; we enter the field of Normative Economics'.

To understand this controversy, let us be clear about the two terms 'positive' and 'normative'; If we say, the price of rice is ₹ 5 per kg., we are only making a positive statement. But if we say, price of rice should not be more than ₹ 4 per kg., we are making a normative statement. Thus, when we are making a positive statement, we are only describing a phenomenon simply. We are not making any judgment; we are totally silent or neutral about the ends. But if we commit ourselves to desirability or otherwise of any end, we are making a judgment, this judgment would constitute a normative statement.

Thus a positive science deals with things as they area. It explains their causes and effects. But it remains strictly neutral as regards as ends. No moral judgment is passed by a positive scientist. A normative science, on the other hand, deals with things as they ought to be. **Lionel Robbins** and others have taken Economics as a pure and positive science. This group of economists is known as 'purists'. Almost all leading economists from **N. Senior** and **J.S. Mill** onwards had declared that "The science of Economics should be concerned only with what is and not what ought to be".

The 'Purists' argue the following in support of positive Economics:

1. For scientific analysis of any problem it is necessary that the two things, viz., 'what is' and 'what ought to be'

should be kept apart. If any scientist tries to mix these two, he will be confused and will not be in a position to go to the root of the problem.

2. There is no such as possibility of disagreement in inquiries regarding what is, because such inquiries are merely expressing the facts as they are. But in the inquiries regarding what ought to be there can be vast scope for disagreement and even controversy.
3. The attempt to combine inquiries regarding what is with inquiries regarding what ought to be shall place the economist in a very awkward position.
4. If the economist attempts to combine the theoretical and practical inquiries, it may tend to mislead the public at a large.

The above view of 'purists' is true for the purely analytical part of Economics. For example, when discussing the theory of consumer behaviour, the economist is not concerned with the morality or legality of the consumer's desires. He is only concerned with the question how the consumer spends his income on his purchases.

Again, a large number of economists insist on treating Economics as a normative science. **Hawtrey** says, "Economics cannot be dissociated from Ethics". Economics is after all a social science. Therefore, economists should make value judgment about the ends of human activity.

In practice, Economics has been developed as both a positive and a normative science. The theoretical foundations of Economics have been continuously strengthened from the day, the science was born. Thus, Positive and Normative Economics have been grown inseparably.

ECONOMICS AS STATIC OR DYNAMIC

Pure economic theory is divided into two broad headings: economic statics and economic dynamics. Economic statics deals with positions of equilibrium between economic quantities at a particulars point at time on the other hand; economic dynamics studies how economic variables at different points of time are functionally related. Under the above two headings, all facts of the economic life are studied in their relations of mutual interdependence. From the intellectual point of view, economic dynamics is much more appropriate than economic statics as the latter cannot faithfully portray the living world which is characterized by dynamism. In real life, we do not come across stationary condition in any economy. We have to readjust our analysis of equilibrium in the context of dynamic nature of economic activities and decisions. Production and consumption are based on time; they involve decision based on future estimates. Future estimates involve guess which logically implies uncertainty. Uncertainty will influence the behaviour and decisions of economic units. In the context of uncertainty we have to admit that there will be errors in production planning or in consumer's decision. A revision of the equilibrium concept is, therefore, necessary in the light of dynamic changes in the economy.

SUBJECT MATTER OF MICROECONOMIC THEORY

Microeconomic theory is concerned with four basic economic questions. They are: (1) What goods shall be produced and in what quantities? (2) By what methods are these goods produced? (3) How shall the goods and services produced be distributed among the members of the society? (4) How efficiently are the resources being used?

The first question arises directly from the scarcity of resources. The scarcity of resources creates a situation in which, when there is full employment of resources, the decision to use more resources to produce more of one thing necessitates producing less of something else. The question concerns the allocation of scarce resources among alternative uses. Any economy in which resources are scarce in relation of human wants whether it be capitalist, socialist or communist, must have some mechanism to make decisions about resource allocation. In free market economies, the majority of decisions concerning the allocation of resources is made through the price system and hence the study of the workings of the price system is an extremely important branch of our subject. This study is dealt with in the theory of price.

The second question arises whenever there are alternative methods of producing same goods. Agricultural goods, for example, can be produced by farming a small quantity of land very intensively, using large quantities of fertilizer, labour and machinery or by farming a large quantity of land extensively, using only small quantities of fertilizer, labour and machinery. Both methods can be used to produce the same quantity of same goods. Similar possibilities are available with manufactured goods; it is usually possible to produce the same output by several different techniques. Questions about why one method of production is used rather than another.

This question is dealt with in the theory of production. The third question is concerned with the distribution of the product produced among various individuals and groups. Different individuals are engaged in the production process in different capacities. They receive income in return from the production process for supplying productive resources. This problem is analysed in the theory of distribution.

The fourth question sub-divides into two questions: Is the production efficient? Is it allocated efficiently? These questions quite naturally arise out of questions 1, 2 and 3. Having asked what quantities of goods are produced, how they are produced and to whom they are allocated, it is natural to go on to ask whether the production and allocation decisions are efficient. Production is said to be inefficient if it would be possible merely to reallocate resources and to produce more of at least one good without simultaneously producing less of any other good. The goods that are produced are said to be inefficiently allocated if it would be possible to redistribute them among the individuals in the society, and make at least one person better off without simultaneously making anyone worse off.

Microeconomics with its Advantages and Limitations

The word 'micro' means small and the word 'macro' means large. From economic point of view the study of Economics is divided by the modern economists into two parts, viz. Microeconomics and Macroeconomics. These terms were first coined and used by **Ragnar Frisch** of Oslo University during the twenties and have now been adopted by all economists throughout the world. The term Microeconomics is derived from the Greek word 'Mikros' which means small and the Macroeconomics from the Greek word 'Makros' which means large. Microeconomics deals with the analysis of small individual units of the economy such as individual consumer, individual firm and small aggregates or group of individual units such as various industries and markets. On the other hand, Macroeconomics concerns itself with the analysis of the economy as a whole or large aggregate such as total national output and income, total employment, total consumption, aggregate investment, etc.

Thus, Microeconomics may be defined as that branch of economic analysis which studies the economic behaviour of the individual unit which may be a person or a particular house hold or a particular firm. It is a study of one particular unit rather than the units combined together. In Microeconomics we study the various units of the economy—how do they function and how do they reach their equilibrium? That is, we attempt only a microscopic study of the national economy but not study of the national economy in detail. For example, we may study an individual behaviour i.e., how a particular person maximises his satisfaction or we may study an individual firm i.e., how a particular firm maximizes its profits or what happens in any particular industry or how a particular family adjusts its expenditure to income—all are in the preview of Microeconomics. Similarly in the analysis of price, we study the price of a particular product or of a particular factor of production but not the general price level in the economy and in the analysis of demand, we discuss the demand of an individual or that of an industry but not the aggregate demand of the entire country. These come under the discussion of Microeconomics. Likewise, the income of an individual or of an industry but not the national income of a country comes within the domain of Microeconomics. In respect of employment, it is the employment in a firm or in an industry but not the aggregate employment in the whole economy. The whole content of Microeconomic theory may be presented in the following chart:

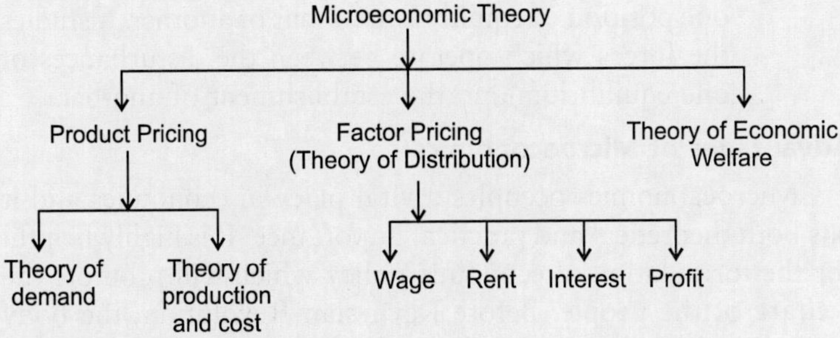

Types of Microeconomics

Microeconomics is of three types discussed below.

1. **Microstatics:** This method of analysis deals with the relationship between different micro variables at a given time under conditions of equilibrium. For example, the price of a commodity in a market is determined by the equilibrium of demand and supply at a given time. Microstatics studies the equilibrium price of a commodity at a given time assuming that the forces of demand and supply do not undergo any change. It does not throw any light on the process by which the forces of demand and supply have reached the position of equilibrium.
2. **Comparative Microstatics:** It compares the equilibrium positions of the relations between micro variables at different points of time. That is, it is a comparative study of different equilibria at different points of time. But it throws no light on the transition from one position of equilibrium to that of another. Suppose, the price of a commodity is ₹ 20 showing the equilibrium price between its demand and supply. If the price of that commodity falls from ₹ 20 to ₹ 18 due to change of equilibrium, it simply compares between the two equilibria but does not explain the reason of occurring new equilibrium.
3. **Micro Dynamics:** It discusses the method on the happenings in the transition from one equilibrium to another. It refers the process by which we reach from

one position of equilibrium to that of another. It studies the forces which operate between the disturbances of one equilibrium and the establishment of another.

Advantages of Microeconomics

Microeconomics occupies a vital place in economics and it has both theoretical and practical importance. It is highly helpful for the formulation of economic policy which will promote the welfare of the people. Before Keynesian Revolution, the body of the economics consisted mainly of Microeconomics. Its advantages are discussed below.

(1) **Determination of prices and allocation of resources:** It tells us how to determine prices and how to allocate resources. How a free market economy with its millions of consumers and producers works to decide about the allocation of resources among the thousands of goods and services and thereby to decide their prices.

(2) **Production and distribution of goods and services:** It shows how goods and services are produced and distributed through market mechanism in the economy.

(3) **Economic policy:** It helps to formulate the policies to promote economic efficiency in production. On the basis of it, we can study the government policies to see how these policies affect prices of goods and wages, allocate the resources, impose taxes and overall how these policies influence the economy.

(4) **Prediction:** It teaches us to predict different market situations as to when and how the situations will prevail in the economy.

(5) **International trade:** The analysis of Microeconomics is applied to show how the gains from international trade can be distributed among the participant countries. It tries to explain the factors which determine the distribution of gains. It finds to solve the various problems of international economies such as devaluation of currency in order to correct the disequilibrium in the balance of payments, foreign exchange rate of

a currency, etc. It studies the elasticities of demand and supply of exports and imports and suggest to do accordingly.

(6) **Social welfare:** It shows how to achieve maximum social welfare for the people. Optimum social welfare can be achieved when there exists perfect competition in all markets. Deviation from perfect competition leads to a lower level of welfare. It also helps to make policy to regulate monopoly so as to attain economic efficiency or maximum welfare of the society.

(7) **Managerial Economics:** It develops a separate branch as Managerial Economics which is mainly followed by the business enterprises for decision-making to achieve maximum profit through optimum level of production. The entrepreneur always tries to avail internal and external economies of scale and always tries to avoid internal and external diseconomies of scale.

From the above discussion it is clear that microeconomic analysis is very useful in every field of Economics.

Limitations

Though microeconomic analysis is very useful in Economics, it has some limitations. These are shown below.

(1) **Individual units and aggregates:** What is true in case of individual units may not be true in case of aggregates. For example, individual thrift may be good, but social thrift is definitely harmful for the community.

(2) **Full employment:** It is based on the assumption of full employment in society assuming other things as constant. This is a highly unrealistic assumption.

(3) **Small parts:** It, instead of studying the total economy, concentrates itself only on small parts of the economy.

(4) **Economic problems:** There are certain economic problems which cannot be analysed with the aid of Microeconomics. For example, problems relating to public finance, monetary and fiscal policy, etc. are beyond the purview of it.

However, it does not mean that Microeconomics is less important in comparison to Macroeconomics. In spite of the popularity of Macroeconomics in these days, Microeconomics retains its importance in theoretical as well as in practical analysis.

SUBJECT MATTER OF MACROECONOMIC THEORY

Macroeconomics may be defined as a branch of economics which is concerned with the aggregates and averages of the entire economy, such as national income, aggregate output, total employment, total consumption, savings and investment, aggregate demand, aggregate supply, general level of prices etc. It is the study of the economic system as a whole. Therefore, macroeconomics is also known as Aggregative Economics. It analyses and establishes the functional relationship between these large aggregates. **Prof. Boulding** says, "Macroeconomics deals not with individual quantities as such but with the aggregates of these quantities' not with individual incomes but with the national income, not with individual prices but with the price level, not with individual output but with the national output." It, thus deals not with one family but with all the families taken together' not with one industry but with the entire industrial structure of an economy. Macroeconomics deals with the averages and aggregates of the system rather than with particular units. It studies the behaviour of macro-quantities or macro-variables.

The fields covered by Macroeconomics may be shown in the following chart:

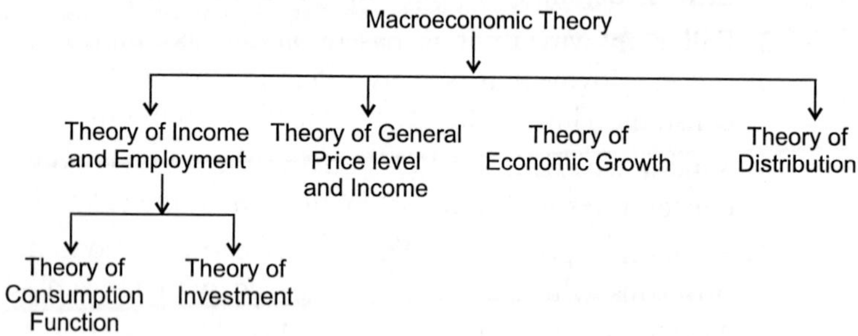

INTERDEPENDENCES BETWEEN MICROECONOMICS AND MACROECONOMICS

Microeconomics and Macroeconomics are complementary to each other rather than being competitive. Actually, Microeconomics and Macroeconomics are so interdependent that one cannot approach without the other; again we cannot attain a complete understanding of the functioning of the economic system unless we integrate the two approaches in a judicious manner. Let us now examine this.

(1) **Macroeconomics depends on Microeconomics:** The theories regarding the behaviour of some Macroeconomic aggregates are derived from the theories of individual behaviour i.e., theories of Microeconomics. The theory of relative prices of products and factors are essential in the explanation of the determination of general price level. Even **Keynes** used Microeconomic theory to explain the rise in price as a result of the increase in the money supply of the country. According to **Keynes,** when as a result of the increase in money supply and consequently the aggregate demand, more output is produced, the cost of production rises. With the rise in the cost of production, the price rises. According to him, cost of production rises because of (i) the law of diminishing returns operates and (ii) wages and prices of raw materials may rise as the economy approaches towards full employment. Now, the influence of cost of production, diminishing returns, etc. to determine the general price level are the parts of Microeconomics. So, Microeconomic theory contributes to Macroeconomic theory in many times.

(2) **Microeconomics depends on Macroeconomics:** The Microeconomic topics, such as the determination of the rate of profit and the rate of interest depend greatly upon the macroeconomic aggregates. The magnitude of profits depends upon the level of aggregate demand, national income and the general price level which are the macroeconomic topics. In the determination of rate of interest, **Keynes** showed that the rate of interest is determined by the liquidity preference function and the stock (or supply) of money, both are macroeconomic topics. Again in the modern interest theory (i.e. intersection of IS-LM curves) along with liquidity preference and the supply of

money, the other two forces, saving and investment function, which are macro terms, are used to explain the determination of interest. Thus, Microeconomics depends to some extend upon Macroeconomics.

Therefore, there is a good deal of interdependences between Micro and Macroeconomics. Microeconomics contributes to Macroeconomics. Macroeconomics, in its turn, contributes to Microeconomics. It is very essential to integrate the two approaches to get correct solution of our main economic problems.

DIFFERENCES BETWEEN MICROECONOMICS AND MACROECONOMICS

Macroeconomics and Microeconomics stand on two different branches of a same tree. Though there is a great deal of interdependences between them, they have many distinctions in their respective approaches.

1. The term Microeconomics is derived from the Greek word 'Mikros' meaning small and the term Macroeconomics from the Greek word 'Makros' meaning large.

2. Microeconomics deals with the analysis of small individual units of the economy, such as individual consumers, individual firms and small aggregates or group of individual units, such as various industries and markets but not aggregate as a whole.

On the other hand, Macroeconomics concerns itself with the analysis of the economy as a whole such as total national output and income, total employment, total consumption, aggregate investment, etc. Therefore, Macroeconomics is also known as aggregative economics. It analyses and establishes the functional relationship among these large aggregates.

3. **K.E. Boulding** makes the distinction between them more clear and more specific when he says, "Microeconomics is the study of particular firms, particular households, individual prices, wages, incomes, individual industries, particular commodities" [K.E. Boulding, *A Reconstruction of Economics* (1950), p. 3]. And "Macroeconomics deals not with individual quantities as such but with aggregates of these quantities; not with individual

incomes but with the national income, not with individual prices but with the price levels; not with individual outputs but with the national output" [K.E. Boulding, *Economic Analysis*, p. 25].

4. Microeconomics should be carefully distinguished from Macroeconomics. Microeconomics also does deal with some 'aggregates' but not of the type with which Macroeconomics concerns. Microeconomics determines the product-price, output and employment of an industry. But industry is also an aggregate of the various firms producing the same product. Similarly, Microeconomics explains the determination of price of a product through the interaction of demand and supply of the market for that product. Market demand is the aggregate of individual demands of all consumers while the market supply is the aggregate of individual productions of all the firms producing the same product.

But the aggregates with which Macroeconomics concerns are of somewhat different variety. It deals with those aggregates which relate to the whole economy. It also discusses the sub-aggregates but these sub-aggregates are not like the aggregates with which Microeconomics deals with. Examples of sub-aggregates with which Macroeconomics concerns itself are the total production of consumer goods and the total production of capital goods, etc.

5. The subject matter of Microeconomics consists in explaining the determination of relative prices of products and factors. The old four divisions of Economics are Consumption, Production, Exchange and Distribution. They are all covered by price theory. Microeconomics seeks to explain that prices are determined by the interaction of demand and supply. The theory of demand covers consumption and supply covers production. According to the old explanation, commodity prices were studied in exchange and factor prices, i.e., rent, wage, interest and profit were studied in distribution. But in price theory we study both product prices (i.e., exchange) and factor prices (i.e., distribution). Thus, the old four divisions of Economics are covered in what we now call Microeconomics.

On the other hand, the subject matter of Macroeconomics is to study aggregates or averages of the entire economy, such as national income, output and employment, total consumption, total savings and investment, aggregate demand and aggregate supply, and so on. It explains what determines the level of national income, output and employment and what causes the fluctuations in the level of national income, output and employment.

The Macro-approach is essential, for what is true of the parts may not be true of the whole. Now-a-days Growth Economics, an important part of Macroeconomics, is a matter of great attention.

6. **Prof. Ackley** says, "Macroeconomics also uses aggregates smaller than for the whole economy but only in a context which makes them subdivisions of an economy-wide total. Microeconomics also uses aggregates, but not in a context which relates them to an economy-wide total".

7. It can be mentioned that classical economic theory of **Adam Smith, Ricardo, Malthus and J.S. Mill** and also attention given by **Lord Keynes** to the analysis of the economy as a whole are mainly based on macro-analysis. On the other hand, neoclassical economics where **Pigou** and **Marshall** predominate is mainly based on micro-analysis.

We, therefore, conclude that separate and distinct microeconomic and macroeconomic analyses are essential to understand the true and the actual working of the economic system of a country as a separate or as a whole. Neither Microeconomics nor Macroeconomics, alone is adequate for the analysis of the economy. It is essential to integrate the two approaches to arrive at a correct solution for better understanding the economic problems.

EXERCISES

1. Define Various Definitions of Economics.
2. What is Wealth Definitions?
3. What is Welfare Definition?

4. What is Scarcity Definition?
5. What is Growth Oriented Definition?
6. What is the Superiority of Robbins' Definition?
7. What are the Implications of Robbins' Definition?
8. Define Scope of Economics.
9. Define Economics as a Science.
10. Define Economics as an Art.
11. Define Economics as Pure or Applied.
12. Define Economics as a Positive or Normative Science.
13. Define Economics as Static or Dynamic.
14. Discuss in brief the subject matter of Microeconomic Theory.
15. Define Microeconomics with its Advantages and Limitations.
16. What are the advantages of Microeconomics?
17. What are the limitations of Microeconomics?
18. Discuss the subject Matter of Macroeconomic Theory.
19. Discuss the interdependences between Microeconomics and Macroeconomics.
20. Discuss the differences between Microeconomics and Macroeconomics.

Chapter 3

Consumer's Behaviour: Cardinal Utility

UTILITY

The concept of utility was evolved by the classical economists of the late 18th and 19th centuries. The 20th century version of the concept is the neoclassical. The utility approach was developed by **W.S. Jevons** of England, **Karl Menger** of Austria and **L. Walras** of France. Later on, in 1890, **Alfred Marshall** defined utility by bringing the concept of price in line with marginal utility.

Utility is generally defined as the capacity or the power of a commodity to satisfy a want. A person takes food; his hunger is satisfied. According to **Wicksteed**, "Utility as an economic concept, means only desireness." It signifies only the fact that a thing is wanted that it is expected to satisfy a given want. Utility resides in the mind of the consumer. The consumer knows it by introspection.

Utility has Certain Features

(i) Utility is different from satisfaction. Utility is the cause, satisfaction is the result.

(ii) Utility is different from pleasure. A medicine is bitter, yet it has utility, though it is not pleasant.

(iii) Utility has no connection with usefulness. Alcohol has utility because it satisfies a want but it is positively harmful for a drunkard.

(iv) Utility is subjective, i.e., it varies from man to man. A blind man has no utility for a lamp, because he cannot see anything.

(v) Production means creation of utility, i.e. the utility contained in something gets enhanced.

(vi) The utility of a commodity must be clearly distinguished from its price. The value of a commodity in terms of money is the same to every person. But other things being equal, utility differs from person to person. For example, one kilogram of wheat to a poor person has greater utility than that of a rich person.

TOTAL UTILITY AND MARGINAL UTILITY AND THEIR RELATIONSHIPS

Total Utility

Total utility is the aggregate or the sum total of the utilities derived from the consumption of the various units of a commodity in a given period of time. That is, the utility derived by a person from the total number of units of a commodity consumed by him is called total utility. For example if u_1, u_2, u_3, ..., u_n represents the utility derived from the first, second, third and up to nth unit of a commodity then total utility (Tu_n) will be

$$Tu_n = u_1 + u_2 + u_3 + \cdots\cdots + u_n$$

In simple words, if a person consumes four loaves of bread, then the total amount of utility will be equal to the sum total of the utility derived from the first, second, third and fourth loaf. Adding up the utility derived from each unit consumed, thus, gives the total utility of a commodity.

Marginal Utility

Marginal utility can be defined as the change in the total utility resulting from one unit change in the consumption of a commodity per unit of time. That is, marginal utility is the utility of one additional unit per unit of time. Again, it can be defined that marginal utility is the additional utility per additional unit of a commodity consumed per unit of time.

Marginal utility means the addition made to total utility by the marginal unit. Thus, if four loaves of bread have been consumed, marginal utility would refer to addition made to the total utility by consumption of this fourth loaf. And this addition would be equal to the total utility of the four loaves of bread minus the total utility of the three loaves of bread consumed. Thus, if four loaves of bread give 56 units of utility, while the three loaves has given 48 units of utility, the addition made by the fourth loaf is 56 – 48 = 8 units. The marginal unit is, therefore, the fourth loaf and the marginal utility is 8 units. Marginal utility is measured by the formula

$$Mu_n = Tu_n - Tu_{n-1}$$

where Mu_n means the marginal utility of nth unit of a commodity when altogether n units have been consumed, Tu_n refers to the total utility of n units and Tu_{n-1} refers to the total utility of (n – 1) units.

Again, the following formula may be used to measure marginal utility:

$$MU = \frac{\text{Change in total utility}}{\text{Change in quantity consumed}}$$

$$= \frac{\Delta TU}{\Delta Q} [\Delta => \text{Change in}]$$

Marginal utility may be positive, zero or negative when the consumption of the marginal unit gives some satisfaction, the marginal utility is positive; when it neither gives satisfaction nor causes any dissatisfaction, the marginal utility is zero; whereas if it causes some dissatisfaction, the marginal utility is negative.

Relationship between Total Utility (TU) and Marginal Utility (MU)

There are some suitable relationships between total utility and marginal utility. Total utility increases because total utility from two units must be more than one and that of three be more than of two and so on. But it increases at a diminishing rate because it is comprised of marginal utility. It increases at a diminishing rate so long as the point of satiety is not reached. The point of satiety is the point where the total utility is maximum and the marginal utility is zero and from where the total utility begins to fall and marginal utility becomes negative. In our example, at fifth and sixth unit, the utility derived from them is constant showing marginal utility is zero, and where TU curve is horizontal to the x-axis. The relationship between total utility and marginal utility can be explained with the help of schedule and Fig. 3.1.

Units	TU	MU
1	10	10
2	18	8
3	25	7
4	30	5
5	34	4
6	34	0
7	32	-2
8	29	-3

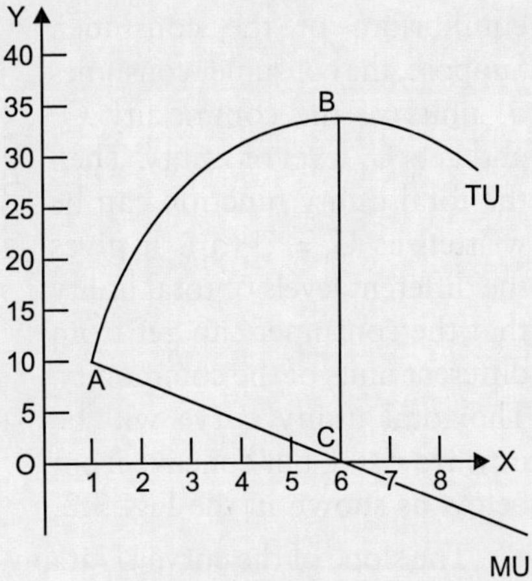

Fig. 3.1

Both the curves start from the point A. TU-curve is maximum at point B at the 6th unit from where it moves downward and where MU-curve cuts the x-axis showing that MU is zero, after which (point C) MU is negative and MU curve is approaching below x-axis.

CONSUMER'S EQUILIBRIUM

The consumer's equilibrium (behaviour) can be studied through two alternative techniques—the utility technique and the indifference curve technique. Here we discuss utility technique.

A consumer at a time needs several goods and services for consumption. His income is limited and it may not be possible for him to buy whatever he desires. He faces fixed prices of commodities in the market. In this situation, how should he decide buying of the commodities? What commodity he should buy and in what amounts, that is to say how should he allocate his limited income on various goods and services so that he gets maximum satisfaction or utility? The problem here is that of maximizing total utility by consuming all goods and services subject to the income constraint.

The solution of this problem will give us the conditions of equilibrium of the consumer. Suppose, the consumer consumes q_1 units of the commodity Q_1 and gets U_1 level of utility. Then the total utility function can be written as $U_1 = U_1(q_1)$. It gives the different levels of total utility that the consumer can get from different units of the commodity. The total utility curve will be upward rising but concave from below as shown in the Fig. 3.2.

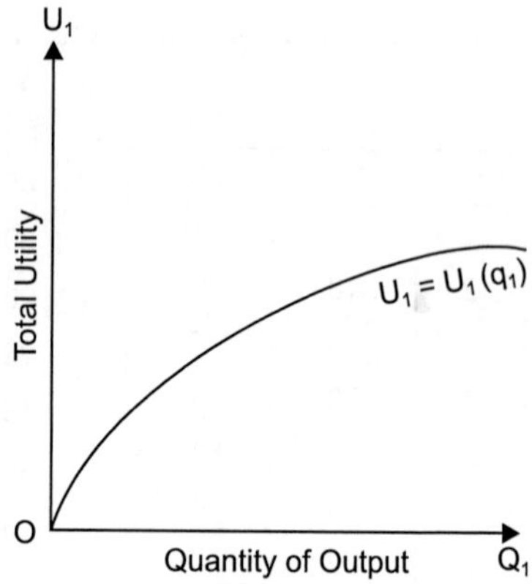

Fig. 3.2

The slope of the curve U_1 at any point represents the marginal utility of Q_1 at that point. Since the curve is concave, it represents that the slopes decrease as we move along the curve from left to right. This means that the marginal utility of Q_1 decreases as more units of Q_1 are consumed.

When the consumer purchases some units of the commodity to get some amount of utility he has to spend some amount of money. Money also possesses some utility, he has to sacrifice the utility of money when he spends. The difference between the total utility obtained and the total utility sacrificed is called the net utility. Suppose, if the consumer purchases q_1 units of the commodity at constant price p_1, the total expenditure is p_1q_1. If λ represents the constant marginal utility of one unit of money, the sacrifice of utility of total money is equal to λp_1q_1. Again, the total utility obtained from q_1 units is equal to $u_1(q_1)$. Therefore, the net utility derived by the consumer is equal to $u_1(q_1) - \lambda p_1q_1$. Let V represents net utility, i.e., $V = u_1(q_1) - \lambda p_1q_1$. Since λ and p_1 are constants, V is a function of q_1 only.

In Fig. 3.3, on the horizontal axis we plot q_1, and on the vertical axis we plot U_1 and λp_1q_1. Here λp_1q_1 is represented by a straight line through origin. It represents the total utility sacrificed while the curve $U_1(q_1)$ represents the total utility obtained. The vertical gap between the total utility curve $U_1(q_1)$ and the total utility sacrificed line $\lambda p_1 q_1$ represent net utility. Net utility will be maximum when the vertical gap between $U_1(q_1)$ and $\lambda p_1 q_1$ is maximum. This happens at point N on the total utility curve where a tangent to the curve $U_1(q_1)$ is parallel to the straight line $\lambda p_1 q_1$. To maximise net utility the consumer will purchase OM units of Q_1 where he gets maximum net utility, NR. If the quantity purchased is more or less than OM, the consumer will derive less net utility. So, the consumer will be in equilibrium at point N on total utility curve $U_1(q_1)$.

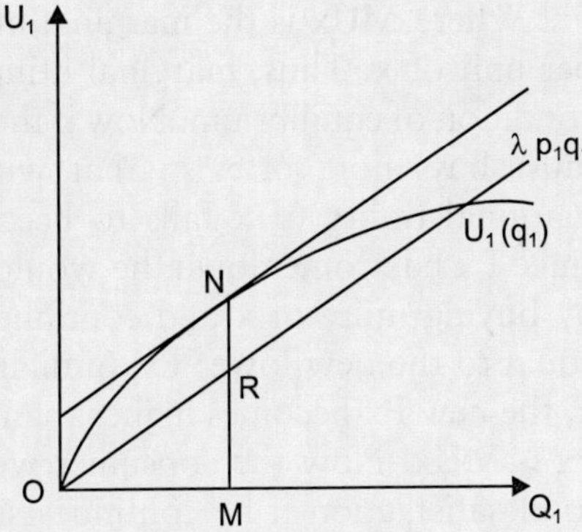

Fig. 3.3

MARSHALLIAN DEMAND CURVE

The demand curve or the law of demand shows the relationship between quantity demanded of a commodity and its price. In the Marshallian analysis, the demand curve for a commodity is derived from its utility function. Since Marshall assumes the utility function of any commodity as being based upon the consumption of this commodity alone, and as independent of the utilities of other goods, the relationship of complementary and substitute goods has thus been ruled out. Further, in deriving the demand curve, Marshall assumes marginal utility of money expenditure to remain constant.

In the law of diminishing utility we have seen that the marginal utility of any commodity say x, declines continuously and becomes negative beyond a point. We also know that the consumer is in equilibrium (i.e., he gets the maximum satisfaction) when marginal utility of a good becomes equal to its market price. Thus, consumer's equilibrium can be expressed as MUx = Px.

Where MUx is the marginal utility of x and Px is the price per unit of x. Thus, marginal utility being equal to price is the condition of equilibrium. Now if the price of x falls, the consumer must buy more of x so that with this additional purchase, marginal utility of x falls to become equal to its price. Now since Px has come down, he would add to his total satisfaction by buying more of x and continue to do so till MUx becomes equal to the new lower Px. Similarly with a rise in the price of x, the new Px becomes higher than the marginal utility of x i.e., Px > MUx. Now the consumer would be making a loss to his total satisfaction if he continues sticking to his earlier level of purchases of x. He must, therefore, readjust his purchases; buy less of x till MUx rises to become equal to Px. Hence, he would buy less at a higher price.

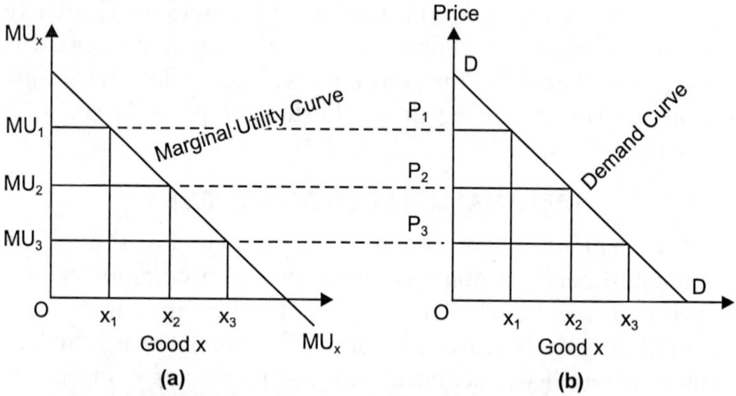

Fig. 3.4

If we measure MUx in monetary units, then the demand curve for x shall be identical to the MUx curve in its positive segment. In the above Fig. 3.4(a) MUx is the marginal utility curve for x. For the quantity OX_1, marginal utility is MU_1. Since the marginal utility itself is being measured in terms of money, MU_1 also corresponds to the price P_1 in Fig. 3.4(b), where quantity bought at this price is Ox_1. Similarly MU_2 in Fig. 3.4(a), shows the marginal utility of the quantity Ox_2. Corresponding to MU_2, price in Fig. 3.4(b) is P_2 and the quantity bought is Ox_2. Again for MU_3 in Fig. 3.4(a), P_3 is the price in Fig. 3.4(b) and the quantity bought is Ox_3. Thus, the curve MUx is itself the demand curve for x. However, the negative segment of the MUx does not form a part of the demand curve because negative prices and negative quantities do not make any sense in economic point of view. Thus, demand curve for x can be derived from its marginal utility curve taking only its positive portion.

Therefore, DD in Fig. 3.4(b) corresponding to the positive portion of MU_x in Fig. 3.4(a) is the Marshallian demand curve.

MARSHALLIAN THEORY

Law of Equi-marginal Utility

Wants are competitive due to multiplicity of wants and scarcity of means. There are more urgent wants and less urgent wants. Therefore, we have innumerable wants whereas our income is limited. We have to think whether to spend money on buying this or that commodity. Money acts as a bridge to purchase from one commodity to another commodity depending on its marginal utility. Consciously or unconsciously we try to balance in our mind the satisfaction which we expect to get from the different commodities. So long as we consider that we shall get more utility from the first than from the other, we shall buy the first commodity. In this way, we go on spending more or less money on this or that commodity until the marginal utility of money is equal on all things. Suppose, there are only two commodities X and Y on which we have to spend our given income. Consumer's behaviour is governed by two factors: first, by the marginal utilities of the goods and secondly, by prices of the two goods. Now, marginal utility of a commodity is proportional to its price.

Therefore, $MU_X \propto P_1$ and $MU_Y \propto P_2$

or, $MUx = \lambda P_1$ and $MU_Y = \lambda P_2$

or, $\dfrac{MUx}{P_1} = \lambda$ and $\dfrac{MUy}{P_2} = \lambda$

$\therefore \quad \dfrac{MUx}{P_1} = \dfrac{MUy}{P_2} = \lambda$ where P_1 and P_2 are the prices of commodity X and Y and λ is the marginal utility of money spent.

This is known as the Marshallian law of equi-marginal utility. This means that we get the same amount of utility by spending one unit of money either on X or Y. Therefore, the law of equi-marginal utility states that to maximize utility the consumer will distribute his money income between the commodities in such a way that the utility derived by spending one unit of money on each commodity is equal.

So long as $\frac{MUx}{P_1} > \frac{MUy}{P_2}$, we shall curtail our expenditure on Y and increase our expenditure on X till $\frac{MUx}{P_1} = \frac{MUy}{P_2}$. Again, if $\frac{MUx}{P_1} < \frac{MUy}{P_2}$ is seen, we shall curtail our expenditure on X and increase our expenditure on Y till $\frac{MUx}{P_1} = \frac{MUy}{P_2}$.

Thus, $\frac{MUx}{P_1} = \frac{MUy}{P_2} = \lambda$

If there are more than two commodities on which we are spending our income, we get

$$\frac{MU_1}{P_1} = \frac{MU_2}{P_2} = \cdots\cdots = \frac{MU_n}{P_n} = \lambda$$

Diagrammatic Representation

The principle of equi-marginal utility can be explained with the help of the following Fig. 3.5. In this figure, we measure commodity X along the X-axis from left to right (i.e., on the portion OX) and also commodity Y along the X-axis from right to left (i.e., on the portion OX′).

Along the OY axis, the amount of money spent on the commodity X and Y is measured. On the right hand side of OY, MU_X is drawn, which slopes downwards from left to right. This curve shows the marginal utility of the money spent on the commodity X. On the other side of OY, MU_Y is drawn, which also slopes downwards from right to left. This curve shows the marginal utility of money spent on the commodity Y.

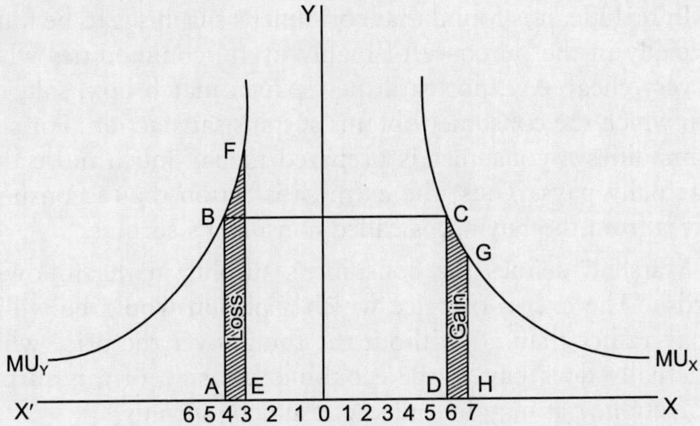

Fig. 3.5

Suppose, we have ₹ 10 to spend on the two commodities X and Y. In the figure, we spend ₹ 6 on X and ₹ 4 on Y and the marginal utilities of both commodities are equal (AB = CD). In this way we get maximum satisfaction. Any other arrangement will reduce our aggregate satisfaction. Suppose, we spend ₹ 7 on X and ₹ 3 on Y. As a result, the marginal utilities will be unequal (FE > GH). The gain in utility by consumption more of X is less than the loss in utility by consumption less of Y and our total utility will be less than before. The gain and the loss of utilities are shown by the shaded area in the Fig. 3.5. Thus, we can conclude that the consumer will get maximum satisfaction and will be in equilibrium if the marginal utilities of money spent on the various goods are equal.

CONSUMER'S SURPLUS

Prof. Alfred Marshall first evolved the concept of consumer's surplus, a very important concept in economic theory, in his book, *Principles of Economics* published in 1890. This concept is important not only in economic theory but also in economic policies, such as taxation by the government and price policy pursued by the monopolistic seller of a product. Consumer's surplus is the extra/surplus satisfaction derived by a consumer from the purchases over the price he actually pays for them.

In real life, it is found that consumer's surplus is to be found especially in the purchase of highly useful commodities which are very cheap e.g., postcard, newspaper, match box, salt, etc. from which the consumer obtains surplus satisfaction. For such commodities a consumer is prepared to pay much more than he actually pays. Thus, the extra satisfaction that a consumer derives from the buying, is called consumer's surplus.

Marshall defines the consumer's surplus in the following words, "The excess of price which a person would be willing to pay rather than go without the thing, over the price which he actually does pay, is the economic measure of this surplus satisfaction.... It may be called consumer's surplus."

The amount of money which a person is prepared to pay for a good indicates the amount of utility he derives from that good, the greater the amount of money he is willing to pay, the greater the satisfaction or utility he will obtain from it. Therefore, the marginal utility (MU) of a unit of a good determines the price which a consumer will be prepared to pay for that unit. The total utility which a person will get from a good will be obtained by sum of marginal utilities (ΣMU) of the units of the good purchased and the money value equals the price per unit multiplied by the number of units purchased. The difference between what a consumer is prepared to pay and what he actually pays or difference between sum of marginal utilities and value of goods purchased is called consumer's surplus. Therefore,

Consumer's surplus = what a consumer is prepared to pay – what he actually pays
= Σ marginal utility – (price × no. of units purchased)
= $\Sigma MU - p \times q$
= Total utility – Total amount spent

Thus, consumer's surplus is the excess of what we are prepared to pay over what we actually pay for a commodity. It is the difference between what we are prepared to pay and what we actually pay.

Illustration: We can illustrate this concept with the help of the table given below.

Units of Oranges (q)	Marginal Utility (p)	Price Per Orange (p)	Consumer's Surplus (p)
1	100	20	80
2	70	20	50
3	50	20	30
4	35	20	15
5	25	20	5
6	20	20	0
Total units purchased = 6	Total utility = 300p	Total money spent = 120p	Total consumer's surplus = 180p

That is, total consumer's surplus = 300p – 120p = 180p.

It is assumed in the above table that the price of each orange in the market is 20p. The consumer will be going to purchase as many oranges one by one till his marginal utility equals to its price. Thus, he will purchase 6 oranges and pay for each 20p. In this way he will spend in all 120p, but the total utility of the 6 oranges is equal to 300p. He thus, gets a consumer's surplus equal to (300 – 120)p = 180p.

The consumer's surplus can also be found from the fourth column of the table shown above. The utility of the first unit of oranges to the consumer is equal to 100p; therefore he would be prepared to pay 100p for it. But he pays for the first orange only 20p, because the price of an orange in the market is 20p. Therefore, from the first unit the consumer gets consumer's surplus equals to (100 – 20)p = 80p shown in the 4th column. Similarly, the utility derived from the second orange is equal to 70p, while the consumer pays 20p for it and therefore obtains (70 – 20) = 50p as consumer's surplus and the like. From the sixth unit, the consumer derives satisfaction equal to 20p and he also pays 20p for it. Thus there is no consumer's surplus from the sixth unit. Now if we add all the consecutive consumer's surplus in the 4th column, we get total consumer's surplus which is equal to 180p.

DIAGRAMMATIC REPRESENTATION

We can show consumer's surplus with the help of the following Fig. 3.6.

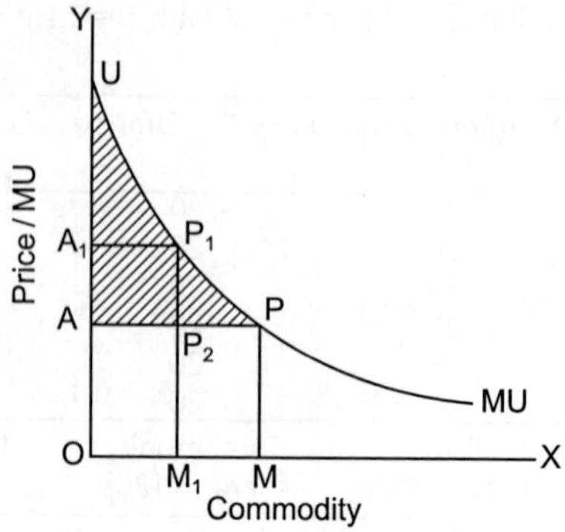

Fig. 3.6

If the market price is OA, the consumer will extend his purchase up to the Mth unit. That is, he will purchase OM quantity. This is so because for this M[th] unit that his marginal utility (MU) is equal to the price. But his marginal utility for the earlier units is more than OA. For M_1[th] unit, for instance, his MU is P_1M_1 but he only pays the market price OA (= P_2M_1) for this unit. He thus, obtains an excess of utility for the M_1[th] unit equal to P_1 P_2. This is consumer's surplus from this unit. Similar surplus arises from the purchase of other units. The total consumer's surplus thus, derived by him when OM units are purchased at OA price is shown by the shaded area UAP.

If the market price rises to P_1M_1, he will purchase only OM_1 quantity of oranges and the consumer's surplus will fall to the smaller triangle UA_1P_1.

We can explain it in another angle also. Suppose in this figure, the total utility derived by the consumer from OM units of the commodity will be equal to the area under the marginal curve up to point M. That is, the total utilities of OM units in this Figure is equal to OUPM. In other words, for OM units of the good the consumer will be prepared to pay the sum equal to Rs. OUPM. But given the price OA, the consumer will actually pay Rs. OAPM for OM units of the good. It is thus clear that the consumer derives extra utilities equal to AUP which is called consumer's surplus.

∴ AUP = OUPM – OAPM. Here, AUP is consumer's surplus shown by shaded area in the Fig. 3.6.

If the market price of the commodity rises above OA, the consumer will buy fewer units of the good than OM. As a result, consumer's surplus obtained by him from his purchase will decline. On the other hand, if the price falls below OA, the consumer purchase more units than before. As a result, the consumer's surplus will increase. Thus, given the marginal utility curve of the consumer, the higher the price, the smaller is the consumer's surplus and the lower the price the greater is the consumer's surplus.

LIMITATIONS OF THE MARSHALLIAN THEORY

The Marshallian theory has been criticised on various grounds. The following shortcomings of marginal utility analysis have been pointed out:

(1) **Cardinal measurability of utility is unrealistic:** Marginal utility analysis of demand is based on the assumption that utility can be measured in quantitative terms i.e., in cardinal numbers such as 1, 2, 3, and so on. But in actual practice utility cannot be measured in such quantitative or cardinal terms. Utility is subjective. It differs from person to person. According to **J.R. Hicks,** we can make order of different utility levels but not exactly measure them.

(2) **Assumption of independent utilities is wrong:** Marshall assumes that utility derived from various goods are independent. This means that different utility functions are independent. Utility obtained from any commodity depends on the amount of that commodity only i.e. $u_1 = u_1(q_1)$ and $u_2 = u_2(q_2)$ and $u = u_1 + u_2$. This assumption is unrealistic. Different utility levels are, in fact, interdependent. Utility obtained from any commodity depends not only on the amount of that commodity but also on the amounts of other commodities. By neglecting interdependence Marshall could not explain the case of substitutes and complements.

(3) **Assumption of constant marginal utility of money is not valid:** Marshall assumes that the marginal utility of money remains constant. It is unrealistic. The constancy of marginal utility of money implies that there is no income effect of a change

in price. But when the price of a commodity changes, the real income of the consumer also changes. With the change in real income, marginal utility of money will change and this would have an effect on the demand for the good though the total money income available with the consumer remains the same. But utility analysis ignores all these and does not take cognizance of the change in real income and its effect on demand for goods. If his assumption is dropped, the demand curve cannot be derived.

(4) **The Marshallian theory is unable to explain Giffen's paradox:** The constancy of marginal utility of money implies that the income effect of a fall in price is zero. It can never be negative or positive. This prevented Marshall from understanding the composite character of the price effect, i.e., price effect is the sum of substitution effect and income effect. As a result, the Giffen's paradox cannot be explained with the help of Marshallian theory. Giffen's paradox takes place when the income effect is negative and stronger than the substitution effect. This is not possible in the Marshallian theory. The demand curve derived from this theory can never be upward rising. It will always be downward sloping.

(5) **Marshallian demand theory cannot genuinely be derived except in one commodity model:** Suppose, the consumer spends all his income on two commodities say, Q_1 and Q_2. Now the price of Q_1 falls but the price of Q_2 remains the same. The demand for Q_1 must then increase from the equilibrium condition of the consumer. The total expenditure on Q_1 may increase or decrease or remain constant. If total expenditure decreases, it means that more money will be left with the consumer to spend on Q_2. On the other hand if total expenditure increases, less money will be left with the consumer to spend on Q_2. In both the cases the demand for Q_2 will be affected. This goes against the assumption of independent utility function.

(6) **Marginal utility analysis does not split up the price effect into substitution and income effects:** We know that when the price of a good falls the consumer becomes better off than before. If with the fall in price the consumer purchases the same quantity of the good as before, he would be left with some income. With this income he would be in a position to

purchase more of this good as well as other goods. This is the income effect due to fall in price. Besides, when the price of a good falls, it becomes relatively cheaper than other goods and as a result the consumer is induced to substitute that good for others. This results in the increase in the quantity demanded of that good. This is the substitution effect of the price change on the quantity demanded of the good.

With the fall in price of a good, the quantity demanded of it rises because of income effect and substitution effect. But marginal utility analysis does not make clear the distinction between the income effect and the substitution effect of the price change. In fact, Marshall ignored income effect of the price change by assuming the constancy of marginal utility of money. Thus, marginal utility analysis does not tell us about how much quantity demanded increases due to income effect and how much due to substitution effect as a result of the fall in price of a good.

(7) **Marginal utility analysis assumes too much and explains too little:** Marginal utility analysis is also criticised on the ground that it takes more assumptions than those of ordinal utility analysis of indifference curve technique.

(1) Marginal utility analysis assumes that utility is cardinally measurable and marginal utility of money remains constant. Hicks-Allen's indifference curve analysis does not take these assumptions and even then it is not only able to deduce all the theorems which cardinal utility analysis can but also deduces a more general theorem of demand.

(2) Without assuming constant marginal utility of money, indifference curve analysis is able to derive the condition of consumer's equilibrium.

(3) Indifference curve analysis is able to explain Giffen paradox which marginal utility analysis could not.

(4) Marginal utility analysis does not split up the price effect into substitution and income effects. But indifference curve analysis is able to split up the price effect into substitution and income effects.

For all these reasons discussed above the marginal utility analysis of Marshall has been rejected by Hicks and Pareto who have developed a new approach to the theory of consumer behaviour which is known as the ordinal approach or the Hicks-Allen indifference curve analysis.

EXERCISES

1. Define Utility.
2. Explain Total Utility and Marginal Utility and also their relationships.
3. Explain critically consumer's equilibrium.

   Or

   A consumer has a given amount of income and faces constant commodity prices. Derive the conditions when its utility is maximised.
4. How do you derive the Marshallian demand curve?

   Or

   Discuss critically the Marshallian technique of deriving demand curve for the good from its utility.

   Or

   By using the cardinal approach to utility analysis, derive the demand curve for the commodity that a consumer buys.
5. Define law of Equi-marginal Utility in the context of Marshallian view.
6. What do you mean by Consumer's Surplus? Illustrate it with the help of a diagram.
7. Discuss critically the limitations of the Marshallian Theory.

   Or

   Evaluate critically the Marginal utility analysis.
8. Marshallian theory of utility analysis assumes too much and explains too little. Explain.

Chapter 4

Consumer's Behaviour: Ordinal Utility

Concept: This is an alternative approach developed by economists like **Edgeworth, Fisher, Slutsky, Hicks** and **Allen** to analyse consumer's behaviour. In this approach, the emphasis is given on comparing different utility levels instead of measuring them through some cardinal scale. In other words, this approach is based on ordinal measurement of utility. Under ordinal measurement scale, the utility can only be ranked such as greater or smaller, higher or lower and the like. Therefore, the alternative approach to explain consumer's behaviour is indifference curve analysis. The approach of indifference curve for analysing consumer behaviour is based on the following axioms:

AXIOMS OF INDIFFERENCE CURVE ANALYSIS

1. **The axiom of completeness:** This axiom states that all commodity bundles can be compared in term of either indifference or preference. That is, for all X and all Y there will be either X ⊗ Y or Y ⊗ X where ⊗ indicates 'is preferred to'. This means that given any two commodity bundles, the consumer can always rank them in his preference scale or will be indifferent in ranking them.

2. **The axiom of transitivity:** The axiom states that for all X, Y and Z if X ⊗ Y and Y ⊗ Z then X ⊗ Z.

3. **The axiom of selection:** The axiom states that within the attainable (or feasible) set the consumer tries to reach the most preferred state. The attainable set or the feasible set represents

those commodity bundles which the consumer can purchase with his given income and the given prices of the commodities.

4. **The axiom of dominance:** If two bundles X and Y are such that X has more of both the commodities than Y, it is said that X dominates Y. If X dominates Y, the consumer will prefer X. That is, the consumer always prefers more of both commodities to less. This axiom can be widened that in the two commodity space if a bundle X contains more of one commodity and same amount of other commodity than the bundle Y, then also X dominates Y. But it is provided the condition that the saturation point with respect to each commodity has not been reached.

5. **The axiom of continuity of preferences:** This axiom says that there exists a set of points on a boundary dividing the commodity space into less preferred and more preferred areas such that these points on the boundary are indifferent to each other. In Fig. 4.1, the line EF divides the space into less preferred area and more preferred area. The point B consisting more of both the commodities, say X and Y than the point A will be preferred. But the consumer will be indifferent on any point along the line EF getting same level of satisfaction.

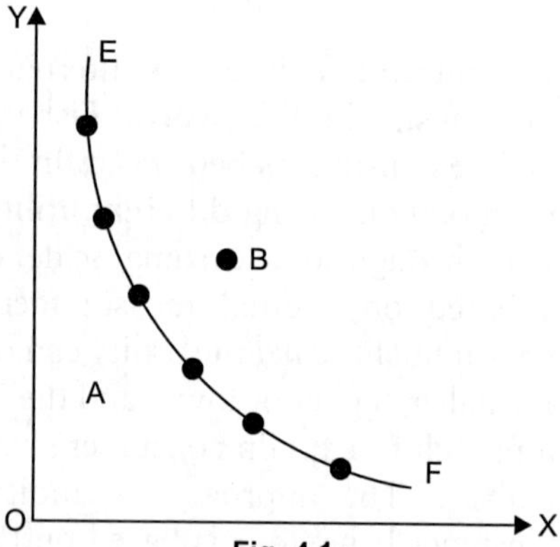

Fig. 4.1

6. **The axiom of convexity of preferences:** This axiom guarantees the convexity of the indifference curves. Convexity may be strong or weak. Weak convexity permits linear indifference curves but strong convexity does not. A curve is said to be strongly convex if the line joining any two points on the curve lies to the right of the curve at a higher distance shown in Fig. 4.2. On the other hand, convexity is weak if the line joining any two points on the curve either lies to the right of the curve at a less distance or coincides shown in Figs. 4.3 and 4.4. These are shown overleaf.

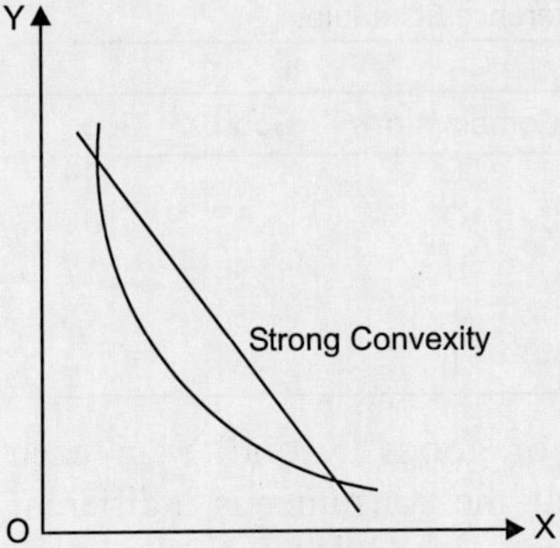

Fig. 4.2

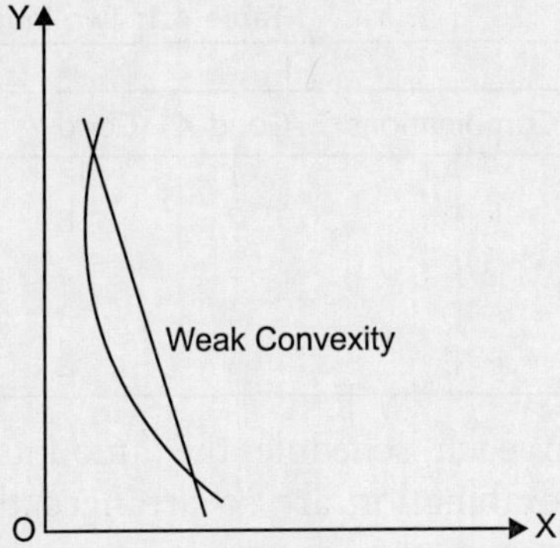

Fig. 4.3

Though there are many goods and multiple combinations of these goods available to the consumer, in the indifference curve analysis, we take only two goods to formulate rules of consumer's behaviour. This is essentially due to the fact that we have only two dimensional diagrams and can, therefore, analyse consumer's behaviour with regard to only two goods and their combinations.

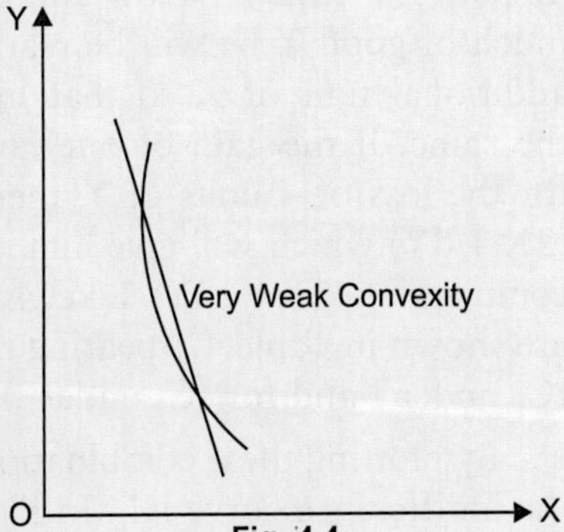

Fig. 4.4

INDIFFERENCE CURVE AND ITS DERIVATION

The basic tool of **Hicks-Allen** ordinal analysis of demand is the indifference curve which represents all those combinations of goods which give same satisfaction to the consumer. That is, an indifference curve is a curve showing the various combinations of two goods among which a consumer is indifferent i.e., he equally prefers these combinations. So, it will not matter to him which one he gets. In other words, all combinations of the goods lying on an indifference curve are equally desirable to or equally preferred by him. To understand indifference curves, it is better to start with indifference schedules. In Table 4.1, two indifference schedules are given.

Table 4.1: Two Indifference Schedules

I			II		
Combinations	Good X	Good Y	Combinations	Good X	Good Y
A	1	12	F	2	14
B	2	8	G	3	10
C	3	5	H	4	7
D	4	3	I	5	5
E	5	2	J	6	4

In each schedule the amounts of goods X and Y in each combination are so arranged that the consumer is indifferent among the combinations in each schedule. In Schedule-I, the consumer has to start with 1 unit of X and 12 units of Y, i.e. (1X + 12Y). Now the consumer is asked to tell how much of good Y he will be ready to give up for the gain of an additional unit of X so that his level of satisfaction remains the same. If the gain of one unit of X compensates him fully for the loss of 4 units of Y, then the next combination will be (2X + 8Y) which will give him the same satisfaction of the first combination (1X + 12Y). Likewise we get the combinations which are shown in Table 4.1 bearing the same level of satisfaction for IC_1 under I and for IC_2 under II.

By plotting these combinations in figure given below, we get the indifference curve IC_1. In Fig. 4.5, units of X are measured on X-axis and that of Y on the Y-axis shown below.

The line joining the points A, B, C, D and E is the indifference curve IC_1. Now if the consumer is given more of X as well as of Y, his satisfaction will increase and he will move on to a higher indifference curve which is above and to the right of the curve IC_1.

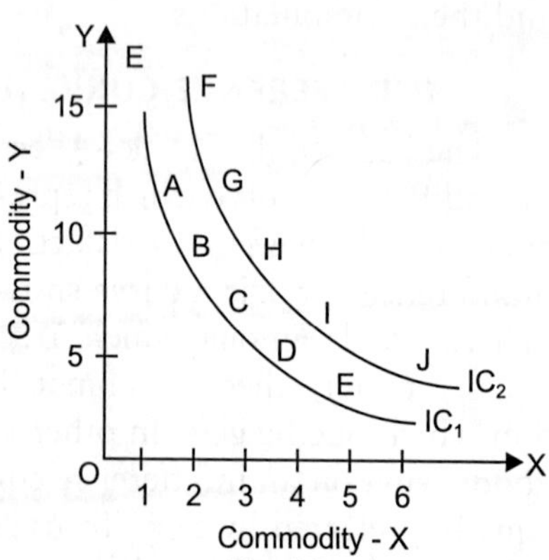

Fig. 4.5

Thus, if the new indifference schedule of the consumer is as shown in

Table 4.1 (II) which contains more of X and Y, he will move on to a higher indifference curve IC_2. By plotting these combinations in the same Fig. 4.5, we get a higher indifference curve by joining the points F, G, H, I and J. This indifference curve IC_2 shows greater satisfaction to the consumer since he has more of X and more of Y than the previous combinations. The curve IC_2 is higher than IC_1 and any point on it shows a higher level of satisfaction compared to that of IC_1. In the same way we can still increase the amount of X and Y available to us and plot those combinations to get a higher curve IC_3. All these curves IC_1, IC_2 and IC_3 show what is called consumer's indifference map. On each curve all the combinations give equal satisfaction. It is, thus clear that the indifference curve lying to the right of an indifference curve will indicate higher level of satisfaction than the lower.

MARGINAL RATE OF SUBSTITUTION (MRS) AND ITS SIGNIFICANCE

The principle of diminishing marginal rate of substitution occupies a key place in the indifference curve analysis in the same way as the principle of diminishing marginal utility is the whole basis of the Marshallian utility analysis of consumer's behaviour. Suppose, the consumer has two commodities say, X and Y for consumption. The term marginal rate of substitution of X for Y represents the amount of Y which the consumer has to give up for the gain of one additional unit of X so that his level of satisfaction remains the same. It is briefly written as MRS_{xy}.

The concept of marginal rate of substitution can be better understood from Table 4.2, which shows various combinations of two goods X and Y that give equal satisfaction to the consumer.

Combination A contains 1 unit of X and 15 units of Y and combination B has 2 units of X and 10 units of Y. Since these two combinations give the same satisfaction to the consumer, it shows that by moving from combination A to combination B, he has added one extra unit of X but has given up 5 units of Y. This means that at this stage he is to prepare to exchange 5 units of Y for 1 unit of X and by doing so he remains on the same level of satisfaction. It follows that 1 unit gain in X fully compensates him for the loss of 5 units of Y. Therefore, at this stage consumer's marginal rate of substitution of X for Y is 5 i.e., MRS_{xy} = 5Y or 5.

Again, when the consumer moves from B to C on his indifference schedule he forgoes 4 units of Y for the additional 1 unit gain in X, i.e., MRS_{xy} = 4Y or 4. Likewise, when the consumer moves from C to D, and then from D to E in his indifference schedule, the MRS_{xy} is 3 and 2 respectively. Thus MRS_{xy} declines. It is shown in Table 4.2.

Table 4.2: Marginal Rate of Substitution

Combinations	Good X	Good Y	MRS_{xy}
A	1	15	–
B	2	10	5
C	3	6	4
D	4	3	3
E	5	1	2

Significance: Naturally a question arises why the magnitude of the marginal rate of substitution of X for Y (MRS_{xy}) declines as we decrease quantity of Y and increase quantity of X. The consumer prefers a balanced consumption of different goods. Too much consumption of one good induces him to substitute it for the other good whose consumption is low. The declining tendency of the MRS can be explained in a better way by using the marginal utility concept. From the law of diminishing marginal utility we know that there is an inverse relationship between quantity of consumption and marginal utility. When we decrease quantity of consumption of a commodity in favour of another, the marginal utility of the commodity increases. On the other hand, the marginal utility of the other commodity decreases. That is, decrease in the quantity of good Y means increase its marginal utility and increase in the quantity of good X means decrease its marginal utility. This is the reason for which MRS_{xy} declines gradually.

Or, following the Table 4.2 shown above an indifference curve is drawn in Fig. 4.6, when the consumer moves from point A to B on this indifference curve he gives up AS of Y and takes up SB of X and remains on the same indifference curve. It means that the loss of satisfaction caused by giving up AS of Y equals the gain in satisfaction due to the increase in good X by SB. It follows that the consumer is to prepare to exchange AS of Y for SB of X. That is, $MRS_{xy} = \frac{AS}{SB}$. Now a small change as AS of Y and as SB of X can be written as ΔY and ΔX respectively. Thus, ΔY shows the amount which the consumer has to give up for the ΔX increase in X remaining on the same indifference curve.

$$\text{So, } MRS_{xy} = \frac{AS}{SB} = \frac{\Delta Y}{\Delta X}$$

An important principle of economic theory is that MRS_{xy} diminishes as more and more of good X is substituted for good Y. Because as the consumer slides down along the curve, the length ΔY becomes shorter and shorter, while the length ΔX is kept the same. It is seen in Fig. 4.6. ΔY_1 is less than ΔY; ΔY_2 is less than ΔY_1; ΔY_3 is less than ΔY_2 while $\Delta X = \Delta X_1 = \Delta X_2 = \Delta X_3$. It means that as the consumer's stock of X increases and his stock of Y decreases, he is willing to forego less and less of Y for a given increment in X.

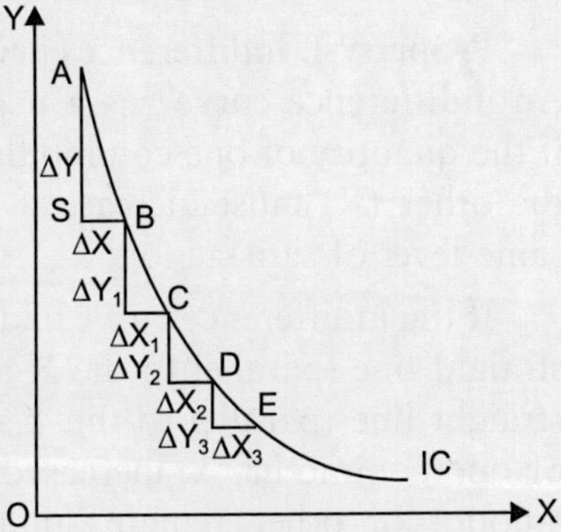

Fig. 4.6

RELATIONSHIP BETWEEN MARGINAL RATE OF SUBSTITUTION AND MARGINAL UTILITIES

To show the relationship we consider the Fig. 4.6. In moving down along the indifference curve from A to B, the consumer gives up ΔY of Y for the gain in X by ΔX and remains on the same level of satisfaction. This means that the total loss in utility by giving up ΔY is equal to the total gain in utilities owing to the increase in X by ΔX. That is, the total loss in utility by surrendering $\Delta Y = \Delta Y \times$ M.U. of Y and, the gain in utility by taking $\Delta X = \Delta X \times$ M.U. of X.

Since the loss is equal to the gain, therefore,

$$\Delta Y \times MU \text{ of } Y = \Delta X \times MU \text{ of } X$$

$$\frac{\Delta Y}{\Delta X} = \frac{\text{M.U. of X}}{\text{M.U. of Y}}$$

$$\therefore \qquad MRS_{xy} = \frac{\text{M.U. of X}}{\text{M.U. of Y}} \left[\because \frac{\Delta Y}{\Delta X} = MRS_{xy}\right]$$

Thus, the marginal rate of substitution between two goods is equal to the ratio between the marginal utilities of two goods.

PROPERTIES OF AN INDIFFERENCE CURVE

Property-I. Indifference curve slopes downward to the right: An indifference curve has a negative slope which denotes that if the quantity of one commodity (Y) decreases, the quantity of the other (X) must increase if the consumer is to stay on the same level of satisfaction, i.e., on the same indifference curve.

If the indifference curve had the shape of either a horizontal straight line (parallel to the X-axis, as in Fig. 4.7) or a vertical straight line (parallel to the Y-axis as in Fig. 4.8), the amount of one commodity is increased in the combination, while the amount of other remains unchanged, the new combination will be preferable to the original one. In Fig. 4.7 in various combinations such as A, B, C and D on indifference curve IC while the amount of good X is successively larger, the amount

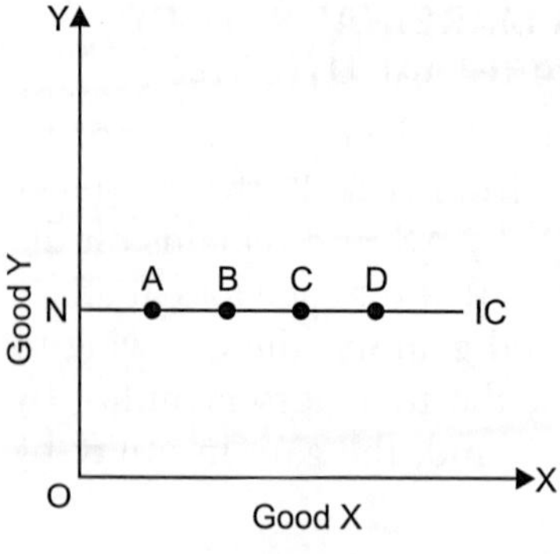

Fig. 4.7

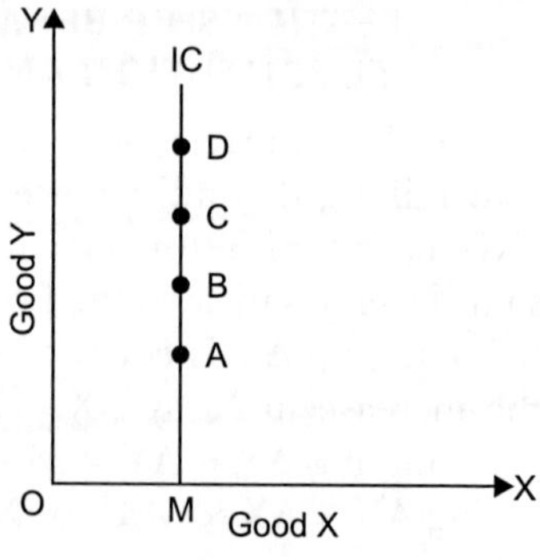

Fig. 4.8

of good Y remains unchanged (ON). If the consumer is to prefer a larger amount of good X to a smaller amount, then how he can be indifferent between combinations A, B, C, and D. It is thus concluded that indifference curve cannot be a horizontal straight line. Likewise, indifference curve cannot be a vertical straight line.

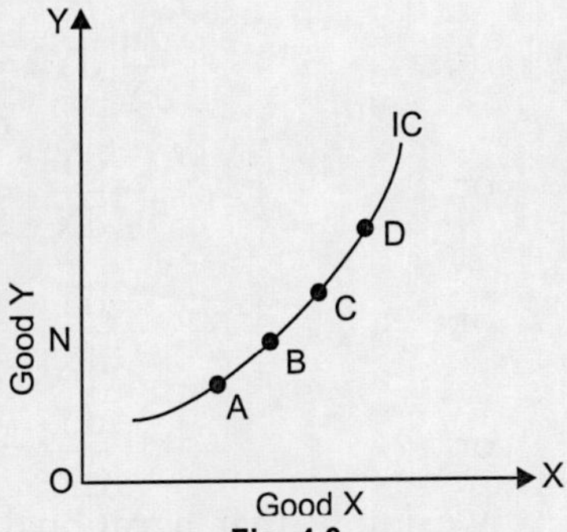

Fig. 4.9

Again if the indifference curves were upward sloping to the right, it means that the amounts of both the goods increase as one moves to the right along the curve as shown in Fig. 4.9. Larger amounts of goods naturally give higher satisfaction which violates the principle of indifference curve analysis. So, indifference curve cannot be a upward sloping curve. An indifference curve represents those combinations which give the same amount of satisfaction to the consumer and he is, therefore, indifferent between them. To maintain his indifference between them, then as the amount of good X is increased, the amount of good Y must be reduced. This is what a downward sloping curve indicates. So the indifference curve slopes downward to the right.

Alternative Explanation

To prove this property mathematically, let us consider the utility function:

$$u = f(X, Y)$$

By taking total derivatives of this function, we have

$$du = \frac{\partial u}{\partial X} dX + \frac{\partial u}{\partial Y} dY$$

From the definition of the indifference curve, we know that utility does not change when we move along the curve, so we can write du = 0.

$$\therefore \quad \frac{\partial u}{\partial X} dX + \frac{\partial u}{\partial Y} dY = 0$$

$$\text{or,} \qquad \frac{\partial u}{\partial Y} dY = -\frac{\partial u}{\partial X} dX$$

$$\text{or,} \qquad -\frac{dY}{dX} = \frac{\partial u/\partial X}{\partial u/\partial Y}$$

$$\text{or,} \qquad -\frac{dY}{dX} = \frac{MU_X}{MU_Y}$$

$$\text{or,} \qquad \frac{dY}{dX} = -MRS_{XY}$$

We know that a rational consumer will not consume a commodity beyond the level when its marginal utility is zero. So, we have $MU_X > 0$ and $MU_Y > 0$. Then MRS_{XY} is always positive. So, to make it positive, the slope must be negative. This proves that the indifference curve is downward sloping.

Property II. An indifference curve must be convex to the origin: This property of indifference curve follows that the marginal rate of substitution of X for Y (MRS_{xy}) diminishes as more and more of X is substituted in place of Y. Only a convex indifference curve can mean a diminishing marginal rate of substitution of X for Y. Let the indifference curve is U_o in Fig. 4.10 shown below. Let A and B be the two points on this indifference curve.

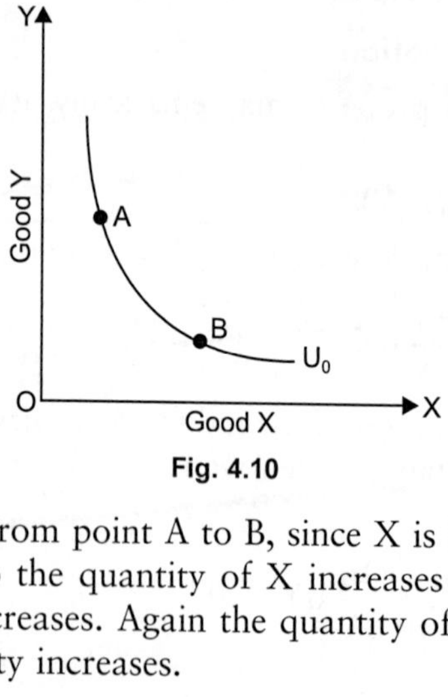

Fig. 4.10

If we move from point A to B, since X is being substituted in place of Y, so the quantity of X increases but its marginal utility (MU_x) decreases. Again the quantity of Y decreases but its marginal utility increases.

That is,

MU_x at point A > MU_x at point B ... (1)

MU_y at point A < MU_y at point B ... (2)

Eqn. (1) ÷ Eqn. (2) gives

$$\frac{MU_x}{MU_y} \text{ at point A} > \frac{MU_x}{MU_y} \text{ at point B}$$

$\therefore$ MRS_{xy} at point A > MRS_{xy} at point B.

$$\left[\therefore \frac{MU_x}{MU_y} = MRS_{xy}\right]$$

It shows that MRS_{xy} decreases as we move from A to B on the same indifference curve. This is possible only when the indifference curve is convex to the origin.

Property III. Two or more indifference curves cannot intersect (or touch) each other: Let us see what happens when two indifference curves intersect each other. Let us suppose that the two indifference curves IC_1 and IC_2 intersect at the point P in Fig. 4.11.

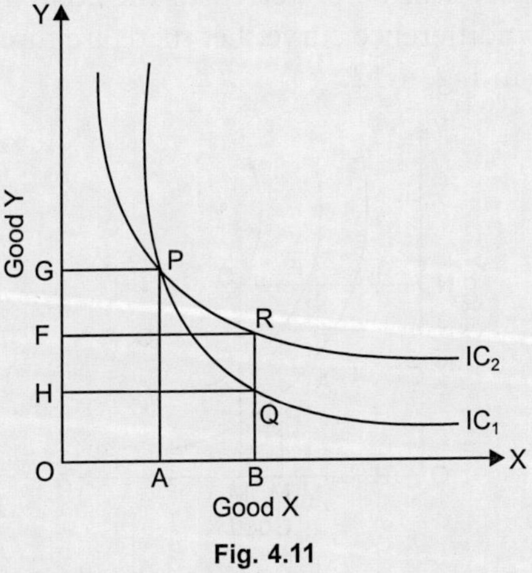

Fig. 4.11

Let us take two more points Q and R on IC_1 and IC_2 respectively. Now since points P and Q are on the same indifference curve IC_1.

Utility of (OA + OG) = utility of (OB + OH) ... (i)

Similarly P and R are on the same indifference curve IC_2.

Utility of (OA + OG) = utility of (OB + OF) ... (ii)

Since the left hand sides of both the equations (i) and (ii) are equal, their right hand sides must also be equal.

Utility of (OB + OH) = Utility of (OB + OF)

or, OB + OH = OB + OF

or, OH = OF

This, however, is impossible, since OF unit of Y is greater than OH unit of Y and as such a greater amount of Y (OF) is definitely preferable to the lesser amount of Y(OH). If OH and OF is equal, it is an absurd proposition because OH is a part of the line OF and the part cannot be equal to the whole. Hence, the two indifference curves cannot intersect (touch) each other.

Property IV. A higher indifference curve represents a higher level of satisfaction than a lower indifference curve: The last property of indifference curve is that every successively higher indifference curve shows a higher level of satisfaction to the consumer. That is, the combinations which lie on a higher indifference curve will be preferred to the combinations which lie on a lower indifference curve. Let there are three indifference curves shown in Fig. 4.12.

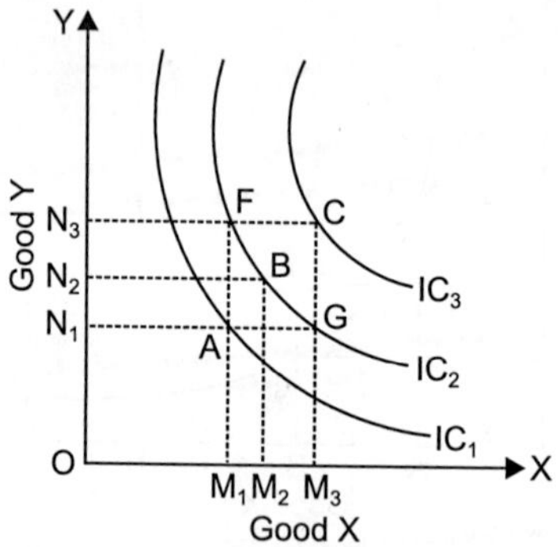

Fig. 4.12

Any point on IC_2 shall give more satisfaction to the consumer than any point on IC_1 and similarly, a point on IC_3 shall have more satisfaction for the consumer than any point on IC_2. Combination A on IC_1 shows that consumer has OM_1 of X and ON_1 of Y. Combination B on IC_2 shows that he has OM_2 of X and ON_2 of Y. Now when consumer has more of both the goods X and Y, he shall have greater satisfaction. Thus combination B is preferable to A as it gives more satisfaction. Again at combination F on IC_2, the consumer gets the same OM_1 of X that he had at combination A, but has more of Y, as now he gets ON_3 while at A he got only ON_1 of Y. Now when the amount of X remains the same and that of Y increases, the consumer shall have greater satisfaction. Similarly, at point G, he gets the same ON_1 of Y, which he had at A but gets OM_3 of X, which is more than OM_1, that he got at A. So G gives him more satisfaction than A. Hence, any combination on a higher indifference curve IC_2 gives more satisfaction than any combination on IC_1. Similarly, point C on IC_3 shows more of X and more of Y. Thus IC_3 curve shows greater satisfaction than IC_2. Hence, every higher indifference curve indicates a greater level of satisfaction than the lower indifference curve.

IMPLICATIONS OF (A) INCREASING MRS, (B) CONSTANT MRS, AND (C) ZERO MRS IN THE INDIFFERENCE CURVE ANALYSIS

(A) **Increasing MRS:** The marginal rate of substitution of X for Y (MRS_{xy}) represents the amount of Y which the consumer has to give up for the gain of one additional unit of X so that his level of satisfaction remains the same. The important property of indifference curve is that the MRS_{xy} diminishes as more and more of X is substituted for Y. Only a convex indifference curve can mean a diminishing MRS_{xy}. If the indifference curve is concave to the origin, it will imply that the MRS_{xy} increases as more and more of X is substituted for Y as shown in Fig. 4.13. In this Figure, it is clear that for each extra unit of X the consumer is willing

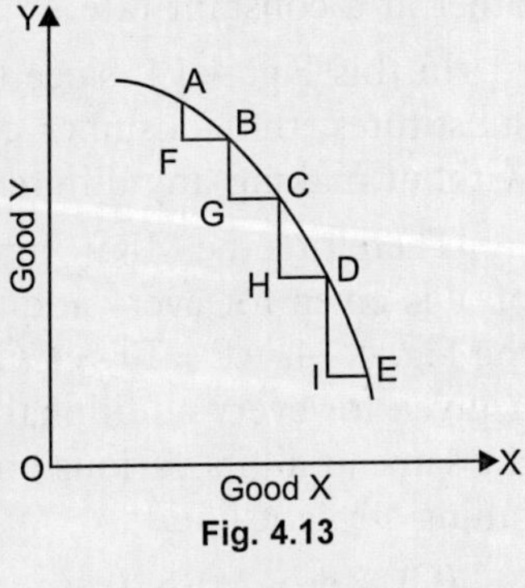

Fig. 4.13

to part with more and more of Y, i.e., MRS_{xy} increases as more and more of X is substituted for Y. It violates the fundamental assumption about the consumer's behaviour. Here in this Fig. 4.13 AF < BG < CH < DI with increase in every additional unit of X. Hence, for every additional unit of X, the consumer is willing to part with more and more of Y when the indifference curve is concave to the origin.

(B) **Constant MRS (case of perfect substitutes):** The curvature of the indifference curve indicates the degree of substitution between the goods. If the goods are perfect substitutes for each other then the indifference curve will be a straight line sloping downward and intersecting the commodity axes. Such line will show constant marginal rate of substitution for the goods. The line intersects the commodity axes which means that the utility level indicated by the line can be attained by consumption of one commodity alone keeping the other one at zero level. This is what perfect substitution implies. Constant MRS means that the consumer is ready to sacrifice one for the other at a constant rate.

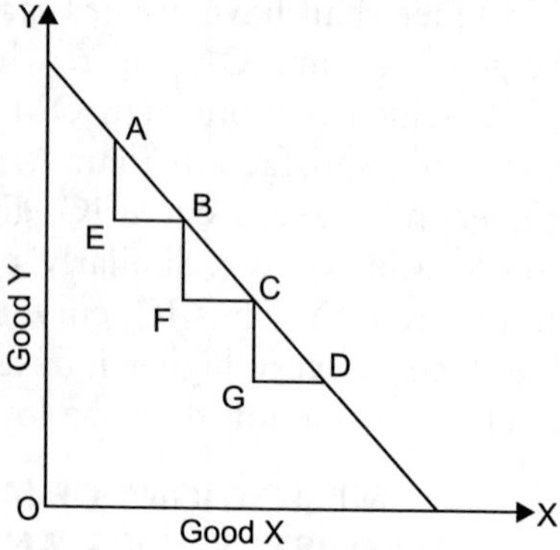

Fig. 4.14

In this Fig. 4.14, since the two goods X and Y are perfect substitutes, the consumer can use either X for Y or Y for X without making any difference of satisfaction.

Therefore, the MRS_{xy} remains constant, i.e., the same amount of Y is given for every additional unit of X. Thus, as shown in the Fig. 4.14, AE = BF = CG which are all the same amounts of Y given for every additional unit of X. Hence, the slope of IC is the same at all its various points and therefore, IC is downward falling straight line.

(C) **Zero MRS (case of perfect complementary goods):** Perfect complementary goods are those goods which are used or consumed by the consumer in a certain fixed ratio (proportion). There is no possibility of substitution of one good for other. For example, for a normal person, a pair of shoes means one right foot shoe to be used with one left foot shoe as both have to be used together and are hence perfectly complementary. For such goods indifference curve is L-shaped or right angle shaped shown in Fig. 4.15.

The MRS is now zero because there is no rate at which the consumer will substitute one kind of shoe for the other. In this Fig. 4.15, on IC_1 if the consumer uses OM of X, he must also have ON of Y, thus IC_1 is an L-shaped or right angle shaped. Similarly, if he uses still more of X, he must have still more of Y, thus making higher indifference curve like IC_2.

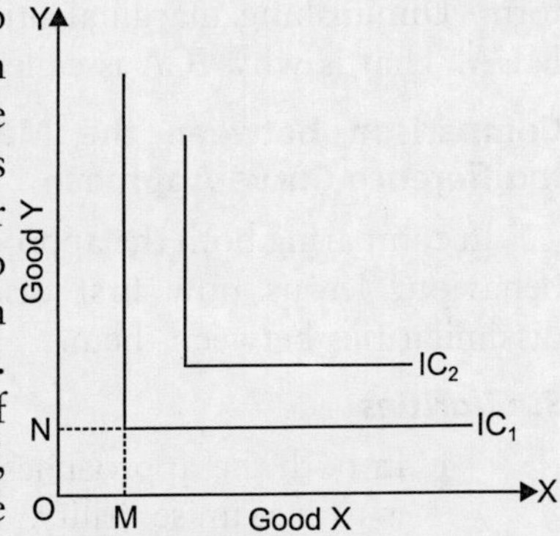

Fig. 4.15

Limitations of the Indifference Curve Analysis

Though the indifference curve analysis is an improvement over the Marshallian utility analysis, it is not free from limitations which are discussed below:

1. **Two commodity model:** The indifference curve analysis (ICA) is applicable only in case of two commodities. When there are more than two commodities the indifference curves cannot be drawn.

2. **Infinite divisibility of commodities:** The indifference curve will be continuous only when both the commodities are perfectly divisible. But in practice they are not always perfectly divisible. That is why, a smooth curve is not possible to draw.

3. **Ranking:** There are infinite number of combinations of the two commodities. The consumer is supposed to rank all the infinite number of combinations. Practically no consumer is able to rank all the available alternatives open to him. So in this sense it is unrealistic.

4. **Introspection:** Indifference curve theory is deduced from introspection, i.e., from what the ideal consumer thinks to do. This assumption is unscientific as it fails to analyse the behaviour of an ordinary consumer. The ICA adopts introspective method not behaviouristic method.

5. **Diminishing MRS:** The ICA assumes the law of diminishing MRS which is the law of diminishing marginal utility in revised form. Diminishing marginal utility is the main assumption of MUA. That is why, ICA is called old wine in a new bottle.

Comparison between the Marshallian Approach and the Indifference Curve Approach

In comparing both the approaches to the theory of consumer behaviour let us now first discuss the similarities and then dissimilarities between them.

Similarities

1. In both the approaches, the objective of the consumer is to maximise utility.
2. Both the approaches are introspective assuming that the consumers are rational.
3. Both the approaches hold the law of equi-marginal utility,

   i.e., $\frac{MU_1}{P_1} = \frac{MU_2}{P_2}$
4. Both the approaches assume that the marginal utility must be diminishing. The indifference curve theory shows the diminishing marginal utility in the form of marginal rate of substitution (MRS).
5. In both the approaches we can derive downward sloping demand curve which means that as price falls, the quantity demanded increases.

Dissimilarities

1. The Marshallian Utility Analysis (MUA) is based on the cardinal measurement of utility while the Indifference Curve Analysis (ICA) is based on the ordinal measurement of utility. But in actual practice

utility cannot be measured in cardinal terms. Utility is subjective, it differs from person to person. It can only be compared. It is followed in ICA.

2. In MUA utility derived from various goods are independent, i.e., different utility functions are independent. Utility obtained from any commodity depends on the amount of that commodity only, i.e., $u_1 = u_1(q_1)$ and $u_2 = u_2(q_2)$ and then $u = u_1 + u_2$. But in the ICA, the utility functions are interdependent. Utility derived from any commodity depends not only on its amount but also on the amounts of the other commodities.
3. In MUA, the marginal utility of money remains constant. It implies that there is no income effect of a change in price, i.e., income effect is zero. So, it is unrealistic. But in ICA, income effect may be positive, zero or negative.
4. In MUA, marginal utility can be measured. But in ICA, it can be measured in terms of MRS.
5. Derivation of demand curve in MUA depends upon the assumptions of constant marginal utility of money and diminishing marginal utility. But in ICA demand curve is drawn without these assumptions.
6. In MUA, the constancy of marginal utility of money implies that the income effect of a fall in price is zero. As a result Marshall cannot explain the Giffen's Paradox. But the ICA can explain the Giffen's Paradox with the help of negative income effect.
7. Marshall explains his theory with taking only one commodity, but two commodities are taken to explain the indifference curve theory.
8. MUA cannot split up the price effect into substitution and income effects. Because Marshall assumes that the income effect of a fall in price is zero. This prevented him from understanding the composite character of the price effect. But in ICA the effect of a price change can be divided into an income effect and a substitution effect.

9. The ICA can explain the welfare effect of the society. Welfare, i.e., level of satisfaction changes due to change in income through the change in price. But the MUA cannot explain it.

   Thus, the ICA is more general and more realistic than the MUA. The MUA is based on too much restrictive assumptions but the ICA is not. Hence, the ICA is regarded as an improvement over the MUA, i.e., the ICA is superior to the MUA.

BUDGET LINE OR PRICE LINE

Let us suppose that a consumer has a fixed money income, Y which he can spend on two commodities, q_1 and q_2 whose prices are P_1 and P_2 respectively. Then the budget equation can be written as $Y = p_1q_1 + p_2q_2$. If he spends his entire income on q_1, he can buy OB amount of q_1. Again if he spends his entire income on q_2, he can buy OA amount of q_2. By joining A and B, we get the budget line. This line shows the maximum amount of q_1 and q_2 that can be purchased with the given income. Any point on the line shows the combination of q_1 and q_2 that the consumer can buy. This is shown in the Fig. 4.16(a).

The line AB is also known as the price line since the slope of this line $\frac{OA}{OB}$ shows the ratio of the commodity prices $\left[OA = \frac{Y}{P_2}\right.$ when $q_1 = 0$, $OB = \frac{Y}{P_1}$ when $q_2 = 0$, then $\left.\frac{OA}{OB} = \frac{Y/P_2}{Y/P_1} = \frac{p_1}{p_2}\right]$.

Thus, a budget line is a locus of all combinations of two goods which can be purchased with fixed income at fixed prices. It is a boundary of consumption for both the commodities. The consumer cannot cross this boundary line since his income would not allow him.

Now, what happens to the price line if either the prices of goods change or the income changes? Let us explain one by one.

Suppose, with the fall in price of q_1, the consumer will purchase more quantity of q_1 than before assuming that the price of q_2 and the income of the consumer remain unchanged.

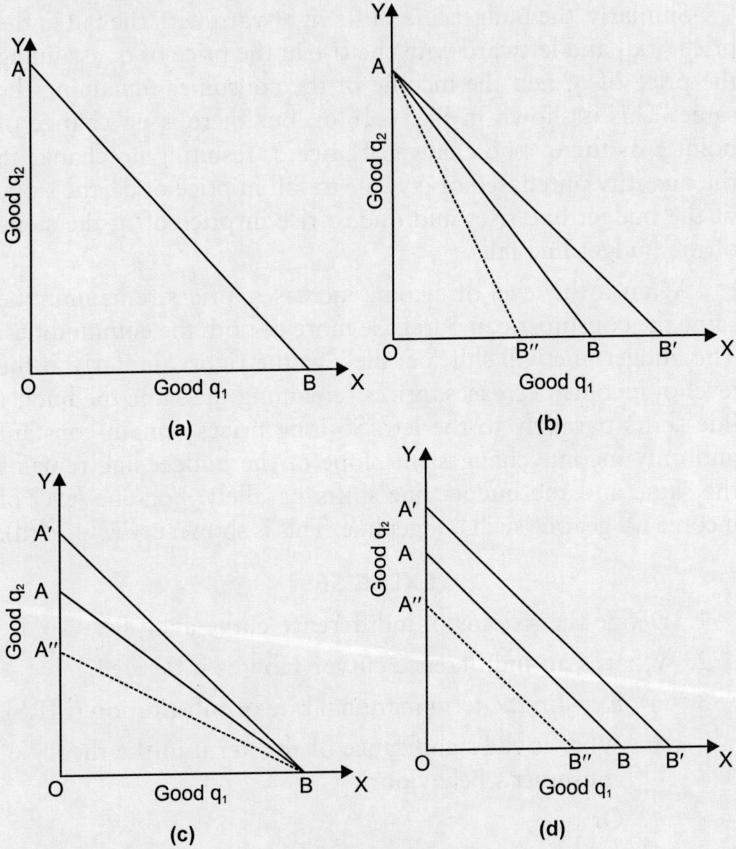

Fig. 4.16

Now he purchases OB′ of q_1 which is greater than OB. So, the price line shifts rightward from the original position, AB and becomes AB′. Likewise if the price of q_1 rises the line shifts leftward from the original position, AB and become AB″ as he purchases smaller quantity of q_1. This is shown in Fig. 4.16(b). But in both the cases, there is no shift of the point A as the price of q_2 remains the same resulting no change in the quantity purchased of q_2. Due to fall in the price of q_1 the slope of the budget line falls and due to rise in the price the slope of the budget line rises.

Similarly, the budget line shifts rightward with the fall in the price of q_2 and leftward with the rise in the price of q_2 assuming the price of q_1 and the income of the consumer remaining the same. This is shown in Fig. 4.16(c). But there is no change of point B as there is no change of price q_1 resulting no change in the quantity purchased of q_1. Due to fall in price of q_2, the slope of the budget line rises and due to rise in price of q_2 the slope of the budget line falls.

Again if the level of income increases, prices remaining the same the consumer can purchase more of both the commodities. The budget line will shift parallely to the right. Similarly, if the level of income decreases, prices remaining the same the budget line shifts parallely to the left. So long prices remain constant and only income changes the slope of the budget line remains the same and the budget line shifts parallely. For one level of income we get one such budget line. This is shown in Fig. 4.16(d).

EXERCISES

1. Define the axioms of indifference curve analysis.
2. What is an indifference curve? How is it derived?
3. (a) Explain the term marginal rate of substitution (MRS).

   (b) What is the significance of this term in the theory of consumer's behaviour?

   Or

   Discuss how to measure marginal rate of substitution on an indifference curve and why does it diminish?
4. Is there any relationship between marginal rate of substitution and marginal utilities?
5. What are the properties of an indifference curve?
6. Explain the implications of (a) increasing MRS, (b) constant MRS and (c) zero MRS in the indifference curve analysis.
7. Write a short note on the budget line or price line.

   Or

   Draw budget line. Distinguish between shift of the budget line and change in slope of the budget line.

Chapter 5

Theory of Consumer's Equilibrium

ORDINAL APPROACH TO CONSUMER'S EQUILIBRIUM

The approach to consumer's equilibrium based on Marshallian utility analysis suffered from the main defect, that utility cannot be measured cardinally. An alternative approach has been provided by **Hicks** in terms of the **"ordinal preference"** or **"indifference curve"**.

The consumer is in equilibrium when he maximizes his utility. His equilibrium is based on the following assumptions:

Assumptions

1. The consumer has a given indifference map.
2. He has fixed money which will be fully spent on the two goods.
3. Prices of the goods are given.
4. Goods are homogeneous and divisible.

Let AB represents a budget line of the consumer and IC_1, IC_2, IC_3, IC_4 and IC_5 are the five indifference curves as shown in Fig. 5.1. The budget line cuts the indifference curve, IC_1 at q_1 and q_4 and cuts the indifference curve IC_2 at q_2 and q_3 and touches the IC_3 at q. All the points like q_1, q_2, q_3, q_4 and q on the budget line are equally costly to the consumer. The consumer can buy any one of them with his given income and given prices. Among these combinations he will select that one where his utility is maximum.

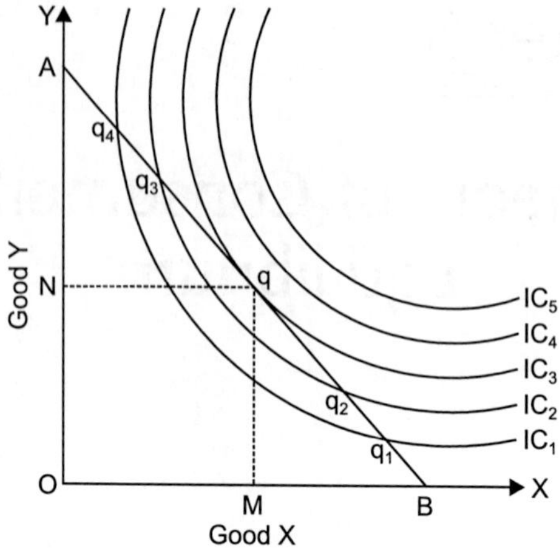

Fig. 5.1

We know that a higher indifference curve represents a higher level of utility. The consumer will try to achieve the highest possible indifference curve while remaining on the budget line. This is possible when the budget line is tangent to one of these indifference curves. This happens at point q where AB touches the IC_3 in the above Figure. Any other point on the budget line AB lies on a lower indifference curve than q. It shows that the utility levels at other points are lower than that at q. The point q, therefore, represents the point on the budget line AB where the consumer can get the highest possible utility. So this point is the equilibrium point of the consumer. In this equilibrium position at q the consumer will buy OM amount of good X and ON amount of good Y. Of course, combinations lying on indifference curves IC_4 and IC_5 will give greater utility to the consumer than q, but they are unattainable by the price line AB with the given money income.

Let us now define the conditions of equilibrium. There are necessary condition and sufficient condition. The necessary condition for the equilibrium of the consumer is that at the equilibrium point the slope of the budget line must be equal to the slope of the indifference curve. But we know that the absolute value of the slope of the indifference curve is the ratio of marginal utilities while the absolute value of the slope of the budget line is equal to the ratio of commodity prices.

Now, the slope of indifference curve = $\frac{MU_x}{MU_y}$

and the slope of budget line = $\frac{P_1}{P_2}$

Therefore, $\frac{MU_x}{MU_y} = \frac{P_1}{P_2}$ $\left[\text{where, } \frac{MU_x}{MU_y} = MRS_{xy}\right]$

That is, $MRS_{xy} = \frac{P_1}{P_2}$

At point q_3 or q_4, the absolute value of the slope of the indifference curves is greater than that of the budget line, i.e., MRS_{xy} is greater than the given price ratio,

i.e. $\frac{MU_x}{MU_y} > \frac{P_1}{P_2}$, i.e., $MRS_{xy} > \frac{P_1}{P_2}$

Now the consumer will substitute X for Y and will come down along the price line towards the equilibrium point q. He will continue to do so till the MRS_{xy} becomes equal to the price ratio.

Again, similarly at points q_1 and q_2,

$\frac{MU_x}{MU_y} < \frac{P_1}{P_2}$, i.e., $MRS_{xy} < \frac{P_1}{P_2}$

The consumer will substitute Y for X thereby moving up towards q along the price line till $MRS_{xy} = \frac{P_1}{P_2}$. Thus, the consumer reaches the equilibrium point q. This is possible only when the indifference curve becomes tangent to the given price line AB.

The sufficient condition is that at the point of equilibrium, the indifference curve must be convex to the origin. We see that in the Fig. 5.1 the indifference curve IC_3 is convex to the origin at q. Thus, at point q both conditions of equilibrium are satisfied. Therefore, q is the equilibrium point where the consumer consumes OM of good X and ON of good Y.

CHANGES IN CONSUMER'S EQUILIBRIUM

The equilibrium of the consumer is obtained on the basis of the assumptions that the income of the consumer, the prices of the goods, tastes and preferences of the consumer remain constant. Let us examine the effects of income and price changes on the consumer equilibrium situation within the indifference map. The equilibrium of the consumer would change according to change in income or change in the price of one good while the price of the other remains the same or changes in the prices of two goods. Accordingly we get income effect, price effect and substitution effect. Now we shall discuss one by one.

INCOME EFFECT: INCOME CONSUMPTION CURVE

A consumer feels better off with an increase in his income and he purchases more of commodities to get more satisfaction. When the prices of commodities remains same, the effect of a change in the consumer's income on his total satisfaction is known as Income Effect.

When income of the consumer increases, prices remaining the same, the budget line shifts parallely to the right. We get a new point of tangency between the budget line and the indifference curve. That is, the equilibrium position of the consumer shifts to a higher indifference curve. Again, if there is a decrease in income, the equilibrium position shifts to a lower indifference curve. The locus of successive equilibrium points between parallel budget lines and indifference curves is called the Income Consumption Curve (ICC). The ICC shows the relationship between income and consumption, i.e., the effect of change in income on consumption. The income effect can be explained with the help of Fig. 5.2.

With the given prices of two commodities X and Y and the given income of the consumer, we have drawn his budget line P_1L_1 and shown his equilibrium point Q_1 on the indifference curve IC_1. He has purchased OM of X and ON of Y. Suppose, the income of the consumer increases while the prices of two commodities remain constant. He would purchase more of X and more of Y. As a result, the budget line shifts upward to a new position P_2L_2.

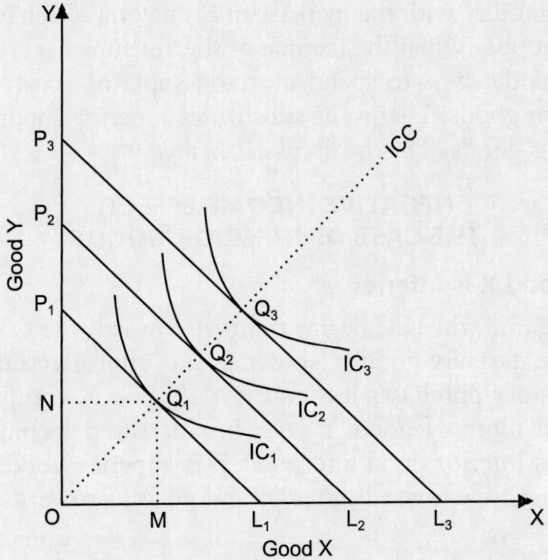

Fig. 5.2

It is parallel to the original budget line P_1L_1. He comes to a new equilibrium point Q_2 on higher IC_2 with this budget line P_2L_2. Again, if his income still further increases, the price line shifts to P_3L_3 and the consumer is in equilibrium at point Q_3 on IC_3. Every new equilibrium shifting upward means to have more quantities of both the commodities than previous equilibrium point and thereby to have more satisfaction. If we join all these equilibrium points Q_1, Q_2 and Q_3 we get a curve called 'Income Consumption Curve', i.e., ICC. Thus, ICC is the locus of equilibrium points at various levels of consumer's income.

The income effect may be either positive or negative. When the ICC slopes upward, the income effect is positive to both commodities. This means that the consumer increases the consumption of both the commodities with the increase in his income. But sometimes, the income effect may be positive towards one commodity and negative towards another. Income effect towards a commodity is positive when the consumer purchases more of that commodity with the increase in his income. This is a case of normal goods. Again, if income effect towards a commodity is negative when the consumer purchases less of that commodity with the increase in his income. Such goods are inferior goods. When the income of the consumer increases, his natural tendency is to spend more on superior goods and less on inferior goods. That is, he substitutes superior goods in place of inferior goods. This is discussed below.

NEGATIVE INCOME EFFECT: THE CASE OF INFERIOR GOODS

When Good X is Inferior

In Fig. 5.3, the ICC begins to move towards the OY-axis on which we measure good Y showing that after a certain point, the consumer purchases less and less of good X and purchases more and more of good Y with his increased income. Here, good X is inferior good and good Y is superior good. Income effect is negative towards good X and positive towards good Y.

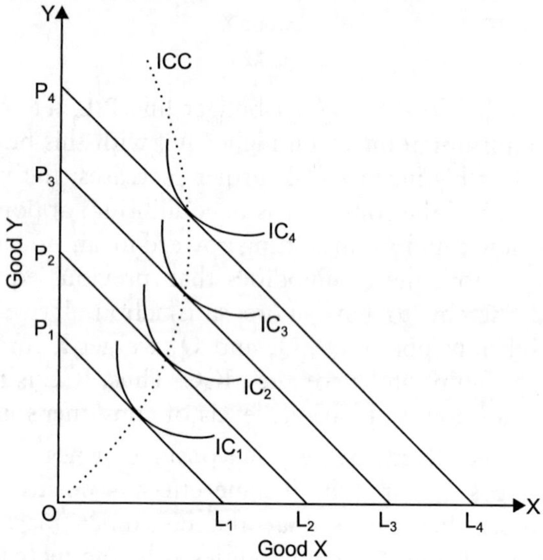

Fig. 5.3

When Good Y is Inferior

Again when good X is superior and good Y is inferior, the ICC will slope towards good X as shown in Fig. 5.4.

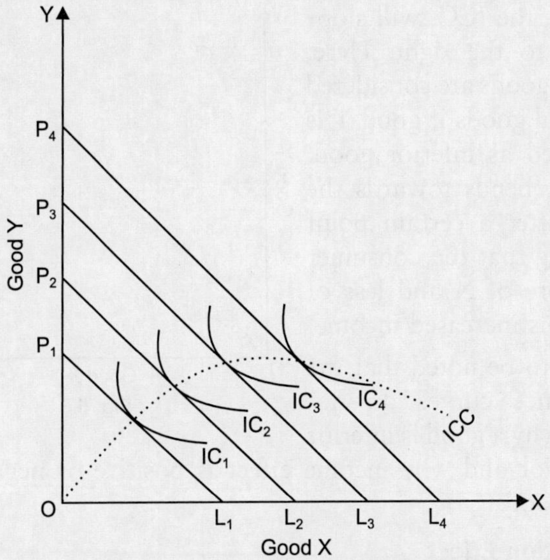

Fig. 5.4

Here, ICC moves towards good X. It shows that good X is purchased more and good Y is purchased less with the increased income. Income effect is positive towards good X and negative towards good Y.

The slope of the ICC will however, depend upon the income elasticity of demand for these two goods. If income elasticity of demand for Y is high and for X is low, the ICC will be sloping upwards to the left more nearer the Y-axis. If income elasticity of demand for X is high and for Y is low, the ICC will be sloping upwards to the right more nearer the X-axis. Thus, we get different shapes of the ICC curve.

Different Shapes of Income Consumption Curves

There are various possible shapes of ICC depending upon the value of income elasticity of demand, i.e., income effect as shown in Fig. 5.5. If the income effect is negative, ICC_1 will slope backward to the left after a certain point showing that the consumer buys less of good X and more of Y with his increased income. So, after certain point on ICC_2 good X is considered as an inferior good. If the income effect is positive for both the goods

X and Y, the ICC_2 will slope upward to the right. Here, both the goods are considered as normal goods if good Y is considered as inferior good, the ICC_3 bends towards the X-axis after a certain point indicating that the consumer buys more of X and less of Y with his increased income.

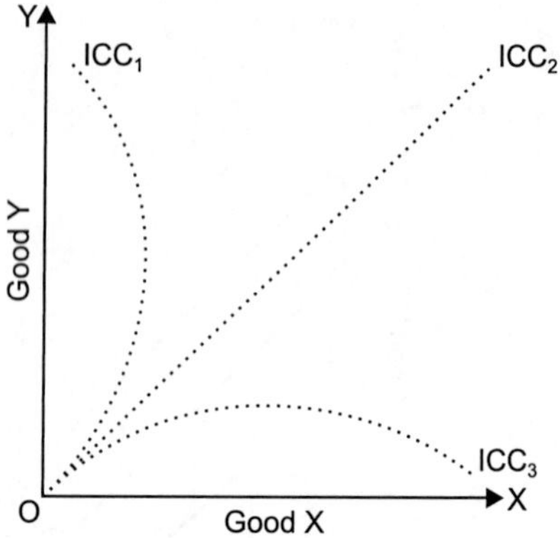

Fig. 5.5

It is to be noted that the indifference curves do not explain why a good is inferior or superior and why income effect is positive or negative for certain goods.

Substitution Effect

The substitution effect shows the change in the quantity of a good purchased due to a change in the relative price of a good, while the income of the consumer remains constant. When the price of a good falls, the real income of the consumers increases. It induces the consumers to buy more of it under the income effect. But with a fall in price of a good, it becomes relatively cheaper and this induces the consumers to buy more to substitute it in place of the other good which is relatively costlier. This is called substitution effect. Thus, a change in price has both income as well as substitution effect.

Hicks-Allen Method (for a fall in price)

Hicks and Allen explained the substitution effect with the principle of compensating variation in income. They make the consumer remain in the same indifference curve and study his equilibrium point due to the price change.

The real income of the consumer increases with a fall in price of a good while his money income remains unchanged. The consumer feels better off than before.

To keep the consumer in his previous position, we make compensatory reduction of his money income to cancel out the gain in real income in such a way that the consumer is neither better off nor worse off. The substitution effect based on **Hicks-Allen** approach is illustrated in the Fig. 5.6.

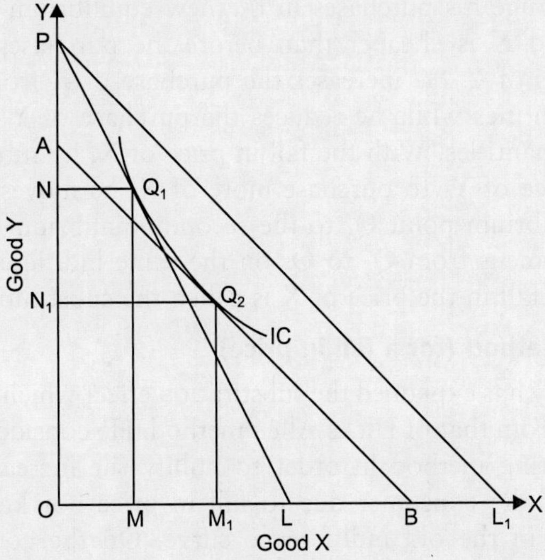

Fig. 5.6

With the given money income and the given prices of two goods X and Y, the price line PL is drawn and the consumer comes to an equilibrium point Q_1 where the price line PL is tangent to the indifference curve IC. Corresponding to this equilibrium point Q_1, he purchases OM units of X and ON units of Y. When the price of good X falls, while the price of good Y and the money income of the consumer remain the same, the price line will shift rightward to PL_1.

Now the consumer's real income or purchasing power increases with the fall in the price of good X. To study the substitution effect, this increase in real income should be nullified by reducing the money income of the consumer by an amount in such a way that the consumer remains on the same indifference curve IC on which he was before. The price line which shifted to the position of PL_1 will come down to the position AB which is parallel to PL_1 and this price line AB will touch, i.e., become tangent to the same indifference curve IC at point Q_2. Thus with the price line AB, the consumer is in equilibrium at Q_2 on IC. At the point Q_2, he gets the same satisfaction as at Q_1 because both Q_1 and Q_2 are on the same indifference curve IC. But he will rearrange his purchases in the new equilibrium point Q_2. Since good X is cheaper than before, he purchases more of X and less of Y. He increases the purchase of X from OM to OM_1 quantities while he reduces the purchase of Y from ON to ON_1 quantities. With the fall in price of X, he substitutes X in the place of Y. To purchase more of X, he moves from the first equilibrium point Q_1 to the second equilibrium point Q_2. The movement from Q_1 to Q_2 on the same indifference curve IC due to fall in the price of X is called the substitution effect.

Slutsky Method (for a fall in price)

Slutsky has explained the substitution effect which is slightly different from that of Hicks-Allen method. He considers neither compensating method in order to nullify the increase in real income of the consumer due to fall in price nor keeping the consumer in the old indifference curve. On the contrary, he considers the increase in the real income of the consumer due to fall in price and makes the consumer go to a higher indifference curve.

Due to fall in price of a commodity, the income of the consumer increases by the cost difference. The cost difference is found out by the difference between the cost of the quantity of a commodity purchased at the old price and the cost of the same quantity of that commodity at the new price. That is, if the old price and the new price per unit of commodity are ₹ 10/- and ₹ 8/- respectively and the unit of the commodity purchased is 10 kg, the cost difference will be ₹ (10 × 10) – ₹ (10 × 8) = ₹ 20/-. Now in order to find out the Slutsky substitution effect, consumer's money income must be reduced by the cost difference which will make him able to purchase the old combination of the goods if he so desires or make him go to higher indifference curve.

Slutsky's substitution effect is illustrated in the Fig. 5.7.

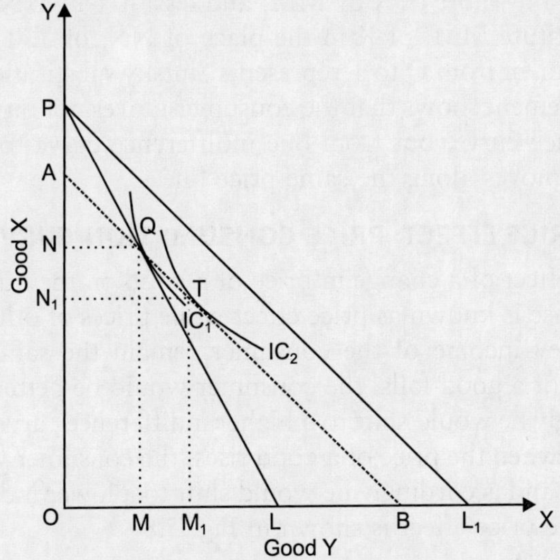

Fig. 5.7

With the given prices of two commodities X and Y and the given income of the consumer, the price line PL is drawn and the consumer is in equilibrium at Q on the indifference curve IC_1 purchasing OM of X and ON of Y. Suppose, the price of X falls, while the price of Y and money income remain unchanged. Due to fall in price of X, the price line shifts to PL_1 and the purchasing power, i.e., the real income of the consumer will increase. To find out the increase in his real income, the cost difference is worked out. The consumer's money income must be reduced by the cost difference and a price line AB parallel to PL_1 is drawn which passes through the point Q and becomes tangent at T to the indifference curve IC_2. The price line AB shows that income equal to AP in terms of Y or BL_1 in terms of X has been taken away from the consumer. As a result, the price line AB is passing through the point Q. The consumer can buy the combination at Q, if he so chooses as Q also lies on the price line AB. But he will not buy the combination at Q since X is now relatively cheaper and Y is relatively dearer than before. A fall in price of X induce him to rearrange the purchases of X and Y at new equilibrium point T on the indifference curve IC_2. At this point T, he will buy more of X by MM_1 and less of Y by NN_1, i.e., he will substitute MM_1 of X in the place of NN_1 of Y. Therefore, the movement from Q to T represents Slutsky substitution effect. This movement shows that the consumer moves not on the same indifference curve, but from one indifference curve to another and also moves along the same price line.

PRICE EFFECT: PRICE CONSUMPTION CURVE

The effect of a change in price of a good on the quantity of its purchase is known as price effect while prices of other goods and money income of the consumer remain the same. When the price of a good falls, the consumer would be better off and accordingly he would shift to a higher indifference curve. On the contrary, when the price of a good rises, the consumer would be worse off and accordingly he would shift to a lower indifference curve. The price effect is shown in Fig. 5.8.

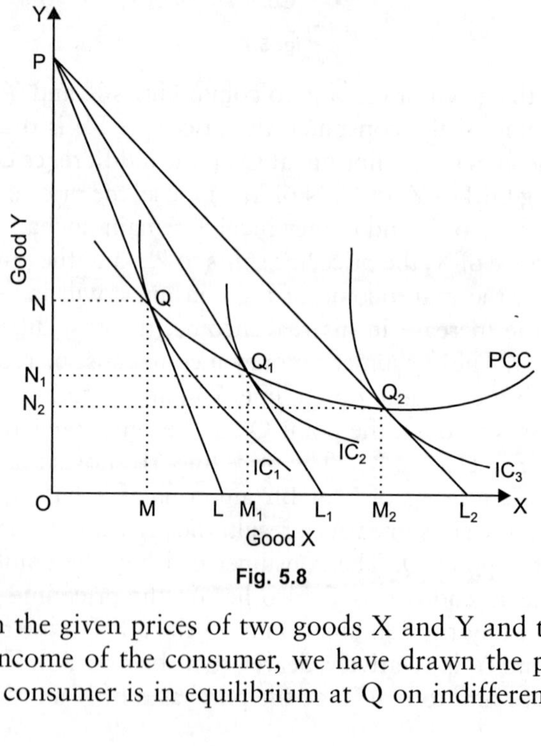

Fig. 5.8

With the given prices of two goods X and Y and the given money income of the consumer, we have drawn the price line PL. The consumer is in equilibrium at Q on indifference curve

IC_1. At Q, he is purchasing OM of X and ON of Y. Let the price of X falls assuming that the price of Y and his money income remain at the same level. With the fall in the price of X, the price line shifts to PL_1 and consequently the consumer reaches a higher indifference curve IC_2 with Q_1 as his equilibrium. At Q_1 he purchases OM_1 of X and ON_1 of Y, suppose, if the price of X still further falls, the price of Y and his income remaining unchanged the price line shifts to PL_2. The consumer will come to equilibrium at Q_2 on IC_3 where he will purchase OM_2 of X and ON_2 of Y. Thus, the consumer will get higher level of satisfaction from higher indifference curves and will feel better off. When all the equilibrium points Q, Q_1 and Q_2 are joined together, we get a curve what is called Price Consumption Curve (PCC). The PCC traces out the price effect. It shows how the changes in price of a good affects the consumer's purchases, other factors like the income of the consumer, his tastes and preferences and prices of other goods remaining unchanged. Here PCC is a downward sloping curve which indicates that the consumer purchases larger quantities of X and lesser quantities of Y due to the fall in the price of X when the demand for X is highly elastic, i.e., price elasticity is greater than one.

PCC may have different shapes. If price of X falls, the demand for Y may increase, may decrease or may remain unchanged. If the demand for Y increases, the PCC will be upward sloping. If the demand for Y decreases, the PCC will be downward sloping. If the demand for Y remains the same, the PCC is horizontal.

Upward Sloping PCC

In case of upward sloping price consumption curve, we see that the quantity purchased of both X and Y rises due to fall in the price of X. We get upward sloping PCC for good X when the demand for X is less elastic (i.e., less than one) as shown in Fig. 5.9.

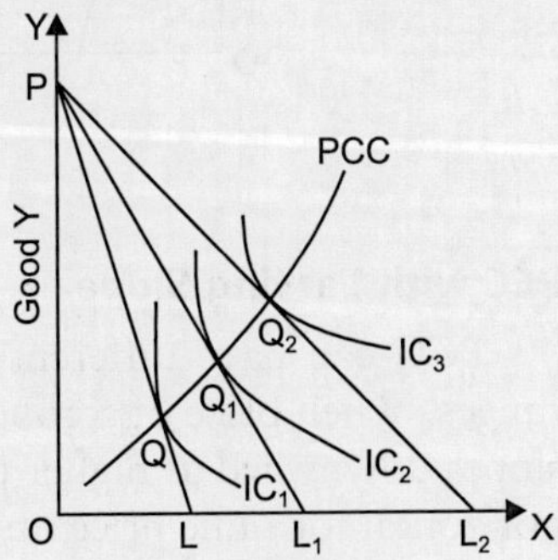

Fig. 5.9

Backward Sloping PCC

When the PCC for X backward sloping curve as shown in Fig. 5.10, we find that the consumer purchases less and less of X and more and more of Y due to fall in the price of X. It is seen in case of Giffen goods.

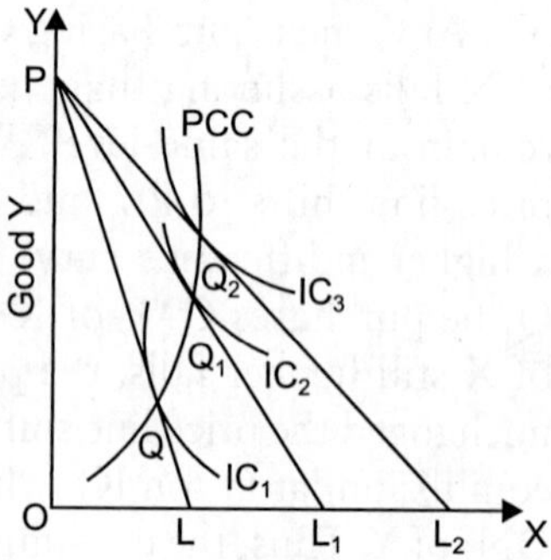

Fig. 5.10

Horizontal PCC

Horizontal PCC for X indicates that when the price of X falls, its quantity purchased increases proportionately, whereas the quantity purchased of Y remains at the same level. In this case, price elasticity of demand for X is equal to unity (i.e., equal to one) as shown in Fig. 5.11.

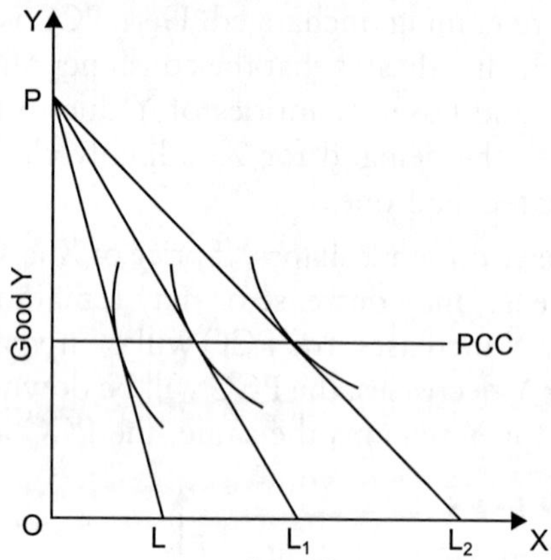

Fig. 5.11

PCC with Varying Slope

PCC can have different shapes or slopes at different price ranges. When price of a good is falling gradually, PCC generally slopes downward at higher price ranges and then it may have a horizontal for same price ranges but ultimately it will be sloping upward for further falling in price. It is illustrated in Fig. 5.12.

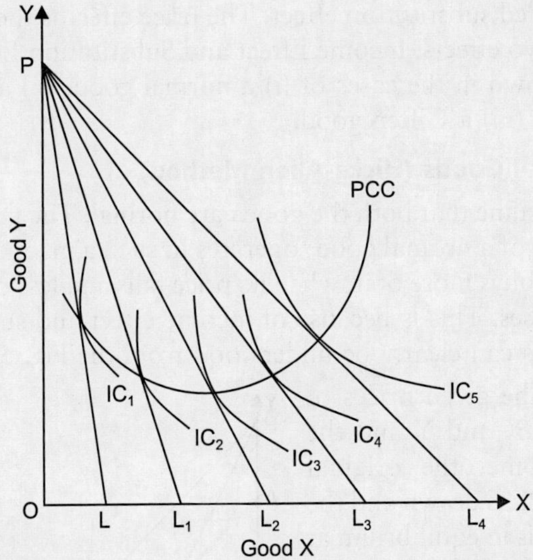

Fig. 5.12

In Fig. 5.12 PC curve has different slopes at different price ranges. When the price of X falls gradually, at higher price ranges from PL to PL_2 it slopes downward and then becomes almost horizontal for some price ranges from PL_2 to PL_3 but ultimately it becomes upward sloping from the price line PL_3 to PL_4.

Decomposition of Price Effect into Substitution Effect and Income Effect *or* Price Effect Combines Substitution Effect and Income Effect

The price effect comprises the income effect and the substitution effect. When the price of a good falls, price of other good and money income remaining unchanged, the real income of the consumer increases. Even if he purchases the previous combination he has some surplus money at his disposal. He can purchase more of both the goods with this surplus money. Thus, the increase in real income induces the consumer to buy more of the goods. This is called income effect due to a fall in price of a good. Again when the price of a good falls, the relative price of the good in terms of other good changes. This good becomes relatively cheaper to other good. The consumer can substitute relatively cheaper good for those which are relatively expensive.

This is called substitution effect. The price effect is the resultant of these two effects: Income Effect and Substitution Effect. This can be shown in the cases of (i) a normal good, (ii) an inferior good, and (iii) a Giffen good.

For Normal Goods (Hicks-Allen Method)

We assume that both the goods are normal. The price effect, in the case of a normal good, operates in such a manner that the consumer buys more of it, when its price falls and less of it, when its price rises. This is because of income effect and substitution effect. This can clearly be understood from the Fig. 5.13.

With the given prices of the goods X and Y and the given income, the original price line PL is drawn and the consumer is in equilibrium at point P_1 on indifference curve IC_1 purchasing OM amount of X. Now price of X falls, the price of good Y and the income of the consumer remaining the same, the price line shifts to the position PL_1 and is tangent to a higher indifference curve IC_2 with equilibrium at point R. Due to fall in price the consumer moves from P_1 to R and buys MM_2 more of X. The movement from P_1 to R is called price effect.

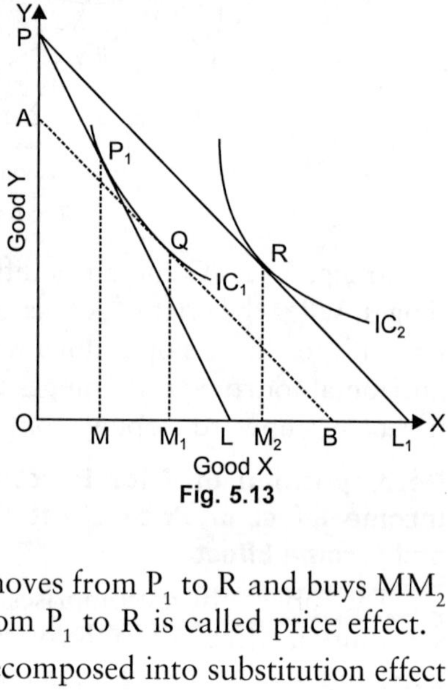

Fig. 5.13

This price effect can be decomposed into substitution effect and income effect.

Due to fall in price of X, the real income of the consumer rises. He can purchase more with this additional income. In Hicksian sense to nullify the gain in real income due to fall in the price of X, the money income of the consumer is so reduced by compensating variation in income in such a way that the price line PL_1 shifts parallel to left position AB and is tangent to the initial indifference curve IC_1 at point Q. Now as X is cheaper, he will substitute X in the place of Y and so he will move from

P_1 to Q on the same indifference curve IC_1. This is substitution effect in Hicksian sense. He will buy MM_1 more of X for Y, i.e., substitute MM_1 of X for Y.

If the amount of money income which was taken away from him is now given back to him, he would move from Q on IC_1 to R on IC_2. The movement from Q to R is called income effect. Due to income effect the consumer will buy M_1M_2 more of X. Thus the price effect (PE), i.e., from P_1 to R is the resultant of the substitution effect (SE), i.e., from P_1 to Q and income effect (IE), i.e., from Q to R. In other way, we can say that with substitution effect, he will increase the purchase of X by MM_1, with income effect he will increase the purchase of X by M_1M_2 and due to price effect he will have purchased MM_2 more of X.

That is, $MM_2 = MM_1 + M_1M_2$ implying that PE = SE + IE.

Therefore, price effect can be decomposed into substitution effect and income effect.

For Inferior Good (Hicks-Allen Method)

The substitution effect for any commodity raises its demand due to fall in its relative price and *vice versa*. That is, substitution effect is always positive. But the income effect is not like that. It depends on the nature of the commodity. It is positive for normal good whereas it is negative for inferior good. Due to increase in income the quantity demanded may increase, may decrease or may remain constant depending on the sign of the income effect.

Suppose, good X is an inferior good and good Y is a normal good. Due to fall in the price of X, the price of Y and the income of the consumer remaining the same, its substitution effect is positive, i.e., its purchase will be increased and its income effect is negative, i.e., its purchase will be decreased. The net result on purchase of X depends on the relative strengths of the two effects. If its substitution effect is stronger than its income effect, the quantity demanded of X increases as its price falls. On the other hand if its substitution effect is weaker than its income effect, its quantity demanded decreases as its price falls. This can be illustrated in the Fig. 5.14.

With the given prices of X and Y and with the money income of the consumer, the price line PL is drawn and is tangent to the indifference curve IC_1 with the equilibrium at point P_1. The consumer is purchasing OM of X. When the price of X falls, the price line PL shifts the position PL_1 as shown in the Fig. 5.14 and his equilibrium shifts to the point R on IC_2 where PL_1 is tangent. Now he purchases MN more of X due to the fall of its price. This is price effect. To separate income effect and substitution effect, the money income of the consumer is reduced to keep his real income as constant by compensating variation in income in such a way that the price line PL_1 shifts parallel to the left position AB which is tangent to the initial indifference curve IC_1 at point Q. The movement from P_1 to Q along the same indifference curve IC_1 is substitution effect in Hicksian sense. It would induce the consumer to buy MT more of X. Now if the amount of money which was taken away from him is given to him, he will move from Q on IC_1 to R on IC_2. The movement from Q to R is the income effect which is in the opposite direction and induces the consumer to purchase NT less of X. This is negative income effect. Since negative income effect (NT) is smaller than the positive substitution effect (MT), the net purchase of X increases by an amount MN.

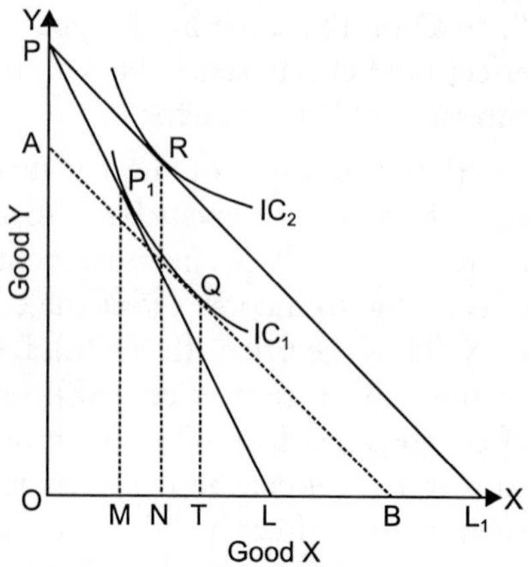

Fig. 5.14

Hence, price effect = substitution effect + negative income effect

That is, MN = MT – NT.

Decomposition of Price Effect into Substitution Effect and Income Effect in Slutsky's View

Slutsky has explained the decomposition of price effect into substitution effect and income effect in slightly different way from the Hicksian view. Let us now suppose that there is a fall in price of a normal good. It is illustrated in Fig. 5.15.

With the given prices of two goods X and Y and the given income of the consumer, the price line PL is drawn and tangent to the indifference curve IC_1 with the equilibrium at point Q. At this equilibrium the consumer is purchasing OM of X. Now the price of X falls, the price of Y and the income of the consumer remaining the same, the price line shifts to the position PL_1 as shown in Fig. 5.15. With price line PL_1, the consumer would now be in equilibrium at R on indifference curve IC_2. He would purchase MS more of X due to fall in price of X. This movement from Q to R is the price effect.

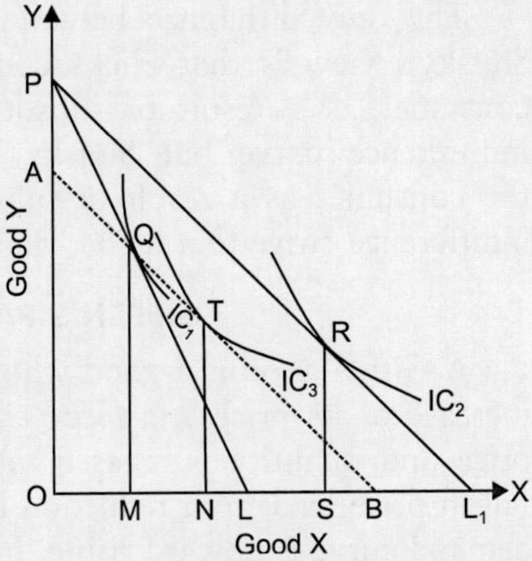

Fig. 5.15

Now to find out the substitution effect, his money income must be reduced by the cost difference in such a way that the price line PL_1 shifts leftward parallel to the position AB which passes through the point Q and is tangent to the indifference curve IC_3 at point T. With price line AB the consumer can buy at Q if he so chooses, but he will not buy the combination at Q since X is now relatively cheaper than before. It will induce him to rearrange the purchases of X and Y at new equilibrium point T on the indifference curve IC_3. At T, he will purchase MN more of X, i.e., he will substitute MN of X in place of Y. The movement from Q to T represents substitution effect in Slutsky's view. Now if the money income which was taken away from him is given to him, he will move from T on indifference curve IC_3 to R on indifference curve IC_2 and will purchase NS more of X. This movement from T to R is called the income effect. Thus movement from Q to R as a result of price effect which can be spilt into the movement from Q to T as a result of substitution effect and from T to R as a result of income effect. Again it can be said in another way that due to price effect he is purchasing MS more of X. Due to substitution effect he is purchasing MN more of X and due to income effect he is purchasing NS more of X, i.e., MS = MN + NS. That is, price effect = substitution effect + income effect.

The only difference between the Hicksian view and the Slutsky's view is that Hicks considers the movement of the consumer as a result of substitution effect along the same indifference curve but Slutsky considers the movement of the consumer as a result of substitution effect from a lower indifference curve to a higher one.

GIFFEN'S PARADOX

A Giffen good is a good whose demand increases with the increase of its price and *vice versa*. Thus, for a Giffen good, price and quantity purchased move in the same direction, a fall in price leads to a reduction in the quantity purchased. Its demand curve is upward rising. It refers to an inferior good. In the case of a Giffen good the income effect is negative which means that the consumer purchases less of this good with the increase of his income. As the price of a Giffen good falls, the real income of the consumer increases. He purchases less of this good due to income effect as it is an inferior good. But the substitution effect is positive. He purchases more of this good due to the substitution effect as its relative price falls. Thus, the income effect and the substitution effect work in the opposite directions for a Giffen good. But the income effect is stronger than the substitution effect. This situation is called Giffen's Paradox. This can be explained with the help of Fig. 5.16 as given on next page.

Initially, the consumer is at equilibrium point G when the price line AB is tangent to the indifference curve IC_1 and purchases OM_1 units of Q_1. With the fall in price of Q_1 the price line shifts to AC and the new equilibrium is established at point F on the higher indifference curve IC_2. At this point the consumer purchases OM_2 units of Q_1. As OM_2 is less than OM_1, it shows that Q_1 is a Giffen good because its quantity demanded decreases with the fall of its price. Hence, movement from G to F is called price effect.

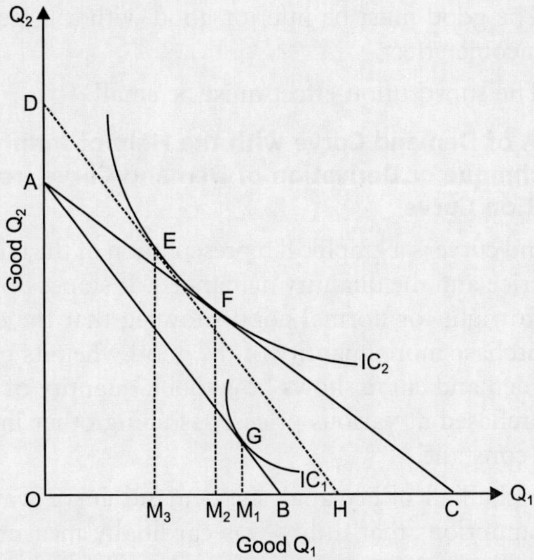

Fig. 5.16

If we assume that price of Q_2 does not fall and income of the consumer is increased in such a way so as to keep him on the same indifference curve IC_2. Then the price line shifts parallel to the right of initial budget line AB and becomes DH which is tangent to the indifference curve IC_2 at point E. At this point E, he purchases OM_3 units of Q_1. Now the movement from G to E is called income effect and due to income effect the consumer purchases M_1M_3 less of Q_1. Again movement from E to F is called substitution effect and due to substitution effect he purchases M_3M_2 more of Q_1. Here, M_1M_3 is greater than M_3M_2. It means that the strength of the income effect is greater than that of the substitution effect. Thus, the consumer purchases M_1M_2 less of Q_1 as its price falls.

The Giffen good is named after the name of **Robert Giffen** who surveyed and found out among the low paid British workers in the 19th century that when the price of bread was high, people bought more of it rather than buying a lower quantity and *vice versa*. The following two conditions are necessary for a good to be a Giffen good:

(i) The good must be inferior good with a large negative income effect.

(ii) The substitution effect must be small.

Derivation of Demand Curve with the Help of Indifference Curve Technique *or* Derivation of Demand Curve from Price Consumption Curve

Demand curve is a graphical representation of the relationship between price and the quantity demanded. It slopes downwards from left to right for normal good showing that the consumer likes to purchase more quantity of the good when its price falls. That is, a demand curve shows how much quantity of the good will be purchased at various prices, assuming other influencing factors as constant.

In Marshallian utility analysis, demand curve was derived on the assumptions that utility was cardinally measurable and marginal utility of money remained constant. With these defects, the conclusions drawn on Marshallian analysis of demand was likely wrong. Therefore, in the modern analysis of demand, the demand curve is derived from the price consumption curve of indifference curve technique.

A price consumption curve represents the successive points of tangency between the different price lines and indifference curves.

That is, it shows the effect of a change in price on the quantity demanded of a good. But it does not directly relate price with quantity demanded. Because indifference curve relates two commodities along the two axes. For the sake of simplicity it is assumed that the consumer is purchasing only one good with his given income. On the vertical axis we plot money income and on the horizontal axis, we plot units of the good. There are different indifference curves between money and the good X. We draw Price Consumption Curve (PCC) with the help of indifference curves and price lines. With the data available in the PCC, we prepare a demand schedule for the good and then with this schedule, we prepare a demand curve. This is illustrated in Fig. 5.17.

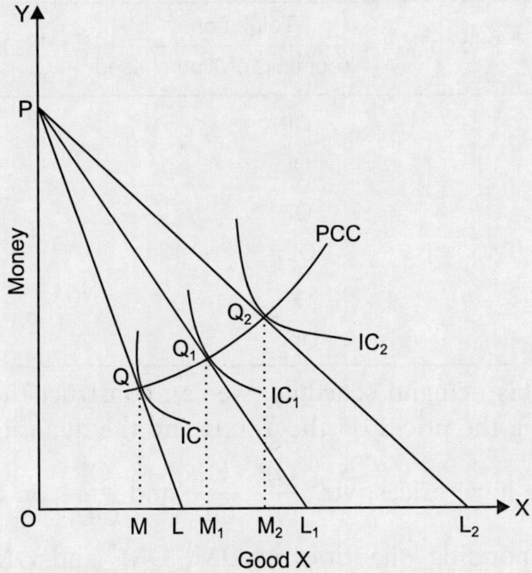

Fig. 5.17

In this Fig. 5.17, we assume that the consumer has OP units of money. He spends this money to purchase the good X. We assume that the price of X continues to fall. PL, PL_1 and PL_2 are the price lines drawn showing the initial and the shifted positions of the price line due to fall in the price of X. We get three tangency points, Q, Q_1 and Q_2 with indifference curves IC, IC_1 and IC_2 respectively. The locus of these points is called PCC.

At first the consumer is in equilibrium at point Q where he purchases OM units of X. At this point, the price per unit of X is OP/OL, i.e., total money income divided by the number of units purchased. At OP/OL price, the consumer can purchase OM units of X.

Similarly at OP/OL_1 price, he purchases OM_1 units of X and at OP/OL_2 price, he purchases OM_2 units of X. In this way, we can draw any number of shifted price lines due to fall in the price of X and find out the price of one unit of X and the quantity purchased at that price in each case.

The whole price-demand schedule based on various price lines can be shown in the following table:

Price Lines	Price of x = $\frac{\text{Total money}}{\text{No. of units of X purchased}}$	Quantity of X demanded
PL	$\frac{OP}{OL}$	OM
PL_1	$\frac{OP}{OL_1}$	OM_1
PL_2	$\frac{OP}{OL_2}$	OM_2

With this demand schedule, we can construct the demand curve taking the prices on the Y-axis and the quantities on the X-axis. We have prices, viz. $\frac{OP}{OL}, \frac{OP}{OL_1}$ and $\frac{OP}{OL_2}$ on the Y-axis and corresponding quantities in OM, OM_1 and OM_2 on the X-axis as shown in Fig. 5.18. In this way we can have three points, A, B and C. If we join the three points, we get DD curve which is called Demand Curve.

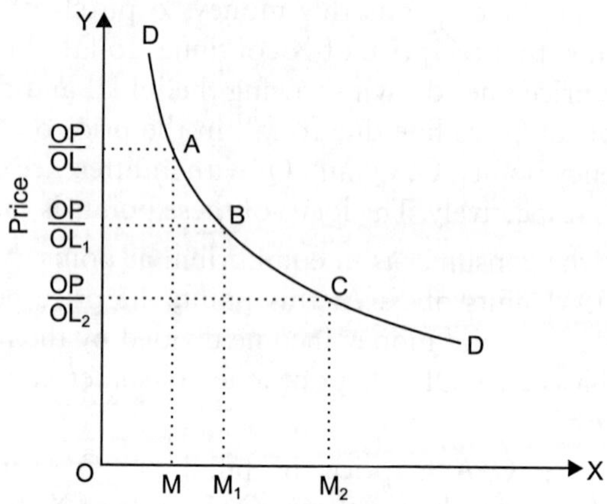

Fig. 5.18

Alternative Way to Draw Demand Curve in the Same Figure

In Fig. 5.18 we have shown demand curve with the help of separate two figures. But we can show this demand curve in the same figure as shown in Fig. 5.19. In the figure, we project the equilibrium points below the X-axis through vertical lines and draw the demand curve in the following way:

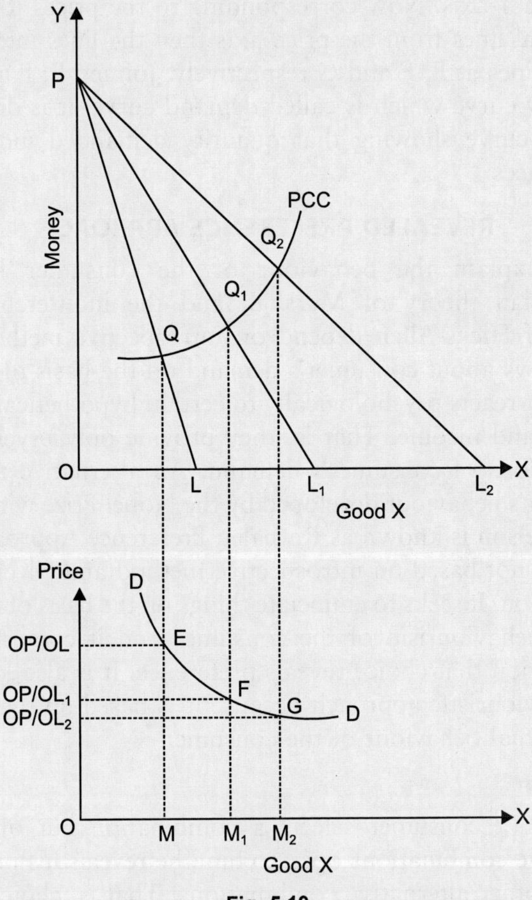

Fig. 5.19

In the lower part of the diagram as shown in Fig. 5.19, price obtained from the above table for the units OM, OM_1 and OM_2 is measured along the Y-axis and the quantity demanded along the X-axis. In the upper part of this figure, the consumer purchases OM, OM_1 and OM_2 quantities of X corresponding to the equilibrium points Q, Q_1 and Q_2 respectively. Now we project QM, Q_1M_1 and Q_2M_2 lines below the X-axis perpendicular to that so as to cut the X-axis of the lower part of the figure and thereby we get the same quantities demanded OM, OM_1 and OM_2 in the lower part for which we have already put prices along the Y-axis. Now corresponding to the prices if we draw horizontal lines from the price axis then the lines intersect the vertical lines at E, F and G respectively. Joining E, F and G we get a DD curve which is called demand curve. It is downward demand curve showing that quantity demanded increases at lower prices.

REVEALED PREFERENCE APPROACH

To explain the behaviour of the consumer both the Marshallian theory of **Marshall** and the indifference curve theory of **Hicks-Allen** depend on introspective method. They derive laws about consumer's demand on the basis of how the consumer reacts psychologically to certain hypothetical changes in price and income. That is, they provide only psychological explanations of consumer's demand. An alternative theory of consumer's behaviour developed by the Nobel Prize winner **Paul A. Samuelson** is known as Revealed Preference Approach. This theory is not based on introspective method and psychological explanation. It seeks to enunciate things on the basis of observed market behaviourism of the consumer and it comprises of a presumption that choice reveals preference. It is also known as the behaviouristic approach because it is based on the analysis of the actual behaviour of the consumer.

Definition

When a consumer selects a combination out of various alternative combinations open to him, he reveals his preference over all other alternative combinations. That is, choice reveals preference.

The definition can be explained with the help of the Fig. 5.20 given on next page. Given the price of two commodities and income of the consumer, the price line PL is drawn. Given the price line PL, the consumer can choose any combination within or on the triangle OPL. Any other point on PL such as A, B and C is equally expensive and any other point such as D, E and F which is to the left of PL is less expensive than any other point like A, B and C on the line PL. Again any point as such G to the right of PL is more expensive than the points on PL. That is, to purchase at point G or at any point to the right of PL is beyond the power of the consumer's purchasing capacity. So, he never chooses the combination at point G or at any point to the right of PL. Again at any point to the left of PL is less preferred to him because it is less expensive or revealed inferior. Therefore, the consumer can purchase at any point lying on the line PL. If the consumer selects the combination at point A, it means that he reveals his preference for A over all other combinations on the line PL. At A, he is buying OM of commodity X and ON of commodity Y. Thus, the basic idea of revealed preference theory is that consumer's choice reveals his preference.

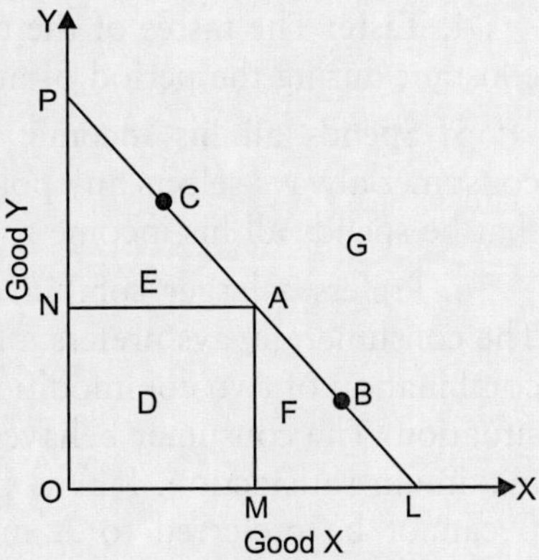

Fig. 5.20

Axioms of Revealed Preference Theorem

Samuelson's revealed preference theorem is based on the following axioms:

1. **Two commodity theorem:** The consumer can buy a combination of two but not more than two commodities.

2. **Income and prices remain constant and the consumer cannot influence prices by his own actions:** The income of the consumer and the prices of the two commodities remain constant throughout the period of action and the consumer cannot influence the prices by his own actions during the period of his preference.

3. **In any given price-income situation the consumer always chooses only one combination:** The consumer's money income enables him to purchase only one of the several combinations available to him.

4. **Taste:** The tastes of the consumer are given and remain constant during the period of analysis.

5. **Spends all his income:** With a given budget line the consumer always selects any point on the budget line indicating that he spends all his income for the combination of the point.

6. **Prefers a larger combination to a smaller combination:** The consumer always prefers a larger combination to a smaller combination of two commodities within the same income-price situation. The consumer behaves rationally always and aims at maximum satisfaction. If A is preferred to B in one situation, B cannot be preferred to A in other situation. It shows the consistency of consumer behaviour.

7. **Choice reveals his preference:** This is the main assumption of revealed preference theorem. That the choice of a particular combination by a consumer reveals his definite preference over all the available combinations.

8. **Demand theorem:** Revealed preference theory obeys the demand theory. A consumer can buy more of a commodity if its price falls. For example, if there is a reduction in the price of commodity X in the market without any fall in the price of commodity Y, the price line will shift to right enabling him to buy more of X when commodity X is put along the X-axis.

9. **Transitivity:** This theory is also based on the assumption of transitivity. If A is preferred to B and B is preferred to C, then the consumer must prefer A to C.

10. **Income elasticity:** This theory assumes that the income elasticity of demand is positive, i.e., as income increases, demand for the commodity must also increase.

Law of Demand and Derivation of the Demand Curve

Prof. Samuelson has established the inverse relationship between price and demand assuming that the income elasticity of demand is positive. He refers to the law of demand as the 'Fundamental Theorem of Consumption Theory'. He states the demand theorem as "Any good that is known always to increase in demand when money income alone rises must definitely shrink in demand when its price alone rises." This statement shows that there is positive income elasticity of demand and inverse relationship between price and quantity demand. His Fundamental Theorem is shown in Fig. 5.21.

We assume that a consumer spends his entire income to purchase two commodities, X and Y. AB is the price line of the consumer. There are so many various combinations of X and Y lying within the triangle OAB or on the line AB. The consumer can buy any of the combinations within his capacity. Suppose, there are three combinations F, G and Q lying on the price line. He chooses the combination Q. This shows that Q selected by him is revealed preferred to any point on or below AB.

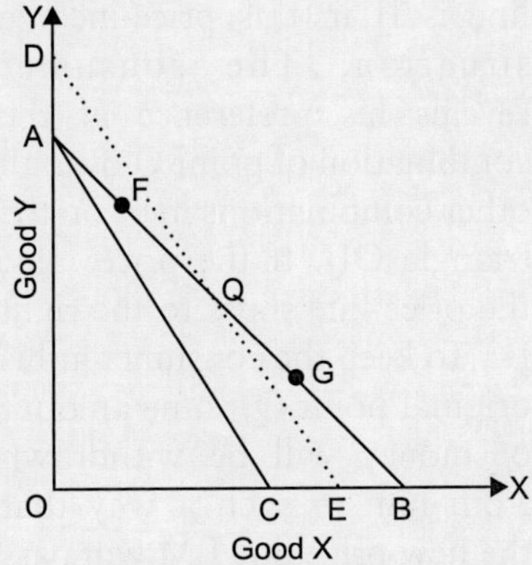

Fig. 5.21

Suppose the price of X rises and the price of Y remains unchanged. The price line will shift to the left new position AC. Now, the combination Q is not available to the consumer due to change in income-price situation. To keep the consumer at previous point Q, we have to compensate him some extra money in such a way that the new price line DE will pass through the point Q in new price-income situation and become parallel to the price line AC. The line DE shows the new income-price situation.

The original combination at Q is also now available in new price-income situation. He will not choose any combination lying below Q on the line DE. If he chooses any combination below Q on the line DE, his choice will be inconsistent as he has already rejected previously the combinations below the line AB. So, he will choose either the point Q (original point) or any point above Q on the portion QD of the new line DE. This implies that he will be buying the same amount of X and Y as before or he will he buying less of X and more of Y than before.

Thus, we see the inverse relationship between price and quantity demand.

Let us now again to see what will be happened in case of a fall in price. It is illustrated in Fig. 5.22.

Here the original price line is IJ in this price-income situation. The consumer reveals his preference at the combination of point Q over all other combinations in or on the triangle OIJ. If the price falls, the price line shifts to the right IK. To keep the consumer at his original point Q, some amount of money will be withdrawn from him in such a way that the new price line LM will pass through the point Q in new price-income situation and become parallel to the price line IK. Here the consumer cannot choose any combination above Q on QL as he has already rejected them earlier in favour of Q. So, in new price-income situation, he will select either Q or any other point below Q on the portion QM of the new price line LM. This shows that he buys the same quantity of X and Y or more X and less Y. Thus, we see that the demand for a product will expand or contract directly with a fall or rise in its price and income elasticity of demand is positive.

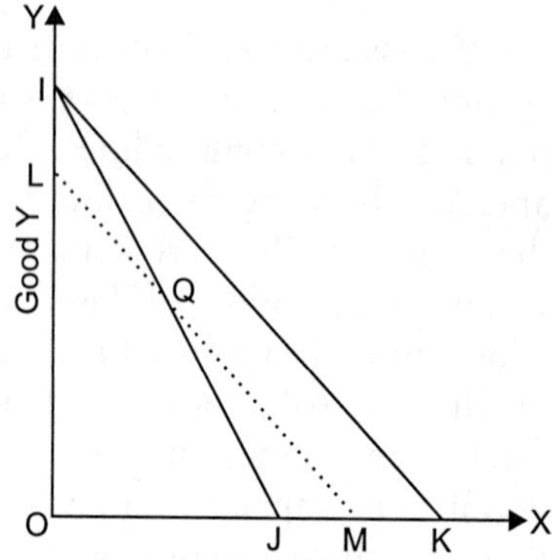

Fig. 5.22

Demand Curve

From Fig. 5.21, it is clear that the consumer can purchase either at point Q or at any point along the portion DQ of the price line DE when the price rises. Again from the above Fig. 5.22, we see that he can purchase at point Q or can choose any point along the portion QM of the price line LM when the price falls. Now we can consider DQ portion of DE as demand curve of the consumer when the price rises and QM portion of LM as the same when the price falls. It is shown in the Fig. 5.23. Here DQM is the demand curve of the consumer. Hence, we can conclude that demand for a good decreases with rise in its price and *vice versa* assuming other influencing factors as constant.

Thus, if we consider so many points along the price line due to small change in price, we get so many combinations of good X and good Y. Putting them in two dimensional graph paper we get a smooth downward sloping demand curve without kink.

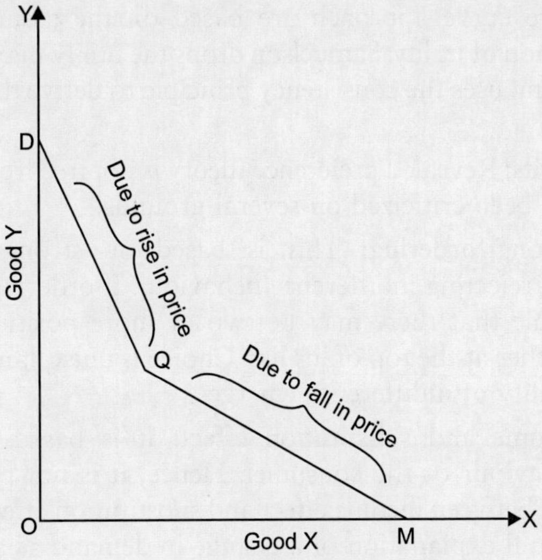

Fig. 5.23

An Appraisal of Revealed Preference Theorem

Merits: Revealed preference theory is an improvement over the Marshallian utility approach and Hicks-Allen indifference curve approach.

1. **More realistic and scientific:** Both **Marshall** and **Hicks-Allen** have used the introspective method to explain consumer behaviour and showed that how consumer reacts psychologically to certain change in prices and incomes. But the revealed preference theory explains consumer's demand on the basis of actual consumer behaviour with the given price and income. Hence, revealed preference theory is more realistic and scientific.

2. **Drop the assumption of continuity**: The indifference curve theory has taken the assumption continuity. But revealed preference theory has given up the continuity assumption and introduced the concept of discontinuity. An indifference curve is a continuous curve and represents all combinations of two goods

whether they are available in the market or not. In the real world we may not have continuity. That is why, revealed preference theory is an improvement over the indifference curve theory.

3. **Consistency:** Both Marshallian utility approach and indifference curve approach are based on the assumption of maximization of utility. **Samuelson** drops the utility maximization principle and uses the consistency principle to derive the demand theorem.

Demerits: Revealed preference theory is not free from defects. It has also been criticized on several grounds.

1. **Strong ordering:** This is based on strong ordering hypothesis rejecting indifference behaviour. If ordering is weak, it is possible that there may be two or more positions which stand together at the top of his list. Choice is unexplained. Now, the possibility of indifference emerges.

2. **Income and substitution effect:** It is based upon the actual behaviour of the consumer. Hence, it is not possible to distinguish between income effect and substitution effect. It gives only a partial explanation of a change in demand as a result of a change in price.

3. **Giffen's paradox:** It shows always positive income elasticity of demand. Hence, it cannot explain Giffen's Paradox when the income effect is negative and stronger than the substitution effect.

4. **Market demand curve:** It deals only with individual demand curve and not market demand curve. Market demand schedule cannot be drawn with the help of this approach. In this regard, Marshallian utility theory and indifference curve theory are more useful.

5. **Welfare purpose:** It does not serve the welfare purpose of the demand theory. It serves only the economic purpose of the demand theory. A perfect demand theory fulfills both the purposes.

In conclusion it can be said that the revealed preference theory is an improvement over the earlier Marshallian utility and indifference curve theory.

EXERCISES

1. Explain consumer's equilibrium condition with the help of indifference curve technique. How will a change in consumer's income and a change in price affect his equilibrium?
2. What is income consumption curve? Show the income consumption curve in the following cases:
   (a) Both X and Y as normal goods.
   (b) Good X is normal good and good Y is inferior good.
   (c) Good X is inferior good and good Y is normal good.
3. What is price consumption curve? What is the relationship between price consumption curve and price elasticity of demand.
4. What is price consumption curve? Show it in the following cases:
   (a) Both X and Y as normal goods.
   (b) Good X is normal good and good Y is inferior good.
   (c) Good X is inferior good and good Y is normal good.
5. With the help of indifference and price consumption curves, derive demand curve for a normal good. Explain why does it slope downward to the right.
6. What is substitution effect? Explain substitution effect in Hicks-Allen method. Also explain that substitution effect is always negative or always positive.
7. Distinguish between Hicksian substitution effect and Slutsky substitution effect. Explain their merits and demerits.
8. Using the indifference curve analysis show how price effect of a commodity is decomposed into income effect and substitution effect.
9. What is a Giffen good? How does indifference curve analysis explain Giffen Paradox? What is the shape of price consumption curve for a Giffen good?

10. Derive demand curve for a Giffen good. Why has it a positive slope?
11. What do you mean by revealed preference theory?
12. Explain, how is demand curve derived from revealed preference theory?
13. Discuss the limitations of the indifference curve analysis.
14. Discuss the comparison between the Marshallian approach and the indifference curve approach.

    Or

    "Indifference curve analysis is an improvement over the Marshallian utility analysis." Discuss.

Chapter 6

Demand and Supply

DEFINITION OF DEMAND

Different economists at different times have given different definitions of demand.

According to Prof. Benham, "The demand for anything, at a given price, is the amount of it which will be bought per unit of time at that price".

In the words of Bobber, "By demand we mean that various quantities of a given commodity or service which consumers would buy in one market in a given period of time at various prices".

Thus, in simple words, by demand we mean the quantity of a given commodity or service which consumers with ability to purchase to purchase wish to purchase in one market in a given period of time and at a given price.

Demand Function

Demand for a commodity depends mainly on four factors: price of the goods, prices of related goods, consumer's income and consumer's taste. This can be expressed by the following formula, which is known as demand function.

Dx = f(Px, Y, Po, T)

Where, Dx = Demand for x good, Px = Price of x good, Y = Consumer's income, Po = Prices of related goods, and T = Taste of the consumer.

KINDS OF DEMAND

Taste of the consumer is a non-monetary concept. It is affected by social, cultural, political, religious, geographical and so many other factors, hence it cannot be measured. Besides, tastes do not change frequently. Hence, we assume them constant in the short-run. Thus, mainly three factors affect the demand accordingly and on account of which there are three main types of demand.

(i) Price-Demand: Other things being constant, the relationship between the demand of x good and its price is known as price-demand. That is, quantity demanded of x good depends upon its price. Demand for x good is function of its price.

$$\text{So, } Dx = f(Px)$$

(ii) Income-Demand: Other things being constant, the relationship between the demand for x good and the consumer's income is known as income-demand. That is, quantity demanded of x good depends upon the income of the consumer. Demand for x good is function of consumer's income.

$$\text{So, } Dx = f(Y)$$

(iii) Cross Demand: Other things being constant, the relationship between the demand for x good and the prices of related goods is known as cross demand. That is, quantity demanded of x good depends upon the prices of related goods. Demand for x good is a function of the prices of related goods.

$$\text{So, } Dx = f(Po)$$

Thus, there are three kinds of demand and they have important effect on the price-output determination by a firm.

DEMAND CURVE

When the consumer's demand is represented by a curve, then it is called demand curve. The demand of the consumer may be changing due to change in price of the commodity, due to change in income of the consumer or due to change in price of the related goods.

SHIFTS IN DEMAND CURVE

Extension of Demand and Increase in Demand and Contraction of Demand and Decrease in Demand

In common usage the terms extension of demand and increase in demand, contraction of demand and decrease in demand are not properly distinguished. But in economics these terms have different meaning which are being explained below.

Extension of Demand

Other things being equal, when a greater quantity is purchased only because of fall in its price, it is called extension of demand. In this case we move along the same demand curve from upward to the downward (or from left to the right). It is shown in Fig. 6.1.

In the diagram the movement from point A to point B along demand curve DD depicts the extension of demand. It shows that quantity demanded is increased from OM to OM_1 due to price falls from OP to OP_1.

Examples and Diagram

Price of x (₹)	Demand for x (units)
10	20
8	25

Here,

Original Price = OP

Original Demand = OM

Changed Price = OP_1

Changed Demand = OM_1

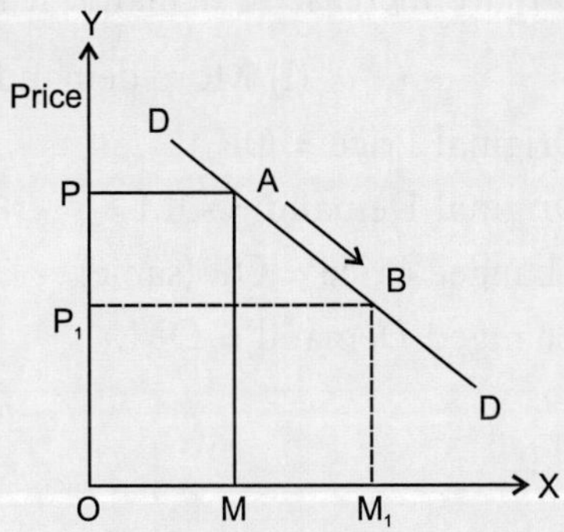

Fig. 6.1: Demand

Increase in Demand

When because of the factors other than the price of the commodity concerned, more quantity at the same price or same quantity at higher price is demanded, it is known as increase in demand. In this case we move from left hand side demand curve to a new right hand side demand curve. In brief, in this situation demand curve shifts to the right. This rightward shift in the demand curve indicates an increase in demand in the sense that more is demanded at a given price or a higher price would be paid for the original quantity.

Thus, the demand curve shifts to the right indicating a large quantity is demanded at each price due to a rise in demand. This can be caused by (i) a rise in income, (ii) a rise in the price of a substitute, (iii) a fall in the price of a complement, (iv) a change in tastes in favour of this commodity.

Example

(I)

Price of x (₹)	Demand for x (units)
10	20
10	25

Or

(II)

Price of x (₹)	Demand for x (units)
10	20
12	20

In our example (I) price remains the same i.e., ₹ 10 but demand increases from 20 to 25 units and in (II) price rise from ₹ 10 to ₹ 12 but demand remains the same i.e., 20 units. Hence both are increase in demand. It is shown in Figs. 6.2 and 6.3.

(I) More demand at the same Price

Original Price = OP

Original Demand = OM

Changed Price = OP (same)

Changed Demand = OM_1

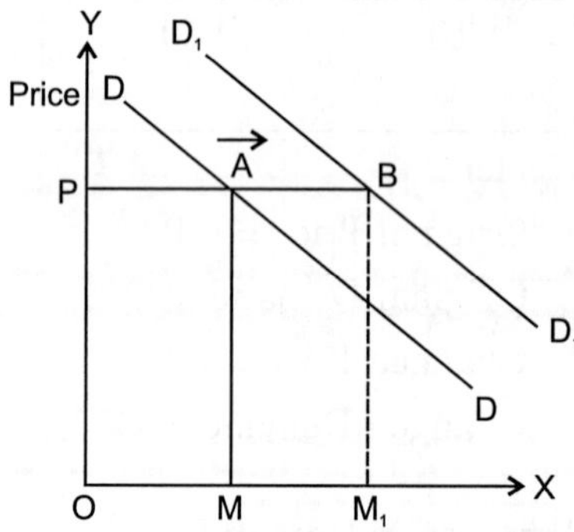

Fig. 6.2: Demand

(II) Same Demand at the higher Price

Original Price = OP

Original Demand = OM

Changed Price = OP_1 (higher)

Changed Demand = OM (same)

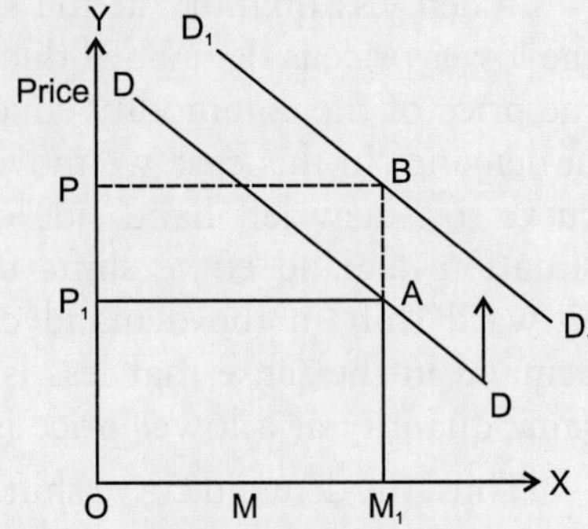

Fig. 6.3: Demand

Contraction of Demand

Other things being equal, when a smaller quantity is purchased only because of rise in its price, it is contraction of demand. In this case we move along the same demand curve from downward to the upward or from right to the left. In the diagram below movement along the demand curve DD from the point A to B (from downward to upward) shows contraction of demand. Here quantity demanded has decreased from OM to OM_1 as price rises from OP to OP_1. It is shown in Fig. 6.4.

Examples and Diagram

Price of x (₹)	Demand for x (units)
10	20
12	15

Here,

Original Price = OP

Original Demand = OM

Changed Price = OP_1 (higher)

Changed Demand = OM_1 (smaller)

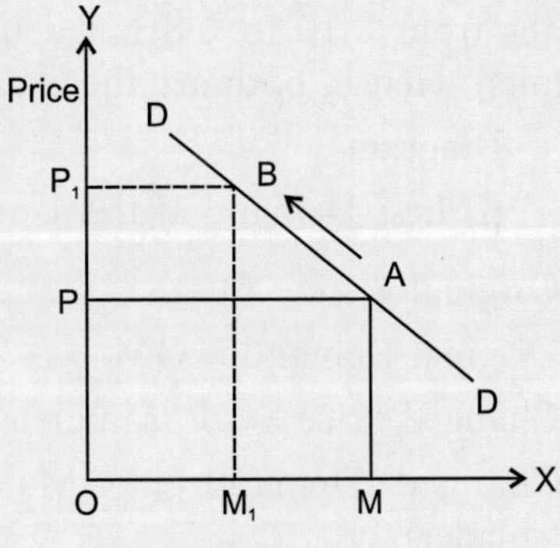

Fig. 6.4: Demand

Decrease in Demand

When less quantity at the same price or same quantity at the lower price is demanded due to the other factors other than the price of the commodity concerned, it is known as decrease in demand. In this case we move from right hand side demand curve to a new left hand side demand curve. In brief, in this situation demand curve shifts from the right to the left. This leftward shift in the demand curve indicates the decrease in demand in the sense that less is demanded at a given price or same quantity at a lower price is demanded.

Thus, the demand curve shifts to the left, indicating a smaller quantity is demanded at each price due to a fall in demand. This can be caused by (i) a fall in income, (ii) a fall in the price of a substitute, (iii) a rise in the price of a substitute, (iv) a rise in the price of a complement, (v) a change in tastes away from this commodity. It is shown in Figs. 6.5 and 6.6.

(I)

Price of x (₹)	Demand for x (units)
10	20
10	15

Or

(II)

Price of x (₹)	Demand for x (units)
10	20
8	20

In our example (I) price remains the same (i.e., ₹ 10) but demand decrease from 20 to 15 units and in example (II) price falls from ₹ 10 to ₹ 8 but demand remains the same (i.e., 20 units). Hence, both are the examples of decrease in demand.

Diagram

(I) Less Demand at the same price

Original Price = OP

Original Demand = OM

Changed Price = OP (same)

Changed Demand = OM_1 (smaller)

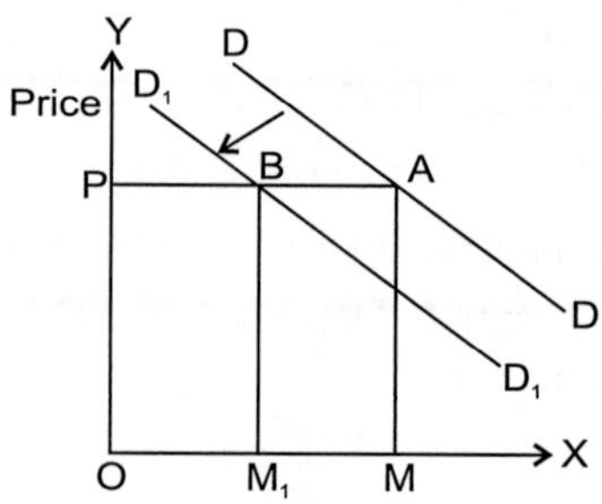

Fig. 6.5: Demand

(II) Same demand at the Lower Price

Original Price = OP

Original Demand = OM

Changed Price = OP_1 (lower)

Changed Demand = OM (same)

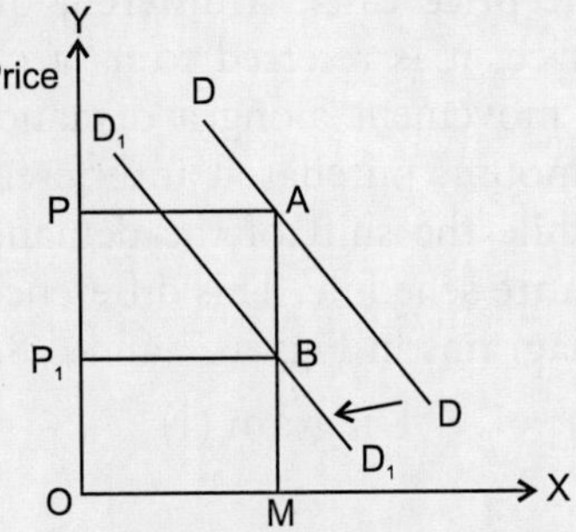

Fig. 6.6: Demand

DIFFERENCE BETWEEN MOVEMENT ALONG A DEMAND CURVE AND SHIFT IN THE DEMAND CURVE

Other things being equal, if the quantity demanded increases or decreases due to fall or rise in the price of a commodity alone, it is known as movement along the demand curve or change in quantity demanded. In this case we move along the same demand curve either upward or downward. Thus, a movement along a demand curve indicates that a different quantity is being demanded because the price of that commodity has changed. A movement down the curve indicates an increase in the quantity demanded because of a fall in price and is known as extension of demand. On the other, a movement up the curve indicates a decrease in the quantity demanded because of a rise in price and is known as contraction of demand.

If more or less quantity of a good is purchased due to changes in factors other than the price, it is called shift in the demand curve or change in demand. In this situation demand curve itself shifts either to the right or to the left. Rightward shift in the demand curve indicates increase in demand while the leftward shift indicates decrease in demand.

Thus, we must clearly understand the difference between a movement along a demand curve and a shift of a whole demand curve. A movement along a demand curve occurs when the quantity demanded changes in response to a change in the commodity's own price. It is referred to as a change in the quantity demanded. On the other, a shift in the whole demand curve occurs when a change in the factors other than the price cause a different quantity to be demanded at every price, it is referred to as a change in demand. Thus, in short a movement along a demand curve represents the changes in amounts purchased at different prices within the same schedule while the shift of the demand curve indicates a change in an entire schedule. This difference has been shown in the following diagrams in Figs. 6.7 and 6.8.

Diagram (I)

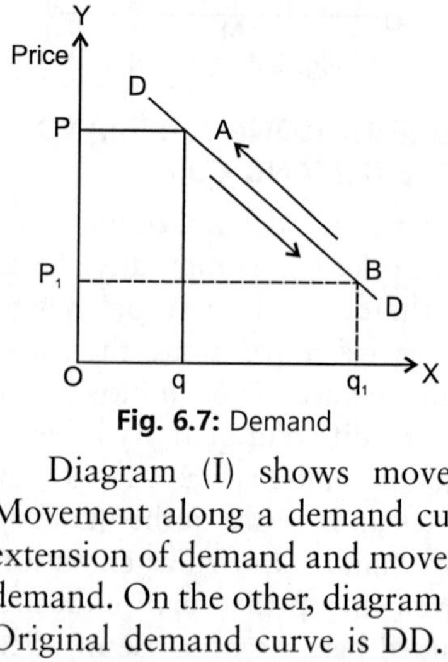

Fig. 6.7: Demand

Diagram (II)

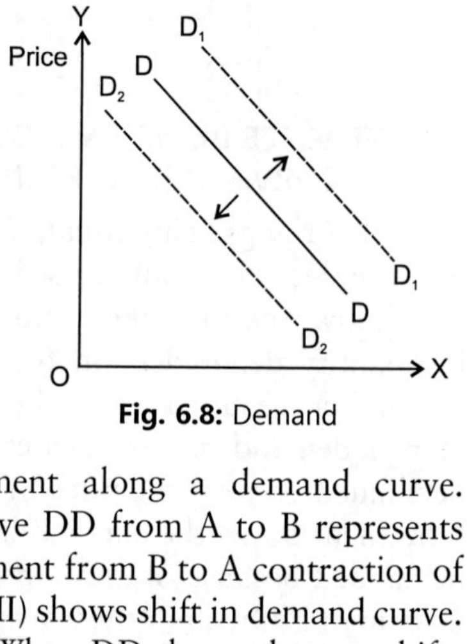

Fig. 6.8: Demand

Diagram (I) shows movement along a demand curve. Movement along a demand curve DD from A to B represents extension of demand and movement from B to A contraction of demand. On the other, diagram (II) shows shift in demand curve. Original demand curve is DD. When DD demand curve shifts to the right and become D_1D_1 demand curve, it is increase in demand. When DD demand curve shifts to the left and becomes D_2D_2 demand curve, it is decrease in demand. In short, rightward shifting shows increase in demand and leftward shifting shows decrease in demand.

LAW OF DEMAND

The law of demand simply expresses a relationship between the quantity demanded of a commodity and its price charged. This law states that other things being equal, the quantity demanded extends with a fall in price and contracts with a rise in price. It shows that the quantity demanded varies inversely with its price not necessarily in proportion. If the price falls, demand will extend and *vice versa*. Thus, the law of demand indicates this inverse relationship between price and quantity demanded. Hence price and demand move in the opposite direction.

So, we can write, the law says that a rise in price of a commodity or service is followed by a reduction in demand and a fall in price is followed by an increase in demand, if conditions of demand remain constant.

Prof. Marshall has defined the law of demand in these words, "The amount demanded increases with a fall in price and diminishes with a rise in price."

According to **Prof. Meyers,** "Under the same conditions of demand, the quantity of a commodity which will be purchased tends to vary inversely with its price."

But the law of demand will operate with given conditions (or assumptions) which are discussed below:

1. There is no change in the tastes and preferences of the consumer.
2. The income of the consumer remains constant.
3. There is no change in customs.
4. The commodity to be used should not confer distinction on the consumer.
5. There should not be any change in the quality of the product.
6. There should not be any substitute of the commodity.
7. There should not be any change in the prices of other related products.
8. The habits of the consumers should remain unchanged.

Given these conditions, the law of demand operates. If there is change even in any one of these conditions, it will stop operating.

EXCEPTIONS TO THE LAW OF DEMAND

In certain cases, the consumer buys more when the price of a commodity rises, and less when the price falls.

1. **War or emergency:** If a shortage of essential commodities is feared in anticipation of war or emergency, people may start buying for stocks even when the price rises.

2. **Speculative effect:** If there is a rise in price of shares and securities, speculators may be induced to buy more of them in the hope of a further rise in price.

3. **Distinctive effect:** In the case of certain commodities, like diamonds, the higher their prices, the greater may be their attractiveness. Display of diamonds is considered to be a mark of distinction by some people as their price is very high. Hence, if their price rises, demand for diamonds may rise rather than fall.

4. **Inferior goods:** Inferior goods are those which are demanded less as the income of the consumer goes up. With an increase in income the consumer shifts his demand away from the inferior goods to some other superior goods. In the case of superior goods, the demand goes up. But in the case of inferior goods the demand falls even in fall of their prices.

5. **Giffen goods:** Giffen goods are those whose demand increases with the increase in its price and decreases with the decrease in its price. Sir Robert Giffen, from his observation of the behaviour of the low paid British workers in the 19th century found out that when the price of bread was high, people bought more of it rather than buying a lower quantity. This is contrary to the law of demand. The reason for such behaviour was that these low paid workers primarily consumed bread with a small quantity of meat. Meat was a relatively more expensive item. When the price of bread went up, they were compelled to spend more on the same quantity of bread and were hence left with much less money to buy that quantity of meat that they were consuming earlier. This reduction in the intake of meat was thus sought to be compensated by buying a little extra bread and hence the demand for bread went up at a higher price. Now if the price of bread were to fall, people would save more money to buy extra meat and use it in place of bread, which would thus cause a reduction in the demand for bread. In this sense bread is a Giffen good whose demand increases with the rise in its price and decreases with the fall in its price.

DETERMINANTS OF DEMAND

Factors which determine the demand in the market are as follows:

1. **Price of the commodity:** General experience says that rise in price of a commodity sells less and fall in price of that commodity sells much. This means that demand has inverse relationship with price.

2. **Income:** A person of less income demands less and of high income demands more for different types of commodities of different values. Demand has more or less direct relationship with income.

3. **Price of related goods:** Prices of related goods affect the demand. Price of substitute goods, say coffee rises, the demand for other related goods, say tea would also increase. In case of complementary goods when the price of one good, say pen falls, the demand for other related goods, say ink, would rise.

4. **Taste, nature and fashion:** Demand for a particular commodity changes with the changes in taste, nature and fashion of the consumers. For example, the demand for pant-shirt has been increasing and the demand for Dhoti-kurta has been decreasing due to the impact of the western civilization.

Besides these major four factors there are also four minor factors which can affect the demand.

1. **Distribution of income and wealth:** Unequal distribution of income and wealth affects the demand for those goods which are naturally purchased by the rich.

2. **Population:** Size of population affects the demand for different types of commodities of different scale. Demand increases with the increase in the size of population and demand decreases with the decrease in the size of population.

3. **Climate and season:** Demand for some commodities depends on climate and season. As such we see the high demand for cold drinks in summer season and hot drinks in winter season.

4. **Expectation:** If there is an expectation of rise in price in near future, demand for different commodities increases and *vice versa*.

ELASTICITY OF DEMAND

The law of demand tells us that with a fall in price of a good, the quantity demanded increases and with a rise in price, quantity demanded decreases assuming other influencing factors remaining as same. Thus, the law of demand shows the direction of the change in quantity demanded due to change in its price. But it does not tell us how much change in quantity demanded will be bought by the change in its price. To measure this 'how much' economists have developed a technical concept known as price elasticity of demand. Law of demand is merely a qualitative statement while the elasticity of demand is a quantitative statement. This concept was first developed by **Prof. Marshall** in his book, *Principles of Economics*. The concept of elasticity of demand refers to the degree of responsiveness of quantity demanded of a good to a change in its price, income or prices of related goods. It is a pure number showing the extent of relationship between the change in price, income or prices of related goods and the change in demand.

Factors Influencing the Elasticity of Demand

1. **Price-level:** The demand of goods having very high prices or very low prices are less elastic and goods of medium level prices have more elastic demand.

2. **Income:** Elasticity of demand will be less in the case of consumers having either a very high income or very low income. But the elasticity of demand will be more elastic of the consumers of middle income group.

3. **Substitute goods:** One of the most important determinants of elasticity is undoubtedly the degree of availability of close substitutes. The demand for commodities having a large number of close substitutes will be more elastic than the commodities having small number of substitutes.

4. **Complementary goods:** The rise or fall of price of a good affects always the demand of its complementary good(s). So, the demand of the complementary goods is always elastic.

5. **Proportion of expenditure:** Elasticity of demand will be less with regard to those goods on which consumer spends a very small fraction of his total expenditure. For instance, salt, matchbox, alpins, etc. on which a consumer spends a very small fraction of his income. On the other hand, elasticity will be greater with regard to those goods on which consumer spends a large portion of his total expenditure.

6. **Nature of the commodity:** Commodities are broadly divided into two groups—necessities and luxuries. Necessities have highly inelastic demand while luxuries have highly elastic demand.

7. **Distribution of wealth:** The distribution of wealth and income also affects the demand. The demand of most of the commodities will be less elastic when the distribution of income and wealth is unequal in the society. If this distribution is equal, the demand becomes more elastic.

8. **Durability:** Perishable goods have less elastic demand while the durable goods have more elastic demand.

9. **Addiction:** When a product is habit forming such as cigarettes, demand will tend to be inelastic. If the price of cigarettes rises, the smokers will find it very difficult to curtail their consumption much, at least in the short run.

USEFULNESS

The concept of price elasticity of demand is not just a theoretical concept. It has various practical uses. The concept is of vital importance to businessmen, farmers, labourers and government policy-makers.

1. **Wage bargaining:** The capacity of trade unions to raise wages depends on the elasticity of demand for the product. If wages are permitted to rise, costs and prices will also rise. If demand is inelastic, sales will not fall much. Again, if demand is elastic, sales will fall.

2. **Bumper crops:** The demand for most agricultural commodities is highly elastic. An increase in the output of wheat or jute due to good harvest may lead to a sharp fall in their prices. This will lead to a fall in the revenue of the farmers. So to help the farmer the government will have to impose restriction on agricultural output.

3. **Excise duty:** The government takes into account the elasticity at the time of selecting goods and services upon which to impose excise duty.

The main purpose of tax on a commodity may be either (a) to raise its price in order to reduce consumers' demand or (b) to raise revenue.

4. **Pricing policy:** The concept of price elasticity has great practical relevance for business pricing policy. Whenever a firm considers to change the price of its product, it has to take into account the effect of the proposed price change on consumers' spending. To the monopolist, the concept has great importance as it helps him to regulate his production and fix his price.

5. **Theory of distribution:** In the field of distribution, the concept of elasticity of demand is useful in the determination of factor prices. The factors having inelastic demand can earn higher remuneration while the factors having more elastic demand would get lower remuneration.

6. **International trade:** If the demand for exports of a country is inelastic, the trader will be gainer in the international trade by raising the price of his product. Again when the demand for exports is more elastic, the trader can sell more by reducing the price of his product if it is permissible.

7. **Fixation of freight and fare:** The concept of elasticity of demand is helpful for the fixation of freight and fare to the transport companies and railways also. Similarly electricity charges are also fixed on the basis of elasticity of demand.

KINDS OF ELASTICITY OF DEMAND

There are three main kinds of elasticity of demand:

(i) Price elasticity of demand,

(ii) Income elasticity of demand, and

(iii) Cross elasticity of demand.

PRICE ELASTICITY OF DEMAND

The term elasticity of demand is generally referred as price elasticity of demand.

According to **Prof. Marshall**, "The elasticity of demand in a market is great or small according as the amount demanded increases much or little for a given fall in price and diminishes much or little for a given rise in price."

In the opinion of **Stonier and Hague**, "Elasticity of demand is a technical term used by economists to describe the degree of responsiveness of the demand for a good to fall in its price."

In the words of **Prof. Meyers,** "The elasticity of demand is a measure of the relative changes in the amount purchased in response to relative change in the price on a demand curve."

Thus, price elasticity means the degree of responsiveness or sensitiveness of quantity demanded of a good to change in its prices or price elasticity of demand is a measure of the relative change in quantity demanded of a good in response to a relative change in its price. Price elasticity can be precisely defined as "The proportionate change in quantity demanded in response to a small change in price, divided by the proportionate change in price" **(Mrs. Robinson).** Thus,

$$\text{Price Elasticity} = \frac{\text{Proportionate change in quantity demanded}}{\text{Proportionate change in price}}$$

$$= \frac{\dfrac{\text{Change in quantity demanded}}{\text{Quantity demanded}}}{\dfrac{\text{Change in price}}{\text{Price}}}$$

$$\text{Symbolically,} \quad e_p = \frac{\dfrac{\Delta q}{q}}{\dfrac{\Delta p}{p}} = \frac{\Delta q}{\Delta p} \cdot \frac{p}{q}$$

where,

e_p stands for price elasticity

q stands for quantity

p stands for price

Δ stands for infinitesimal change.

In percentage form, it can be written as the percentage change in quantity demanded divided by the percentage change in price. That is,

$$e_p = \frac{\%\text{ change in quantity demanded}}{\%\text{ change in price}}$$

Sign of e_p: The sign of e_p is negative since the change in quantity demanded is in opposite direction to the change in price. But we ignore the negative sign and take into account only the numerical value for the sake of better understanding.

For example, if 2% change in price leads to 4% change in quantity demanded of good A and 8% change in quantity demanded of good B.

Therefore, e_p for good A = $\frac{4}{2}$ = 2 and e_p for good B = $\frac{8}{2}$ = 4.

The result show that the quantity demanded of good B changes much more than that of good A in response to a given change in price. But if we consider the minus signs, we get –2 and –4. It indicates that the quantity demanded of good B changes much less than that of good A since –2 > –4. It gives opposite results. In practical sense, the response of demand for B to the given change in price is greater than that of A. So, it is better to ignore minus signs and draw conclusion from the numerical values of elasticities. Hence minus sign before the value of price elasticity of demand is generally ignored in economics.

DEGREES OF PRICE ELASTICITY OF DEMAND

The responses of quantity demanded of different commodities to changes in each respective price are different in character. That is why, in the case of some goods the quantity demanded responds very high or very little or not at all to their price changes. Thus, the degree of responsiveness of the quantity demanded to change in the price may differ, accordingly elasticity of demand will also differ. They are discussed below:

1. **Perfectly elastic demand:** When demand changes infinitely with a very small change in price, it is known as perfectly elastic demand. Here elasticity of demand is equal to infinity and demand curve becomes horizontal, i.e., parallel to the X-axis as shown in the diagram (Fig. 6.9).

Quantity demanded (q) is zero at all prices above OP, but at price (p) OP or a small less than OP, quantity demanded is infinite. Here, $e_p = \infty$

That is, $e_p = \frac{\Delta q/q}{\Delta p/p} = \infty$

When $\frac{\Delta p}{p} = 0 \Rightarrow$ almost no change.

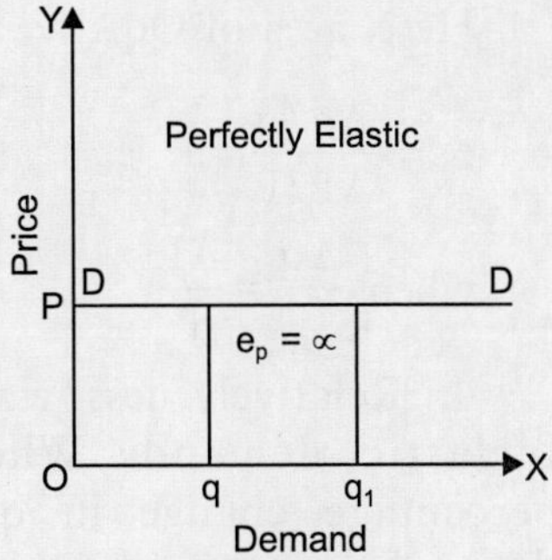

Fig. 6.9

2. **Highly elastic demand:** If the percentage change in quantity demanded (q) is more than the percentage change in price (P), it is known as highly elastic demand.

$$\text{Here, } e_p = \frac{\%\text{ change in q}}{\%\text{ change in p}}$$

$\therefore e_p > 1$ when % change in q > % change in P.

This is shown in the Fig. 6.10. Here change in quantity demanded is greater than the change in price. It is seen in case of luxury goods.

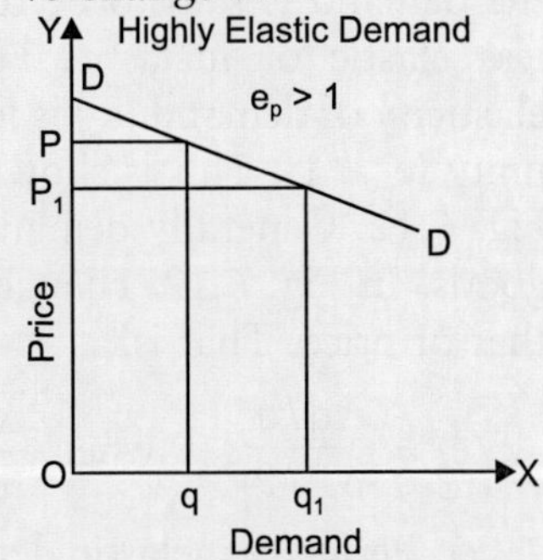

Fig. 6.10

$$e_p = \frac{\Delta q / q}{\Delta p / p} > 1$$

$$\text{when } \frac{\Delta q}{q} > \frac{\Delta p}{p}$$

3. **Unitary elastic of demand:** When a percentage change in price (P) results in an exactly compensating percentage change in quantity demanded (q) so as to keep total expenditure (P × q) exactly unchanged. For instance, if the rise in price is 20%, the decline in the quantity demanded will exactly be 20%. In this case, the shape of the demand curve is rectangular hyperbola. Any area under this curve always remains the same showing the total expenditure as constant. In this case e_p will be one ($e_p = 1$) showing unitary elasticity of demand. This is shown in the Fig. 6.11.

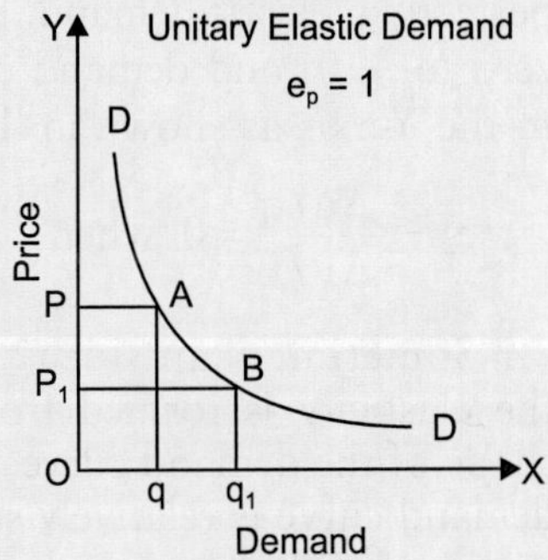

Fig. 6.11

Here, area of OqAP = area of Oq_1BP_1

$$e_p = \frac{\Delta q/q}{\Delta P/P} = 1$$

when $\frac{\Delta q}{q} = \frac{\Delta P}{P}$

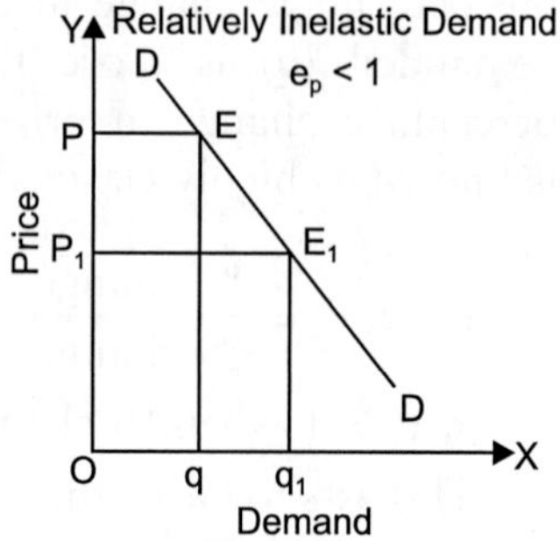

Fig. 6.12

4. **Relatively less elastic or inelastic demand:** When the percentage change in quantity demanded (q) is less than the percentage change in price (P), the demand is said to be relatively less elastic or inelastic. Here the elasticity of demand (e_p) is less than unity ($e_p < 1$). This is shown in the Fig. 6.12. Generally demand is inelastic in case of compulsory goods. In Fig. 6.12, change in quantity demanded is less than that of price. That is,

$$e_p = \frac{\Delta q/q}{\Delta P/P} < 1 \text{ when } \frac{\Delta q}{q} < \frac{\Delta P}{P}$$

5. **Perfectly inelastic demand:** If there is no change at all in quantity demanded (q) when price (P) changes, this is known as perfectly inelastic demand. Here elasticity of demand is equal to zero ($e_p = 0$) and demand curve becomes vertical, i.e., parallel to the Y-axis as shown in the following Fig. 6.13.

$$e_p = \frac{\Delta q/q}{\Delta P/P} = 0 \text{ when } \frac{\Delta q}{q} = 0 \Rightarrow \text{ no change in demand.}$$

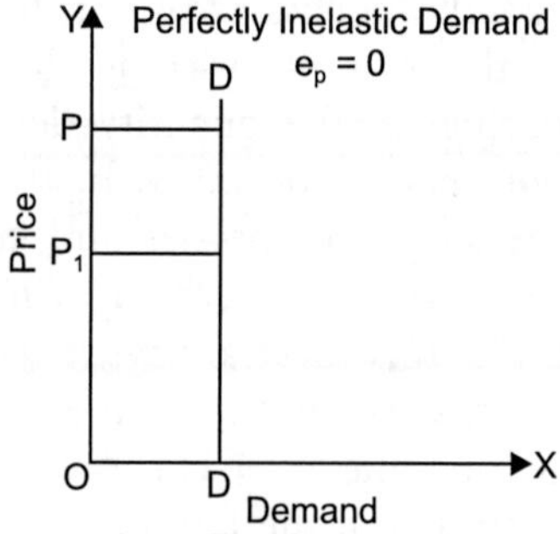

Fig. 6.13

Sometimes an idea about the elasticity is formed from the shape of the demand curve. When demand curve is relatively steeper, it is said that demand is less elastic. And when its slope is less steeper or flatter, it is said to be a more elastic demand curve. In the extreme cases, a vertical straight line demand curve would show zero elasticity while a horizontal straight line demand curve would denote infinite elasticity.

Ranges of Values of the Price Elasticity of Demand

The ranges of values of the price elasticity of demand are

$$0 \leq e_p \leq \propto$$

where,

If $e_p = 0$, the demand is perfectly inelastic (Fig. 6.14)

If $e_p = 1$, the demand has unitary elasticity (Fig. 6.15)

If $e_p = \propto$, the demand is perfectly elastic (Fig. 6.16)

If $0 < e_p < 1$, the demand is inelastic (Fig. 6.17)

If $1 < e_p < \propto$, the demand is elastic (Fig. 6.18)

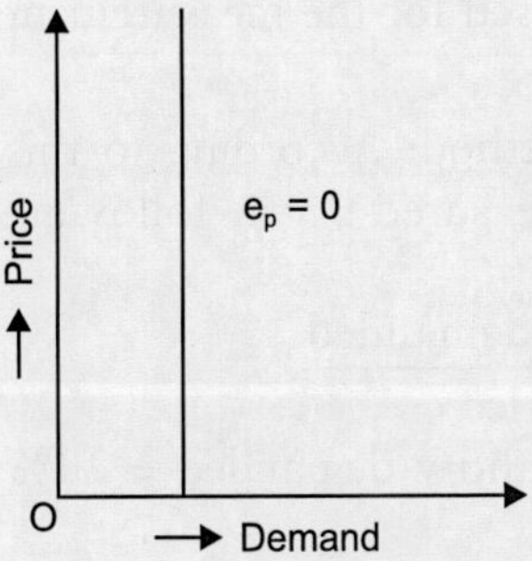

Fig. 6.14

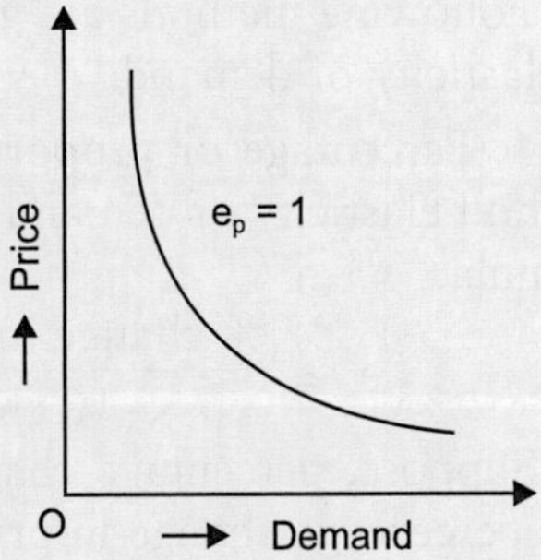

Fig. 6.15

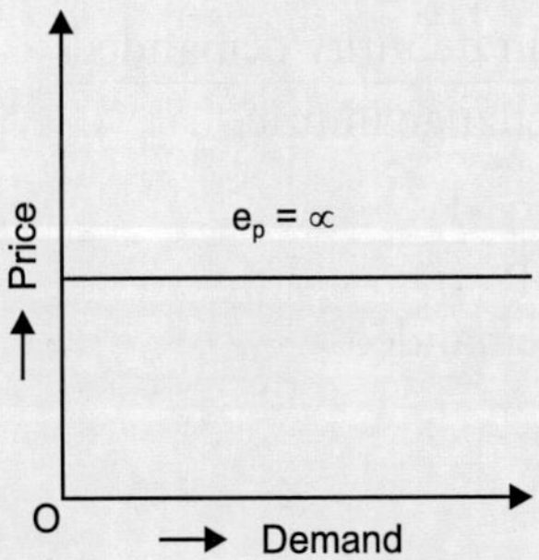

Fig. 6.16

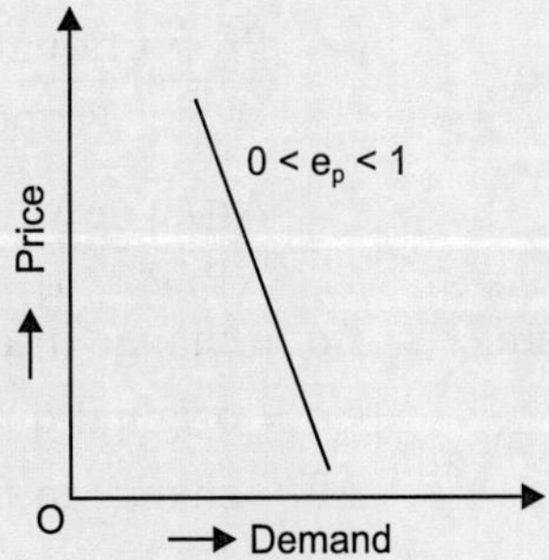

Fig. 6.17

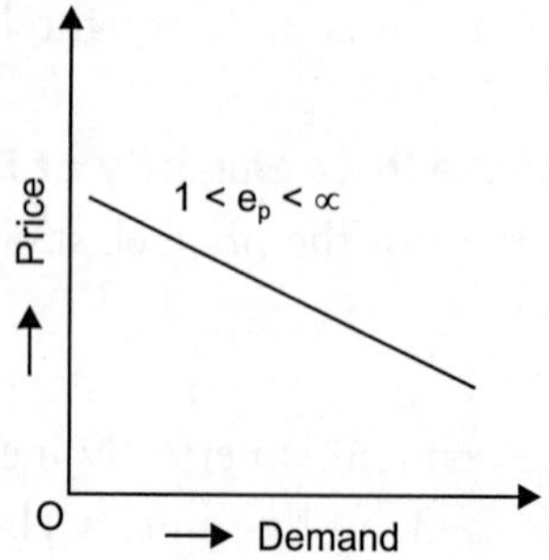

Fig. 6.18

DIFFERENT METHODS OF MEASURING PRICE ELASTICITY OF DEMAND

Following methods are generally used for the measurement of elasticity of demand:

1. **Percentage or proportionate method:** According to this method elasticity of demand can be measured by the following formula:

$$e_p = \frac{\%\text{ change in quantity demanded}}{\%\text{ change in price}}$$

Suppose, percentage change in quantity demanded = 20% and percentage change in price = 10%

Then $e_p = \frac{20\%}{10\%} = 2$

or, $e_p = \frac{\text{Proportionate change in quantity demanded}}{\text{Proportionate change in price}}$

$$= \frac{\Delta q/q}{\Delta P/P} = \frac{\Delta q}{q} \times \frac{P}{\Delta P} = \frac{\Delta q}{\Delta P} \cdot \frac{P}{q}$$

where, Δq = change in quantity demanded

q = original quantity

ΔP = change in price

P = original price

We shall use only this formula to calculate elasticity of demand from different demand schedules.

Example-I

P_x (₹)	q_x (Kg.)
6	10
4	15

Here $\Delta q_x = 10 - 15 = -5$

$\Delta P_x = 6 - 4 = 2$

$P_x = 6; q_x = 10$

$$e_p = \frac{\Delta q_x}{\Delta P_x} \cdot \frac{P_x}{q_x} = \frac{-5}{2} \cdot \frac{6}{10} = -\frac{3}{2}$$

As we have already said that minus sign is customarily dropped hence, the $e_p = 1.5$.

Example - II: Find elasticity of demand on the basis of data given in the Table when (i) price falls from ₹ 7.00 per kg to ₹ 5.00 per kg, (ii) price rises from ₹ 5.00 per kg to ₹ 7.00 per kg. Comment the results.

Price of X per kg (₹)	Total outlay (₹)
8	0
7	7000
6	12000
5	15000
4	16000

Solution: On the basis of information given in the Table we should construct first our demand schedule. If we divide total outlay by the price, we get quantity demanded at various prices. Thus, our demand schedule will be

P_x per kg. (₹)	Total outlay (₹)	q_x (Units)
8	0	0
7	7000	1000
6	12000	2000
5	15000	3000
4	16000	4000

We know,

$$e_p = \frac{\Delta q_x}{\Delta P} \cdot \frac{P}{q_x}$$

(i) When price falls from ₹ 7.00 to ₹ 5.00

$\Delta q_x = 1000 - 3000 = -2000$

$\Delta P = 7 - 5 = 2;\ q_x = 1000$

$P = 7$

Hence, $e_p = \frac{-2000}{2} \cdot \frac{7}{1000} = 7 > 1$ (negative sign omitted)

(ii) When price rises from ₹ 5.00 to ₹ 7.00

$\Delta q_x = 3000 - 1000 = 2000;\ \Delta P = 5 - 7 = -2;\ q_x = 3000;$
$P = 5$

Hence, $e_p = \frac{2000}{-2} \cdot \frac{5}{3000} = -\frac{5}{3} = 1.67 > 1$ (negative sign omitted)

Both the values of e_p are greater than one. Hence, it implies that both have highly elastic demand, i.e., elasticity of demand in both the cases are highly elastic. Again it shows that 1% change in price brings more than 1% change in quantity demanded. But case-I is more responsive than case-II.

Example-III: Demand schedules of good X and good Y.

P_x (Rs.)	q_x (Units)
8	10
4	12

P_y (Rs.)	q_y (Units)
8	10
6	25

Find out the elasticities of demand on the basis of these schedules and tell which is more elastic and comment.

Here,

$$e_p \text{ for good X} = \frac{\Delta q_x}{\Delta P_x} \cdot \frac{q_x}{P_x}$$

where $\Delta q_x = 10 - 12 = -2$

$\Delta P_x = 8 - 4 = 4$

$P_x = 8;\ q_x = 10$

$$= \frac{-2}{4} \cdot \frac{8}{10} = -\frac{2}{5}$$

$$= \frac{2}{5} \text{ (negative sign is omitted)}$$

$\therefore \frac{2}{5} < 1 => $ inelastic demand

Again,

$$e_p \text{ for good Y} = \frac{\Delta q_y}{\Delta P_y} \cdot \frac{P_y}{q_y} \quad \text{where } \Delta q_y = 10 - 25 = -15$$

$$\Delta P_y = 8 - 6 = 2$$

$$P_y = 8;\ q_y = 10$$

$$= \frac{-15}{2} \cdot \frac{8}{10} = 6 \text{ (–ve sign is omitted)}$$

Here 6 > 1 = > elastic demand.

Thus, the demand for good Y is more elastic than the demand for good X. Demand schedule of good X is an example of inelastic demand schedule while the demand schedule of good Y is an example of elastic demand schedule.

2. **Point elasticity method or geometrical method:** Point elasticity of demand is a measure of elasticity at different points on a demand curve. It is a measure of responsiveness of demand to very small change of price level in the vicinity of the point. The change in price is assumed to be so small that the original price and the changed price are depicted by the same point on the demand curve.

Let DD′ be a demand curve as shown in Fig. 6.19. We want to measure elasticity of demand at point R on this demand curve. We draw a tanget tT through the point R, meeting OY at t and OX at T.

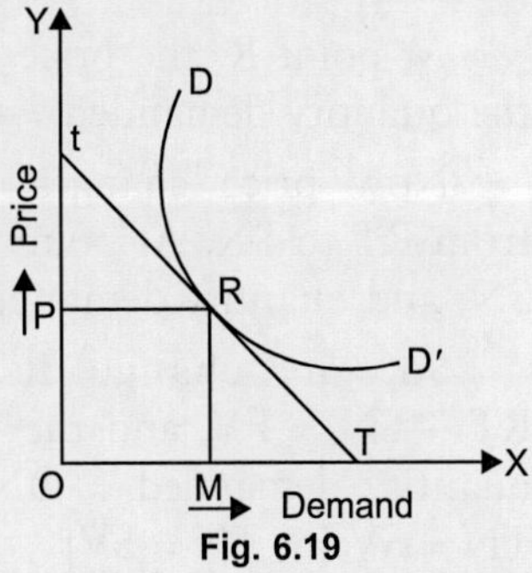

Fig. 6.19

$$\text{We know, } e_p = \frac{\Delta q}{\Delta P} \cdot \frac{P}{q} \qquad \text{... (1)}$$

Here, P = RM (OP) and q = OM $\therefore \frac{P}{q} = \frac{RM}{OM}$

$$\frac{\Delta P}{\Delta q} = \frac{RM}{MT} \text{ where } \frac{\Delta P}{\Delta q} \text{ is the slope of the line tT}$$

$$\therefore \quad \frac{\Delta q}{\Delta P} = \frac{MT}{RM}$$

Putting these values in (1), we get

$$e_p = \frac{MT}{RM} \cdot \frac{RM}{OM} = \frac{MT}{OM}$$

Since ΔRMT and ΔtOT are similar, therefore,

$$\frac{MT}{OM} = \frac{RT}{Rt}$$

$$\therefore \quad e_p = \frac{RT}{Rt} = \frac{\text{Lower portion below R}}{\text{Upper portion above R}}$$

In the same way we can measure the elasticity at different points on a straight line demand curve.

Alternative Method

Let a linear demand curve be Dd as shown in Fig. 6.20 on next page. We measure elasticity of demand at point R on this demand curve.

At point R, the price = TR and the quantity demanded = OT.

Now price changes, i.e., falls from RT to SN. At point S, price = SN, and quantity demanded = ON.

So, the change in price = RT – SN = RV, and the change in quantity demanded = ON – OT = TN = SV [∵ TN = SV]

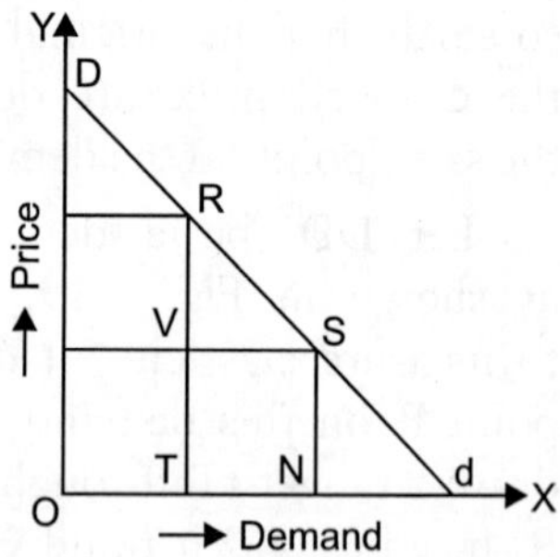

Fig. 6.20

We know, $e_p = \frac{\Delta q}{\Delta P} \cdot \frac{P}{q}$

where, Δq = SV; ΔP = RV; P = RT; q = OT

$$\therefore \quad e_p = \frac{SV}{RV} \cdot \frac{RT}{OT} \qquad \text{... (1)}$$

From the Figure we can also see that the triangles RVS and RTd are similar (because each corresponding angle is equal) then $\frac{SV}{RV} = \frac{Td}{RT}$ putting in eqn. (1), we get

$$e_p = \frac{Td}{RT} \cdot \frac{RT}{OT} = \frac{Td}{OT}$$

Again, ΔDOd and ΔRTd are similar. Again, we get

$$\frac{Td}{OT} = \frac{Rd}{RD}$$

Therefore, e_p at point R = $\frac{Rd}{RD}$

It means that the elasticity of demand at point R

$$= \frac{\text{Lower segment of the linear demand curve below R}}{\text{Upper segment of the linear demand curve above R}}$$

Given this graphical measurement of point elasticity it is obvious that at the mid-point of a linear demand curve $e_p = 1$ (point R is the mid-point in Fig. 6.21). At any point to the right of R the point elasticity is less than unity ($e_p < 1$). At any point to the left of R, $e_p > 1$, at point D, $e_p = \infty$ while at point d, $e_p = 0$.

In mathematical expression, we can write the following:

R is the mid-point on the linear demand curve Dd.

At point D, $e_p = \frac{Dd}{O} = \infty$

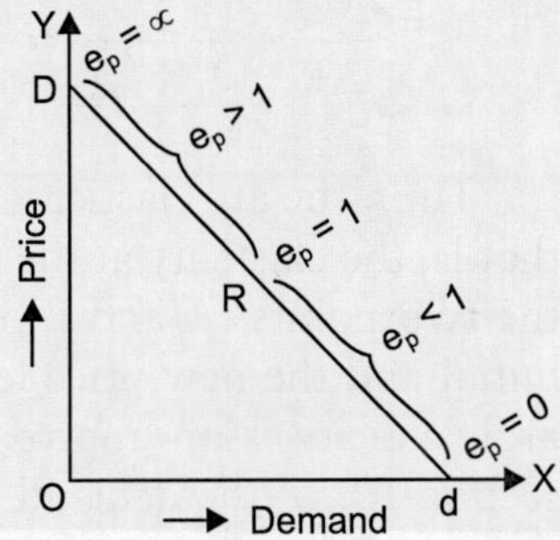

Fig. 6.21

At any point in between D and R,

$$e_p = \frac{\text{Greater than Rd}}{\text{Smaller than RD}} > 1$$

At point R, $e_p = \frac{Rd}{RD} = 1$

[∵ Rd = RD]

At any point in between R and d, $e_p = \frac{\text{Smaller than Rd}}{\text{Greater than RD}} < 1.$

At point d, $e_p = \frac{O}{Dd} = 0.$

3. **Arc method (Arc elasticity of demand):** The point method for measuring price elasticity is applicable only for infinitesimal changes in the price. But when the price change is somewhat large, we have to measure elasticity over an arc of the demand

curve rather than at a specific point on it. In this case the point method to measure price elasticity does not provide us the true and correct figure. In such a situation, elasticity of demand is measured by the arc method. Arc method measures the arc elasticity of demand. In this method the price is measured as an average of the original price and changed price and similarly quantity is also measured by taking an average of the original quantity and the changed quantity. In Fig. 6.22, P_1 is the original price and P_2 is the price after change, then the average price is $\frac{P_1 + P_2}{2}$.

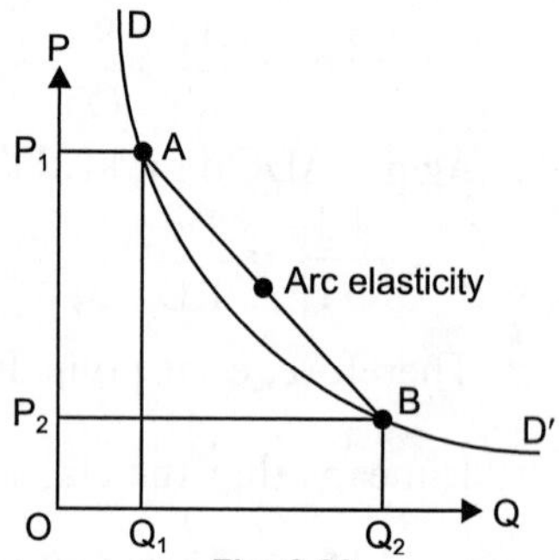

Fig. 6.22

Similarly, the average quantity will be $\frac{Q_1 + Q_2}{2}$, where Q_1 is the original quantity and Q_2 is the changed quantity. Now the formula for measuring the arc elasticity of demand is

$$e_p = \frac{\Delta Q}{\Delta P} \cdot \frac{\frac{P_1 + P_2}{2}}{\frac{Q_1 + Q_2}{2}} = \frac{\Delta Q}{\Delta P} \cdot \frac{(P_1 + P_2)}{(Q_1 + Q_2)}$$

Thus, the arc elasticity is a measure of the average elasticity, that is, the elasticity at the mid-point of the chord that connects the two points (A and B) on the demand curve defined by the initial and the new price levels (Fig. 6.22). The measure of the arc elasticity is an approximation of the true elasticity of the section AB of the demand curve.

4. **Total outlay method (Total expenditure method):**
   1. If the total expenditure remains the same with the fall or rise in price, price elasticity of demand is equal to unity ($e_p = 1$).
   2. If the total expenditure will increase with the fall in price and will decrease with the rise in price, price elasticity of demand is greater than one ($e_p > 1$).

3. If the total expenditure will decrease with the fall in price and will increase with the rise in price, price elasticity of demand is less than one ($e_p < 1$).

We shall now prove the above propositions which state the relationship between price elasticity of demand and total expenditure.

Proof 1. If the total expenditure remains the same with the fall or rise in price, price elasticity is equal to unity ($e_p = 1$).

With fall in price

$TE_b = PQ$ and $TE_a = (P - \Delta P)(Q + \Delta Q)$

where, TE_b = total expenditure before change in price
TE_a = total expenditure after change in price
P = initial price
Q = quantity demanded of the good at price P
ΔP = change in price
ΔQ = change in quantity demanded

By condition,

$$TE_a = TE_b$$

$$\therefore \quad (P - \Delta P)(Q + \Delta Q) = PQ$$

or, $PQ + P\Delta Q - Q\Delta P - \Delta P\Delta Q = PQ$ [$\Delta P\Delta Q$ will be infinitesimally small quantity which can be ignored]

or, $P\Delta Q - Q\Delta P = 0$

or, $P\Delta Q = Q\Delta P$

or, $\frac{\Delta Q}{\Delta P} \cdot \frac{P}{Q} = 1 \therefore e_p = 1$

With rise in price

By condition,

$$TE_a = TE_b$$

$$(P + \Delta P)(Q - \Delta Q) = PQ$$ [$\Delta P\Delta Q$ will be infinitesimally small quantity which can be ignored]

or, $PQ - P\Delta Q + Q\Delta P - \Delta P\Delta Q = PQ$

or, $-P\Delta Q + Q\Delta P = 0$

or, $P\Delta Q = Q\Delta P$

$$\text{or, } \frac{\Delta Q}{\Delta P} \cdot \frac{P}{Q} = 1 \therefore e_p = 1$$

Hence, total expenditure remains the same with the fall or rise in price when price elasticity of demand is equal to one. In other words, if price elasticity is equal to one, there is no change in total expenditure with the change in price.

Proof 2. If the total expenditure will increase with the fall in price and will decrease with the rise in price, price elasticity of demand is greater than one ($e_p > 1$).

With fall in price

$$TE_a > TE_b$$

$$(P - \Delta P)(Q + \Delta Q) > PQ$$

$$\text{or, } PQ + P\Delta Q - Q\Delta P - \Delta P\Delta Q > PQ$$

$$\text{or, } P\Delta Q - Q\Delta P > 0$$

$$\text{or, } P\Delta Q > Q\Delta P$$

[$\Delta P \Delta Q$ will be infinitesimally small quantity which can be ignored]

$$\text{or, } \frac{\Delta Q}{\Delta P} \frac{P}{Q} > 1 \therefore e_p > 1$$

With rise in price

$$TE_a < TE_b$$

$$(P + \Delta P)(Q - \Delta Q) < PQ$$

$$\text{or, } PQ - P\Delta Q + Q\Delta P - \Delta P\Delta Q < PQ$$

$$\text{or, } -P\Delta Q + Q\Delta P < 0$$

$$\text{or } -P\Delta Q < -Q\Delta P$$

$$\text{or, } P\Delta Q > Q\Delta P$$

[$\Delta P \Delta Q$ will be infinitesimally small quantity which can be ignored]

$$\text{or, } \frac{\Delta Q}{\Delta P} \cdot \frac{P}{Q} > 1 \therefore e_p > 1$$

Hence total expenditure will increase with the fall in price and will decrease with the rise in price when price elasticity of demand is greater than one.

Proof 3. If the total expenditure will decrease with the fall in price and will increase with the rise in price, price elasticity of demand is less than one ($e_p < 1$).

With fall in price

$$TE_a < TE_b$$

$$(P - \Delta P)\,(Q + \Delta Q) < PQ$$

$$\text{or, } PQ + P\Delta Q - Q\Delta P - \Delta P\Delta Q < PQ$$

$$\text{or, } P\Delta Q - Q\Delta P < 0$$

$$\text{or, } P\Delta Q < Q\Delta P$$

$$\text{or, } \frac{\Delta Q}{\Delta P}\cdot\frac{P}{Q} < 1 \therefore e_p < 1$$

[$\Delta P\Delta Q$ will be infinitesimally small quantity which can be ignored]

With rise in price

$$TE_a > TE_b$$

$$(P + \Delta P)\,(Q - \Delta Q) > PQ$$

$$\text{or, } PQ - P\Delta Q + Q\Delta P - P\Delta Q > PQ$$

$$\text{or, } -P\Delta Q + Q\Delta P > 0$$

$$\text{or, } -P\Delta Q > -Q\Delta P$$

$$\text{or, } P\Delta Q < Q\Delta P$$

$$\text{or, } \frac{\Delta Q}{\Delta P}\cdot\frac{P}{Q} < 1 \therefore e_p < 1$$

[$\Delta P\Delta Q$ will be infinitesimally small quantity which can be ignored]

Hence when total expenditure will decrease with the fall in price and will increase with the rise in price, price elasticity of demand is less than one ($e_p < 1$).

The above can be explained with the help of the table and diagram given below (Fig. 6.23):

Price	Demand	Total expenditure	Elasticity
1	80	80	
2	70	140	$e_p < 1$
3	55	165	
4	45	180	
5	36	180	$e_p = 1$
6	30	180	
7	20	140	
8	15	120	$e_p > 1$
9	9	81	

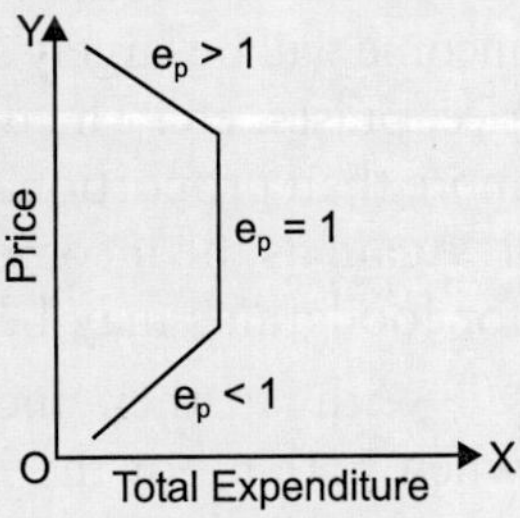

Fig. 6.23

INCOME ELASTICITY OF DEMAND

As we know, change in demand not only depends upon the change in price but also on the change in the level of income of buyers. Suppose that all prices are assumed to remain constant while income is variable. As income changes quantity demanded will change. The quantity demanded will, therefore, be a function of income.

So, income elasticity of demand is a measure of the degree of responsiveness of the demand for a good to a small change in consumer's income. Thus the income elasticity of demand may be defined as the ratio of the proportionate change in quantity demanded of a good to the proportionate change in income.

$$\text{That is, } e_y = \frac{\text{Proportionate change in quantity demanded}}{\text{Proportionate change in income}}$$

$$= \frac{\frac{\Delta Q}{Q}}{\frac{\Delta Y}{Y}} = \frac{\Delta Q}{\Delta Y} \cdot \frac{Y}{Q}$$

Thus, income elasticity of demand can be measured as the percentage change in quantity demanded divided by the percentage change in consumer's income.

$$\text{That is, } e_y = \frac{\text{\% change in quantity demanded}}{\text{\% change in consumer's income}}$$

Income elasticity of demand for a commodity may be different at different levels of income. For example, at extremely low levels of income where a person is underfed, any increase in income will be largely spent upon buying the foodgrains—wheat, rice, pulses, etc. The demand for foodgrains may, thus, increase more than proportionately to increase in income and we get, $e_y > 1$. Again as the income rises still further, the increase in demand for foodgrains may be less and then we get $e_y < 1$, but $e_y > 0$.

With further increase in income, a state may come when nothing of the increased income is spent on foodgrains, then $e_y = 0$. Again, with further increase in income, the person would start substituting the traditional items of food—wheat, rice, etc. by superior items like butter, milk, fruit, mutton, etc. Thus, foodgrains now being regarded as inferior goods, their demand will fall with the increase in income i.e. $e_y < 0$. This can be explained with the help of the Fig. 6.24.

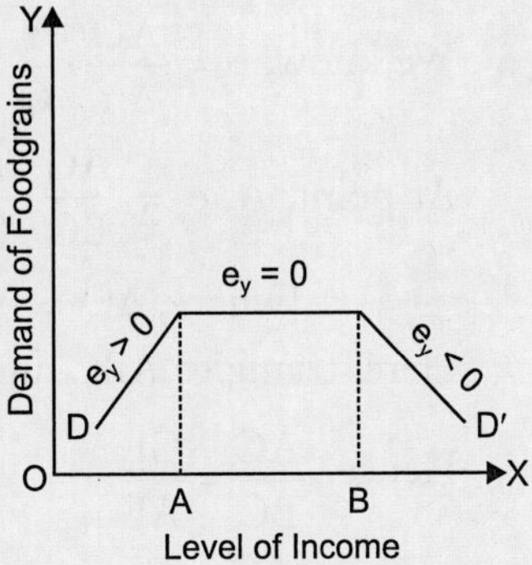

Fig. 6.24

The curve DD′ shows the demand for foodgrains at various levels of income. As the income level rises from O to A there is an increase in demand for foodgrains, then $e_y > 0$. Between income levels A and B, there is no additional demand for foodgrains, then $e_y = 0$ which implies that income elasticity of demand is inelastic. Beyond B level of income, the demand for foodgrains decreases with an increase in income. In this situation, foodgrains is regarded as inferior goods then, $e_y < 0$.

The concept of income elasticity of demand (e_y) can be used for classifying commodities shown in the following table:

Values of the income elasticity	Type of goods
$e_y > 1$	Luxury (or foodgrains in the condition of underfeeding)
$0 < e_y < 1$	Normal goods
$e_y < 0$	Inferior goods

Measurement of Income Elasticity of Demand (e_y) at a Point on an Income Demand Curve

Income demand curve shows the quantity demanded of a good at different levels of income. Let DD′ is a demand curve having positive slope as shown in Fig. 6.25. We want to measure income elasticity at point A on it where quantity demanded is OE at the income level AE. Suppose, income increases from AE to BF and as a result quantity demanded increases by EF or AC. Now, we extend DD′ curve downward so as to meet the X-axis at point G.

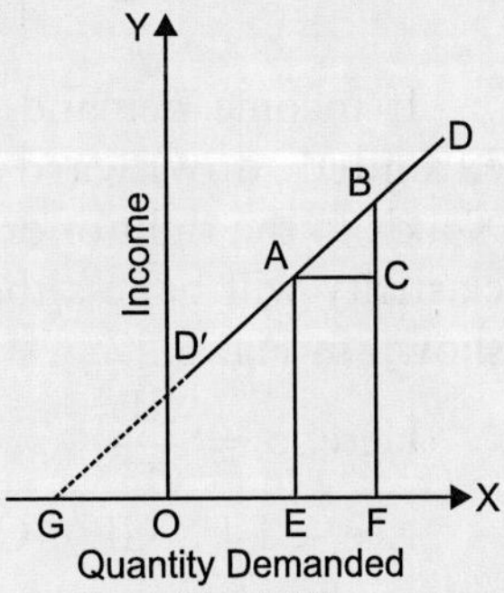

Fig. 6.25

We know, $e_y = \frac{\Delta Q}{\Delta Y} \cdot \frac{Y}{Q}$

At point, A, $e_y = \frac{AC}{BC} \cdot \frac{AE}{OE}$ ... (1)

[where, $\Delta Q = AC$, $\Delta Y = BC$, $Y = AE$ and $Q = OE$]

Here, triangles ABC and AEG are similar.

Hence, $\frac{AC}{BC} = \frac{GE}{AE}$

Putting $\frac{AC}{BC} = \frac{GE}{AE}$ in eqn. (1), we get

$$e_y = \frac{GE}{AE} \cdot \frac{AE}{OE} = \frac{GE}{OE}$$

Here GE > OE ∴ $e_y > 1$ i.e., income elasticity of demand is greater than one.

Here income demand curve when extended downward meets the X-axis to the left of origin. If income demand curve when extended downward meets the X-axis at its origin, income elasticity will be equal to one. It is shown in Fig. 6.26.

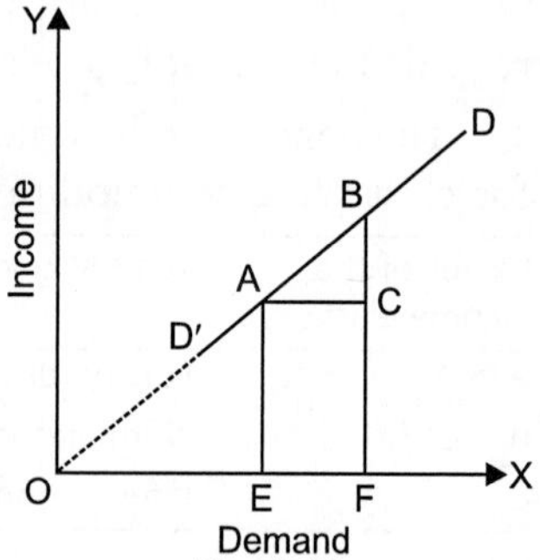

Fig. 6.26

Here, $e_y = \frac{OE}{OE} = 1$

[∵ GE = OE]

If income demand curve when extended downward meets the X-axis to the right of origin, income elasticity will be less than one. It is shown in Fig. 6.27.

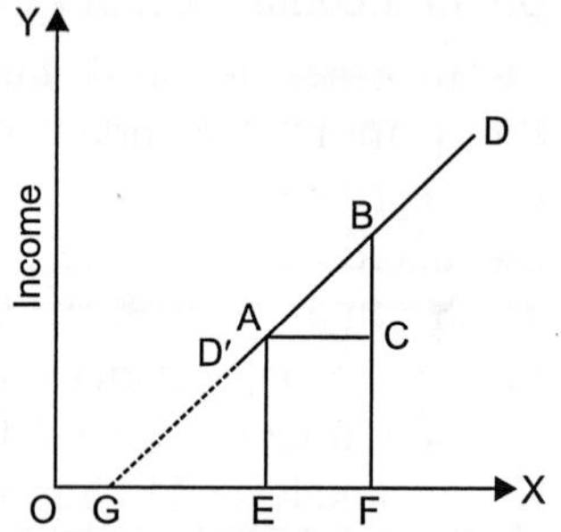

Fig. 6.27

Here, $e_y = \frac{GE}{OE}$

∴ $e_y < 1$ [∵ GE < OE]

Income Elasticity of Demand from the Proportion of Income Spent on a Good

There is a useful relationship between income elasticity for a good and proportion of income spent on it. It is described in the following three propositions:

Proposition I: If proportion of income spent on a good increases as income increases, the income elasticity for the good is greater than one i.e., $e_y > 1$.

The proportion of income spent is $\frac{X}{Y}$ where Y is for income and X is for the income spent on a good at that level of income. If the income increases by ΔY and as a result expenditure on the good rises by ΔX, then the new proportion of income spent on the good will be $\frac{X+\Delta X}{Y+\Delta Y}$. Now, if the proportion of income spent on the good increases with the increase in income then,

$$p_a > p_b \text{ i.e. } \frac{X+\Delta X}{Y+\Delta Y} > \frac{X}{Y}$$

$$\text{or, } XY + Y\Delta X > XY + X\Delta Y$$

$$\text{or, } Y\Delta X > X\Delta Y$$

$$\text{or, } \frac{\Delta X}{\Delta Y} \cdot \frac{Y}{X} > 1$$

$$\therefore e_y > 1$$

[where P_a = proportion of income spent after change
P_b = Proportion of income spent before change
Y = income, X = expenditure
X + ΔX = changed expenditure
Y + ΔY = changed income]

Hence, when the proportion of income spent on a good increases as income increases, income elasticity is greater than one.

Proposition II: If proportion of income spent on a good remains the same as income increases, then income elasticity for the good is equal to one.

Here, $P_a = P_b$, i.e., $\frac{X+\Delta X}{Y+\Delta Y} = \frac{X}{Y}$

or, $XY + Y\Delta X = XY + X\Delta Y$, or, $Y\Delta X = X\Delta Y$

or, $\frac{\Delta X}{\Delta Y} \cdot \frac{Y}{X} = 1 \therefore e_y = 1$

Hence, when the proportion of income spent on a good remains the same as income increases, income elasticity is equal to one.

Proposition III: If proportion of income spent on a good decreases as income increases, then income elasticity for the good is less than one.

Here, $P_a < P_b$, i.e., $\frac{X + \Delta X}{Y + \Delta Y} < \frac{X}{Y}$

or, $XY + Y\Delta X < XY + X\Delta Y$, or, $Y\Delta X < X\Delta Y$

or, $\frac{\Delta X}{\Delta Y} \cdot \frac{Y}{X} < 1 \therefore e_y < 1$

Hence, when proportion of income spent on a good falls as income increases, the income elasticity is less than one.

Problem I: Calculate the income elasticity of demand from the following table and comment the result:

Income (₹)	200	250
Demand (Units)	10	12

Here, $\Delta Q = 10 - 12 = -2$, $\Delta Y = 200 - 250 = -50$ $Q = 10$; $Y = 200$

$$e_y = \frac{\Delta Q}{\Delta Y} \cdot \frac{Y}{Q} = \frac{-2}{-50} \cdot \frac{200}{10} = 0.8 > 0$$

Here $e_y = 0.8 > 0$ but < 1 means that proportionate change in quantity demanded is smaller than proportionate change in income. Hence, it is the demand for normal good.

Cross Elasticity of Demand and Comments in Different Values of it

The concept of cross elasticity of demand is based upon the fact that some commodities are close substitutes and, therefore, the consumer can use one in place of another. Now we can take the example of tea and coffee. A person in need of hot drink can take either tea or coffee. Now suppose the price of coffee goes up. Then some people may start taking less of coffee and to meet their need for a hot drink, may start taking tea. Thus, the demand for tea goes up not because the price of tea has gone down, but because the price of a close substitute, i.e., coffee has gone up.

Again some commodities are complementary. A person cannot use one without the use of another at a time. We take the example of tea and sugar. If the price of tea goes up, the demand for sugar would fall and *vice versa*.

The degree of change in the demand for one commodity with the change in price of another commodity is called cross elasticity of demand. In other words, the cross elasticity of demand is defined as the proportionate change in the quantity demanded of X resulting from a proportionate change in the price of Y. Symbolically, we have

$$e_{xy} = \frac{\frac{\Delta Q_x}{Q_x}}{\frac{\Delta P_y}{P_y}} = \frac{\Delta Q_x}{\Delta P_y} \cdot \frac{P_y}{Q_x}$$

Again in percentage form, it is defined as the ratio of the percentage change in the demand for X to the percentage change in the price of Y.

That is, $e_{xy} = \dfrac{\%\text{ change in the demand for X}}{\%\text{ change in the price of Y}}$

Sign: Three possibilities may be seen as far as the numerical value of the elasticity coefficient is concerned. e_{xy} is negative if X and Y are complementary goods. For example, if the price of petroleum increases, the market demand for motor-cars is likely to fall. If e_{xy} is positive, in general, the two products are substitutes. For example, an increase in the price of coffee will lead to an increase in the demand for tea. If e_{xy} is zero, then the two products are neither substitutes nor complementary, e.g. computer and car.

Values of the cross elasticity	Type of goods
$e_{xy} < 0$	Complementary goods
$e_{xy} > 0$	Substitute goods
$e_{xy} = 0$	Neither substitute nor complementary goods

Thus, the concept of cross elasticity of demand is very important in economic theory. The substitutes and complementary goods are defined in terms of cross elasticity of demand. The goods between which cross elasticity of demand is positive are known as substitute goods and the goods between which cross elasticity of demand is negative are complementary goods. The higher the value of the cross elasticity the stronger will be the degree of substitutability or complementarity between two goods.

NUMERICAL PROBLEMS AND SOLUTIONS

1. If the price of coffee rises from ₹ 25.00 per hundred grams to ₹ 30.00 per hundred grams and as a result the consumers' demand for tea increases from 60 kg to 70 kg in a locality, then what will be the cross elasticity of demand of tea for coffee?

We know, cross elasticity of demand $(e_{xy}) = \frac{\Delta q_x}{\Delta P_y} \times \frac{P_y}{q_x}$

where, $\Delta q_x = 60 - 70 = -10$ kg, $q_x = 60$ kg

$\Delta P_y = 25 - 30 = ₹\ -5$, $P_y = ₹\ 25$

$$\therefore\ e_{xy} = \frac{-10}{-5} \times \frac{25}{60} = \frac{5}{6} = 0.83$$

2. Calculate the price elasticity of demand in the following situations:

(i)

P_x (₹)	q_x (Unit)
20	300
22	240

(ii) When the price of a commodity goes up by 10%, a consumer's demand falls from 500 units to 400 units.

(iii) When the price of commodity falls by 80%, the quantity demanded of it increases by 100%.

We know,

(i) $e_p = \frac{\Delta q_x}{\Delta P_x} \cdot \frac{P_x}{q_x}$ [where $\Delta q_x = 300 - 240 = 60$ units

$\Delta P_x = 20 - 22 = ₹\ -2$

$e_p = \frac{20}{300} \cdot \frac{60}{-2}$ $P_x = ₹\ 20$

or, $e_p = -2$ $q_x = 300$ units]

Therefore, e_p = 2 (negative sign omitted) which is more than one. So, price elasticity of demand is elastic.

(ii) Percentage change in demand $= \frac{(500 - 400) \times 100}{500}$

$$= \frac{100 \times 100}{500} = 20\%$$

We know, $e_p = \frac{\text{\% change in demand}}{\text{\% change in price}}$

$$= \frac{20}{10} = 2 > 1$$

Therefore, price elasticity of demand is more elastic.

(iii) We know, $e_p = \frac{\text{\% change in demand}}{\text{\% change in price}}$

$$= \frac{100}{80} = \frac{2}{5} = 2.5 > 1$$

Therefore, price elasticity of demand is more elastic.

3. Following are the demand schedules for commodity A and commodity B. Which of them has a more elastic demand? Explain your answer.

Commodity - A		Commodity - B	
Price (₹)	Quantity (Unit)	Price (₹)	Quantity (Unit)
100	1000	200	1000
102	900	198	1100

We know,

e_p for com. = A $= \frac{\Delta q_x}{\Delta P_x} \cdot \frac{P_x}{q_x}$

$$= \frac{100}{-2} \cdot \frac{100}{1000}$$

= 5 (–ve sign omitted)

[where

Δq_x = 1000 – 900

= 100 (units)

ΔP_x = 100 – 102

= ₹ –2

P_x = ₹ 100

q_x = 1000 units]

Again,

$$e_p \text{ for com.} = B = \frac{\Delta q_x}{\Delta P_x} \cdot \frac{P_x}{q_x}$$

$$= \frac{-100}{2} \cdot \frac{200}{1000}$$

$$= 10 \text{ (–ve sign omitted)}$$

[where
$\Delta q_x = 1000 - 1100$
$= -100$ (units)
$\Delta P_x = 200 - 198$
$=$ ₹ 2
$P_x =$ ₹ 200
$q_x = 1000$ units]

Here, the value of the price elasticity of demand (e_p) for commodity B > the value of price elasticity of demand for commodity A. It implies that the commodity B is more elastic.

4. A consumer was consuming 4 kg of sugar per month when his income was ₹ 1000 per month. When his income increases to ₹ 1200 per month, he starts consuming 5 kg of sugar per month. Is the demand for sugar elastic or inelastic with respect to income? (Assuming no change in other determinants of demand.)

We know,

$$e_y = \frac{\Delta Q}{\Delta Y} \cdot \frac{Y}{Q}$$

$$e_y = \frac{-1}{-200} \frac{1000}{4}$$

$$= \frac{5}{4} = 1.25$$

[where $\Delta Q = 4 - 5 = -1$ kg
$\Delta Y = 1000 - 1200 = -$ ₹ 200
$Y =$ ₹ 1000, $Q = 4$ kg]

Here, $e_y = 1.25 > 1$

Hence, the demand for sugar with respect to income is elastic.

5. On the basis of information given below, calculate the co-efficient of income elasticity of commodity 'X' and comment upon the result.

Income (₹)	800	1000
Expenditure on 'X' (₹)	25	40

We know, income elasticity of demand,

$$e_y = \frac{\Delta E}{\Delta Y} \cdot \frac{Y}{E}$$

[where $\Delta E = 25 - 40 = -$ ₹ 15

$$\Delta Y = 800 - 1000 = -₹\ 200$$

$$\therefore \quad e_y = \frac{-15}{-200} \cdot \frac{800}{25} = 2.4 > 1 \quad Y = ₹\ 800,\ E = 25]$$

The result shows that income elasticity of demand is more than one. That is, demand increases with the increase in income of the consumer. So, the good is luxury good.

6. Given that the quantity previously demanded was 100 units, decrease in quantity demanded is 5 units, increase in price is ₹ 5 and price elasticity of demand is 1.2. Calculate the price before the change.

We know,

$$e_p = \frac{\Delta q_x}{\Delta P_x} \cdot \frac{P_x}{q_x}$$

[where $\Delta q_x = 5$ units
$\Delta P_x = ₹\ 5$
$q_x = 100$ units
$e_p = 1.2,\ P = ?$]

$$\therefore \quad 1.2 = \frac{5}{5} \cdot \frac{P_x}{100}$$

$$\text{or} \quad 1.2 = \frac{P_x}{100}$$

or, $P_x = 100 \times 1.2 = ₹\ 120$.

So, the price before the change was ₹ 120 per unit.

Relationship between Slope and Elasticity of Demand

Before examining the relationship between slope and elasticity of demand, let us define the terms first. Slope of a demand curve is the tangent of the angle produced by the line with the horizontal and vertical axes. Symbolically, slope = $\frac{dp}{dq}$ when Y-axis measures price and X-axis measures quantity demanded.

Price elasticity of demand (e_p) is the proportionate change in quantity demanded with respect to proportionate change in price.

Symbolically, $e_p = \frac{p}{q}\frac{dq}{dp}$.

Apparently, we see that there exists an inverse relationship between slope and absolute value of elasticity of demand. Let us now prove it in the following cases:

(i) When the demand curve is horizontal straight line and parallel to the x-axis like in the perfect competitive market shown in the Fig. 6.28. Here slope $\frac{dp}{dq} = 0,$

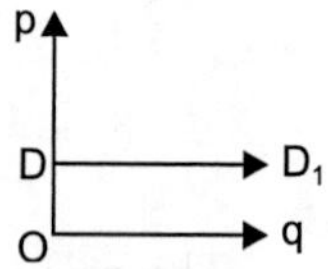

Fig. 6.28

then $e_p = \frac{p}{q}\frac{dq}{dp} = \infty$

(ii) When the slope, $\frac{dp}{dq} > 1$, it is shown in the Fig. 6.29, then $e_p < 1$

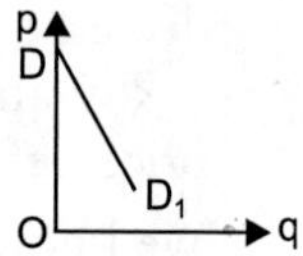

Fig. 6.29

(iii) When the slope $\frac{dp}{dq} < 1$, it is shown in the Fig. 6.30, then $e_p > 1$

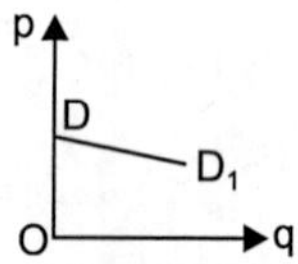

Fig. 6.30

(iv) When the slope, $\frac{dp}{dq} = \infty$, it is shown in the Fig. 6.31, then $e_p = 0$. The demand curve is vertical straight line and parallel to the Y-axis like in the monopoly market. Thus, we can show when slope = 0, then $e_p = \infty$ and when slope = ∞, then $e_p = 0$ in a single Fig. 6.32. In this figure at point D, slope = 0 then $e_p = \infty$ and at point D_1, slope = ∞ then $e_p = 0$.

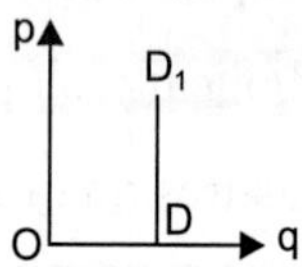

Fig. 6.31

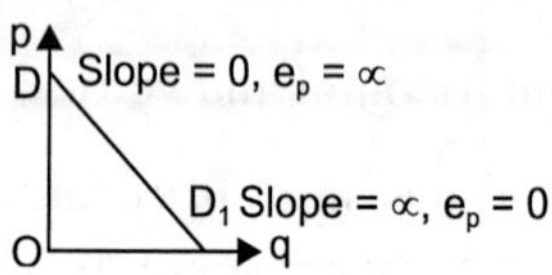

Fig. 6.32

(v) If two demand curves intersect each other, their absolute elasticities can be compared at the point of intersection by comparing their slopes. The greater the slope the lower will be the absolute value of elasticity and *vice versa*.

Let the two demand curves AB and CD intersect each other at point E in Fig. 6.33 where price is OP and quantity is OM. We know, the absolute value of elasticity of demand is $e_p = \frac{p}{q}\frac{dq}{dp}$.

Here, $\frac{p}{q}$ is the same at the point of their intersection point E, but the slope $\frac{dp}{dq}$ differs. The greater the absolute slope, the lower will be value of $\frac{dq}{dp}$ and *vice versa*. Here, tan m of AB > tan n of CD, then $\frac{dq}{dp}$ of AB < $\frac{dq}{dp}$ of CD.

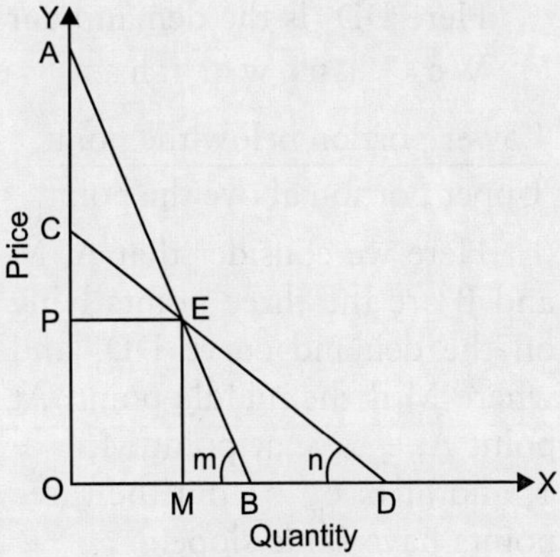

Fig. 6.33

$\therefore$ As $\frac{p}{q}$ is same, then e_p of AB < e_p of CD.

Again, it can be proved in the following way,

$$e_p \text{ of AB at E} = \frac{EB}{EA} = \frac{OP}{PA}$$

$$\text{and } e_p \text{ of CD at E} = \frac{ED}{EC} = \frac{OP}{CP}$$

$$\text{Since PA > CP, } \frac{OP}{PA} < \frac{OP}{CP} \Rightarrow e_p \text{ of AB} < e_p \text{ of CD}$$

Thus it is proved that the greater the slope the lower will be absolute value of elasticity and *vice versa*.

From the explanation of the above five cases, one may conclude that an inverse relationship exists between the slope of a demand curve and its absolute value of price elasticity of demand. However, it is not true in real sense. Let us now examine it.

Case - I: Different points on a straight line demand curve have same slope but different absolute value of price elasticity of demand.

Here DD_1 is the demand curve as shown in Fig. 6.34.

We know that e_p at a point = $\frac{\text{Lower portion below the point}}{\text{Upper portion above the point}}$.

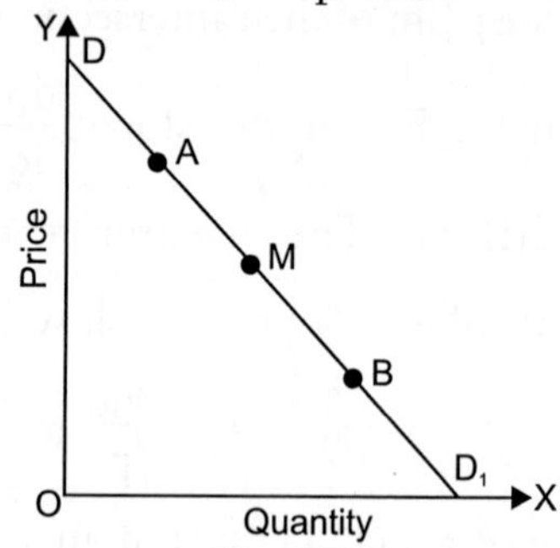

Fig. 6.34

Here we consider that A, M and B are the three points lying on the demand curve DD_1 and where M is the middle point. At point A, $e_p > 1$; at point M, $e_p = 1$, and at B, $e_p < 1$ but the three points have same slope.

Hence, three different points on a straight line demand curve have same slope, but different absolute value of price elasticities of demand.

Case - II: Two demand curves may have different slopes, but the same elasticity of demand if they have equal price or quantity intercept.

Let us assume, there are two demand curves AB and AC having the same intercept OA from the price axis shown in Fig. 6.35(a). Let us take D on AB and E on AC having the same price OP.

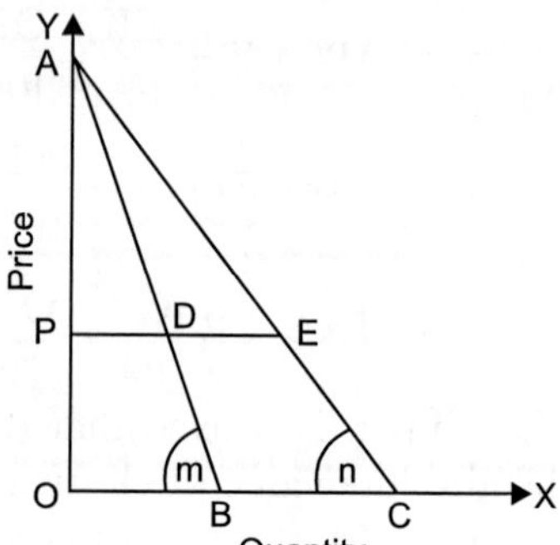

Fig. 6.35(a)

Here,

$$e_p \text{ at D on AB} = \frac{DB}{DA} = \frac{OP}{PA}$$

and

$$e_p \text{ at E on AC} = \frac{EC}{EA} = \frac{OP}{PA}$$

e_p at D = e_p at E. So, we get that two demand curves have the same elasticity at each price, but they have different slopes since tan m > tan n.

Again, in Fig. 6.35(b), the demand curves AB and BC have same intercept OB from the quantity axis, but they have different slopes since tan v > tan r. Let us take one point E on BC and another point D on AB having the same quantity OM.

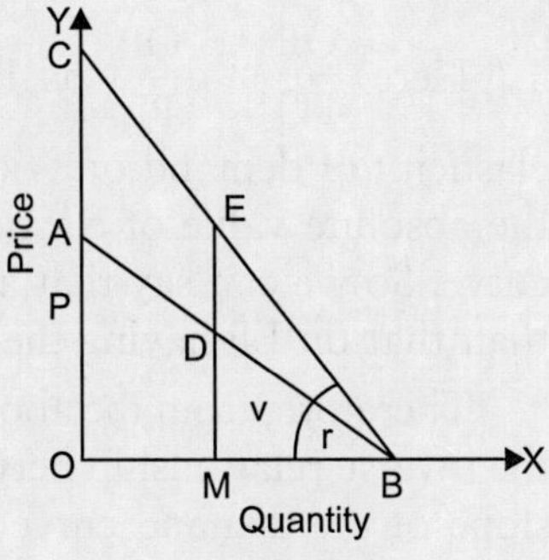

Fig. 6.35(b)

Now,

$$e_p \text{ at D on AB} = \frac{DB}{DA} = \frac{MB}{OM}$$

$$\text{and } e_p \text{ at E on BC} = \frac{EB}{EC} = \frac{MB}{OM}$$

$$e_p \text{ at D on AB} = e_p \text{ at E on BC}$$

Hence, the two demand curves may have different slopes, but the same absolute elasticity of demand.

Case - III: Two demand curves may have the same slope, but different elasticities at each price.

Let us take there are two parallel demand curves CD and EF shown in Fig. 6.36.

Since CD and EF are parallel, they have same slopes. Let us now consider any price OP, at this price, A is a point on CD and B is a point on EF.

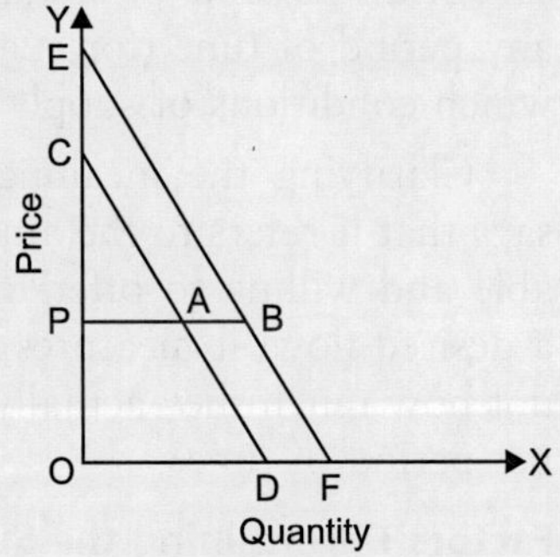

Fig. 6.36

At point A on CD, the elasticity of demand $= \frac{AD}{AC} = \frac{OP}{PC}$.

At point B on EF, the elasticity of demand $= \frac{BF}{BE} = \frac{OP}{PE}$

Here $\frac{OP}{PC} > \frac{OP}{PE}$ as PC < PE i.e., the absolute value of elasticity of demand on A of CD demand curve is greater than the absolute value of elasticity of demand on B of EF demand curve. So we can say that at any point on CD, the e_p is greater than that on EF having the same price.

Therefore, from the above three cases, we may conclude that the inverse relationship between absolute value of elasticity and slope of the demand curve does not hold true. Hence, there is no exact relationship between the absolute value of elasticity of demand and the slope of a demand curve.

SUPPLY FUNCTION, SHIFTS IN SUPPLY CURVE

Meaning of Supply

The amount of a commodity offered for sale in a market at a given price in a given period of time is called supply.

Prof. Benham defines supply in these words, "supply may mean the amount offered for sale per unit of time."

According to Prof. Meyers, "We may define supply as a schedule of the amount of a good that would be offered for sale at all possible prices at any one instant of time, or during any period of time (for example, a day, a week, and so on, in which conditions of supply remain the same)."

Clarifying the meaning of the term supply, Prof. Lipsey says that it refers to the amount of a commodity that firms are able and willing to offer for sale. According to him supply is a desired flow; it measures how much firms would like to sell, not how much they actually sell, and it measures it as so much per period of time.

Factors Determining the Supply

Supply of a commodity depends mainly on five factors: price of the commodity, prices of other commodities, prices of factors of production, production technique and goal of the producer.

(i) **Price of the Commodity:** Ordinarily, when the price of the commodity falls, sellers reduce the supply of the commodity in the market and when its price rises, sellers increase the supply. We expect, therefore, that the higher the price, the greater will be the quantity supplied.

(ii) **Price of other Commodities:** Generally, an increased in the prices of other commodities will make production of the commodity whose price does not rise relatively less attractive than it was previously. The supply of a commodity. The supply of a commodity, other things remining the same, is inversely related with the prices of all other commodities.

(iii) **Prices of Factors of Production:** A change in the price of one factor of production will cause changes in the relative profitability of different lines of production. This will cause producers to shift from one line to another, and so cause changes in the quantities of the various commodities that are supplied. Similarly if there is an increase in the prices of all factors of production, it will make the production of goods costlier and cause reduction in the supply of commodities at various prices.

(iv) **Production Technique:** If improved and advanced technology is used for the production of a commodity, it reduces its cost of production and increases the supply. On the other hand, supply of those goods will be less whose production depends on inferior and old technology. There had been a substantial improvement and changes in the state of technology during the last two centuries especially in the industrially advanced countries. Countries having high level of technology can supply more goods than countries of low level technology.

(v) **Goal of the Producer:** Generally it is presumed that the goal of a firm is to maximise its profits. However besides it, maximum sales, maximum output or maximum employment can also be the goals of firm. The supply of goods also depends on the priority of a firm regarding these various goals and the extent to which it is prepared to sacrifice one goal to the other.

Supply Function

Factors affecting the supply of a commodity can be summarised in mathematical form known as supply function. That is, supply of x good is a function of its price, prices of other goods, prices of factors of production, technique of production, goal of the producer. Mathematically, it can be written as:

$S_x = f(p_x, p_o, F_p, T, G)$

Where, S_x = supply of x good, P_x = price of x good,

P_o = prices of other goods, F_p = prices of factors of production,

T = Technique of production and G = Goal of the producer.

Supply Schedule

A supply schedule shows the various amounts of a commodity that producers wish to sell in the market at different prices during a given period of time. Thus, supply schedule indicates the relation between market prices and the amounts of the goods that producers are willing to supply. An imaginary supply schedule and diagram in Fig. 6.37 are given below.

Supply Schedule

Px (₹)	Sx (Units)
1	2
2	5
3	10
4	14

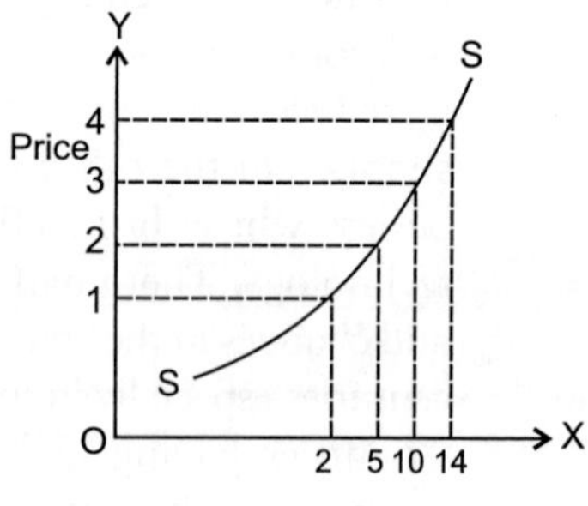

Fig. 6.37: Supply

As with demand schedule supply schedule is also of two types:

(i) **Individual Supply Schedule:** It shows the various quantities of a commodity that a particular firm (or a particular producer) wants to sell at different prices in the market.

(ii) **Market Supply Schedule:** A schedule showing the various amounts of goods that all the firms (or all the producers) in the market wish to sell at different prices is known as market supply schedule. Market supply schedule can be obtained by adding all individual supply schedules. This is explained in the example below. There are three individual supply schedules of firms 'A', 'B' and 'C' and then by adding these schedules we have obtained market supply schedule.

Supply Curve of a Market

A graphical representation of supply schedule is the supply curve as shown in the diagram. It shows the quantity offered for sale at each price. Supply curve is also of two types: individual supply curve and market supply curve. Market supply curve can be obtained through horizontal summation of all individual supply curves. This is shown in the diagrams given below in which market supply curve SS is obtained by adding two individual supply curves of firm 'A' and firm 'B'. For simplicity, we assume there are only two firms in the market.

Thus, the market supply curve for a commodity shows the relation between its price and the quantity sold by the seller per period of time. The shape of the supply curve is upward sloping from left to the right which indicates that the higher the price, the more the sellers wish to sell. It is shown in Market Supply Schedule and Fig. 6.38.

Market Supply Schedule

Px (₹)	Supply of firm 'A' (units)	Supply of firm 'B' (units)	Market Supply (units)
1	4	5	4 +5= 9
2	8	7	8 + 7 = 15
3	10	8	10 + 8 = 18

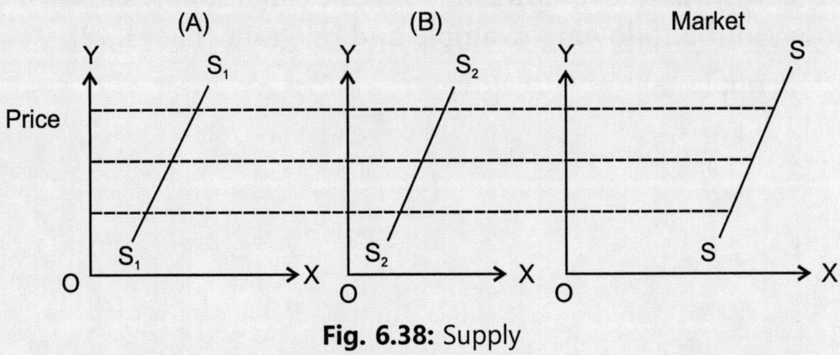

Fig. 6.38: Supply

Law of Supply

Law of supply states that other things remaining unchanged, the quantity supplied decreases with the fall in price and increases with the rise in price. In other words, sellers want to sell more quantity at higher prices and less quantity at lower prices.

When other things remaining unchanged, the amount of supply largely depends on its price only, then the supply function is written as: $S_x = f(P_x)$

Exceptions

There are some situations under which the law of supply does not operate; they are called exceptions of the law. For instance, if there is an expectation for further change in prices, this law may not operate. On the output of agricultural goods also this law does not hold well because agriculture largely depends on the nature. In backward countries also production and supply cannot be increased merely with the rise in prices because of the lack of resources. This law cannot be applied frequently on the high quality artistic goods also.

Distinction between Extension of Supply and Increase in Supply, Contraction of Supply and Decrease in Supply

In common usage distinction between these terms- extension of supply and increase in supply, contraction of supply and decrease in supply is not made. But in economics we make distinctions between them which explained below.

Extension of Supply

Other things being equal, when more quantity is supplied with the rise is price of the commodity, it is extension of supply. In this way, we move upward along the same supply curve. It is shown in the following example and diagram (Fig. 6.39).

Example

P_x (₹)	S_x (units)
10	100
15	125

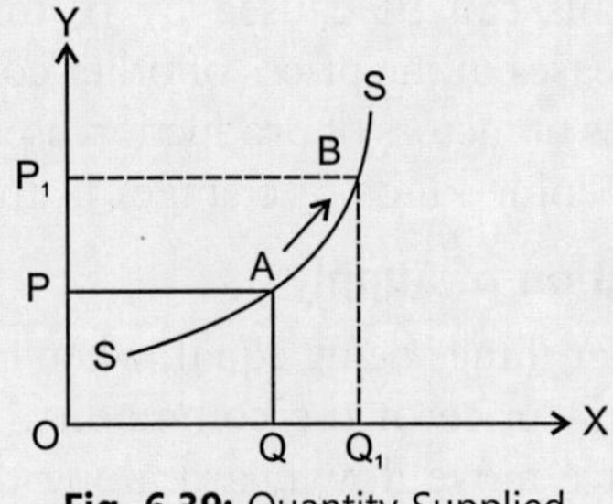

Fig. 6.39: Quantity Supplied

Increase in Supply

When as a result of changes of prices of other factors other than the price of the commodity concerned, more quantity at the same price or the same quantity at a lower price is supplied, it is increase in supply. In this situation we move form leftward supply curve to the new right ward supply curve, i.e., supply cure itself shifts to the rightward. This is explained in the following examples and diagrams (Figs. 6.40 and 6.41).

(i) Example for Fig. 6.40

Px (₹)	Sx (Units)
10	80
10	100

Or

(ii) Example for Fig. 6.41

Px (₹)	Sx (units)
10	100
12	100

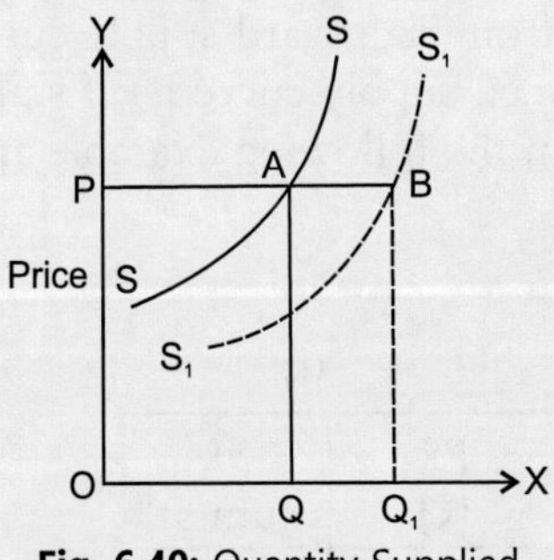

Fig. 6.40: Quantity Supplied

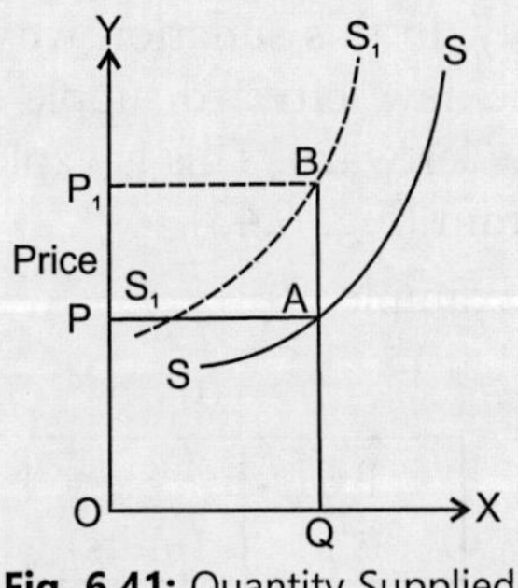

Fig. 6.41: Quantity Supplied

Reasons for the Increase in Supply

For an increase in supply, the supply curve shifts to the right, indicating that producers wish to make and sell more at each price. This can be caused by (i) improvements in technology, (ii) decreases in the prices of other commodities, (iii) decreases in the prices of factors of production used in making this commodity, and (iv) some kinds of changes in the goals of producers.

Contraction of Supply

Other things being equal, when less quantity is supplied with the fall in price of the commodity, it is contraction of supply. In this we move downward along the same supply curve. It is shown in the following example and diagram (Fig. 6.42).

Example

Px (₹)	Sx (Units)
10	100
8	80

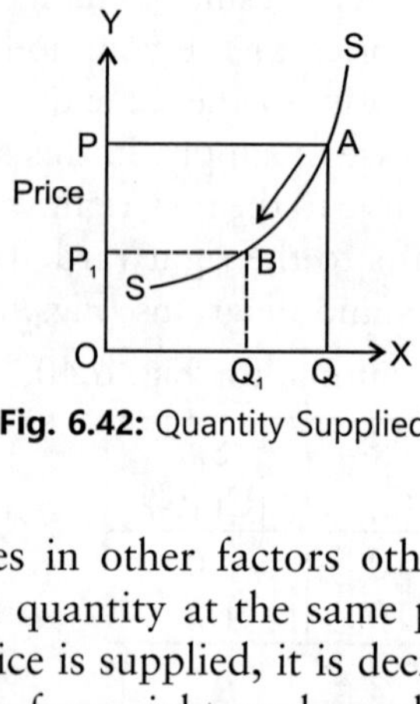

Fig. 6.42: Quantity Supplied

Decrease in Supply

When as a result of changes in other factors other than the price of the commodity, less quantity at the same price or the same quantity at a higher price is supplied, it is decrease in supply. In this sudation we move from rightward supply curve to the new leftward supple curve, i.e., supply curve itself shifts to the leftward. This is explained in the following example and diagram (Fig. 6.43).

Example

(i)

Px (₹)	Sx (units)
10	100
10	80

(ii)

Px (₹)	Sx (units)
10	100
15	100

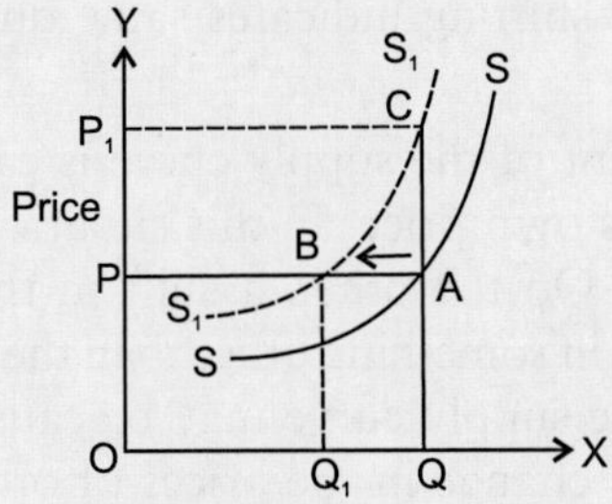

Fig. 6.43: Quantity Supplied

Reasons for the Decrease in Supply

For a decrease in supply, the supply curve shifts to the left, indicating that producers wish to make and sell less at each price. This can be caused by (i) loss of technical knowledge, (ii) increase in the price of other commodities, (iii) increase in the price of factors of production used to make the product, and (iv) some kinds of change in the goals of the producers.

Difference between movement along a supply curve and shifting of supply curve

Other things being equal, when more or less quantity is offered for sale in response to change in the price of the commodity, it is movement along a same supply curve for change in the quantity supplied. In this we move along the same supply curve either upward or downward. Upward movement along a supply curve is known as extensions of supply i.e., more quantity supplied at a higher price while the downward movement is known as contraction of supply i.e., less quantity supplied at a lower price.

When because of changes in some other factors other than the price of the commodity, different quantities are supplied at same price, it is a shift in the supply curve. It occurs when more or less quantity is supplied at the same price. In this situation supply curve itself shifts either to the right or to the left. Rightward shifting of supply curve indicates **increase in supply** at same price and leftward shifting indicates **decrease in supply** at same price.

Again same quantity is supplied at different prices. Rightward shifting of supply curve indicates same quantity supplied at lower price and leftward shifting indicates same quantity supplied at higher price.

Thus, movement of the supply curve is caused by a change in the commodity's own price. In this situation supply schedule remains the same. On the other, a shift in the supply curve is caused by a change in something other than the commodity's own price. A shift in the supply curve may be caused by any one of the factors such as change in the prices of other goods, change in the prices of factors of production, change in techniques of production or change in the goal of the producer.

Following diagrams Figs. 6.44 and 6.45 show the difference between movement along a supply curve and a shift in the supply curve.

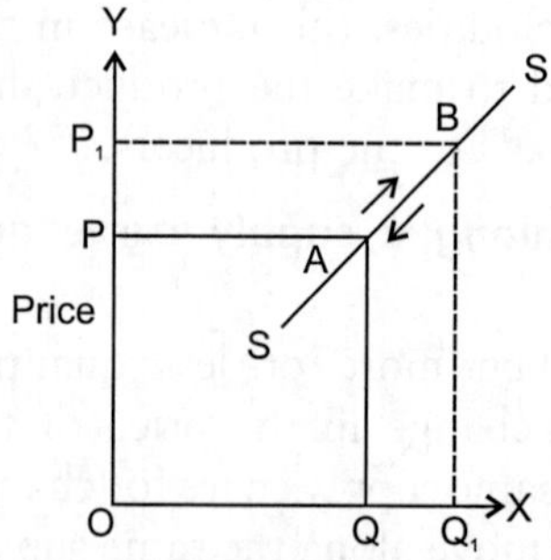

Fig. 6.44: Quantity Supplied

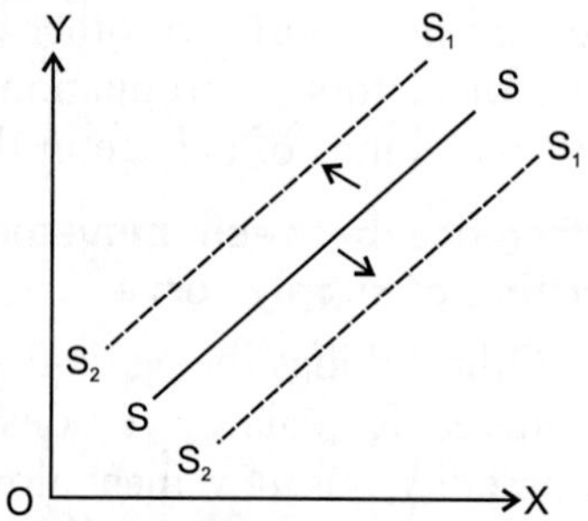

Fig. 6.45: Quantity Supplied

Fig. 6.44 shows the movement along the same supply curve SS either upward from point A to B (extension of supply) or downward from point B to A (contraction of supply). On the other hands, Fig. 6.45 shows the shift in the supply curve. The original supply curve SS both shifts rightward and becomes S_1S_1 supply curve (increase in supply) or leftward becoming S_2S_2 supply curve (decrease in supply).

Causes of Changes in Supply

Change in supply occurs when there are changes in the conditions of supply itself. This change may be because of following factors:

(1) **Changes in Self-consumption by the Producers:** If the producers of the commodity themselves start consuming

more of the commodity, supply is reduced and if they reduce the quantum of their self-consumption, supply is increased.

(2) **Change in the Cost of Production:** If a producer is forced to pay more to the factors of production, its production cost would rise. Other things being equal, if production cost increases, supply will fall at each price and if production cost decreases, supply will increase.

(3) **Change in Production-Technique:** Adoption of advanced and improved technology may lead to increase in production and thereby supply.

(4) **Effect of Change in Season:** Especially in the field of agriculture good rainfall and favorable weather conditions may increase production of agricultural goods. On the contrary, draught or heavy rainfall may destroy the crops and may reduce the output of agricultural goods.

(5) **Effect of Taxations:** Imposition of tax on commodity has the same effect as the increase in cost of production. Hence, other things being equal, increase in taxes reduces supply and decrease in taxes increases the supply.

(6) **Change in the Prices of Other Goods:** As we have already discussed that rise in the prices of other goods increases the supply of the commodity and fall in the prices of other goods decreases the supply of the commodity.

(7) **Other Reasons:** Means of transport and communications, political atmosphere of the country and the level of development etc. also affect the supply of the commodity in a country. Similarly, changes in the goal of the producer may also cause change in the supply.

ELASTICITY OF SUPPLY

Definition: Law of supply indicates merely the direction of supply in response to change in the price. This law does not tell us how much change in the quantity supplied occurs in response to change in its price. To know and measure this 'how much' the concept of elasticity of supply has been evolved.

Elasticity of supply can be defined as a measure of the degree of responsiveness of quantity supplied to changes in the commodity's own price. In simple words it is the percentage change in quantity supplied divided by the percentage change in the price of the commodity.

Degrees of Elasticity of Supply

Depending upon the value of the co-efficient, there are five types of elasticity of supply. They are known as degrees of elasticity of supply (Es). These are explained below.

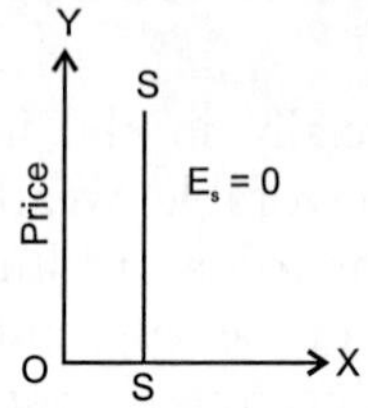

Fig. (i): Supply
Perfectly inelastic supply

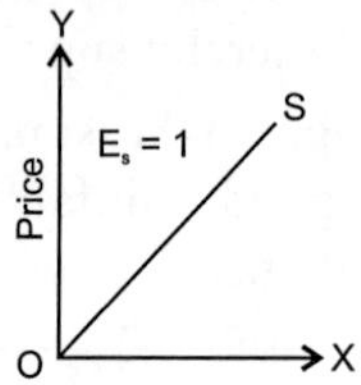

Fig. (ii): Supply
Unitary inelastic supply

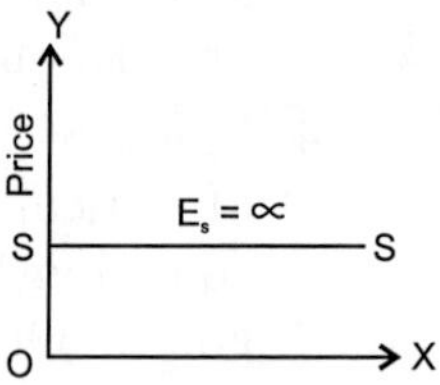

Fig. (iii): Supply
Perfectly elastic supply

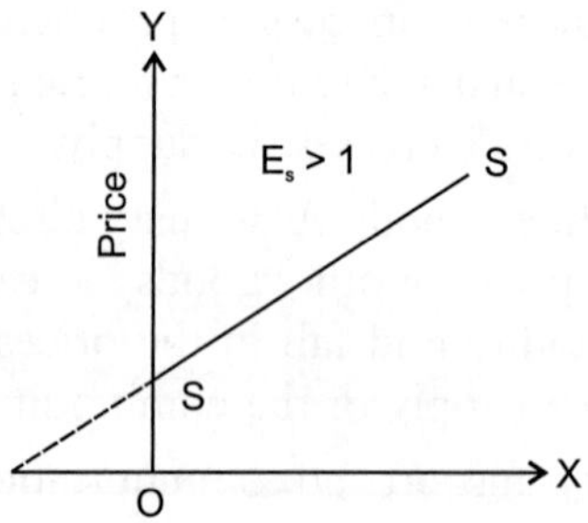

Fig. (iv): Supply
Highly

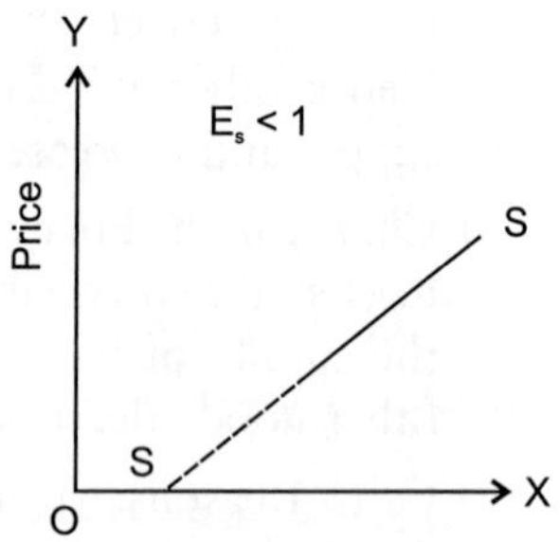

Fig. (v): Supply
Less Elastic

(i) When there is no change in quantity supplied in response to change in price, it is known as perfectly inelastic supply or zero elasticity of supply ($E_s = 0$). Supply curve in this case becomes vertical or parallel to the Y-axis as shown in the Fig. (i). It may happen in the situation when a perishable commodity say fish, or milk is brought to today's market for sale at whatever price, it will fetch. It is shown in the Fig. (i).

(ii) When the proportionate change in quantity supplied is just equal to the proportionate change in price, it is unity elasticity of supply ($E_s = 1$). In this case, a straight line supply curve passes through the origin as shown in the Fig. (ii).

(iii) When at a particular level of price, sellers are willing to supply infinite amounts of supply but nothing will be supplied at a price lower than this, it is the case of perfectly elastic supply or infinite elasticity of supply ($E_s = \infty$). Here supply curve becomes horizontal or parallel to the X-axis which is shown in the Fig. (iii).

(iv) When the proportionate change in supply is more than that of proportionate change in price, it is the case of highly elastic supply. In this situation, elasticity of supply is greater than one ($E_s > 1$). Here the positively sloped straight line supply curve meets the line of the Y-axis above the origin (O) which is shown in the Fig. (iv).

(v) When the proportionate change in supply is less than that of proportionate change in price, it is the case of inelastic supply. In this situation, elasticity of supply is less than one ($E_s < 1$). Here the positively sloped straight line supply curve meets the line of the X-axis to the right of the origin (O) which is shown in the Fig. (v).

Measurement of Elasticity of Supply

Elasticity of supply can be measured with the help of the following method known as proportionate or percentage method:

$$= \frac{\text{Proportionate change in quantity supplied}}{\text{Proportionate change in price}}$$

$$= \frac{\frac{\Delta S}{S}}{\frac{\Delta P}{P}}$$

$$= \frac{\Delta S}{S} \times \frac{P}{\Delta P} = \frac{\Delta S}{\Delta P} \times \frac{P}{S}$$

Where, ΔS = change in quantity supplied, ΔP = change in price

S = original supply and P = original price

This method of measurement can be explained more clearly with the help of following examples:

In percentage form, elasticity of supply can be written as

$$E_s = \frac{\%\text{ change in quantity supplied}}{\%\text{ change in price}}$$

Factors Affecting the Elasticity of Supply

1. **Nature of the Commodity:** Elasticity of supply to some extent depends on the nature of the commodity. Elasticity of supply in the case of durable goods is more than perishable goods. Similarly, elasticity of supply of agricultural goods is less than the industrial goods.
2. **Cost of Production:** Elasticity of supply depends to a great extent on how costs behave as output is varied. If unit cost rises rapidly as output rises, the stimulus to expand production in response to a price rise will quickly be chocked off by this increase in production cost. In this case, supply will tend to be rather inelastic. If, on the other hand, unit cost rises slowly as production increases, a rise in price will induce producers to produce more and thus in this case supply will tend to be rather elastic.
3. **Time Period:** Elasticity of supply also varies with the time period involved. Elasticity of supply tends to be grater in the long run, when all adjustments to the higher price have been made than in shorter periods of time.

NUMERICAL EXAMPLE

Case of Perfectly Inelastic Supply

Price (Px) (₹)	Supply (Sx) (Units)
10	20
15	20

In this example

Here, $\Delta P = 10 - 15 = -5$

$\Delta S = 20 - 20 = 0$

$P = 10$ and $S = 20$

We know,

$E_s = \Delta S/\Delta P \times P/S$

That is, $E_s = 0/-5 \times 10/20 = 0$

It is a case of perfectly inelastic supply. The supplier will supply fixed quantity at different prices.

Case of Unitary elastic supply

Price (Px) (₹)	Supply (Sx) (Units)
5	50
4	40

In this example

Here, $\Delta P = 5 - 4 = 1$

$\Delta S = 50 - 40 = 10$

$P = 5$ and $S = 50$

We Know,

$E_s = \Delta S/\Delta P \times P/S$

$= 10/0 \times 5/50 = 1$

It is a case of unitary elastic supply.

Case of Perfectly elastic supply

Price (Px) (₹)	Supply (Sx) (Units)
5	50
5	60

In this example

Here, $\Delta P = 5 - 5 = 0$

$\Delta S = 50 - 60 = -10$

$P = 5$ and $S = 50$

We know

$E_s = \Delta S/\Delta P \times P/S$

$= -10/0 \times 5/10 = \propto$

It is a case of perfectly elastic supply. The supplier will supply whatever he wishes at fixed price.

Case of Highly Elastic Supply

Price (Px) (₹)	Supply (Sx) (Units)
5	50
6	100

In this example

Here, $\Delta P = 5 - 6 = -1$

$\Delta S = 50 - 100 = -50$

$P = 5$ and $S = 50$

We Know,

$E_s = \Delta S/\Delta P \times P/S$

$E_s = -50/-1 \times 5/50 = 5 > 1$

It is a case of highly elastic supply.

Case of Less Elastic Supply

Price (Px) (₹)	Supply (Sx) (Units)
8	20
6	16

In this example

Here, $\Delta P = 8 - 6 = 2$

$\Delta S = 20 - 16 = 4$

$P = 8$ and $S = 20$

We Know,

$E_s = \Delta S/\Delta P \times P/S$

$E_s = 4/2 \times 8/20 = 0.80$

Therefore, it is a case of less elastic supply.

EXERCISES

1. Define demand.
2. What is demand function?
3. Define demand curve.
4. Define shifts of demand curve.
5. Define increase in demand.
6. Define decrease in demand.
7. Discuss the difference between movement along a demand curve and shift in the demand curve.
8. Define contraction of demand.
9. Explain the law of demand. What are the exceptions to the law of demand?
10. What are the determinants of demand?

    Or

    Define demand. Mention also the factors influencing the demand for a good.
11. What do you understand by elasticity of demand? What are the factors on which elasticity depends?

    Or

    Explain the concept of elasticity of demand and point out its usefulness.
12. What is price elasticity of demand? Define different degrees of price elasticity of demand.
13. What are the ranges of values of the price elasticity of demand? Show with figures.
14. Explain the concept of income elasticity of demand.
15. What are the different methods of measuring price elasticity of demand?
16. How will you measure income elasticity of demand (e_y) at a point on an income demand curve?
17. How will you find out the income elasticity of demand from the proportion of income spent on a good?

18. Define cross elasticity of demand. Comment different values of it.
19. Is there any relationship between slope and elasticity of demand? Discuss.
20. What do you mean by supply?
21. Define supply function.
22. Define law of supply.
23. What is elasticity of supply?
24. What is demand function?
25. What is elasticity of demand?
26. How many types of elasticity of demand are there?
27. Define price elasticity of demand.
28. Define income elasticity of demand.
29. Define cross elasticity of demand.
30. Define unitary elastic of demand.

Chapter 7

Theory of Production

PRODUCTION FUNCTION

Production function is a technical relationship between inputs and output expressed in a mathematical form. It describes the manner in which the physical quantities of inputs are related to the physical quantities of output. The act of production is simply the process of transforming inputs into output. In simple words, production or output is a function of inputs. This functional relationship between inputs and the output can be written as

$$Q = f(a, b, c, \ldots\ldots, n)$$

where Q is the quantity of output and a, b, c, ..., n are the quantities of various inputs, and f denotes the functional relationship between the output and the inputs. If labour and capital are the only inputs used in the production process, production function can be written as

$$Q = f(L, K)$$

where L denotes the quantity of labour and K denotes the quantity of capital used in production. The production function is, thus an algebraic expression of the relationship between the quantities of inputs and the quantity of output of a given product.

In the short run, some factors are fixed while the others are variable. Hence, some inputs in the production function remain fixed, while the others can be varied. Therefore, to obtain an increase in the quantity of output of a product, more of variable factors have to be combined with the fixed factors. This results in the operation of the law of variable proportions. But in the long run, all factors can be varied. This enables a firm to maintain the proportion between various factor inputs even when it expands the scale of its operations. The resulting output from this change in scale is subject to the 'law of returns to scale'.

A production function provides:

(i) When the physical quantities of inputs are specified, production function helps to estimate the level of production.

(ii) When Q is fixed, production function gives the different combination of inputs which yields the same level of output.

(iii) Production functions helps to determine the technically efficient combination of inputs and also to select the least cost combination of inputs when the budget constraint is given.

(iv) Production function helps to estimate the degree of returns to scale prevailing in the process of production.

(v) The marginal product of different factors can be obtained from production function.

Production function can be fitted to a particular farm or to a sector or to a firm, industry or to an economy as a whole. Generally, for a given technology, production function remains the same. As the technology changes, production function will also change. The nature and type of production function depends upon the data, time period of investigation and the type of technology employed.

ISOQUANT (EQUAL PRODUCT CURVE)

It is well-known fact that factors of production are to some extent substitutable for each other. We assume that there are two factors of production, say labour and capital which are substitutable in place of another. We can employ more labour and less capital or less labour and more capital to get the same level of output. An isoquant, i.e., an equal product curve shows all possible input (factor) combinations which give the same level of output. Here the various combinations of labour (L) and capital (K) give the same level of output. If the output level is constant at q_0, the equation of the isoquant is given by $q_0 = f(L, K)$. For one possible level of output we shall get one isoquant. A higher output level is represented by a higher isoquant and a lower output level is represented by a lower isoquant. It will be clear from the following example:

Factor Combinations Yielding Equal Product

Factor Combination	Capital (K)	Labour (L)
A	1	15
B	2	10
C	3	06
D	4	03
E	5	01

It is clear that combinations A, B, C, D and E represent different amounts of labour and capital to give the same level of output. If we plot all these combinations in a diagram and join the various points, we get the equal product curve (isoquant) as shown in Fig. 7.1. This curve is also known as production indifference curve as the producer will be indifferent between all these combinations that yield equal output.

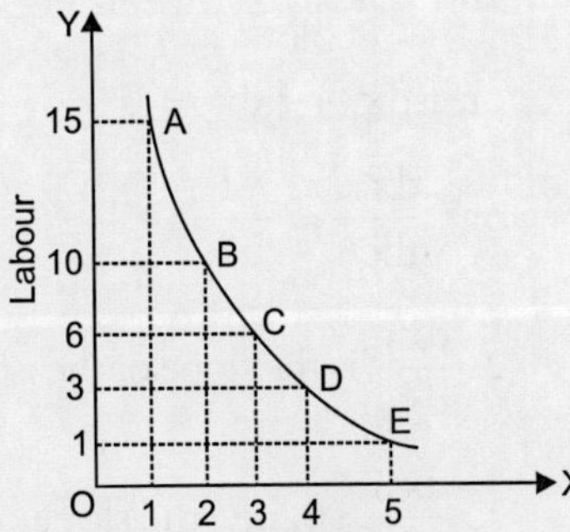

Fig. 7.1

An increase in the quantity of both the inputs viz. labour and capital, would yield a larger quantity of output and hence the isoquant would move upward. Thus, we can draw a number of isoquants, one above the other, showing each higher level of output that could be obtained by various combinations of labour and capital. As shown in the

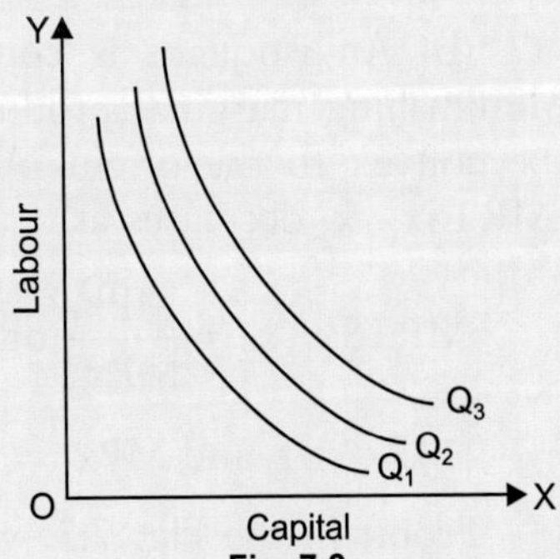

Fig. 7.2

Fig. 7.2 Q_1, Q_2 and Q_3 are the isoquants showing successively higher quantities of output i.e., $Q_1 < Q_2 < Q_3$.

PROPERTIES OF ISOQUANT

(a) **The slope of an isoquant is negative.** Let the equation of an isoquant be $q = f(x_1, x_2)$. For one possible level of output we shall get one isoquant. If we assume that the marginal productivities of both the factors are positive and decreasing as more of factors are used, the isoquant will be downward sloping. Let us prove it.

From the total differential of the equation of the isoquant, we get $dq = f_1 dx_1 + f_2 dx_2$ where $f_1 = \frac{\delta q}{\delta x_1} = MPx_1$

and $f_2 = \frac{\delta q}{\delta x_2} = MPx_2$

or, $f_1 dx_1 + f_2 dx_2 = 0$ [$\therefore$ dq = 0 since q_0 is constant]

or $\frac{dx_2}{dx_1} = -\frac{f_1}{f_2}$

$\therefore \frac{dx_2}{dx_1}$ is the slope of the isoquant. By assumption, $f_1 > 0, f_2 > 0$

$\therefore \frac{dx_2}{dx_1} < 0$, i.e., the slope of an isoquant is negative. It means that the isoquant is downward sloping. It implies that to obtain a given level of output if the entrepreneur employs more of one factor, he must employ less of another factor.

(b) **An isoquant is convex to the origin.** If the law of diminishing marginal productivity operates, the isoquant will be convex to the origin. A convex isoquant means that the $MRTSx_1, x_2$ decreases as x_1 is substituted for x_2. Here,

$$MRTSx_1, x_2 = \frac{MPx_1}{MPx_2} \text{ or, } MRTSx_1, x_2 = \frac{f_1}{f_2}$$

$[MPx_1 = f_1 \text{ and } MPx_2 = f_2]$

Proof: In the Fig. 7.3, when we move from A to B along the isoquant, we employ BC units more of x_1 and AC units less of x_2. As a result MPx_1 decreases while MPx_2 increases. That is, f_1 at point A > f_1 at point B and f_2 at point A < f_2 at point B

$$\therefore \frac{f_1}{f_2} \text{ at point A} > \frac{f_1}{f_2} \text{ at point B.}$$

i.e., $MRTSx_1,x_2$ at point A > $MRTSx_1,x_2$ at point B. It shows, $MRTSx_1,x_2$ decreases from point A to point B. Hence, the shape of the isoquant is convex to the origin.

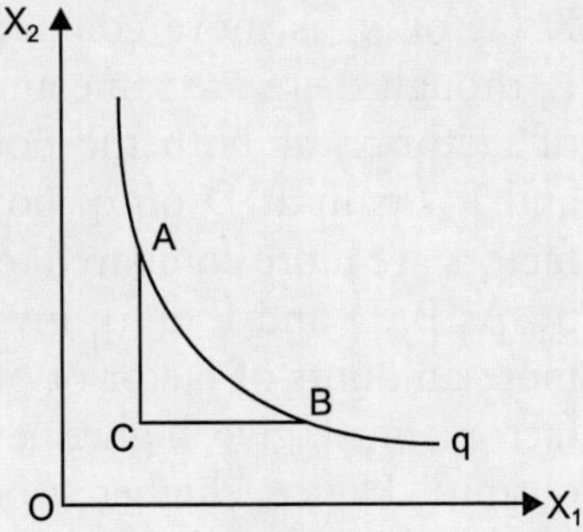

Fig. 7.3

(c) **No two isoquants can cut each other or touch each other:** Let there are two isoquants say q_0 and q_1 in the Fig. 7.4, they intersect at point A. Let B be the point on the isoquant q_0 and C on the isoquant q_1. But C stands vertically above B.

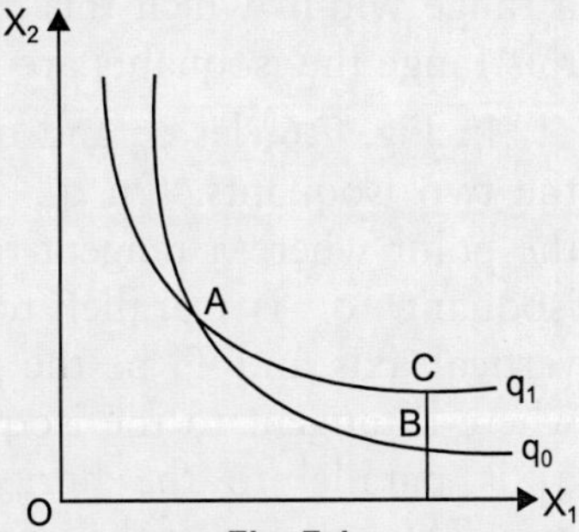

Fig. 7.4

Since A and B stand on the same isoquant q_0, by definition we can write the following:

Output at A = Output at B ... (1)

Again, A and C stand on the same isoquant q_1, we get

Output at A = Output at C ... (2)

From (1) and (2), we can write that, output at B = output at C since left hand sides of both the equations are equal. But it is absurd. Because C stands vertically above B employing more of factor x_2 in comparison to B. So output level at C must be greater than that at B. Hence, two isoquants can never intersect (or touch) each other.

(d) **Higher isoquant represents higher level of output:** Let there are two isoquants, say q_0 and q_1 shown in the Fig. 7.5. We assume A, C, and E are the points on q_0 and B, D and F on q_1. At point B, factor x_1 is more compared to A, though there are same amounts of factor x_2 at both the points. Similarly at

F, factor x_2 is more compared to E, though there are same amounts of factor x_1 at both the points E and F. Again at D on q_1 both the factors are more compared to C on q_0. As B, D and F on q_1 involving more amounts of factor or of both factors must give higher level of output. Hence, higher isoquant represents higher level of output.

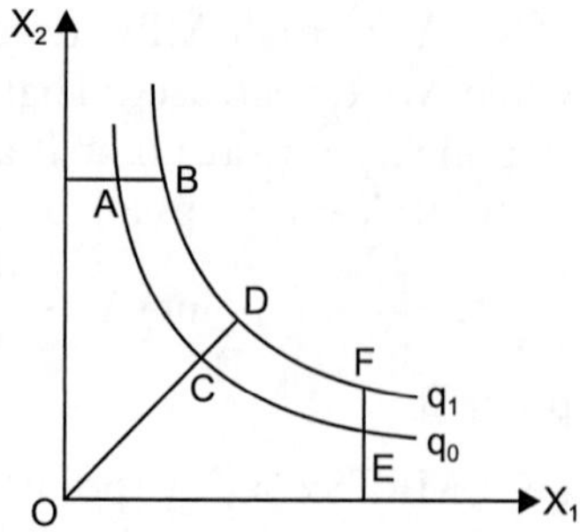

Fig. 7.5

(e) **Economic region of production:** Though on an isoquant one input can be substituted in place of another input, there is a range within which this substitution can take place. Within this range the isoquants are negatively sloped.

In Fig. 7.6, let q_0 and q_1 are the two isoquants. On q_0, T_1 be the point where a tangent to the isoquant, q_0 is parallel to the vertical axis and T_2 be the point where a tangent to the isoquant, q_0 is parallel to the horizontal axis. This portion of the isoquant which lies between T_1 and T_2 is the portion over which the marginal products of factors are diminishing but positive. At T_1 on q_0 and S_1 on q_1, $MPx_2 = 0$ and at T_2 on q_0 and S_2 on q_1, $MPx_1 = 0$. The locus of points of isoquants where the marginal products of the factors are zero form the ridge lines. The upper ridge line implies that the MP of factor x_2 is zero. The lower ridge line implies that the MP of factor x_1 is zero. Production techniques are only efficient inside the ridge line. Outside the ridge lines the marginal products of factors are negative and the methods of production are inefficient since they require more quantity of both factors for producing same level of output. Here at any point in between T_1 and T_3 or T_2 and T_4 on isoquant q_0 more of both the factors are required to produce the same level of output. Such inefficient methods are not considered by the theory of production, since they imply

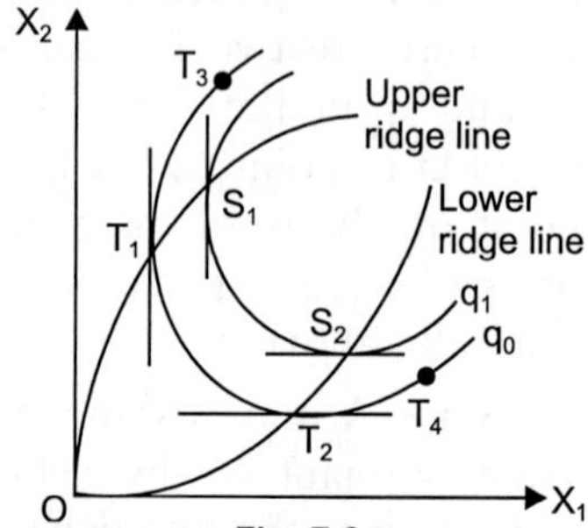

Fig. 7.6

irrational behaviour of the firm. The condition of positive but declining marginal products of the factors defines the range of efficient production, i.e., the range of isoquants over which they are convex to the origin.

Therefore, the producer will produce only within the ridge lines. The region between the ridge lines is called production region. The ridge lines separate the economic region from the uneconomic region of production.

EXCEPTIONAL CASE TO THE NORMAL SHAPE OF ISOQUANT

There are two exceptions to the general property of the convexity of isoquant. One is the case of factors which are substitutes of each other. When the two factors are perfect substitutes of each other, then each of them can be used equally in place of the other. For all purposes they can be regarded as the same factor. Therefore, the marginal rate of technical substitution between two perfect substitute factors remains constant. Since marginal rate of technical substitution remains the same throughout, the isoquants of the perfect substitute factors are straight lines instead of being convex to the origin. It is shown in Fig. 7.7. Here X and Y are two perfect substitute factors.

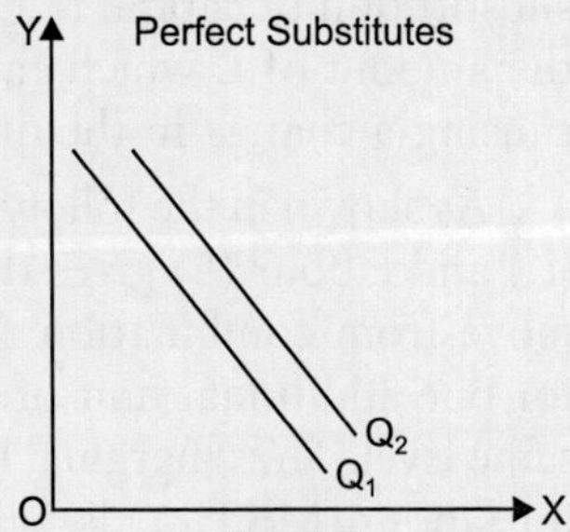

Fig. 7.7

Another exceptional case is of factors which are perfect complements and used jointly for the production in a fixed proportion. Hence, no amount of one factor can be substituted for any unit of the other. It is a case when the isoquants take the shape of right angles as shown in Fig. 7.8. The two factors are perfectly complementary factors

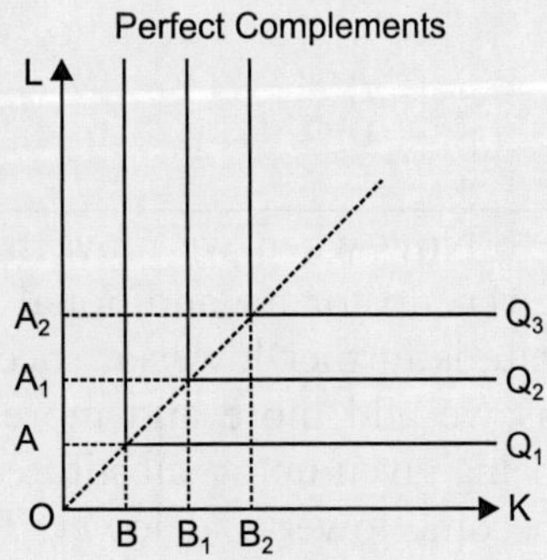

Fig. 7.8

where each one has to be used in a fixed proportion with the other to get a given level of output. If more output is to be produced, increase in one must be accompanied by an increase in the other. Thus, for example, if factor K is increased from OB to OB_1 or OB_2 output will not increase unless factor L is increased from OA to OA_1 or OA_2. Hence, in case of two perfectly complementary factors, we cannot draw the usual convex isoquant, it is of a different shape, i.e., it forms right angles whose sides are parallel to both the axes.

DIMINISHING MARGINAL RATE OF TECHNICAL SUBSTITUTION (MRTS)

The marginal rate of technical substitution (MRTS) between two factors (inputs) is the rate at which one factor can be substituted for another at the margin without change in the quantity of output produced. Thus, the marginal rate of technical substitution of capital (K) for labour (L) ($MRTS_{KL}$) is defined as the amount of L which can be replaced by a unit of K without causing a change in the quantum of output produced.

As shown in the following Table, each combination of capital (K) and labour (L) gives the same amount of output. But as we move from combination A to B, we give up 5 units of labour for one additional unit of capital to maintain the output at the same level. Thus marginal rate of technical substitution of capital for labour ($MRTS_{KL}$) is 5 units of labour for one unit of capital.

Marginal Rate of Technical Substitution

Factor Combination	Capital (K)	Labour (L)	$MRTS_{kL}$
A	1	15	–
B	2	10	5
C	3	6	4
D	4	3	3
E	5	1	2

Now when we move from B to C, the amount of labour given up for an additional unit of capital is lower at 4. This rate is further lower at successive combination D and E. Thus as we add more and more of capital, the amount of labour being given up or substituted by each additional unit of capital become lower and lower. This is called diminishing marginal rate of technical substitution.

The marginal rate of technical substitution can be measured from the equal product curve (isoquant) as the rate of the amount of labour (L) is given up for an additional unit of capital (K). This is shown in Fig. 7.9.

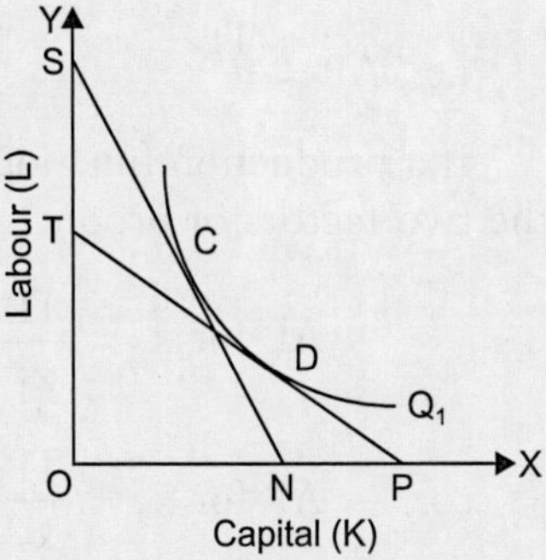

Fig. 7.9

If we want to measure the $MRTS_{KL}$ at point C on the isoquant Q_1, this is equal to the slope of the tangent drawn from that point C. For example, SN is tangent to the isoquant Q_1 at point C. The slope of the tangent line SN is equal to $\frac{OS}{ON}$.

Hence, $MRTS_{KL}$ at the point C = $\frac{OS}{ON}$.

Similarly, at a lower point D on the isoquant Q_1, the slope of the tangent line TP is equal to $\frac{OT}{OP}$. Hence, $MRTS_{KL}$ at point D = $\frac{OT}{OP}$.

Clearly, $\frac{OS}{ON} > \frac{OT}{OP}$ as OS > OT and ON < OP

$\therefore$ $MRTS_{K,L}$ at C > $MRTS_{K,L}$ at D

Hence, $MRTS_{KL}$ is higher at point C and becomes smaller at point D. In other words, the marginal rate of technical substitution goes on diminishing as we move down on the isoquant, showing that successively smaller amount of labour is being given up for every additional unit of capital for keeping production at the same level.

AVERAGE AND MARGINAL PRODUCTIVITY AND THEIR RELATIONSHIPS

Average Product (AP): Average product of a factor is the total product (TP) divided by the number of units of a factor (x). Thus, average product means the output per unit of factor employed.

i.e., $AP = \frac{TP}{x}$

If a production function is $q = f(x_1, x_2)$, where x_1 and x_2 are the two factors of production. Then

$$\text{AP for } x_1 = \frac{TP}{x_1} = \frac{q}{x_1} = \frac{f(x_1, x_2)}{x_1}$$

$$\text{or,} \quad \text{AP for } x_2 = \frac{TP}{x_2} = \frac{q}{x_2} = \frac{f(x_1, x_2)}{x_2}$$

Thus, the average product (AP) of x_1 or x_2 is its total product divided by its quantity employed.

Marginal Product (MP): Marginal product is the change in total product resulting from the use of one more unit of the variable factor. It measures the rate at which total product is changing as one factor is varied.

Hence, $MP = \frac{\Delta TP}{\Delta L}$ where ΔTP = change in TP and ΔL = change in labour input.

The term marginal product can be defined in another form also. The marginal product of a factor is the extra product per extra unit of that factor employed in the process of production, while other factors are being held constant. Hence, marginal product can be calculated with the help of following formula:

$MP_n = TP_n - TP_{n-1}$ where, MP_n = MP for n^{th} unit of a factor, TP_n = TP of n units of a factor

TP_{n-1} = TP of (n – 1) units of a factor

Again, if a production function is $q = f(x_1, x_2)$,

$$MPx_1 = \frac{\delta q}{\delta x_1} = f_1(x_1, x_2)$$

$$\text{or,} \quad MPx_2 = \frac{\delta q}{\delta x_2} = f_2(x_1, x_2)$$

That is, partial derivative of this production function with respect to x_1 or x_2 is called the marginal product of that factor, say x_1 or x_2.

This will be more clear in the following table and diagram:

Land (Fixed factor) (Acre)	Labour (Variable factor) (Units)	TP (Units)	MP (Units)	AP (Units) TP/L
1	1	20	20	20
1	2	50	30	25
1	3	90	40	30
1	4	120	30	30
1	5	140	20	28
1	6	150	10	25
1	7	150	0	21.43
1	8	140	–10	17.5

With the increase in the units of labour both average product and marginal product first rise, then after reaching their maximum start to decline. Hence, the average product and marginal product curves are inversely U-shaped curves. With the increase in the units of a variable factor marginal product continues to decline after reaching its maximum point and with its declining trend it becomes zero, even negative. Hence, marginal product curve after cutting X-axis goes below. But average product, no doubt, declines with the increase in the variable factor but it never becomes zero or negative, hence, average product curve always remains above X-axis.

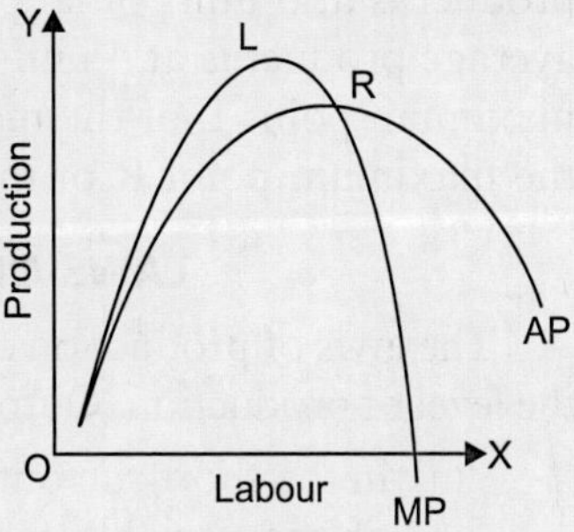

Fig. 7.10

The Average Product—Marginal Product Relationship

Following are the main points concerning the relationship between average product and marginal product:

(i) MP > AP = > AP↑

When marginal product is greater than the average product, the average product rises. This is the case up to 3 units of labour in our example.

(ii) MP = AP = > AP max.

When marginal product becomes equal to average product, the average product reaches its maximum. This stage is shown at 4 units of labour in our example and at point R in our diagram. Thus, marginal product curve cuts average product curve from above at a point R where the average product curve is at its maximum.

(iii) MP < AP = > AP↓

When marginal product is less than the average product, the average product starts to decline. This stage starts from 5 units of labour in our example and after point R in our diagram.

(iv) Both the average product and the marginal product increase in the beginning then after reaching their maximum start to decline. But the maximum point of the marginal product comes first and the maximum point of the average product comes later. As our example shows that the maximum point of the marginal product is at 3 units of labour while the maximum point of the average product is at 4 units of labour. In our diagram also, the maximum point L of the marginal product curve stands before the maximum point R of the average product curve.

LAWS OF PRODUCTION

The laws of production describe the possible ways to increase the level of production. Output may be increased in various ways:

(a) In the short run output may be increased by using more of the variable factor(s), while capital (and possibly other factors as well) are kept constant. The marginal product of the variable factor(s) will decline eventually as more and more quantities of this factor are combined with the other constant factors. The expansion of output by variable factor with other factor as constant is referred to the law of variable proportions.

(b) In the long run output can be increased by changing all factors of production. Because all the factors in the long run are variable factors. This refers to the law of returns to scale.

LAW OF VARIABLE PROPORTIONS

Law of variable proportions has an important place in economic theory. This explains the production function in which one factor is variable and other factors are fixed. When one factor is varied keeping other factors as constant, the factor proportion undergoes a change. For instance, there are 10 acres land and 1 labour, the land labour ratio is 10:1. If labour increases from 1 to 2, land-labour ratio becomes 5:1 and so on. Thus, this law shows the effect of change in factor proportions on the amount of output.

Again it can be explained in another way also. It states the relationship between variable factor and output. The input-output ratio changes due to change in variable factor. Suppose 10 acres of land and 1 labour give 20 quintals of paddy, then the ratio between labour and output is 1:20. If 2 labours are employed, output increases to 30 quintals, then the labour-output ratio becomes 1:15. It is clear that the ratio between variable factor and output changes and that is why, it is termed as law of variable proportion.

Thus, the law of variable proportion states that output varies with the variation of variable factor keeping other factors as constant. That is, it simply shows the relationship between the changes in the units of a variable factor and the changes in the quantities of output.

The extra output obtained by applying extra unit of a variable factor can be greater than, equal to and less than the output of previous period. That is why, this law has three stages: Increasing, diminishing and negative returns. So this law is also called as the law of returns to a variable factor.

Assumptions

(i) One is variable factor and others are the fixed factors.
(ii) It is possible to change the factor proportions.
(iii) No change in technique of production and organisation.
(iv) All units of the variable factor are homogeneous.
(v) Factors of production are not perfect substitutes.
(vi) Factors of production are scarce.
(vii) It is based on short run situation.

Explanation of the Law: This law can be illustrated with the following schedule and Fig. 7.11:

Land (acre)	Labour (units)	T.P. (qnt.)	A.P. (qnt.)	M.P.	Stages
1	0	0	0	–	
1	1	2	2	2	I
1	2	6	3	4	
1	3	12	4	6	
1	4	16	4	4	
1	5	18	3.6	2	II
1	6	18	3	0	
1	7	14	2	-4	
1	8	8	1	-6	III

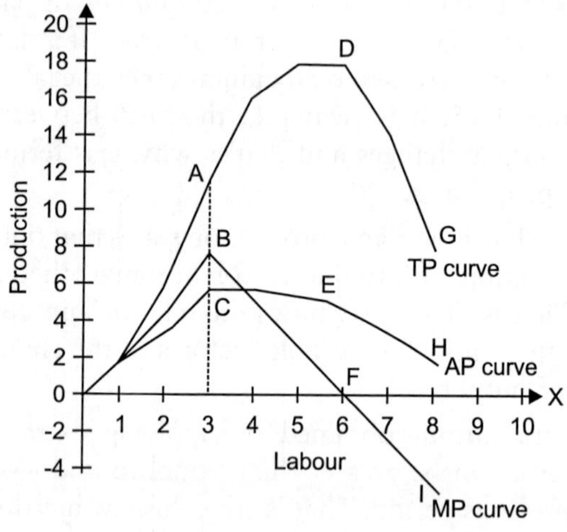

Fig. 7.11

In this example, we have assumed that land is a fixed factor and labour is a variable factor. Here different amounts of output are obtained by applying different units of labour on one acre of land.

Three stages of the law: The relation between variable factor and output shows three stages which are shown in the schedule and also in the diagram.

Stage-I: Increasing returns: In the beginning of this stage total product (TP) increases at an increasing rate. Average

Product (AP) and Marginal Product (MP) also increase but all increase up to a point beyond which they start to decline. Here AP continues to increase till MP is greater than AP up to that point. This particular point is called outer limit of the Stage-I. In our example, the first stage of the law runs up to 3 units of labour. In the diagram, this limit is shown by the points A, B and C on TP, MP and AP respectively corresponding to 3 units of labour. In this figure from the origin to the point A on TP curve, its slope is increasing at an increasing rate meaning that MP rises. It is concave upwards up to the point A. 'A' where the TP stops increasing at an increasing rate and starts increasing at a diminishing rate is called the point of inflexion at which MP is highest showing the ends of Stage-I.

Stage-II: Diminishing returns: In this stage, the TP continues to increase at a diminishing rate until it reaches its maximum point D where the Stage-II ends and MP is zero corresponding to 6 units of labour. Both AP and MP declines but remain positive. It is in between A and D on TP-curve, C and E on AP-curve and B and F on MP-curve. This stage is known as the stage of diminishing returns. This is very crucial and important because the firm will seek to produce in this stage.

Stage-III: Negative returns: TP declines and slopes downward showing MP is negative. MP-curve goes below the X-axis. This stage starts from D on TP, E on AP and F on MP-curves.

A rational producer will never choose first and third stage for his production, he will always operate in the second stage.

RETURNS TO SCALE

The laws of production describe the possible ways to increase the level of production. In the short run output may be increased by using more of the variable factor(s) while capital and other possible fixed factors as well are kept constant. The expansion of output by a variable factor with other factors as constant is referred to the law of variable proportions.

But in the long run output can be increased by changing all factors of production. Because all the factors in the long run are variable factors. This refers to the law of returns to scale. A change in scale means proportionate change in all inputs (factors). An increase in the scale means that all inputs or factors are increased in the same proportion. Thus, increase in the scale occurs when all inputs are increased keeping input proportions unchanged. So returns to scale refer to the relation between the change in the output level and the change in the scale of the production process. Thus, all factors in the production process can be changed. When all factors can be varied, keeping their proportion unchanged, it is called the scale of operation (production process). Therefore, when we study the change in output due to change in all factors, it refers to the returns to scale.

Suppose, two factors x_1 and x_2 are required to produce a commodity, q. An equal product map is drawn taking x_1 along the X-axis and x_2 along the Y-axis as shown in Fig. 7.12. The particular quantities of two inputs produce a particular quantity of output. If we increase both the inputs in the same proportion, their ratio will remain the same but the output level will change. In this case we move along a straight line passing through the origin. Now straight lines OP and OR are drawn passing through the origin.

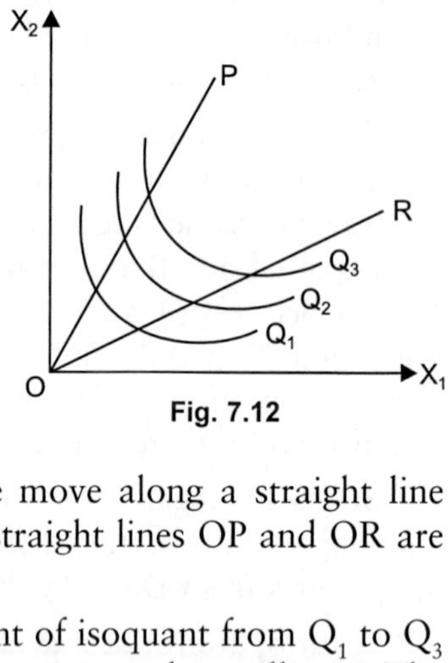

Fig. 7.12

Now, we see that the movement of isoquant from Q_1 to Q_3 along OP shows that the input factors, x_1 and x_2 will vary. The ratio between the two factors will remain the same throughout OP as this line passes through the origin. An upward movement along OP indicates the increase of two factors in absolute amounts with the proportion between the two remaining unaltered. But the scale of the production process is changed. Similarly, a movement along OR represents change in scale with a given proportion between these two factors which remains unchanged. Thus, different straight lines passing through the origin will indicate different proportions between the two factors keeping their proportion unchanged in each line.

THREE PHASES OF RETURNS TO SCALE

There are three phases (or stages) of returns to scale. These are increasing returns to scale, constant returns to scale and decreasing returns to scale.

Increasing returns to scale occur when we increase all the inputs in a given proportion, output increases in a more than proportion. That is, by doubling the inputs, output is produced more than double.

Constant returns to scale refer to the situation when all inputs are increased in a given proportion, output increases in the same proportion. That is, doubling of inputs results in doubling of output (returns).

Decreasing returns to scale show when we increase all the inputs in a given proportion, output increases in a less than proportion. By doubling the inputs, output increases by less than twice its original level.

We can explain the three stages of returns to scale with the following example and Fig. 7.13.

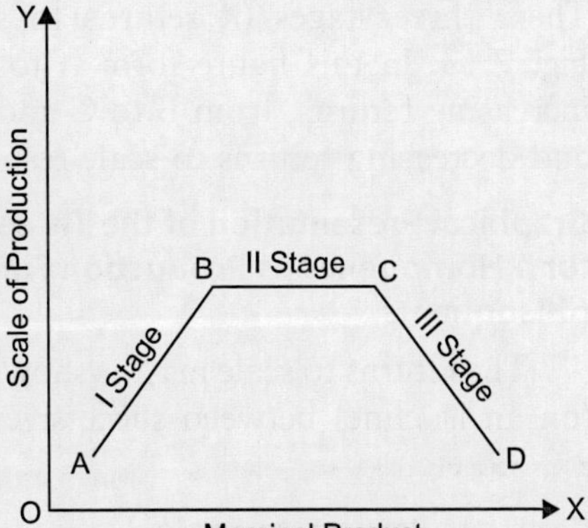

Fig. 7.13

Returns to Scale Shown in the Table

Sl. No.	Scale of Production (workers and land)	Total Product (in units)	Marginal Product (in units)	
1.	1 w + 2 acres of land	4	4	Stage I (Increasing returns)
2.	2 w + 4 acres of land	10	6	
3.	3 w + 6 acres of land	18	8	
4.	4 w + 8 acres of land	28	10	Stage II (Constant returns)
5.	5 w + 10 acres of land	38	10	
6.	6 w + 12 acres of land	48	10	Stage III (Decreasing returns)
7.	7 w + 14 acres of land	56	8	
8.	8 w + 16 acres of land	62	6	

In this table we have increased the workers and acres of land in a given proportion. In the beginning when the input scale is doubled, i.e., 2 workers and 4 acres of land are employed from 1 worker and 2 acres of land, the output is produced more than double. When the scale is trebled, the output is more than treble. That is why, marginal product is increasing from Sl. No. 1 to Sl. No. 4 showing that we have increasing returns up to this stage. Again if the scale of proportion is further increased, the marginal product remains constant up to a certain point and beyond it, marginal product starts diminishing. From Sl. No. 4 to Sl. No. 6 marginal product (i.e., returns) remains constant at 10 units. This stage is constant returns to scale. Afterwards, the marginal product declines. It is decreasing returns to scale. These three stages of returns to scale are illustrated in the Fig. 7.13. In this figure form A to B, this stage is referred to increasing returns, from B to C and C to D show the constant and decreasing returns to scale respectively.

Graphical Presentation of the Three Phases of Returns to Scale for a Homogeneous Production Function with the Application of Isoquants

The returns to scale may be shown graphically by the distance (on an isocline) between successive multiple isoquants, e.g. x, 2x, 3x, etc.

Constant Returns to Scale

Along any isocline the distance between successive multiple isoquants is constant. Doubling the factor inputs achieves double the level of the initial output; trebling inputs achieves treble output and so on (Fig. 7.14).

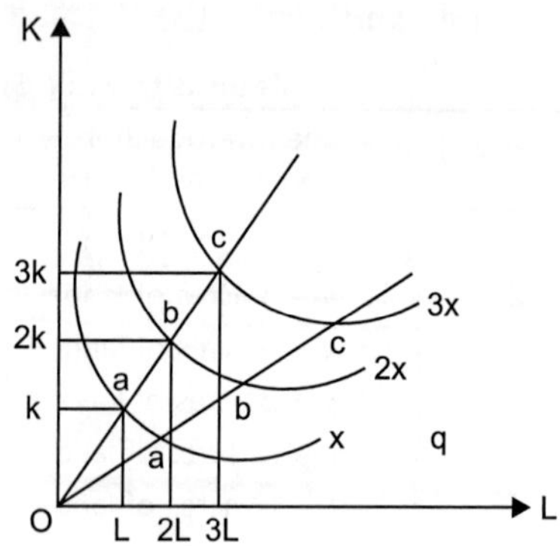

Fig. 7.14

Here the distance between x and 2x isoquants and the distance between 2x and 3x isoquants are equal, i.e., Oa =

ab = bc. It shows that to get the isoquant 2x, we have to increase the inputs just double.

Decreasing Returns to Scale

The distance between consecutive multiple isoquants increases. By doubling the inputs, output increases by less than twice its original level. In Fig. 7.15 the point a′ defined by 2k and 2L, lies on a dotted isoquant below the isoquant, 2x. Decreasing returns to scale shows Oa < ab < bc. If it were constant return to scale we get the dotted isoquant achieving by doubling the labour and capital. But due to decreasing returns to scale, the actual isoquant stands after the dotted isoquant. It implies that to get the isoquant 2x, we have to increase the inputs more than double.

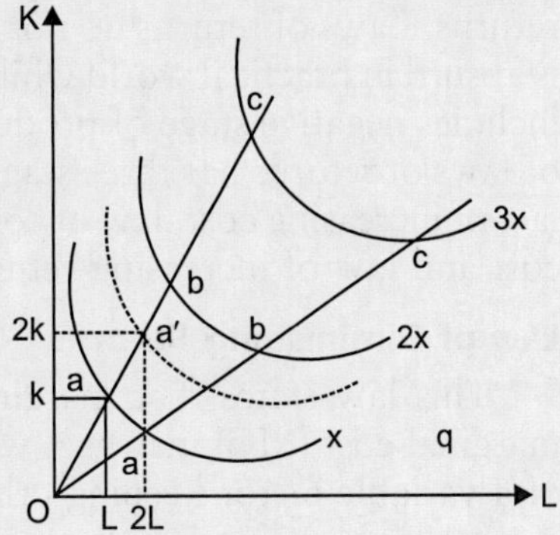

Fig. 7.15

Increasing Returns to Scale

The distance between consecutive multiple isoquants decreases. By doubling the inputs, output increases more than double. In Fig. 7.16 doubling K and L leads to point b′ which lies on a dotted isoquant above the isoquant 2x. Due to increasing returns to scale, we get oa > ab > bc. It indicates that to get the isoquant 2x we have to increase inputs less than double.

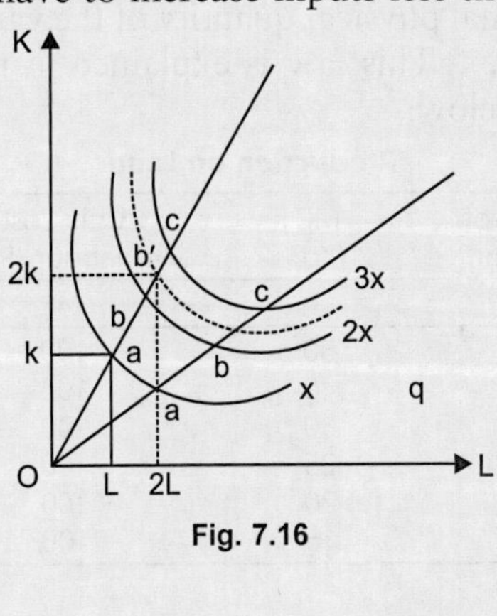

Fig. 7.16

LAWS OF PRODUCTION OR LAWS OF RETURNS

From the three stages of the law of variable proportions generally, three laws of returns are prescribed. They are law of increasing returns, law of constant returns and law of diminishing returns. Actually, laws of returns are simple form of the law of variable propositions. This is a minor difference between the three stages of the law of variable proportions and the three laws of returns. Laws of returns do not include the negative stage which is absurd in practical world while the law of variable proportions includes negative stage of production. Thus, laws of production or laws of returns has three stages: law of diminishing returns or law of increasing cost, law of constant returns or law of constant cost and law of increasing returns or law of diminishing cost.

Law of Diminishing Returns

This law states that marginal product (MP) diminishes or marginal cost (MC) increases with the increase in the quantities of a variable factor keeping other factor as constant.

According to classical version, this law is mainly concerned with land and agriculture. As **Marshall** puts it, "An increase in the capital or labour applied in the cultivation of land causes in general, a less than proportionate increase in the amount of product raised, unless it happens to coincide with an improvement in the art of agriculture."

According to modern version, it is applicable not only in agriculture but in all fields of production. **Prof. Boulding** has defined this law in the way, "As we increase the quantity of anyone input which is combined with a fixed quantity of other inputs, the marginal physical quantity of the variable input must eventually decline." This law is explained in the schedule and Fig. 7.17 given below:

Production on Land

Land	Units of labour	MP (Kg)	Unit Cost of labour (Rs.)	MC (Rs.) (4 ÷ 3)
(1)	(2)	(3)	(4)	(5)
1	1	50	100	2
1	2	40	100	2.5
1	3	30	100	3.33
1	4	25	100	4
1	5	20	100	5
1	6	15	100	6.66

It is clear from the above schedule and diagram that MP decreases and MC increases gradually with the increase in labour keeping other factor (land) as constant. In Fig. 7.17(a) the MP curve slopes downward from left to right indicating the diminishing of returns while in Fig. 7.17(b) MC curve slopes upward from left to right showing the increase in cost with the increase in the units of labour in both cases.

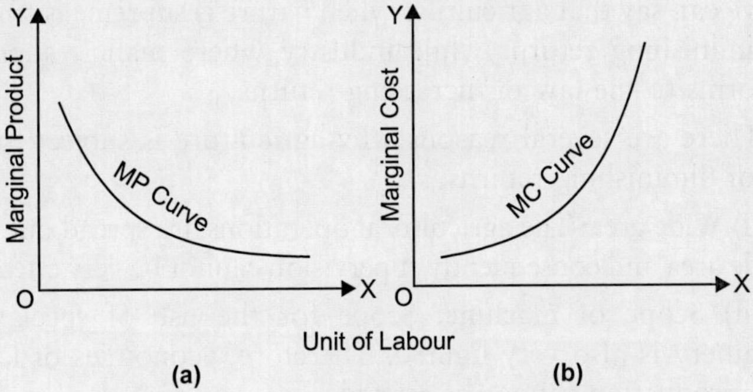

Fig. 7.17

CAUSES OF THE OPERATION OF THIS LAW

There are some vital reasons for which the law is bound to operate. These are given below:

1. **Fixed factor:** We increase the amount of variable factor to increase production keeping other factor as constant. The amount of fixed factor input per unit of variable factor falls as more and more of the later is put to use. As a result the output begins to decline.

2. **Scarcity of factors:** Factors of production are scarce and limited in supply. This law has come into existence due to scarcity of factors.

3. **Imperfect substitution:** Factors of production cannot fully be substituted. For example, labour or capital cannot be substituted in place of other.

4. **Optimum combination:** Optimum combination is a best level of combination of different factors of production producing optimum output. At this combination output is maximum. If we increase a particular factor of production to get higher output beyond this optimum production, marginal product of that factor declines.

WHY DOES THIS LAW SPECIALLY APPLY TO AGRICULTURE?

Though it is applied to all fields of production but it is specially applied to agriculture. Because in agriculture, it is easily seen to be applied within a short period of time. Production where nature is supreme is subject to this law and production where man plays as supremacy is subject to increasing returns. So, we can say that agriculture when nature is supreme is subject to diminishing returns while industry where man is supreme conforms to the law of increasing returns.

There are several reasons why agriculture is subject to the law of diminishing returns:

(i) **Wide area:** The agricultural operations are spread out over a wide area and consequently supervision cannot be very effective.

(ii) **Scope of machine:** Scope for the use of specialized machinery is also very limited. Therefore, economies of large-scale production cannot be reaped.

(iii) **Interruption:** There are further limitations arising from the seasonal nature. Agricultural operations are likely to be interrupted by rain and other climate changes. Man is not a complete master of nature. Thus, the law of diminishing returns operates in agriculture easily.

But, we cannot say that agriculture is always subject to diminishing returns and manufacturing is always to increasing returns. This law applies everywhere. In **Wicksteed**'s words, "This law is as universal as the law of life itself." Its application is not confined to agriculture only; it applies to manufacturing industries too. If the industry is expanded too much, there will be lack of supervision and the costs will go up. This law will, therefore, set in. The only difference is that in agriculture it sets in earlier and in industry much later. Agriculture also has increasing returns in the beginning. Hence, it is applied in both agriculture and manufacturing.

LIMITATIONS OF THE LAW OF DIMINISHING RETURNS

There are some limitations on account of which this law cannot operate for a time being.

(i) **Improved methods of cultivation:** Scientific rotation of crops, improved seeds, modern implements, artificial manures, better irrigation facilities, modern techniques, etc. are bound to give increasing returns. But, it will not be found for a long period of time. The law must operate sooner or later.

(ii) **New soil:** When a virgin soil is brought under cultivation, in the beginning the additional returns for each successive dose of labour and capital may increase for a time. But, after a time, the tendency of diminishing returns will set in.

(iii) **Sufficient capital:** Application of sufficient capital may yield more returns than before. Later, the marginal returns will decrease. Thus, the early state is an exception to the law of diminishing returns.

IMPORTANCE OF THIS LAW

Cairnes says that in the absence of the law of diminishing returns the science of political economy would be completely as revolutionized as if human nature itself were altered. Upto **Marshall**, it was thought that this law is applied to agriculture whereas the laws of increasing or constant returns is applied to manufacture. But, this law is applied in all fields of production, whether agriculture, mining or manufacture. In the words of **Wicksteed**, "The law of diminishing returns is as universal as the law of life itself." So, it has great importance in real life. Again, it forms the basis of a number of economic doctrines propounded by the English classical economists, especially **Malthus** and **Ricardo**.

Malthusian theory of population: The **Malthusian** theory of population, which says that population increases faster than the food supply, is obviously based on the fact that the production of food is subject to the law of diminishing returns.

Ricardian theory of rent: The **Ricardian** theory of rent explains the determination of rent on the assumption that inferior lands have to be cultivated on account of the operation of the law of diminishing returns. The margin of cultivation descends, and rent rises.

Theory of distribution: The marginal productivity theory, which determines the share of a factor of production in the national dividend, is also based on the operation of this law.

Hence, the law of diminishing returns occupies a very important place in the realm of production system.

LAW OF CONSTANT RETURNS

This law states that marginal product (MP) and marginal cost (MC) remain constant with the increase in the quantities of a variable factor keeping other factor as constant. That is, production increases in the same proportion as the increase in variable factor keeping other factor as constant. In this situation, both of marginal product and average product (AP) are same and constant. From the cost point of view it is called the law of constant cost, because with the increase in the units of a variable factor marginal cost (MC) and average cost (AC) remain constant.

According to **Marshall**, the stage of constant returns comes at the point where the effects of increasing returns and diminishing returns balance each other. Thus, the relationship between increasing returns and diminishing returns is not direct, they are related with the law of constant returns.

This law is illustrated in the following example and Fig. 7.18:

Example:

Production

Units of labour	Total product (kg.)	MP (kg.)	AP (kg.)	Unit cost of labour (Rs.)	MC (Rs.) (5 ÷ 3)	AC (Rs.) (5 ÷ 4)
1	2	3	4	5	6	7
1	25	25	25	100	4	4
2	50	25	25	100	4	4
3	75	25	25	100	4	4
4	100	25	25	100	4	4
5	125	25	25	100	4	4

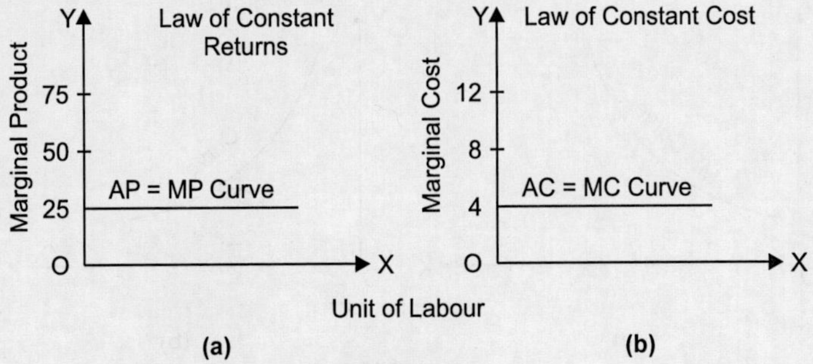

Fig. 7.18

From the above example and Figure, it is seen that output increases in the same proportion as the increasing in the variable factor (labour) keeping other factor as constant. Hence, average product and marginal product curve become one, horizontal and parallel to the X-axis under constant returns. Average product and marginal product both remain same at ₹ 25. Again, in case of cost condition, average cost and marginal cost both are same at ₹ 4. They become also one, horizontal and parallel to the X-axis. These are shown in Figs. 7.18(a) and 7.18(b).

LAW OF INCREASING RETURNS

This law states that product increases in the increasing proportion with the increase in variable factor keeping other factor as constant. That is, marginal product (MP) increases or marginal cost (MC) decreases with the increase in quantities of a variable factor keeping other factor as constant. From the cost point of view, it is termed as law of diminishing cost. This law is explained in the following example and Fig. 7.19:

Example:

Production

Units of labour	Total product (kg.)	MP (kg.)	Unit cost of labour (Rs.)	MC (Rs.) (4 ÷ 3)
1	2	3	4	5
1	20	20	100	5.00
2	45	25	100	4.00
3	75	30	100	3.33
4	115	40	100	2.50
5	165	50	100	2.00

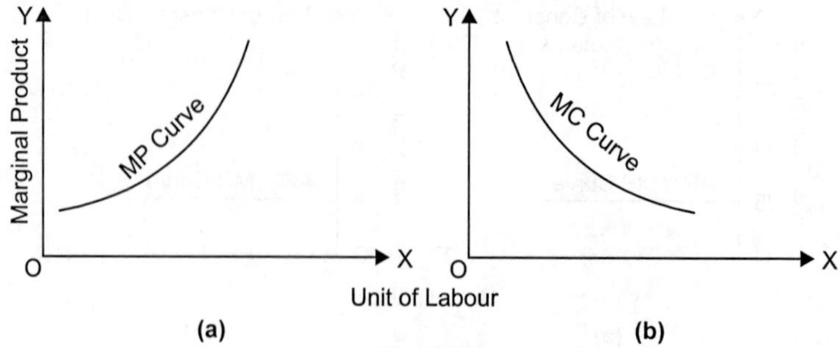

Fig. 7.19

From the above example and figure, it is clear that output increases in the increasing proportion with the increase in variable factor (labour) keeping other factor as constant. With the increase in the units of labour, marginal product increases. This is shown by the upward slopping MP curve in Fig. 7.19(a). On the other hand, marginal cost decreases with the increase in the units of labour. This is also depicted by the downward slopping MC curve in Fig. 7.19(b). This law is mostly applicable in manufacturing industries where men are supreme. But this stage is possible only before the point of optimum combination after which this law breaks down eventually.

CAUSES OF THE OPERATION OF THIS LAW

1. **Indivisibility of factor:** There are some factors which cannot be used in parts. Such as a generator of 5 horse power is not used in part. With the increase in production marginal cost will decline using the generator to its full capacity.

2. **Increase in efficiency:** If the efficiency of fixed factor increases with the increase of variable factor, the law of increasing returns will operate.

3. **Fixed factor:** The cost of fixed factor is fixed. With the increase in output, per unit fixed cost will decline which will lower the overall average cost.

4. **Division of labour:** Proper division of labour and specialisation in the production will lower the cost of production and thereby create the conditions of increasing returns.

5. **Optimum combination:** Before arriving the point of optimum combination of various factors of production, the law of increasing returns will generally operate.

6. **Economies:** At the beginning firm gets some economies in favour of production which reduces the average cost with the increase in output. As a result, the law of increasing returns to scale operates.

DIFFERENCES BETWEEN THE LAWS OF RETURNS TO THE VARIABLE FACTOR AND THE LAWS OF RETURNS TO SCALE

1. The law of returns to the variable factor or the law of variable proportion shows the effect of the changes in the quantities of a variable factor on the output keeping other fixed factors as constant. But the law of returns to scale shows the effect on output when all the factor-inputs are varied simultaneously.
2. The law of returns to the variable factor has three stages: increasing, diminishing and negative while the law of returns to scale has also three stages: increasing, constant and diminishing.
3. Returns to the variable factor is a phenomenon of short period, while the returns to scale are concerned with long period.
4. In the case of returns to the variable factor only one factor is varied keeping other factors as constant, while in the case of returns to scale all the factors of production are varied simultaneously. In the first case there is no change in the scale of production, while in the second case the scale of production itself is changed.

EQUILIBRIUM OF THE FIRM (OPTIMIZING BEHAVIOUR)

To find out the optimizing behaviour of a firm, we have to know first about isocost line. Let us first define what is isocost line? We assume that a firm produces one output q using two inputs x_1 and x_2. The entrepreneur purchases x_1 and x_2 in perfectly competitive markets at constant unit prices. His total cost of production is given by the linear equation $C = r_1x_1 + r_2x_2$ where r_1 and r_2 are the respective prices of x_1 and x_2.

This equation will be satisfied by different combinations of x_1 and x_2. The isocost line is defined as the locus of all such combinations of two factors (inputs) which the firm can purchase with its given outlay. For example, a firm, with its given outlay, can purchase either OB of x_1 or OA of x_2 as shown in Fig. 7.20. Joining the two points A and B, we get the isocost line AB. This isocost line AB shows that the firm can purchase any combination of x_1 and x_2 on this line with its given level of cost. When it is purchasing OB of x_1, it is purchasing nothing of x_2 and *vice versa*.

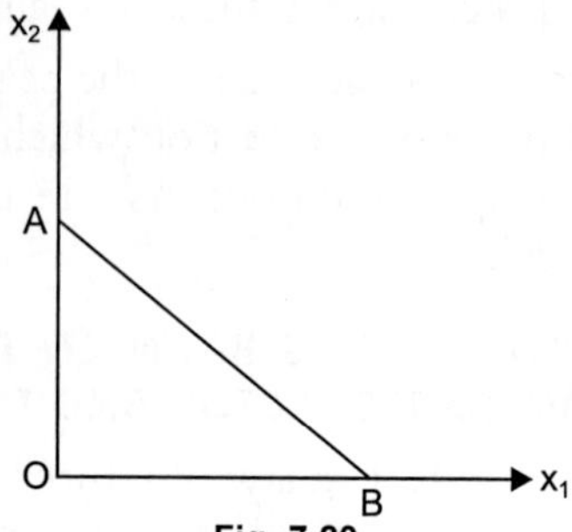

Fig. 7.20

Slope of the Isocost Line

The slope of the isocost line is the price ratio of two factors x_1 and x_2. Now the isocost equation is $C = r_1x_1 + r_2x_2$ which can be written as $x_1 = \frac{c}{r_1} - \frac{r_2}{r_1}x_2$, where $\frac{c}{r_1}$ represents the intercept (OB) of the isocost line on the x_1 axis and this intercept is the amount of x_1 if the entire cost is incurred on purchasing x_1, i.e., $\frac{c}{r_1} = OB$.

Similarly, the intercept on the x_2 axis is $\frac{c}{r_2}\left[x_2 = \frac{c}{r_2} - \frac{r_1}{r_2}x_1\right]$ which is the amount of x_2 (AO) if the entire cost is expended upon x_2,

i.e., $\frac{c}{r_2} = OA$

Now, the slope of the isocost line is

$$\frac{OA}{OB} = \frac{c}{r_2} \div \frac{c}{r_1} = \frac{r_1}{r_2}$$

$$\therefore \quad \frac{OA}{OB} = \frac{r_1}{r_2}$$

Thus, the price ratio, $\frac{r_1}{r_2}$ of two factors x_1 and x_2 is the slope of the isocost line AB. But it is negative, i.e., $\frac{OA}{OB} = -\frac{r_1}{r_2}$ or, we can directly show the slope from the cost equation, $x_2 = \frac{c}{r_2} - \frac{r_1}{r_2}x_1$ where the slope is $-\frac{r_1}{r_2}$.

Shift of the Isocost Line

Any change either in the factor prices or in the cost level would cause shift in the isocost line. For example, if the input prices remain constant but the cost level changes, the isocost line will shift parallely. The slopes of parallel shifted isocost lines remain the same. It is shown in Fig. 7.21. In this figure the isocost line AB shifts to CD and CD shifts to EF due to increase in the level of cost of the firm. But the slopes of the lines are the same. Similarly, the isocost line will shift to the left due to decrease in the cost level.

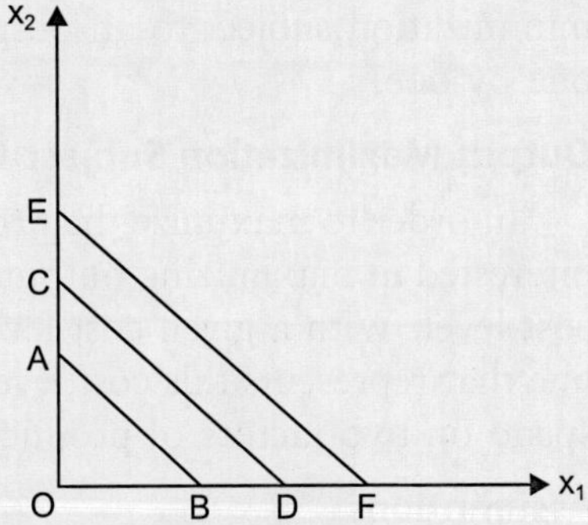

Fig. 7.21

Again if, the price of x_1 falls while the price of x_2 remains the same and the cost level is also kept as constant, the isocost line changes from AB to AC in the rightward direction. If the price of x_1 rises, the cost line shifts to AD in the leftward direction. It is shown in Fig. 7.22.

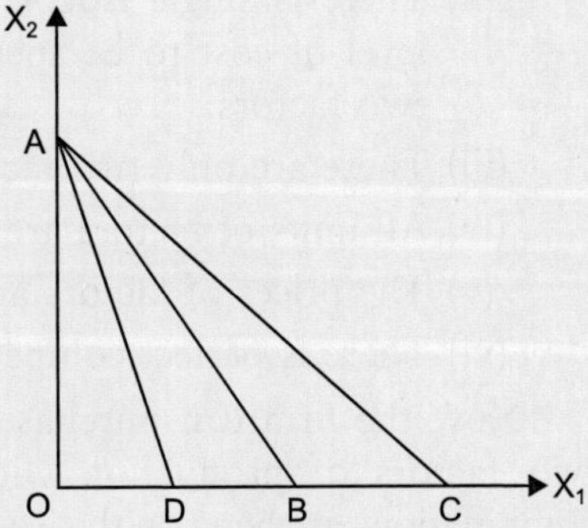

Fig. 7.22

Likewise, if the price of x_2 changes, the cost level and the price of x_1 remaining the same, the isocost line will shift. From the above explanation it is clear that the isocost line depends upon two things: (i) prices of the factors and (ii) the cost level of the firm.

EQUILIBRIUM OF THE FIRM USING ISOQUANTS

In the theory of consumer's behaviour, we see that the consumer is in equilibrium when he maximizes his satisfaction with his given income and given the prices of two commodities. Similarly, in the theory of production, the producer is in equilibrium when he maximizes his profits on the basis of (i) output maximization subject to a cost constraint, or (ii) cost minimization subject to an output constraint. Now we discuss one by one.

Output Maximization Subject to a Cost Constraint

In order to maximize the profits, a rational producer will be interested in maximizing output of the commodity with a given cost level. With a given cost level, there will be a single isocost line that represents this cost level which the firm has decided to spend on two factors of production.

Assumptions

The assumptions, on which the producer tries to maximize his output with the given cost level, are given below:

(i) There is isoquant map in which different isoquants show different levels of output.

(ii) There is single isocost line which represents a given level of cost to be spent on different combination of two factors.

(iii) There are only two factors of production.

(iv) All units of factors are homogeneous.

(v) The prices of factors are given and constant.

(vi) There is perfect competition in the factor markets.

Now the firm can purchase different combinations of the two factors of production with his given outlay. All these combinations are lying on the isocost line. But question arises: On which isoquant in the isoquant map and on which point along the isocost line, the producer will maximize the level of output with his given level of cost, i.e., which combination of factors the producer will choose to produce so that he can maximize the level of output.

Let us suppose that there are four isoquants, say q, q_1, q_2 and q_3, AB is a single isocost line and x_1 and x_2 are two factors. It is illustrated in the Fig. 7.23.

In Fig. 7.23, we put x_1 along the X-axis and x_2 along the Y-axis. The isoquant q intersects the isocost line AB at P_1 and P_2 and the isoquant q_1 intersects the isocost line AB at P_3 and P_4 while the isoquant q_2 touches the isocost line AB at point P. But the isoquant q_3 cannot touch the isocost line AB standing above the AB line. Now all the point P, P_1, P_2, P_3 and P_4 are lying on the AB line. All are equally costly. The firm can purchase any one of these combinations of the two factors at any point along the isocost line AB but by moving from P_1 to P_3 and from P_3 to P, the firm can increase the level of output because, P_3 is on a higher isoquant compared to P_1 and P is also on a higher isoquant compared to P_3. P is a point of tangency between the isoquant q_2 and the isocost line AB. The producer gets highest possible level of output at point P on isoquant q_2 with his given cost level. Again, the movement from P to P_4 or P_4 to P_2 is not desirable since the rational producer can never move from a higher isoquant to a lower isoquant. But the producer cannot reach the isoquant q_3 since it is beyond the isocost line AB. The producer producing highest possible level of output subject to the cost constraint is said to be in equilibrium at the point P where the isoquant q_2 is tangent to the isocost line AB.

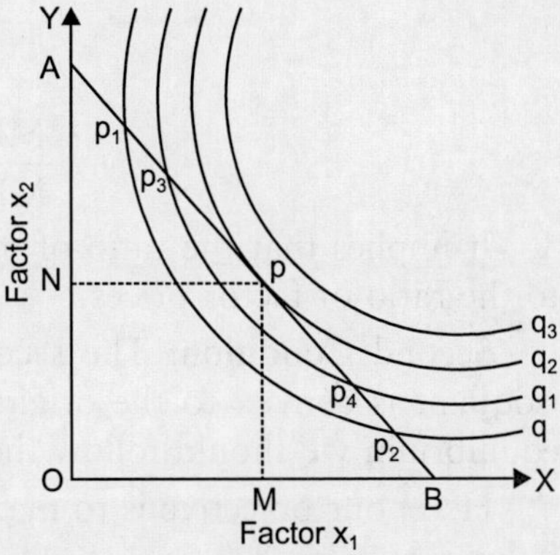

Fig. 7.23

Conditions for Equilibrium

There are two conditions for equilibrium:

First Condition: The first condition for equilibrium is that the isocost line is tangent to the isoquant. At the point of tangency, the slope of the isoquant is equal to the slope of the isocost line.

$$\text{The slope of the isoquant} = \frac{-\delta q/\delta x_1}{\delta q/\delta x_2} \quad \frac{-MPx_1}{MPx_2}$$

$$\text{And the slope of the isocost line} = -\frac{r_1}{r_2}$$

$$= -\frac{\text{Price of } x_1}{\text{Price of } x_2}$$

$$\therefore \quad \frac{MPx_1}{MPx_2} = \frac{r_1}{r_2}$$

It implies that the ratio of marginal productivities is equal to the ratio of factor prices.

Second Condition: The second condition proves that the isoquant is convex to the origin. For the second condition of equilibrium we should follow the Lagrange multiplier method.

Here, our objective is to maximize $q = f(x_1, x_2)$ subject to $C = r_1x_1 + r_2x_2$

According to this method, we have

$$L = q + \lambda (c - r_1 x_1 - r_2 x_2)$$

Or, $L = f(x_1, x_2) + \lambda (c - r_1 x_1 - r_2 x_2)$ where λ is Lagrangian multiplier.

The first order conditions of maximization require

$$\frac{\delta L}{\delta x_1} = f_1 - \lambda r_1 = 0 \quad \text{... (1)}$$

$$\frac{\delta L}{\delta x_2} = f_2 - \lambda r_2 = 0 \quad \text{... (2)}$$

$$\frac{\delta L}{\delta \lambda} = c - r_1x_1 - r_2x_2 = 0 \quad \text{... (3)}$$

The second condition for equilibrium is the second order condition of Lagrangian multiplier method which requires that the relevant bordered Hessian determinant should be positive.

That is,

$$\begin{vmatrix} f_{11} & f_{12} & -r_1 \\ f_{21} & f_{22} & -r_2 \\ -r_1 & -r_2 & 0 \end{vmatrix} > 0$$

It implies that the isoquant must be convex to the origin.

If the isoquants are concave to the origin, the point of tangency of the isocost and the isoquant curves does not define an equilibrium position. It is shown in Fig. 7.24.

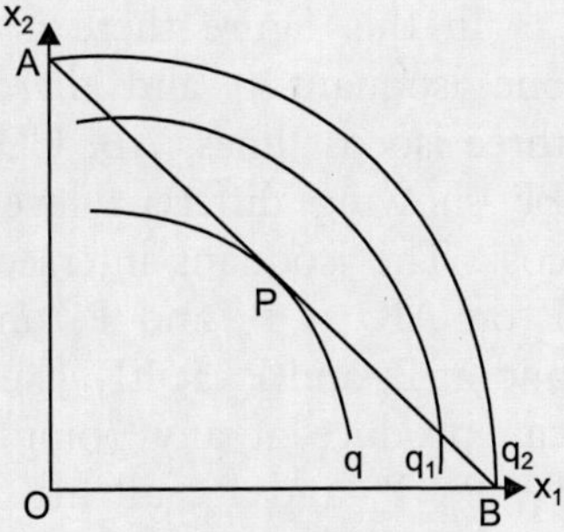

Fig. 7.24

In this case, highest level of output will be produced at the corner point of the isocost line. Here output will be maximum at any one of the corner points A and B.

COST MINIMIZATION SUBJECT TO AN OUTPUT CONSTRAINT

In order to maximize the profits, a rational producer will be interested in minimising the cost level to be spent on the different combinations of the two factors keeping the output level as constant. With a given output level there will be a single isoquant which represents a same level of output from different combinations of two factors of production.

Assumptions

(i) There are large number of isocost lines representing different levels of cost.

(ii) There is a single isoquant.

(iii) There are only two factors of production.

(iv) All units of factors are homogeneous.

(v) The prices of factors are given and constant.

(vi) There is perfect competition in the factor market.

Let us assume that the single isoquant intersects several isocost lines at several points. Each and every point on the isoquant shows the same level of output. Now question arises on which point of which isocost line along the isoquant, the producer will produce so that he can minimize the level of cost for a given level of output. He will always try to produce the given level of output at the lowest possible cost of production. That is, he will select the point on the isoquant which is least costly. It is illustrated in Fig. 7.25.

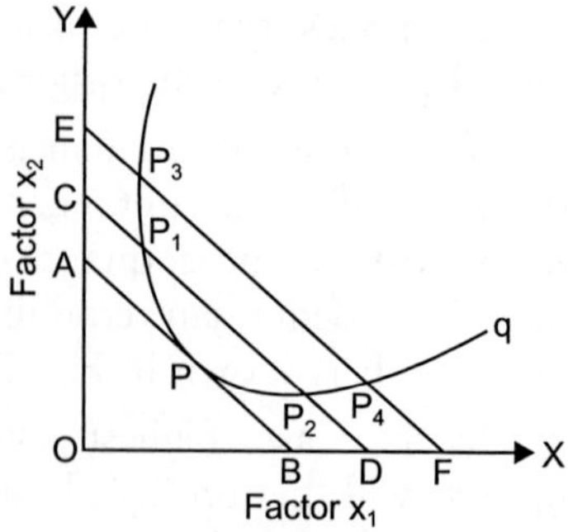

Fig. 7.25

In this figure there is only one isoquant q and there are three isocost lines, AB, CD and EF showing different levels of cost. The isoquant intersects at P on AB, at P_1 and P_2 on CD and at P_3 and P_4 at EF. The firm can produce at any point of P, P_1, P_2, P_3 and P_4, all are lying on the same isoquant q showing the same level of output. But a rational producer will try to produce at the lowest isocost line. By moving either from P_3 or P_4 of the isocost line EF either to P_1 or P_2 of the isocost line CD, the firm can minimize the level of cost. Again, by moving either from P_1 or P_2 of CD to P on the isocost line AB, the producer can reach the lowest possible cost level to produce the output level q. Here P is a tangency point between the isocost line AB and the isoquant q. So, the producer producing a given level of output at the lowest possible cost is said to be in equilibrium at the point P where the isoquant q is tangent to the isocost line AB.

Conditions for Equilibrium

There are two conditions for equilibrium in order to minimise the cost subject to output constraint.

First Condition: The first condition for equilibrium is that the isocost line is tangent to the isoquant. At the point of tangency, the slope of the isoquant is equal to the slope of the isocost line.

$$\text{The slope of the isoquant} = \frac{-\delta q/\delta x_1}{\delta q/\delta x_2} = \frac{-MPx_1}{MPx_2}$$

$$\text{And the slope of the isocost line} = -\frac{r_1}{r_2}$$

$$= -\frac{\text{Price of } x_1}{\text{Price of } x_2}$$

$$\therefore \frac{MPx_1}{MPx_2} = -\frac{r_1}{r_2}$$

Therefore, the first condition implies that the ratio of marginal productivities is equal to the ratio of factor prices.

Second Condition: The second condition shows that the isoquant is convex to the origin. For the second condition of equilibrium, we should follow the Lagrange multiplier method. Here, our problem is to minimize $C = r_1 x_1 + r_2 x_2$ subject to $q = f(x_1, x_2)$. This problem can be solved by the Lagrangian multiplier method.

According to this method, we have

$$L = C + \lambda\left[q - f(x_1, x_2)\right]$$

Or, $$L = r_1 x_1 + r_2 x_2 + \lambda\left[q - f(x_1, x_2)\right]$$

$$\frac{\delta L}{\delta x_1} = r_1 - \lambda f_1 = 0 \qquad \text{... (1)}$$

$$\frac{\delta L}{\delta x_2} = r_2 - \lambda f_2 = 0 \qquad \text{... (2)}$$

$$\frac{\delta L}{\delta \lambda} = q - f(x_1, x_2) = 0 \qquad \text{... (3)}$$

The second condition for equilibrium is the second order condition of Lagrangian multiplier method which requires that the relevant bordered Hessian determinant should be negative.

That is,

$$\begin{vmatrix} -\lambda f_{11} & -\lambda f_{12} & -f_1 \\ -\lambda f_{21} & -\lambda f_{22} & -f_2 \\ -f_1 & -f_2 & 0 \end{vmatrix} < 0$$

Putting $f_1 = \frac{r_1}{\lambda}$ and $f_2 = \frac{r_2}{\lambda}$, we get

$$\begin{vmatrix} f_{11} & f_{12} & -r_1 \\ f_{21} & f_{22} & -r_2 \\ -r_1 & -r_2 & 0 \end{vmatrix} > 0, \text{ since } \lambda > 0$$

This bordered Hessian determinant is greater than zero implying that the isoquant must be convex to the origin.

If the isoquant is concave to the origin, the highest isocost line will be tangent to the isoquant. It is shown in Fig. 7.26. In this case, to produce a given level of output at the lowest possible cost will be at the corner point of the isocost line. Here the given level of output is possible at any one of the corner points A and B which show the lowest possible cost.

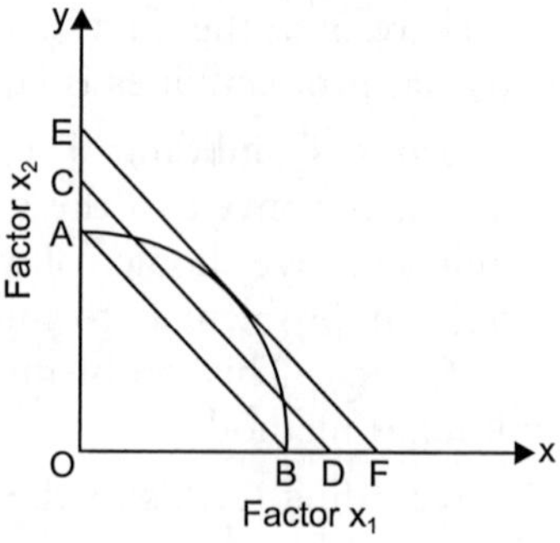

Fig. 7.26

EXPANSION PATH

The objective of a producer is to maximize his profit. In order to maximize his profit, we have seen that a producer tries to produce highest possible output with a given outlay or to produce a given level of output with a lowest possible outlay. Every time the producer is in equilibrium at a tangency point between the isoquant and the isocost line. At tangency point the slope of the isoquant is equal to the slope of the isocost line. This means that the ratio of marginal productivities of two factors, i.e., the marginal rate of technical substitution is equal to the factor price ratio of the two factors.

Assumptions

1. There are two factors of production.
2. The price of the factors is assumed to be constant.
3. The producer likes to expand his level of output by increasing the total outlay.
4. There is perfect competition in the factor market.

This is illustrated in Fig. 7.27. Suppose, the factors of production are x_1 and x_2. We plot x_1 along the X-axis and x_2 along the Y-axis. With higher budget outlay, the firm can buy more of x_1 and more of x_2. As a result, the isocost line or price line moves from AB to CD and they are parallel to each other showing that their price ratio and slope remain the same. With isocost line AB, the equilibrium point is E at the isoquant q.

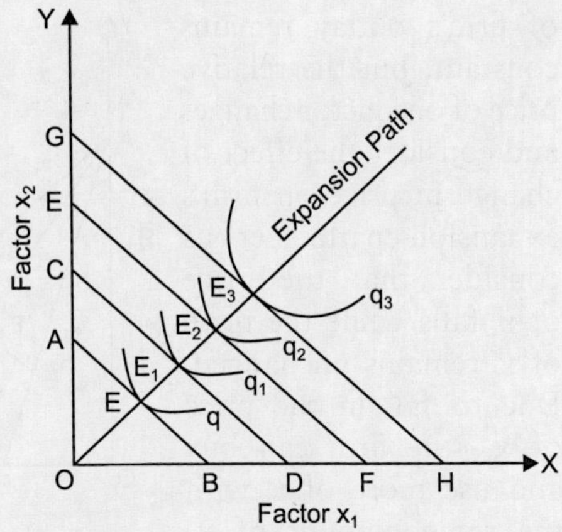

Fig. 7.27

With shifting the isocost line from AB to CD, the equilibrium point E also shifts to E_1 at new isoquant q_1. That is, the producer reaches the new equilibrium point E_1 at which the isocost line CD is tangent to the new isoquant q_1. Likewise, with further increases in outlay, he reaches successively higher isoquants q_2 and q_3 with equilibrium points E_2 and E_3. The line joining these successive points of equilibrium is called the expansion path of the firm. That is, the expansion path is the locus of tangency points between isocost lines and isoquants.

The expansion path, here, is moving upward from the origin showing the way in which factor proportions change in response to output changes with the factor price ratio remaining unchanged. This indicates that to reach successively higher levels of output, the firm will use greater quantities of both factors. Each successive point of equilibrium will show the least cost combination of producing that level of output. Thus, the expansion path shows the locus of points of successive least cost combinations depending on which the firm can achieve successively higher level of output. The expansion path is also known as scale-line because it indicates how the producer will change the quantities of the two factors when it increases the level of output.

The expansion path can have different shapes and slopes depending upon the relative prices of the factors used.

Changes in Factor Prices and Expansion Path

For the construction of expansion path, so far we have assumed that factor prices remain unchanged and only the level of firm's outlay is changed. Now we assume that the level of firm's outlay remains constant, but the relative price of one factor changes and consider the effect of change in price on firm's expansion path. Let us consider that the price of x_1 falls while the price of x_2 remains unchanged. Due to fall in the price of x_1, the firm can buy and use more of it with the same amount of x_2 when the level of outlay of the firm remain the same. As a result the isocost line shifts from its position AB to the position AC as shown in Fig. 7.28. The firm reaches a new equilibrium point (new point of least cost combination) from E to E_1 and produces a higher level of output. Again if the price of x_1 continues to fall, the price of x_2 remaining the same, the isocost line also continues to shift in rightward direction and similarly the equilibrium point also shifts from its previous position to new position E_2 as shown in Fig. 7.28. If we join the equilibrium points, E, E_1 and E_2 we get expansion path. It is clear that due to fall in the price of x_1, the firm will use more of it, but whether it will use some more of x_2 or not, it will depend upon the elasticity of substitution between x_1 and x_2.

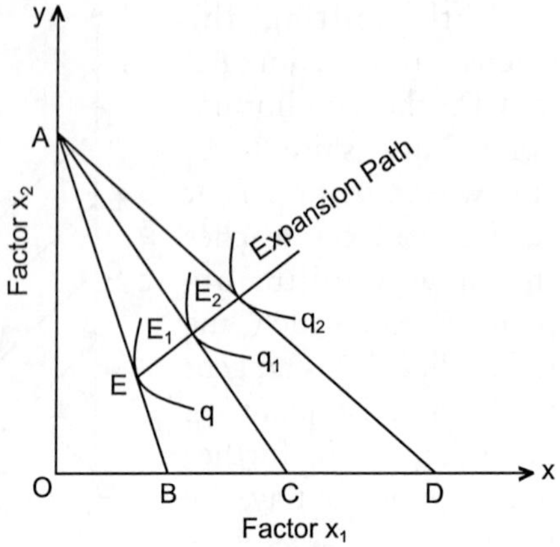

Fig. 7.28

Similarly, if the price of x_2 falls but the price of x_1 and the level of outlay remain the same, the firm will use more of x_2. As a result, the isocost line will shift rightward and likewise we get the expansion path as shown in Fig. 7.29. But how much more of x_2 and x_1 the firm will use depends upon the elasticity of substitution between x_2 and x_1.

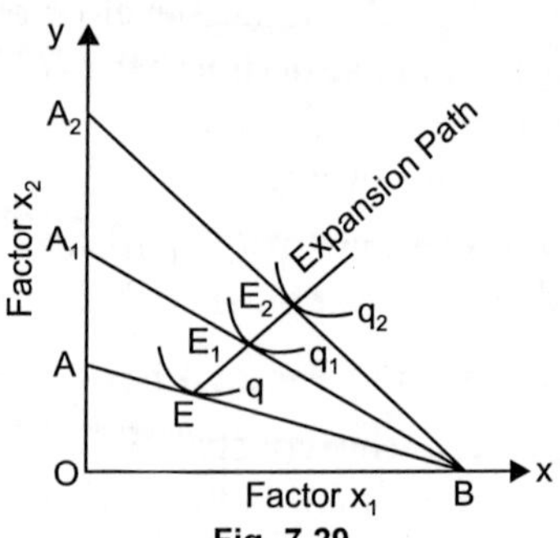

Fig. 7.29

Expansion Path and Production Function

Let us assume that x_1 and x_2 are two factors of production and the prices of x_1 and x_2 are r_1 and r_2 which are fixed.

If the production function is $q = f(x_1, x_2)$ which is homogeneous of degree one, we get, $q = x_1 g\left(\frac{x_2}{x_1}\right)$ where q is the level of output.

$$\therefore \; MPx_1 = \frac{\delta q}{\delta x_1} = g\left(\frac{x_2}{x_1}\right) - \frac{x_2}{x_1} g'\left(\frac{x_2}{x_1}\right)$$

$$MPx_1 = h\left(\frac{x_2}{x_1}\right), \text{(say)}$$

Similarly, $$MPx_2 = g'\left(\frac{x_2}{x_1}\right)$$

Therefore, both the marginal productivities of x_1 and x_2 depend only on the input ratio. In this case, the slopes of the successive isoquants along any ray from the origin remain constant. If we imagine three points, p, p_1 and p_2 successively on the ray OR form the origin, and on each point there are successively three isoquants q, q_1 and q_2 as shown in Fig. 7.30, we get slope of q at p = slope of q_1 at p_1 = slope of q_2 at p_2. Again if we imagine three successive parallel isocost lines AB, CD and EF through the point p, p_1 and p_2, then the ray OR will be expansion path. Each isocost line will be tangent to each isoquant. At any tangency point we know that the slope of isocost line is equal to the slope of isoquant. If r_1 and r_2 be the prices of factors x_1 and x_2, the slope of isocost line is $\frac{r_1}{r_2}$ and the slope of isoquant is $\frac{MPx_1}{MPx_2}$.

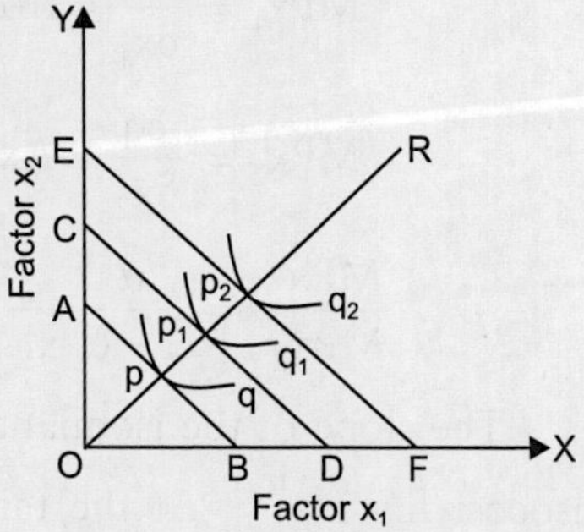

Fig. 7.30

Therefore, $$\frac{MPx_1}{MPx_2} = \frac{r_1}{r_2}$$

$$\text{or,} \qquad \frac{h\left(\frac{x_2}{x_1}\right)}{g'\left(\frac{x_2}{x_1}\right)} = \frac{r_1}{r_2}$$

$$\text{or} \qquad h\left(\frac{x_2}{x_1}\right) = \frac{r_1}{r_2} g'\left(\frac{x_2}{x_1}\right)$$

This is the equation of the expansion path. Clearly this is a equation of a straight line passing through the origin. So the line OR is the expansion path which is a straight line starting from the origin. So it is clear that the input proportion does not change with the expansion of output if input prices are given.

Let us now consider the Cobb-Douglas (C-D) production function as a linear homogeneous production function.

Now the C-D production function is $q = A x_1^{\alpha} x_2^{1-\alpha}$ where A and α are constants.

$$MPx_1 = \frac{\delta q}{\delta x_1} = A\alpha x_1^{\alpha-1} x_2^{1-\alpha}$$

$$MPx_2 = \frac{\delta q}{\delta x_2} = A x_1^{\alpha}(1-\alpha)x_2^{-\alpha} = A(1-\alpha)x_1^{\alpha}x_2^{-\alpha}$$

$$\therefore \frac{MPx_1}{MPx_2} = \frac{\alpha}{1-\alpha}\frac{x_2}{x_1}$$

The slope of the isoquant = $\frac{\alpha}{1-\alpha}\frac{x_2}{x_1}$ and the slope of the isocost line = $\frac{r_1}{r_2}$. At the tangency point between the isocost line and the isoquant, we get slope of the isoquant = slope of the isocost line.

Therefore, $\frac{\alpha}{1-\alpha}\frac{x_2}{x_1} = \frac{r_1}{r_2}$

or, $x_2 = \frac{r_1}{r_2}\frac{(1-\alpha)}{\alpha} x_1$ which is a equation of a straight line starting from the origin. This straight line is nothing but a line of expansion path.

PRODUCTION POSSIBILITY CURVE

Generally, we study production function with two inputs and one output, i.e., output is a function of two inputs. It can be written in functional way that $q = f(x_1, x_2)$ where q is an output produced from two inputs x_1 and x_2.

But some firms can produce two products such as milk and butter using only one input milk. Now let us consider that a producer is producing two products q_1 and q_2 using a single input x. We can express the relationship between the input quantity and the output quantities through a production function as

$$x = g(q_1, q_2)$$

It expresses the cost of production in terms of x as a function of the quantities of the two products, q_1 and q_2. Suppose x is fixed as $x = x_0$ then we have the production function as $x_0 = g(q_1, q_2)$.

The concept of production possibility curve is based on the following assumptions:

(i) The firm has a fixed quantity of an input with which it produces two products in different proportions.

(ii) There is no change in the production technique.

Suppose the firm uses a fixed quantity of input x_0 and produces two products q_1 and q_2 in different proportions.

The production possibility curve shows the locus of different points of combinations of two products q_1 and q_2 that the firm can produce with the fixed input x_0. It shows all possible combinations of two products that can be produced by making full use of given resource and technology in an economy. It is illustrated in the Fig. 7.31, where we plot q_1 along the x-axis and q_2 along the y-axis.

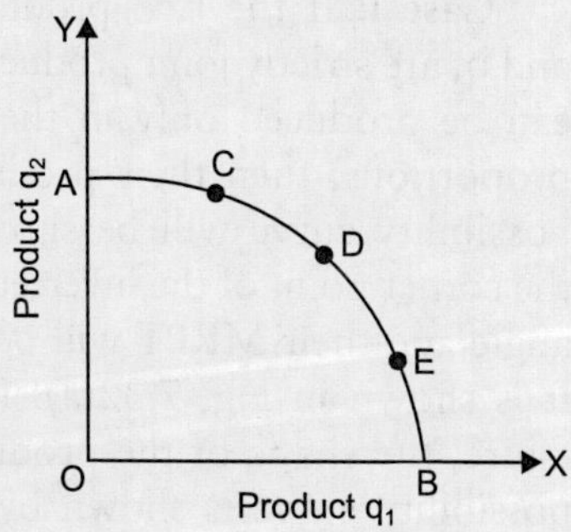

Fig. 7.31

In this figure, the production possibility curve AB is concave towards the origin. It indicates that with the fixed input, the firm can produce either OA quantity of product q_2 and zero quantity of product q_1 or OB quantity of product q_1 and zero quantity of product q_2 or various possible combinations between these two extremes, such as C, D, and E. It is concave which indicates that for every additional unit of product q_1 produced, the sacrifice of product q_2 goes on increasing and *vice versa*. That is why, it is also known as product transformation curve, because, when the firm moves from one point to another point along this curve, it transforms one product into another product by transferring some portion of the fixed input there.

So, this curve not only shows production possibilities but also the rate of transformation of one product into another product when the firm moves from one point to another point along this curve. With given fixed quantity of the input, the rate at which one product is transformed into another is called the marginal rate of product transformation (MRPT). The MRPT at any point on this curve is the slope of this curve at that point. The slope of this curve, i.e., MRPT is always negative, which indicates that to increase the quantity of one product, the firm has to produce less of another product with the fixed amount of that input.

Some exceptions: The production possibility curve is not concave to the origin in the following two cases:

Case I: If the two products q_1 and q_2 are strictly joint products and can be produced only in the fixed proportions, then their production possibility curve will be shown by the corner point of the inverted right angle and their MRPT will be zero. It is shown in Fig. 7.32(a). In this figure, the shape of the production possibility curve is shown by ACB where C shows the fixed quantities of q_1 and q_2 products.

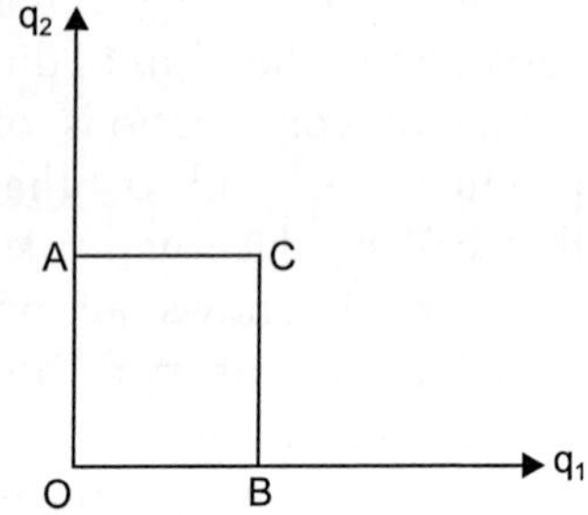

Fig. 7.32(a)

Case II: If the two products are perfect substitutes, the production possibility curve will be a downward sloping straight line as shown in the Fig. 7.32(b). It shows constant rate of product transformation between them, i.e., their MRPT is unity. In this figure, AB is the production possibility curve for the two products q_1 and q_2.

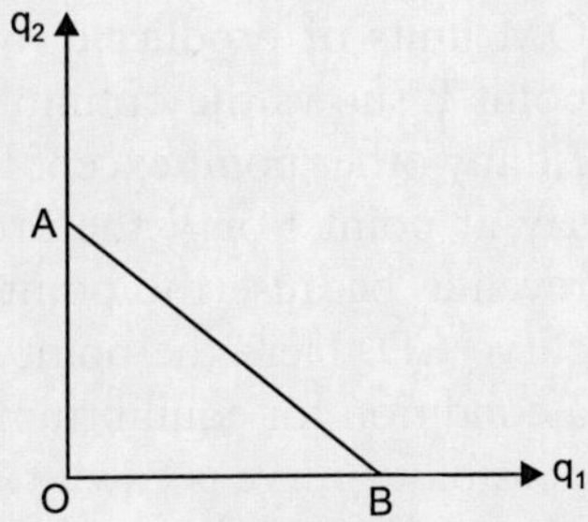

Fig. 7.32(b)

Optimum Combination of Two Products

To find out the optimum combination of two products from the given amount of the input, we need further explanation of the iso-revenue curves. An iso-revenue curve is defined as a straight line curve which shows the equal revenue from all combinations of the two products by selling them. In other words, the iso-revenue curve shows the locus of points of combinations of the two products, q_1 and q_2 yielding the same level of revenue. The higher iso-revenue curve shows the higher level of revenue and *vice versa*. The iso-revenue curve is a downward straight line because the prices of the two products are fixed. The slope of the iso-revenue curve of the two products is their price ratio.

If p_1 and p_2 are the prices of the two products q_1 and q_2 respectively, the slope of iso-revenue curve is equal to $\frac{p_1}{p_2}$.

The objective of the firm is to earn maximum revenue from the selling of the optimum combinations of the two products. The firm will get optimum combination of two products on the production possibility curve at the point where the iso-revenue curve will be tangent to the production possibility curve. This is illustrated in Fig. 7.33. In this figure, the iso-revenue curve EF is tangent to the production possibility curve AB at point P. The point P gives maximum revenue by selling

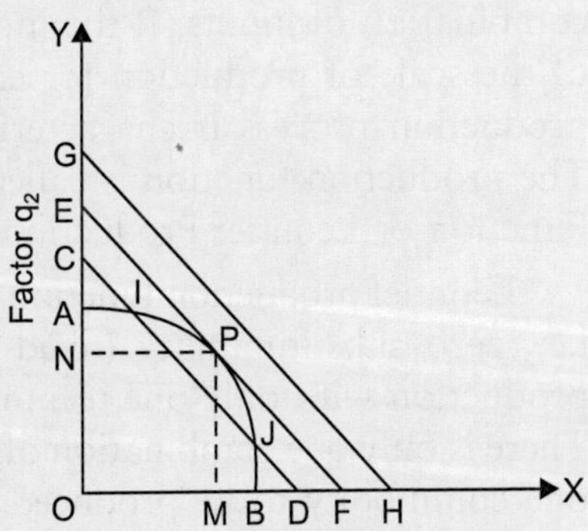

Fig. 7.33

OM units of product q_1 and ON units of product q_2. So, the point P shows the optimum combination of the two products. At any other point except P on the production possibility curve, say at point I or J, the firm will not be able to get maximum revenue because the point I and J lie on a lower iso-revenue curve CD. Here the point P is the equilibrium point where, as a condition for equilibrium, we get that the slope of production possibility curve is equal to the slope of iso-revenue curve. That is, the slope of the production possibility curve AB = MRPT = $\frac{\Delta q_1}{\Delta q_2}$ and the slope of the iso-revenue EF = $\frac{p_1}{p_2}$.

By the condition, we get at point P, $\frac{\Delta q_1}{\Delta q_2} = \frac{p_1}{p_2}$

Thus, the firm is in equilibrium at the point P where the iso-revenue curve EF is tangent to the production possibility curve AB and gets maximum revenue.

LEONTIEF PRODUCTION FUNCTION

There are two broad classes of production function: (i) fixed proportions production function and (ii) variable proportions production function.

A production process is characterized by fixed proportions if each level of output technologically requires a unique combination of inputs. If the input-output ratio is independent of the scale of production for each input-output, such type of production process is characterized by fixed input coefficient. The production function is called Fixed Proportion Production Function or Leontief Production Function.

Leontief production function assumes strict complementarity i.e., zero substitutability (fixed coefficients) of the factors of production with only one technique of producing each output. There is only one combination of the production method for any one commodity to be produced. The isoquant of such type of production function takes the shape of a right angle. This type of production function requires a fixed minimum amount of factors. This production function is named Leontief production function after name of **W. Wassily Leontief** who evolved it first. With the help of this production function, he developed Input-Output Analysis. The input-output analysis is called as the analysis of inter-industry or inter-sector flows or the analysis of inter-industry relations. The production function for each industry is the constant-coefficient type, i.e., fixed proportion type.

This type of production function can be written as $q = \min\left(\frac{x}{a}, \frac{y}{b}\right)$. It implies that q is equal to the minimum of the two ratios $\frac{x}{a}$ and $\frac{y}{b}$. If we have $\frac{x}{a} = \frac{y}{b}$ both the inputs will be fully utilized, but if we have $\frac{x}{a} \neq \frac{y}{b}$ one input is fully utilized, but some amount of the other input will be redundant.

Now if we consider $\frac{x}{a} = \frac{y}{b}$ or $\frac{x}{y} = \frac{a}{b}$ or $x = \left(\frac{a}{b}\right)y$ which is the equation of a straight line passing through the origin. It is shown in Fig. 7.34 where we take x along the x-axis and y along the y-axis. Here this straight line is OC. Now all the points along the line OC satisfy the relation x : y = a : b. As there is fixed proportion between the two factors i.e., there is no possibility of substitution between the two factors, we have only one process of production. In this process we can imagine an L shaped isoquant. In Fig. 7.34, we have shown two isoquants, viz. EFG and HIJ. One isoquant shows one output level. The corner points of the L-shaped isoquants stand on the line OC. At point F on OC where we employ OM units of x and ON units of y and get the output level q_1. If we keep the input x constant at OM units and increase y beyond ON units, total output will not be increased. The excess of y over ON will be redundant. Thus, the output q_1 at any point along EFG will be same, i.e., it will be same at any point either on EF or on FG. So, EFG showing

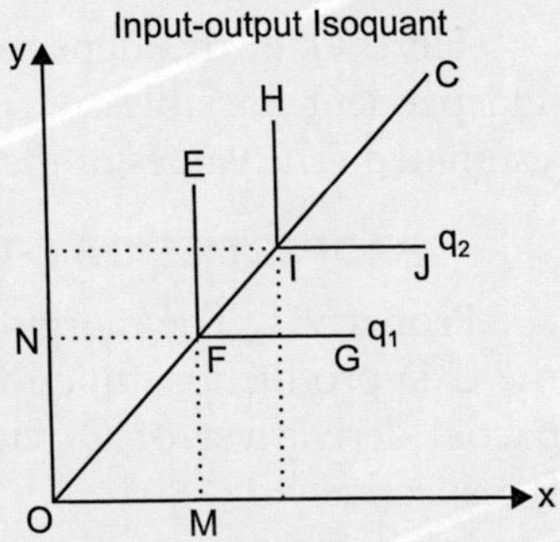

Fig. 7.34

the same level of output on any point of it is an isoquant. For higher output level we have to go to a higher isoquant, like HIJ lying to the right of the initial isoquant. There are only the points F and I where all units of the factors x and y are fully utilized. The producer will always produce at points F and I, i.e., at corner points. This L-shaped isoquant is also called input-output isoquant.

COBB-DOUGLAS PRODUCTION FUNCTION

Cobb-Douglas production function is the familiar form of production function used most frequently in economic research works. This function assumes that output is a function of two factors, viz. capital and labour. In its original version Cobb-Douglas (C-D) production function is a linear homogeneous production function in variables K and L. The general version of the C-D production function is $Q = AK^{\alpha} L^{\beta}$

where, Q is the quantity of output

K is the quantity of capital

L is the quantity of labour

A is the efficiency parameter

α is the elasticity of output with respect to capital

β is the elasticity of output with respect to labour

Here Q is the dependent variable and K and L are the independent variables. A, α and β are the parameters to be estimated. The values of these parameters vary from firm to firm.

PROPERTIES OF C-D PRODUCTION FUNCTION

Property 1. The marginal products of capital and labour in the C-D production function can be obtained by the first order partial derivatives of Q with respect to capital, K and labour, L respectively.

$$\text{Marginal product of capital} = \alpha\left(\frac{Q}{K}\right)$$

$$\text{Marginal product of labour} = \beta\left(\frac{Q}{L}\right)$$

Proof: We have, $Q = AK^{\alpha} L^{\beta}$

$$MP_k = \frac{\delta Q}{\delta K} = \frac{\delta}{\delta K}\left(AK^{\alpha}L^{\beta}\right) = A\alpha K^{\alpha-1}L^{\beta}$$

$$= A\alpha\frac{K^{\alpha}L^{\beta}}{K} = \frac{\alpha\left(AK^{\alpha}L^{\beta}\right)}{K} = \alpha\left(\frac{Q}{K}\right)$$

And $$MP_L = \frac{\delta Q}{\delta L} = \frac{\delta}{\delta L}\left(AK^{\alpha}L^{\beta}\right) = \beta AK^{\alpha}L^{\beta-1}$$

$$= \frac{\beta\left(AK^{\alpha}L^{\beta}\right)}{L} = \beta\left(\frac{Q}{L}\right)$$

$$\therefore MP_k = \alpha\left(\frac{Q}{K}\right)$$

and $$MP_L = \beta\left(\frac{Q}{L}\right)$$

Property 2. C-D production function is a homogeneous function of degree $(\alpha + \beta)$.

If $Q = AK^{\alpha} L^{\beta}$

Suppose new output, $Q^* = A (\lambda K)^{\alpha} (\lambda L)^{\beta}$

$= A\lambda^{\alpha} K^{\alpha} \lambda^{\beta} L^{\beta}$

$= \lambda^{\alpha+\beta} AK^{\alpha} L^{\beta}$

$\therefore$ $= \lambda^{\alpha+\beta} Q$

Therefore, C-D production function is a homogeneous of degree $(\alpha + \beta)$.

Property 3. C-D production function becomes linear in logarithm.

Here, $Q = AK^{\alpha} L^{\beta}$.

Taking logarithm on both the sides, we have

$$\log Q = \log (AK^{\alpha} L^{\beta})$$
$$= \log A + \log K^{\alpha} + \log L^{\beta}$$
$$= \log A + \alpha \log K + \beta \log L$$

Property 4. The value of $(\alpha + \beta)$ is the returns to scale. If the capital (K) and labour (L) are increased by 100%, i.e., doubled, the new production will be

$$Q^1 = A(2K)^{\alpha}(2L)^{\beta}$$
$$= A\,2^{\alpha}K^{\alpha}2^{\beta}L^{\beta}$$
$$= 2^{\alpha+\beta}A\,K^{\alpha}L^{\beta}$$
$$\therefore\ Q^1 = 2^{\alpha+\beta}Q \qquad \text{(where } Q = AK^{\alpha}L^{\beta}\text{)}$$

Case I: If $\alpha + \beta = 1$, $Q^1 = 2\,Q$ output is also doubled and this represent constant returns to scale.

Case II: If $\alpha + \beta > 1$ then, $Q^1 > 2\,Q$, it implies that increase in output is more than 100% and this represents increasing return to scale.

Case III: If $\alpha + \beta < 1$, then $Q^1 < 2\,Q$, it implies that increase in output is less than 100% and this represents diminishing returns to scale.

Property 5. Elasticity of substitution (σ) in C-D production function is equal to one. The elasticity of substitution is defined as:

$$\sigma = \frac{\text{Proportionate change in capital-labour ratio}}{\text{Proportionate change in } MRS_{LK}} = 1$$

Proof:

$$\sigma = \frac{d\,(K/L)/(K/L)}{d\,(MRS_{LK})/MRS_{LK}}$$

$$= \frac{d\,(K/L)}{(K/L)} \times \frac{MRS_{LK}}{d\,(MRS_{LK})}$$

$$= \frac{MRS_{LK}}{(K/L)} \times \frac{d(K/L)}{d\,(MRS_{LK})}$$

where, $MRS_{LK} = \dfrac{MP_L}{MR_K}$

Here, $MP_L = \dfrac{dQ}{dL} = \dfrac{d}{dL}\left(AK^{\alpha}L^{\beta}\right) = A\beta\,K^{\alpha}L^{\beta-1}$

$$= \frac{\beta\,AK^{\alpha}L^{\beta}}{L} = \frac{\beta Q}{L}$$

$$\text{And} \quad MP_K = \frac{dQ}{dK} = \frac{d}{dK}\left(AK^{\alpha}L^{\beta}\right) = A\alpha K^{\alpha-1}L^{\beta}$$

$$= \frac{\alpha A K^{\alpha} L^{\beta}}{K} = \frac{\alpha Q}{K}$$

$$\therefore \quad MRS_{LK} = \frac{MP_L}{MP_K} = \frac{\frac{\beta Q}{L}}{\frac{\alpha Q}{K}} = \frac{\beta Q}{L} \times \frac{K}{\alpha Q} = \frac{\beta}{\alpha}\frac{K}{L}$$

$$\text{Therefore,} \quad \sigma = \frac{(\beta/\alpha)\cdot(K/L)}{K/L}\,\frac{d(K/L)}{d(\beta K/\alpha L)}$$

$$= \frac{\beta/\alpha\,(K/L)}{\beta/\alpha\,(K/L)} \cdot \frac{d\,(K/L)}{d\,(K/L)}$$

$$= 1$$

Property 6. Expansion path generated by the C-D production function is linear and passes through the origin.

We know, under perfect competition at equilibrium,

$$\frac{MP_K}{MP_L} = \frac{P_K}{P_L} \quad \text{... (1)}$$

(where P_K= price of capital and P_L = price of labour)

For the C-D production function, we get

$$MP_K = \frac{\alpha Q}{K}$$

$$\text{and} \quad MP_L = \frac{\beta Q}{L}$$

$$\therefore \quad \frac{MP_K}{MP_L} = \frac{\frac{\alpha Q}{K}}{\frac{\beta Q}{L}} = \frac{\alpha Q}{K} \times \frac{L}{\beta Q} = \frac{\alpha}{\beta}\frac{L}{K}$$

$$\therefore \quad \frac{\alpha L}{\beta K} = \frac{P_K}{P_L} \quad \text{[From (1)]}$$

Or, $\beta P_K K - \alpha P_L L = 0$

This is the form like ax – by = 0, i.e. $y = \frac{\alpha}{\beta}x + c$ which represents the equation of a straight line passing through the origin where c = 0.

The above equation in K and L represents the expansion path generated by the C-D production function and this is a straight line passing through the origin.

Property 7. α and β represent the capital share and labour share of the output respectively.

Under perfect competition at equilibrium, we get

$$P_K = MP_K \cdot P_Q \quad \text{(where } P_Q \text{ is the price of the output and } P_K \text{ is the price of capital)}$$

i.e., $$MP_K = \frac{P_K}{P_Q}$$

or, $$\alpha\frac{Q}{K} = \frac{P_K}{P_Q} \qquad \left[\because MP_K = \alpha\left(\frac{Q}{K}\right)\right]$$

∴ $$\alpha = \frac{K}{Q}\cdot\frac{P_K}{P_Q} = \frac{\text{Value of capital}}{\text{Total income}}$$

$$= \text{Share of capital}$$

Similarly, $$\beta = \frac{L}{Q}\cdot\frac{P_L}{P_Q} = \frac{\text{Value of labour}}{\text{Total income}}$$

$$= \text{Share of labour}$$

Property 8. α and β are the elasticities of output with respect to capital and labour respectively.

$$\text{Elasticity of output with respect to capital} = \frac{\text{Proportionate change in output}}{\text{Proportionate change in capital}}$$

$$= \frac{\Delta Q/Q}{\Delta K/K} = \frac{K}{Q}\frac{\Delta Q}{\Delta K} = \frac{K}{Q}\cdot MP_K$$

Since as limit $\Delta K \to O$, $\frac{\Delta Q}{\Delta K}$ equals to $\frac{\delta Q}{\delta K} = MP_K$

$$\therefore \qquad \frac{K}{Q} MP_K = \frac{K}{Q} \alpha \left(\frac{Q}{K}\right) \left[\because MP_K = \alpha\left(\frac{Q}{K}\right)\right]$$

$$= \frac{K}{Q} \alpha \frac{Q}{K} = \alpha$$

Thus, the elasticity of output with respect to capital is α. Similarly, the elasticity of output with respect to labour is β.

Therefore, α and β are the elasticities of output with respect to capital and labour respectively.

Property 9. C-D production function satisfies the Euler's Theorem when it follows CRS.

Euler's Theorem is $MP_k K + MP_L \cdot L = Q$

According to this theorem, total output Q is exhausted by the distributive shares of all factors when each factor is paid equal to its marginal product. Here MP_K = rate of return on capital (K) and MP_L = Wage rate of labour.

For the C-D production function, we have

$$MP_K = \alpha\left(\frac{Q}{K}\right) \text{and } MP_L = \beta\left(\frac{Q}{L}\right)$$

Therefore, $MP_K \cdot K + MP_L \cdot L = \alpha\left(\frac{Q}{K}\right)K + \beta\left(\frac{Q}{L}\right)L$

$$= \alpha \frac{Q}{K} K + \beta\left(\frac{Q}{L}\right)L$$

$$= \alpha Q + \beta Q$$

or, $\qquad MP_k \cdot K + MP_L \cdot L = (\alpha + \beta) Q$

(where $\alpha + \beta = 1$)

$\therefore \qquad MP_k \cdot K + MP_L \cdot L = Q$

Hence, the Euler's theorem is proved.

Property 10. If one of the inputs is zero, output will be zero. This property states that both the inputs are necessary for production and one input cannot be substituted perfectly for another.

If, K = 0, then, $Q = A K^{\alpha} L^{\beta} = A (0)^{\alpha} L^{\beta} = 0$

Similarly, if L = 0, Q also becomes zero.

Property 11. The marginal product of an input in C-D production function decreases when the quantity of that input rises.

We have,

$$Q = AK^{\alpha} L^{\beta}$$

Now, $$\frac{\delta Q}{\delta K} = \alpha AK^{\alpha-1} L^{\beta}$$

and $$\frac{\delta^2 Q}{\delta K^2} = \alpha(\alpha - 1) AK^{\alpha-2} L^{\beta}$$

Since α is a positive fraction, $(\alpha - 1)$ is negative. Thus, the rate of change of the marginal product of input, K is negative and MP_k declines.

Property 12. The C-D production function in form of logarithm is a type of linearly homogeneous production function which has proved particularly useful for empirical work.

In general, $\log Q = \log A + \alpha \log K + \beta \log L$.

This means that one having a C-D production function can take advantage of the many simplifications in the process of statistical estimation that are possible in the case of a linear relationship.

Property 13. C-D production function helps in finding out the economic viability of a firm.

Under perfect competition, the C-D production function implies that the value of each factor in total revenue is constant and equal to the elasticity of output with respect to that factor. This property of the C-D production function holds only in the case of constant returns to scale.

By fitting the data of a firm/farm in the C-D production function, we can easily find out whether the firm has constant returns to scale at the prevailing level of output or not. If we get so, then the factor shares for the specified factors exhaust the total product, i.e., the output elasticities of the factors add up to unity. It means that the firm is viable. But there are certain limitations to C-D production function analysis. These are discussed below:

(i) It does not take into consideration the relative importance to the input in the production process.

(ii) Owing to practical and institutional difficulties, resources in the agricultural sector cannot be adjusted according to their marginal value productivities.

(iii) Factors are not perfectly mobile. Therefore, factor prices are not determined by a free play of market forces under perfect competition.

(iv) C-D production function does not tell us that which specific practices or resources to be used. At best, it is a broad rough approximation examining resource efficiency.

RETURNS TO SCALE AND HOMOGENEOUS PRODUCTION FUNCTION

The concept of returns to scale can be explained with the help of homogeneous production function.

Suppose, a production function at an initial level of input and output is

$$q_o = f(x, y)$$

If we increase all the factors by the same proportion K^r, we will get a new level of output q which is higher than the original level q_o, i.e.,

$$q = f(k^r x, k^r y)$$

If K^r can be factored out, the new level of output q can be expressed as a function of K^r (to any power r) and the level of output will be

$$q = K^r f(x, y)$$

or $$q = K^r q_o \left[\because q_o = f(x, y)\right]$$

It shows that if the values of inputs x and y are increased by K^r times, the initial level of output q_o will be increased by K^r times. The power r of K is called the degree of homogeneity of the function and is a measure of the returns to scale.

This kind of production function is known as homogeneous production function and in case K^r cannot be factored out, the production function is known as non-homogeneous production function.

Thus, the production function, $q = f(x, y)$ is said to be a homogeneous production function of degree r when the values of each such variables x and y are multiplied by the same number K^r, then the value of the function q_o is multiplied by K^r.

Since r is a measure of the returns to scale, we get following three types of returns to scale depending on the value of it.

If $r = 1$, the production function is homogeneous of degree one and represents constant returns to scale.

If $r > 1$, the production will yield increasing returns to scale.

If $r < 1$, the production will yield decreasing returns to scale.

PROPERTIES OF HOMOGENEOUS PRODUCTION FUNCTION

Homogeneous production function plays an important role in various areas of economic analysis. It is used in Linear Programming Model of Production and Input-Output Theory. It is important in the theory of distribution. Homogeneity of degree zero has a significant place in monetary analysis. So, it has occupied an important place in the field of economics because of having its certain mathematical properties. Some properties of homogeneous production function are discussed below.

Property 1. If $q = f(x, y)$ is a homogeneous production function of degree r, then

$$q = x^r g\left(\frac{y}{x}\right)$$

$$\text{or } q = y^r h\left(\frac{x}{y}\right)$$

Proof: $q = f(x, y)$ is a production function

By definition,

$$K^r q = f(Kx, Ky) \text{ for any value of K} \qquad \dots (1)$$

Putting $K = \dfrac{1}{x}$ in (1),

$$\therefore \quad \left(\frac{1}{x}\right)^r q = f\left(1, \frac{y}{x}\right)$$

$$\text{or,} \quad q = x^r g\left(\frac{y}{x}\right) \qquad \text{(Proved)}$$

Again putting $K = \dfrac{1}{y}$ in (1),

$$\therefore \quad \left(\frac{1}{y}\right)^r q = f\left(\frac{x}{y}, 1\right)$$

$$\text{or,} \quad q = y^r f\left(\frac{x}{y}, 1\right)$$

$$\text{or,} \quad q = y^r h\left(\frac{x}{y}\right) \qquad \text{(Proved)}$$

Property 2. If a production function is homogeneous of degree r, the marginal product of each input will be homogeneous function of degree, i.e., r – 1.

Proof: Suppose, the production function is $q = f(x, y)$ which is homogeneous of degree r. By definition,

$K^r q = f(Kx, Ky)$ for any value of K

Putting $K = \dfrac{1}{x}$

$$\therefore \quad \left(\frac{1}{x}\right)^r q = f\left(1, \frac{y}{x}\right) \text{or, } q = x^r f\left(1, \frac{y}{x}\right)$$

$$\text{or,} \quad q = x^r g\left(\frac{y}{x}\right)$$

We know, the marginal productivity (MP) of x is $\dfrac{\delta q}{\delta x}$.

$$\therefore \quad \frac{\delta q}{\delta x} = r x^{r-1} g\left(\frac{y}{x}\right) - x^r g'\left(\frac{y}{x}\right)\frac{y}{x^2}$$

$$= r x^{r-1} g\left(\frac{y}{x}\right) \quad x^{r-2} g'\left(\frac{y}{x}\right) y$$

$$= x^{r-1}\left[r g\left(\frac{y}{x}\right) - \frac{y}{x} g'\left(\frac{y}{x}\right)\right]$$

$$\therefore \quad \frac{\delta q}{\delta x} = x^{r-1} h\left(\frac{y}{x}\right) \qquad \dots (1)$$

Again, the marginal productivity (MP) of y is $\frac{\delta q}{\delta y}$

$$\therefore \quad \frac{\delta q}{\delta y} = x^{r} g'\left(\frac{y}{x}\right) \cdot \frac{1}{x}$$

$$\text{or,} \quad \frac{\delta q}{\delta y} = x^{r-1} g'\left(\frac{y}{x}\right) \qquad \dots (2)$$

Equations (1) and (2) represent the MPs of x and y respectively. Both are homogeneous function of degree (r – 1). It tells us that if the production function is homogeneous of degree r, the MPs will also be homogeneous function of degree (r – 1).

Property 3. Homogeneous production function satisfies the Euler's Theorem. **Euler's Theorem** states that total output equals the MP of x multiplied by its quantity plus the MP of y multiplied by its quantity when the firm is using two inputs x and y.

$$\text{That is,} \quad \frac{\delta q}{\delta x} x + \frac{\delta q}{\delta y} y = q \qquad \dots (1)$$

where the degree of homogeneity of the homogeneous production function is one.

$$\text{And} \quad \frac{\delta q}{\delta x} x + \frac{\delta q}{\delta y} y = rq \qquad \dots (2)$$

where r is the degree of homogeneity of the homogeneous production function.

Proof: Let q = *f* (x, y) is a homogeneous production function of degree one.

We have to prove $\frac{\delta q}{\delta x} x + \frac{\delta q}{\delta y} y = q$

From property 1, we have $q = x^r g\left(\frac{y}{x}\right)$

Now if degree r = 1, then $q = xg\left(\frac{y}{x}\right)$

$$\text{Now} \quad \frac{\delta q}{\delta x} = x^{1-1}g\left(\frac{y}{x}\right) - xg'\left(\frac{y}{x}\right)\frac{y}{x^2}$$

$$= x^0 g\left(\frac{y}{x}\right) - x^{1-2}g'\left(\frac{y}{x}\right)y$$

$$= g\left(\frac{y}{x}\right) - x^{-1}g'\left(\frac{y}{x}\right)y$$

$$\text{and} \quad \frac{\delta q}{\delta y} = xg'\left(\frac{y}{x}\right)\frac{1}{x} = g'\left(\frac{y}{x}\right)$$

$$\therefore \quad \frac{\delta q}{\delta x}x + \frac{\delta q}{\delta y}y = \left[g\left(\frac{y}{x}\right) - x^{-1}g'\left(\frac{y}{x}\right)y\right]x + g'\left(\frac{y}{x}\right)y$$

$$= xg\left(\frac{y}{x}\right) - yg'\left(\frac{y}{x}\right) + yg'\left(\frac{y}{x}\right)$$

$$= xg\left(\frac{y}{x}\right) = q$$

$$\therefore \quad \frac{\delta q}{\delta x}x + \frac{\delta q}{\delta y}y = q$$

This proves **Euler's Theorem** when the degree of homogeneity is one.

Now, we shall prove it when degree of homogeneity is r.

From property 1, we have

$$q = x^r g\left(\frac{y}{x}\right)$$

$$\text{Now} \quad \frac{\delta q}{\delta x} = rx^{r-1}g\left(\frac{y}{x}\right) - x^r g'\left(\frac{y}{x}\right)\frac{y}{x^2}$$

$$= rx^{r-1}g\left(\frac{y}{x}\right) - x^{r-2}g'\left(\frac{y}{x}\right)y$$

and $\quad \dfrac{\delta q}{\delta y} = x^r g'\left(\dfrac{y}{x}\right)\dfrac{1}{x} = x^{r-1} g'\left(\dfrac{y}{x}\right)$

$$\therefore \quad \frac{\delta q}{\delta x}x + \frac{\delta q}{\delta y}y = r x^r g\left(\frac{y}{x}\right) - x^{r-1} g'\left(\frac{y}{x}\right)y + x^{r-1} g'\left(\frac{y}{x}\right)y$$

$$= r x^r g\left(\frac{y}{x}\right) = rq$$

$$\therefore \quad \frac{\delta q}{\delta x}x + \frac{\delta q}{\delta x}y = rq$$

This proves **Euler's Theorem.** This is very useful in the theory of distribution. If the production function involves more than two inputs, i.e., $q = f\ (x, y, \ldots\ldots, z)$ and is homogeneous of degree r, then it can be proved likewise that

$$\frac{\delta q}{\delta x}x + \frac{\delta q}{\delta y}y + \ldots\ldots + \frac{\delta q}{\delta z}z = rq$$

Property 4. Given two functions of the same variables, the first of which is homogeneous of degree s and the second homogeneous of degree t, then a third function obtained by dividing the first function by the second will be homogeneous of degree s – t.

Proof: From the property –1, we get

$$q_1 = x^s g_1\left(\frac{y}{x}\right) \text{and } q_2 = x^t g_2\left(\frac{y}{x}\right)$$

Dividing the first by the second, we get

$$\frac{q_1}{q_2} = \frac{x^s}{x^t}\,\frac{g_1\left(\frac{y}{x}\right)}{g_2\left(\frac{y}{x}\right)}$$

$q = x^{s-t} g\left(\dfrac{y}{x}\right)$ which is a homogeneous of degree s – t. If in particular s = t, the function obtained by this division process will be homogeneous of degree zero, i.e., multiplication of each variable by R will leave the value of the new function totally unaffected.

Property 5. For any homogeneous production function in two input variables, the expansion path will be a ray.

Property 6. If the production function is homogeneous of any degree s, then along any ray (straight line through the origin) the slopes of all the isoproduct curves will be identical.

Property 7. Linear Homogeneous Production Function: In any homogeneous production function, if the degree of homogeneity is equal to one, i.e., r = 1, the production function is known as linear homogeneous production function. This type of production function will always represent the operation of constant returns to scale. Generally, the marginal product of factors under this production function is constant. Mathematically, linear homogeneous production function may be defined as follows:

If $q = f(x, y)$ is a production function, $q = x^r g\left(\frac{x}{y}\right)$ is a homogeneous production function of degree r.

Now if r = 1, then $q = x\, g\left(\frac{x}{y}\right)$ is a linear homogeneous production function.

That is, if $q = f(x, y)$, then $f(kx, ky) = k\, f(x, y)$

Or, $f(kx, ky) = kq$ for any value of k.

The linear homogeneous production function has the following properties:

(i) One isoquant is sufficient to deduce all other isoquants because it obeys the constant returns to scale. Here the distance between the origin and the first isoquant will be equal to that between any two consecutive isoquants.

(ii) If the isoquants are convex, the marginal productivity will be diminishing and the two factors will be complements to each other.

CONSTANT ELASTICITY OF SUBSTITUTION (C.E.S.) PRODUCTION FUNCTION

One of the crucial implications of a production function is the degree of elasticity of substitution between two inputs.

For a long time, the theory of production had focused on two convenient values for the elasticity of substitution (σ). These two values are σ = 1 and σ = 0. In **Cobb-Douglas** production function with constant returns to scale, the value of σ is one. On the other extreme, in the **Leontief** input-output production function, the value of σ is zero. In many cases, the value of elasticity of substitution of a production function may be constant but not necessarily be equal to one or zero. The constant elasticity of substitution (C.E.S.) production function assumes that the elasticity of substitution is a constant. The form of the C.E.S. production function is

$$Q = A\left[\delta k^{-\rho} + (1-\partial)\, L^{-\rho}\right]^{\frac{-1}{\rho}}$$

where, Q = output, L = labour, K = capital, A = efficiency parameter (A > 0), δ = distribution parameter or capital intensity coefficient (0 < ∂ < 1), (1 – ∂) = labour intensity co-efficient and ρ = substitution parameter (ρ ≥ – 1).

PROPERTIES OF C.E.S. PRODUCTION FUNCTION

Property 1: The C.E.S. production function is linearly homogeneous or homogeneous of degree one, i.e., the production function always obeys the law of constant returns to scale. This can be proved in the following way:

Proof: The original form is $Q = A\left[\partial k^{-\rho} + (1-\partial)\, L^{-\rho}\right]^{\frac{-1}{\rho}}$

Now if we increase both the factors, labour and capital in a fixed proportion, say λ, then the output will be increased by the same proportion according to this property.

$$\text{Now,} \quad Q^* = A\left[\partial(\lambda k)^{-\rho} + (1-\partial)(\lambda L)^{-\rho}\right]^{\frac{-1}{\rho}}$$

$$= A\left[\lambda^{-\rho}\partial k^{-\rho} + \lambda^{-\rho}(1-\partial)L^{-\rho}\right]^{\frac{-1}{\rho}}$$

$$= A\left[\lambda^{-\rho}\left\{\partial k^{-\rho} + (1-\partial)L^{-\rho}\right\}\right]^{\frac{-1}{\rho}}$$

$$= A\lambda^{-\rho\frac{-1}{\rho}}\left[\partial k^{-\rho} + (1-\partial)L^{-\rho}\right]^{\frac{-1}{\rho}}$$

$$= \lambda A\left[\partial k^{-\rho} + (1-\partial)L^{-\rho}\right]^{\frac{-1}{\rho}}$$

$$\therefore \quad Q^* = \lambda Q$$

Therefore, this proves that the C.E.S. production function obeys the law of constant returns to scale.

Property 2: The MPP_K and MPP_L equations or functions are homogeneous of degree zero, i.e., if we increase both the factors L and K by a fixed proportion, say λ, in the MPP_K and MPP_L function, then the MPP_K and MPP_L will be unaltered where MPP_K is marginal physical productivity of capital and MPP_L is marginal physical productivity of labour.

Proof: The original form of C.E.S. production function is

$$Q = A\left[\partial k^{-\rho} + (1-\partial)L^{-\rho}\right]^{\frac{-1}{\rho}}$$

$$MPP_K = \frac{\partial Q}{\partial K}$$

$$= \left(-\frac{1}{\rho}\right)A\left[\partial k^{-\rho} + (1-\partial)L^{-\rho}\right]^{\frac{-1}{\rho}-1}\partial(-\rho)K^{-\rho-1}$$

$$\therefore \quad MPP_K = A\left[\partial k^{-\rho} + (1-\partial)L^{-\rho}\right]^{\frac{-1}{\rho}-1}\partial K^{-\rho-1}$$

Now, if we increase k (capital) and L (labour) by λ proportion, we get

$$\left(\frac{\partial Q}{\partial K}\right)^* = A\left[\partial(\lambda k)^{-\rho} + (1-\partial)(\lambda L)^{-\rho}\right]^{\frac{-1}{\rho}-1}\partial(\lambda K)^{-\rho-1}$$

$$= A\left[\lambda^{-\rho}\partial k^{-\rho} + \lambda^{-\rho}(1-\partial)L^{-\rho}\right]^{\frac{-1}{\rho}-1}\lambda^{-\rho-1}\partial K^{-\rho-1}$$

$$= \left(\lambda^{-\rho}\right)^{\frac{-1}{\rho}-1}A\left[\partial k^{-\rho} + (1-\partial)L^{-\rho}\right]^{\frac{-1}{\rho}-1}\lambda^{-\rho-1}\partial K^{-\rho-1}$$

$$= \left(\lambda^{+1+\rho-\rho-1}\right)A\left[\partial k^{-\rho} + (1-\partial)L^{-\rho}\right]^{\frac{-1}{\rho}-1}\partial K^{-\rho-1}$$

$$\therefore \left(\frac{\partial Q}{\partial K}\right)^* = \lambda^0 \frac{\partial Q}{\partial K} = \frac{\partial Q}{\partial K} \text{ showing no change}$$

Similarly,

$$MPP_L = \frac{\partial Q}{\partial L} = \left(-\frac{1}{\rho}\right) A\left[\partial k^{-\rho} + (1-\partial)L^{-\rho}\right]^{\frac{-1}{\rho}-1} \times (1-\partial)(-\rho)L^{-\rho-1}$$

$$\therefore \quad MPP_L = \frac{\partial Q}{\partial L} = A\left[\partial k^{-\rho} + (1-\partial)L^{-\rho}\right]^{-\frac{1}{\rho}-1} \times (1-\partial)L^{-\rho-1}$$

Now, we increase K and L by λ proportion, we get

$$\left(\frac{\partial Q}{\partial L}\right)^* = A\left[\partial(\lambda k)^{-\rho} + (1-\partial)(\lambda L)^{-\rho}\right]^{\frac{-1}{\rho}-1} (1-\partial)(\lambda K)^{-\rho-1}$$

$$= A\left[\lambda^{-\rho}\partial k^{-\rho} + \lambda^{-\rho}(1-\partial)L^{-\rho}\right]^{\frac{-1}{\rho}-1} \lambda^{-\rho-1}(1-\partial)L^{-\rho-1}$$

$$= \left(\lambda^{-\rho}\right)^{\frac{-1}{\rho}-1} A\left[\partial k^{-\rho} + (1-\partial)L^{-\rho}\right]^{-\frac{1}{\rho}-1} (1-\partial)L^{-\rho-1}\lambda^{-\rho-1}$$

$$= \left(\lambda^{+1+\rho-\rho-1}\right) A\left[\partial k^{-\rho} + (1-\partial)L^{-\rho}\right]^{-\frac{1}{\rho}-1} (1-\partial)L^{-\rho-1}$$

$$\therefore \left(\frac{\partial Q}{\partial L}\right)^* = \lambda^0 \frac{\partial Q}{\partial L} = \frac{\partial Q}{\partial L} \text{ showing no change.}$$

Therefore, MPP_K and MPP_L are homogeneous of degree zero.

Property 3: The C.E.S. production function satisfies the **Euler's Theorem** or 'Adding up' problem or 'Product Exhaustion Theorem'. **Euler's Theorem** states that if all the factors are paid according to their respective marginal productivities, then the total product will be exhausted among the factors of production.

Proof: C.E.S. Production Function is

$$Q = A\left[\partial k^{-\rho} + (1-\partial)L^{-\rho}\right]^{\frac{-1}{\rho}}$$

Now the Euler's form is $\frac{\partial Q}{\partial K}K + \frac{\partial Q}{\partial L}L = Q$

$$\therefore \quad \frac{\partial Q}{\partial K} = \left(\frac{-1}{\rho}\right)A\left[\partial k^{-\rho} + (1-\partial)L^{-\rho}\right]^{-\frac{1}{\rho}-1} \times -\rho\partial K^{-\rho-1}$$

$$= A\left[\partial k^{-\rho} + (1-\partial)L^{-\rho}\right]^{-\frac{1}{\rho}-1} \partial K^{-\rho-1}$$

$$\therefore \quad \frac{\partial Q}{\partial L} = \left(\frac{-1}{\rho}\right)A\left[\partial k^{-\rho} + (1-\partial)L^{-\rho}\right]^{-\frac{1}{\rho}-1} \times -\rho\,(1-\partial)\,L^{-\rho-1}$$

$$= A\left[\partial k^{-\rho} + (1-\partial)L^{-\rho}\right]^{-\frac{1}{\rho}-1}(1-\partial)L^{-\rho-1}$$

Now,

$$\frac{\partial Q}{\partial K}K + \frac{\partial Q}{\partial L}L = A\left[\partial k^{-\rho} + (1-\partial)L^{-\rho}\right]^{-\frac{1}{\rho}-1} \times \partial K^{-\rho-1}K + A\left[\partial A^{-\rho} + (1-\partial)L^{-\rho}\right]^{-\frac{1}{\rho}-1} \times (1-\partial)L^{-\rho-1} \times L$$

$$= A\left[\partial k^{-\rho} + (1-\partial)L^{-\rho}\right]^{-\frac{1}{\rho}-1} \times \left[\partial K^{-\rho-1+1} + (1-\partial)L^{-\rho-1+1}\right]$$

$$= A\left[\partial k^{-\rho} + (1-\partial)L^{-\rho}\right]^{-\frac{1}{\rho}-1} \times \left[\partial K^{-\rho} + (1-\partial)L^{-\rho}\right]$$

$$= A\left[\partial k^{-\rho} + (1-\partial)L^{-\rho}\right]^{-\frac{1}{\rho}-1+1} = Q$$

$$\therefore \frac{\partial Q}{\partial K} K + \frac{\partial Q}{\partial L} L = Q$$

Therefore, if all the factors are paid according to their respective marginal productivities, then the total product is exhausted among the factors of production. Hence, **Euler's Theorem** is proved.

Property 4: The elasticity of substitution of C.E.S. production function is a constant and in this particular form it is,

$$\sigma = \frac{1}{1+\rho}$$

The σ is defined as the ratio of proportionate change of the input ratio to proportionate change of the MRTS's ratio.

Proof: According to formula,

$$\sigma = \frac{\dfrac{\partial(K/L)}{(K/L)}}{\dfrac{\partial(MRTS_{LK})}{(MRTS_{LK})}}$$

$$\sigma = \frac{\dfrac{\partial(K/L)}{(K/L)}}{\dfrac{\partial(F_L/F_K)}{(F_L/F_K)}} \qquad \left[\text{Since, } MRTS_{LK} = \frac{F_L}{F_K}\right]$$

Here,

$$\frac{F_L}{F_K} = \frac{\partial Q/\partial L}{\partial Q/\partial k} \frac{\left(-\dfrac{1}{\rho}\right) A\left[\partial k^{-\rho} + (1-\partial)L^{-\rho}\right]^{\frac{-1}{\rho}-1}(1-\partial)L^{-\rho-1}}{\left(-\dfrac{1}{\rho}\right) A\left[\partial k^{-\rho} + (1-\partial)L^{-\rho}\right]^{-\frac{1}{\rho}-1}\partial k^{-\rho-1}}$$

where $F_L = MPP_L = \dfrac{\partial Q}{\partial L}$ and $F_K = MPP_K = \dfrac{\partial Q}{\partial K}$

$$\therefore \quad \frac{F_L}{F_K} = \frac{(1-\partial)}{\partial}\left(\frac{L}{K}\right)^{-\rho-1} = \frac{(1-\partial)}{\partial}\left(\frac{K}{L}\right)^{\rho+1}$$

Now,

$$\sigma = \frac{\dfrac{\partial\left(\dfrac{K}{L}\right)}{\left(\dfrac{K}{L}\right)}}{\dfrac{\partial\left(\dfrac{1-\partial}{\partial}\right)\left(\dfrac{K}{L}\right)^{\rho+1}}{\left(\dfrac{1-\partial}{\partial}\right)\left(\dfrac{K}{L}\right)^{\rho+1}}} = \frac{\dfrac{\partial\left(\dfrac{K}{L}\right)}{\left(\dfrac{K}{L}\right)}}{\dfrac{\partial\left(\dfrac{K}{L}\right)^{\rho+1}}{\left(\dfrac{K}{L}\right)^{\rho+1}}}$$

$$= \frac{\partial\left(\dfrac{K}{L}\right)}{\left(\dfrac{K}{L}\right)} \times \frac{\left(\dfrac{K}{L}\right)^{\rho+1}}{\partial\left(\dfrac{K}{L}\right)^{\rho+1}} = \left(\frac{K}{L}\right)^{\rho+1-1} \frac{\partial\left(\dfrac{K}{L}\right)}{\partial\left(\dfrac{K}{L}\right)^{\rho+1}}$$

$$= \left(\frac{K}{L}\right)^{\rho} \frac{1}{\dfrac{\partial\left(\dfrac{K}{L}\right)^{\rho+1}}{\partial\left(\dfrac{K}{L}\right)}} = \left(\frac{K}{L}\right)^{\rho} \frac{1}{(\rho+1)\left(\dfrac{K}{L}\right)^{\rho+1-1}}$$

$$\therefore \qquad \sigma = \frac{1}{(\rho+1)}$$

So, σ (elasticity of substitution) of the C.E.S. production function bears a constant value which is equal to $\frac{1}{\rho+1}$.

Property 5: The isoquants generated by the C.E.S. production function are always negatively sloped and strictly convex to the origin for the positive values of K and L. This will be proved if we can prove that

$$\frac{\partial K}{\partial L} < 0 \text{ and } \frac{\partial^2 K}{\partial L^2} > 0$$

Proof: Now,

$$\frac{\partial K}{\partial L} = -\frac{\frac{\partial Q}{\partial L}}{\frac{\partial Q}{\partial K}}$$

$$= -\frac{\left(\frac{1}{-\rho}\right)A\left[\partial k^{-\rho} + (1-\partial)L^{-\rho}\right]^{-\frac{1}{\rho}-1}(-\rho)(1-\partial)L^{-\rho-1}}{\left(\frac{1}{-\rho}\right)A\left[\partial k^{-\rho} + (1-\partial)L^{-\rho}\right]^{-\frac{1}{\rho}-1}(-\rho)\partial k^{-\rho-1}}$$

$$= -\frac{(1-\partial)}{\partial}\frac{L^{-\rho-1}}{K^{-\rho-1}}$$

$$= -\frac{(1-\partial)}{\partial}\left(\frac{K}{L}\right)^{\rho+1}$$

$\therefore \quad \frac{\partial K}{\partial L} = -\text{ve}$ as ∂ and $(1 - \partial) > 0$.

It implies that the C.E.S. production function is a negative slope curve as the value of $\frac{\partial K}{\partial L}$ is negative.

Again, we will prove that $\frac{\partial^2 K}{\partial L^2} > 0$.

Now,

$$\frac{\partial K}{\partial L} = -\frac{(1-\partial)}{\partial}\left(\frac{K}{L}\right)^{\rho+1}$$

$$\frac{\partial^2 K}{\partial L^2} = \frac{\partial}{\partial L}\left(\frac{\partial K}{\partial L}\right) = -\frac{(1-\partial)}{\partial}(\rho+1)\left(\frac{K}{L}\right)^{\rho+1-1} \times -\frac{K}{L^2}$$

$$\therefore \quad \frac{\partial^2 K}{\partial L^2} = +\frac{(1-\partial)}{\partial}(\rho+1)\left(\frac{K}{L}\right)^{\rho}\frac{K}{L^2} > 0$$

as $(1 - \partial) > 0$, since $0 < \partial < 1$.

The positive value of $\frac{\partial^2 K}{\partial L^2}$ shows that the isoquants generated by C.E.S. production function is convex to the origin.

Property 6: The C.E.S. production function represents a family of production functions which include the special cases, i.e., linear production function, input-output production function and Cobb-Douglas production function for different values of ρ.

Proof: For different extreme values of ρ, we get three different types of production function for three different values of ρ, we get three different shapes of isoquants.

Here C.E.S. production function is

$$Q = A\left[\partial K^{-\rho} + (1-\partial)L^{-\rho}\right]^{-\frac{1}{\rho}}$$

(i) When ρ = –1, then we get

$$Q = A\left[\partial K + (1-\partial)L\right]$$

$$\therefore \quad \partial K + (1-\partial)L = \frac{Q}{A}$$

$$\text{or,} \quad \frac{\partial K}{\frac{Q}{A}} + \frac{(1-\partial)L}{\frac{Q}{A}} = 1$$

$$\text{or,} \quad \frac{K}{\frac{\frac{Q}{A}}{\partial}} + \frac{L}{\frac{\frac{Q}{A}}{1-\partial}} = 1$$

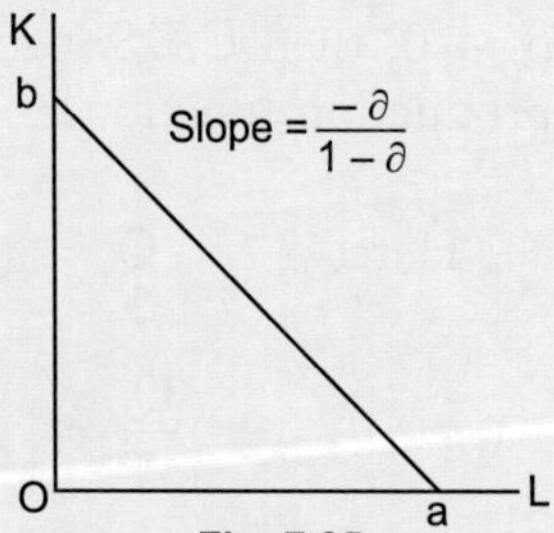

Fig. 7.35

This is equation of a straight line in the form of $\frac{x}{a} + \frac{y}{b} = 1$ which intercepts X-axis at a distance of oa and Y-axis at a distance of ob. This is shown in Fig. 7.35. Thus, it implies a linear downward production function.

$$\text{Again, } \sigma = \frac{1}{1+\rho} = \frac{1}{0} = \infty \text{ when } \rho = -1$$

It implies that certain slight change in wage and interest would lead to continuous changes in K and L.

(ii) When ρ = ∞, then we get σ = 0 showing the case of **Leontief's** input-output production function (fixed coefficient production function).

That is, $Q = \min.\left(\frac{L}{a}, \frac{K}{b}\right)$

In this production function, there is no scope for substitution between labour and capital as $\sigma = 0$. Production is done always at corner point shown in Fig. 7.36.

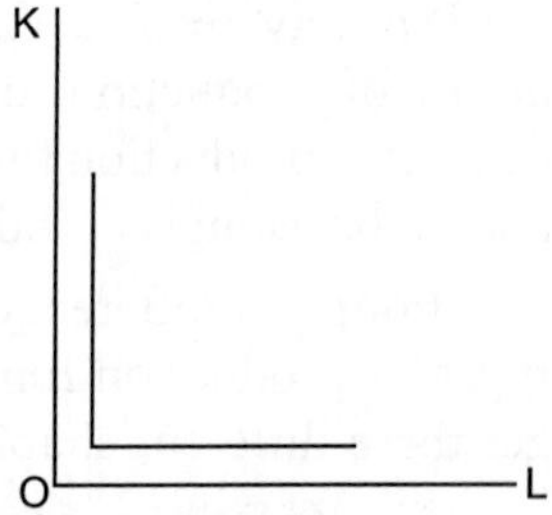

Fig. 7.36

(iii) When $\rho = 0$, $\sigma = 1$ which is the characteristics of the **Cobb-Douglas** production function. This suggests that the (linearly homogeneous) **Cobb-Douglas** production function is a special case of (linearly homogeneous) C.E.S. production function. But the difficulty is that, when $\rho = 0$, then the C.E.S. production function is undefined because of division by zero. Nevertheless, we can show that as $\rho \to 0$, then C.E.S. production function $\to$ the **Cobb-Douglas** production function.

Here,
$$Q = A\left[\partial k^{-\rho} + (1-\partial)L^{-\rho}\right]^{\frac{-1}{\rho}}$$

$$\frac{Q}{A} = \left[\partial k^{-\rho} + (1-\partial)L^{-\rho}\right]^{\frac{-1}{\rho}}$$

$$\log\left(\frac{Q}{A}\right) = -\frac{1}{\rho}\log\left[\partial k^{-\rho} + (1-\partial)L^{-\rho}\right]$$

$$\log\left(\frac{Q}{A}\right) = \underset{\rho\to 0}{\text{Lt}}\ \frac{-\log\left[\partial k^{-\rho} + (1-\partial)L^{-\rho}\right]}{\rho}\quad\left[\frac{0}{0}\text{ form}\right]$$

Applying L-Hospital rule, we get

$$\log\left(\frac{Q}{A}\right) = \underset{\rho\to 0}{\text{Lt}}\ \frac{-\frac{\partial}{\partial\rho}\left[\partial k^{-\rho} + (1-\partial)L^{-\rho}\right]}{\left[\partial k^{-\rho} + (1-\partial)L^{-\rho}\right]}$$

$$= \underset{\rho\to 0}{\text{Lt}}\ \frac{-\left[-\partial k^{-\rho}\log K - (1-\partial)L^{-\rho}\log L\right]}{\left[\partial k^{-\rho} + (1-\partial)L^{-\rho}\right]}$$

$$\left[\text{Where } \frac{d}{dx}\left(a^x\right) = a^x \log a\right]$$

$$= \frac{+\left[\partial \log K + (1-\partial) \log L\right]}{\partial + 1 - \partial}$$

$$= \log K^{\partial} + \log L^{(\partial - 1)}$$

Or, $\log \frac{Q}{A} = \log K^{\partial} L^{\partial - 1}$

Or, $\frac{Q}{A} = K^{\partial} L^{\partial - 1}$

$\therefore$ $Q = AK^{\partial} L^{\partial - 1}$

It is implies **Cobb-Douglas** production function.

Now, if we put $\rho = 0$ in the elasticity of substitution of C.E.S. production function, we get the elasticity of substitution of **Cobb-Douglas** production function. That is, $\partial = \frac{1}{1+\rho} = \frac{1}{1+0} = 1$ which is the elasticity of substation of **Cobb-Douglas** production function.

Thus, the C.E.S. production function represents a family of production functions within the values of $0 \leq \sigma \leq \propto$ that include the special cases shown in Fig. 7.37.

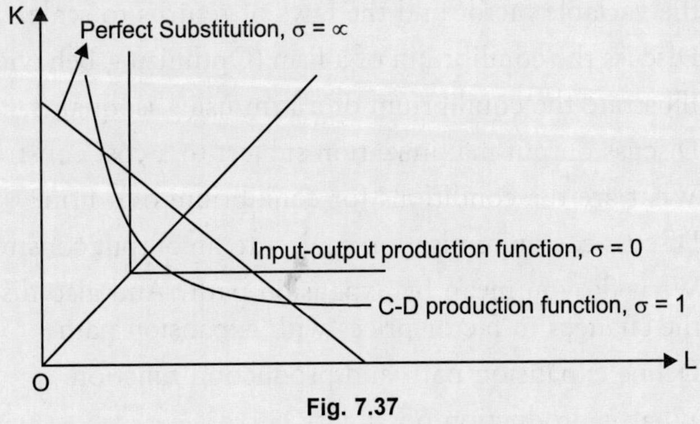

Fig. 7.37

EXERCISES

1. Define Production Function.
2. What do you mean Isoquant (Equal product curve)?
3. What are the properties of isoquant?
4. Explain the exceptional cases to the normal shape of isoquant.
5. What is the diminishing Marginal Rate of Technical Substitution (MRTS)?
6. Explain the relationship between average and marginal productivity.
7. Explain the laws of production.
8. What are the law of variable proportions? Explain it with its different stages.
9. Explain returns to scale and also its three phases.
10. Explain graphical presentation of the three phases of returns to scale for a homogeneous production function with the application of Isoquants.
11. Explain the laws of production or laws of returns.
12. Explain the causes of the Operation of Law of Diminishing Returns. Why does this law specially apply to agriculture?
13. What are the limitations of the Law of Diminishing Returns? What are the importances of this law?
14. What are the differences between the laws of returns to the variable factor and the laws of returns to scale?
15. Discuss the equilibrium of a firm (Optimizing Behaviour).
16. Illustrate the equilibrium of a firm using isoquants.
17. Discuss output maximization subject to a cost constraint.
18. What are the conditions for equilibrium of a firm?
19. Discuss cost minimisation subject to an output constraint.
20. What do you mean by expansion path? And also discuss the changes in factor prices with expansion path.
21. Define expansion path and production function.
22. What is production possibility curve?

23. Define Leontief production function with its properties.
24. Define Cobb-Douglas production function with its properties.
25. Prove that C-D production function satisfies the Euler's Theorem.
26. Explain if one of the inputs is zero, output will be zero. This property states that both the inputs are necessary for production and one input cannot be substituted perfectly for another in C-D production function.
27. Explain returns to scale and homogeneous production function.
28. Discuss the properties of homogeneous production function.
29. Define constant elasticity of substitution (C.E.S.) production function.
30. Discuss the properties of C.E.S. production function.
31. Prove that C.E.S. production function represents a family of production functions which include the special cases, i.e., linear production function, input-output production function and Cobb-Douglas production function for different values of ρ (substitution parameter).

Chapter 8

Theory of Cost

SHORT RUN COST AND LONG RUN COST

Short run is a period of time during which a firm can vary its output by varying only the amount of variable factors, such as labour, raw materials, etc. but not by varying the fixed factors, such as capital equipment, management personnel, etc. The cost relating to short run is called short run cost. In the short run a firm employs two types of factors—fixed factor and variable factor. Hence, the cost corresponding to fixed factor is called fixed cost and cost corresponding to variable factor is called variable cost. In the short run we get total fixed cost, total variable cost, total cost, average fixed cost, average variable cost, average cost and marginal cost.

Long run is a period of time during which a producer gets enough time to change the scale of production through an adjustment of the quantity of the various factors employed. The quantity of all the factors can be increased or decreased according to the requirements of production. Thus in the long run, all factors are variable. There is nothing like fixed factor. If the scale of production is to be expanded, new building can be constructed or hired, new machinery items can be installed and the administrative or sale staff can be increased or decreased as per requirement. The cost relating to long run is called long run cost. In the long run, we get long run total cost, long run average cost and long run marginal cost.

SHORT RUN COST

Total Fixed Cost (TFC)

Payments for fixed factors of production in the short run are known as fixed cost or total fixed cost. That is, total fixed cost is the cost of all fixed factors paid by the producer in the short run. Fixed cost does not change with the change in the quantity of production. It remains fixed whether the output is increased or decreased or even zero. Thus, it is totally unaffected by the changes in the rate of output. Even when a firm temporarily suspends its production, this cost continues unchanged. This cost also often refers to as supplementary cost or unavoidable cost. Examples of fixed cost are rent of the land, insurance premium, salaries of the permanent employees, etc. Total fixed cost (TFC) of a firm is illustrated in the following Table and Fig. 8.1. It is evident from the Table that TFC always remains the same (₹ 25) at all levels of output (i.e., from 0 unit to 8 units). Therefore, TFC-curve is parallel to the X-axis as shown in Fig. 8.1.

Units of output (Qnt.)	TFC (₹)
0	25
1	25
2	25
3	25
4	25
5	25
6	25
7	25
8	25

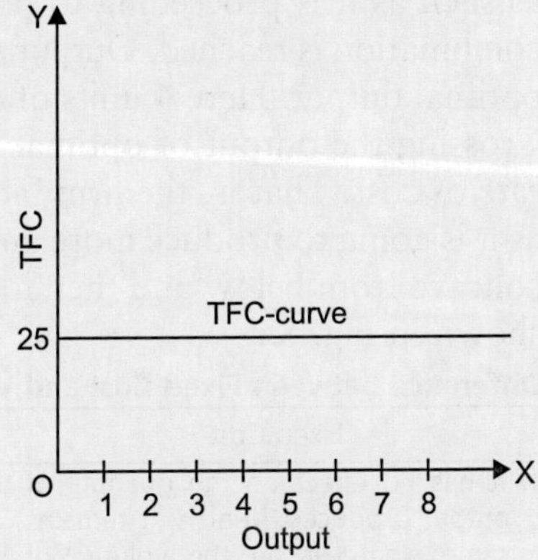

Fig. 8.1

Total Variable Cost (TVC)

The payments made to the total variable factors of production are called Total Variable Cost (TVC). Variable costs are those costs which vary more or less proportionately with the variations in the volume of output. They are also referred as prime costs or direct costs. Examples of TVC are the cost of raw material, fuel, electric power, temporary labourers, etc. Such costs are ceased as soon as the production is stopped. TVC is illustrated in the following Table and Fig. 8.2.

Unit of output (Qnt.)	TVC (₹)
0	0
1	20
2	35
3	42
4	48
5	65
6	90
7	120
8	180

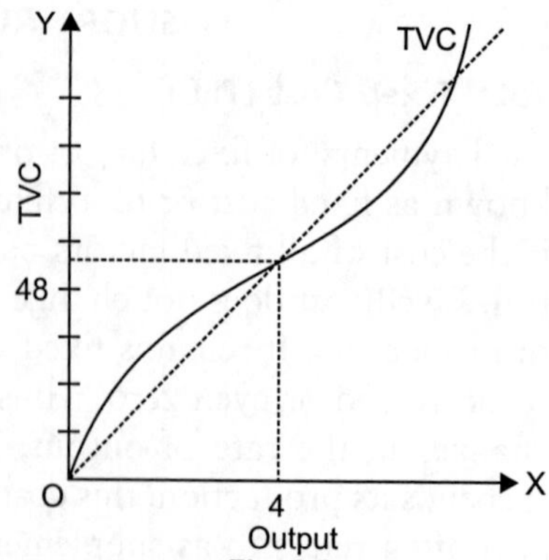

Fig. 8.2

This table and Fig. 8.2 show that TVC varies directly with the volume of output. TVC is zero at zero level of output and rises at a diminishing rate but up to the four units of output. These four units of output are the output of optimal combination of variable factors. That is why, the firm faces gradually low cost as such as it is proceeding to produce output until the optimal combination is reached. Output of optimal combination is called optimal output. Here 4 units of output is called optimal output. Crossing the output of optimal combination it faces increasing rate of cost. That is, the firm faces gradually high cost as much as it is going to produce more and more. Thus TVC curve is first concave from below and then it becomes convex from below as shown in Fig. 8.2.

Difference between Fixed Cost and Variable Cost

Fixed Cost	Variable Cost
1. It has no effect on the quantity of output produced. That is, it remains same whatever be the volume of output produced.	1. It varies with the variation of the volume of output produced.
2. It never becomes zero.	2. It becomes zero when the firm shuts down its production. That is, it is nil when production is nil.
3. It is the cost of fixed factor.	3. It is the cost of variable factor.
4. A firm can continue its production even at the loss of entire fixed costs.	4. Production is done by a firm only if its variable costs are fulfilled.
5. Fixed cost curve starts from a particular point above the origin and are horizontal to the x-axis.	5. It starts from origin. It is first concave and then convex from below.

Relationship among Short Run Total Cost, Total Fixed Cost and Total Variable Cost

The payments made for fixed, and variable factors to produce a given amount of output in a given time period are called Total Cost (TC). That is, total cost is the cost of production for producing a given amount of output in a given time period. It is obtained by the summation of TFC and TVC like TC = TFC + TVC. So, TC is the sum total of TFC and TVC.

The relationship among these three TFC, TVC and TC is illustrated in the following Table and Fig. 8.3:

Units of Output (Qnt.)	TFC (₹)	TVC (₹)	TC (₹)
0	5	0	5
1	5	5	10
2	5	8	13
3	5	10	15
4	5	11	16
5	5	13	18
6	5	16	21
7	5	20	25
8	5	25	30
9	5	32	37
10	5	42	47

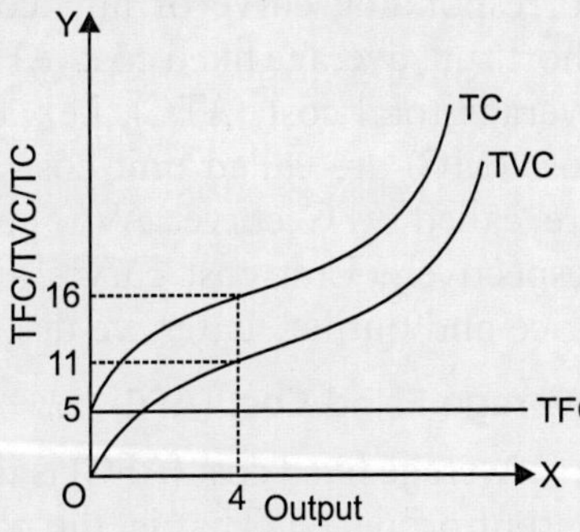

Fig. 8.3

The above table and figure show the changes in fixed and variable costs corresponding to different levels of output. Total fixed cost remains fixed at ₹ 5 irrespective of the level of output produced. Total variable cost is zero, when output is zero and this increases with an increase in output initially at decreasing rate and after facing optimal combination of output this increases at increasing rate. Total cost starts from the particular point from where TFC starts above the origin showing the same characteristics of TVC.

Since total fixed cost, by definition, remains constant, the changes in total cost are entirely due to the change in total variable cost. TC and TVC curves, therefore, have the similar shape, the only difference is that TVC curve starts from the origin while TC curve starts from a point above the origin, from where TFC curve starts.

Since TC = TFC + TVC, it shows that TC is also obtained by adding up vertically TFC and TVC in Fig. 8.3. Again, TC – TVC = TFC shows that vertical distance between TC and TVC gives TFC which is constant from the beginning to end. Again TC – TFC = TVC indicates that the vertical distance between TC and TFC gives the amount of TVC and this difference goes on increasing as output rises shown in Fig. 8.3.

UNIT COST AND UNIT COST CURVE IN SHORT RUN

Unit cost is the cost per unit of output produced and the corresponding curve of unit cost is called unit cost curve. In short run, average fixed cost (AFC), average variable cost (AVC), average total cost (ATC), i.e., average cost (AC) and marginal cost (MC) are called unit cost and their corresponding curves are called AFC curve, AVC curve, AC curve and MC curve respectively. Unit cost curves are very useful to determine the price and output. Later we discuss one by one in detail.

Average Fixed Cost (AFC)

Average fixed cost (AFC) is the cost of fixed factor per unit of output produced. That is, the payment made to the fixed factor per unit of output produced is called AFC. Since the total fixed cost of a firm remains fixed irrespective of the level of output produced, the AFC would fall and fall as the firm produces its output more and more. That is why, the curve corresponding to AFC would continue to fall with the expansion of production. AFC is found by dividing TFC by the level of output (Q) : AFC $= \frac{TFC}{Q}$.

Features of AFC: There are some special features of AFC in comparison to AVC, AC and MC. These are discussed below:

1. AFC $= \frac{TFC}{Q}$ since TFC is a constant quantity as Q $\uparrow$ $\Rightarrow$ AFC $\downarrow$.

It means that since TFC is a constant quantity AFC falls steadily with increase in output. Therefore, AFC curve slopes downward throughout its length.

2. $AFC = \frac{TFC}{Q}$ as $Q \to \infty \Rightarrow AFC \to 0$ when TFC is constant.

It implies that when output is produced in very large amount, AFC becomes less and less approaching towards zero but never reduces itself to zero. It always remains positive. Hence AFC curve tends to downward and downward but never touches the X-axis.

3. $AFC = \frac{TFC}{Q}$ as $Q \to 0 \Rightarrow AFC \to \infty$ when TFC is constant.

It indicates that when output is being produced in very small quantity gradually towards one unit. AFC rises itself very large and large and tends to become equal to TFC. In this case AFC curve starts from the point from where TFC starts.

Thus AFC curve approaches both the axes asymptotically. If we pick up any point on the AFC curve and multiply the average fixed cost at that point with the corresponding quantity of output produced, we get the total fixed cost which is same at any point on AFC curve throughout. A curve with such a property is called rectangular hyperbola. It is shown in the following Table and Fig. 8.4:

Units of Output (Qnt.)	TFC (₹)	$AFC = \frac{TFC}{Q}$ (₹)
1	20	20
2	20	10
3	20	6.67
4	20	5.0
5	20	4.0
6	20	3.33
7	20	2.86
8	20	2.5
9	20	2.22
10	20	2.00

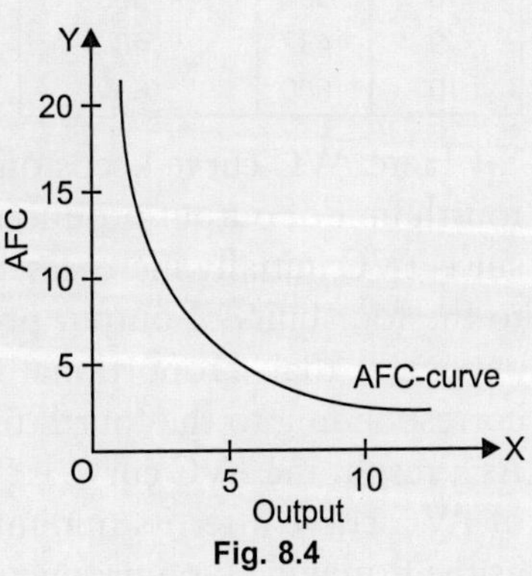

Fig. 8.4

Short Run Average Variable Cost (AVC)

Average variable cost (AVC) is the variable cost per unit of output produced. It is obtained by dividing the total variable cost (TVC) by the corresponding level of output (Q), i.e., $AVC = \frac{TVC}{Q}$.

AVC is different at different levels of output since the TVC is different at different levels of output because of the operation of the law of variable proportion. The TVC increases first at a less than proportional rate and beyond a certain amount of output it increases at a more than proportional rate to the expansion of output. Following these, the AVC curve first falls, reaches a minimum and then begins to rise. These are explained in the following Table and Fig. 8.5:

Units of Output	TVC (₹)	$AVC = \frac{TVC}{Q}$ (₹)
1	25	25
2	40	20
3	54	18
4	60	15
5	90	18
6	138	23
7	210	30
8	304	38
9	432	48
10	600	60

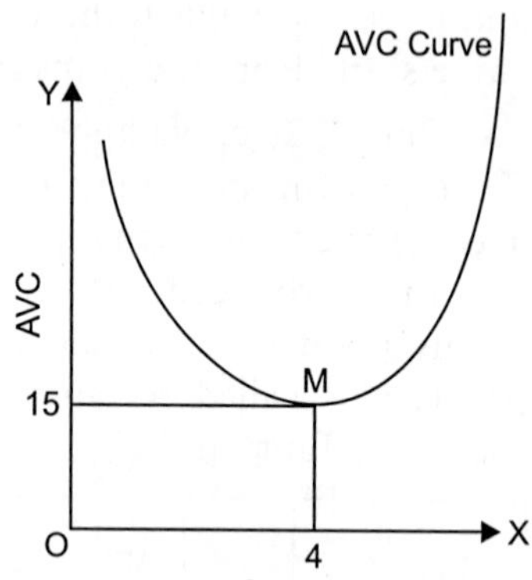

Fig. 8.5

Here AVC curve keeps on falling sharply but it is up to the fourth unit of output produced after which it rises quite sharply since TVC initially increases at a less than proportional rate up to the four units of output produced beyond which it increases at a more than proportional rate. Its minimum point is at 'M' corresponding to the fourth unit of output at the cost of ₹ 15/-. As a result, the AVC curve is 'U' shaped. But the right hand side of AVC curve after its minimum point will be steeper as much as the firm will go on production in comparison to the left hand side of AVC curve.

Relationship among Different Short Run Cost Curves: AC, AVC and AFC

Average cost (AC) or average total cost (ATC) is the cost per unit of output produced. The average cost (AC) is found by dividing TC by the level of output produced (Q):

$$AC = \frac{TC}{Q} = \frac{TFC + TVC}{Q} \qquad [\because TC = TFC + TVC]$$

$$= \frac{TFC}{Q} + \frac{TVC}{Q} \qquad \therefore AC = AFC + AVC$$

Thus, AC is equal to the sum total of AFC and AVC. AC being the sum of AFC and AVC shows the same characteristics of AVC. The only difference is that having kept AFC, the AC curve stands above the AVC curve. Likewise of AVC curve, the AC curve first falls and beyond a certain point it starts rising. This is explained in the following Table and Fig. 8.6:

Output (Qnt.)	TFC (₹)	TVC (₹)	TC (₹) (2+3)	AFC (₹) (2÷1)	AVC (₹) (3÷1)	AC (₹) (4÷1) or, (5+6)
1	2	3	4	5	6	7
1	20	18	38	20	18	38
2	20	30	50	10	15	25
3	20	40	60	6.66	13.33	20
(4)	20	52	72	5	(13)	18
(5)	20	65	85	4	13	(17)
6	20	84	104	3.33	14	17.3
7	20	105	125	2.86	15	18
8	20	144	164	2.5	18	20.5
9	20	189	209	2.22	21	23.2
10	20	260	280	2	26	28

Here AC curve keeps on falling sharply but it is up to fifth unit of output produced after which it rises quite sharply as the total cost initially increases at a less than proportional rate upto the five units of output produced beyond which it increases at more than proportional rate. That is why, the

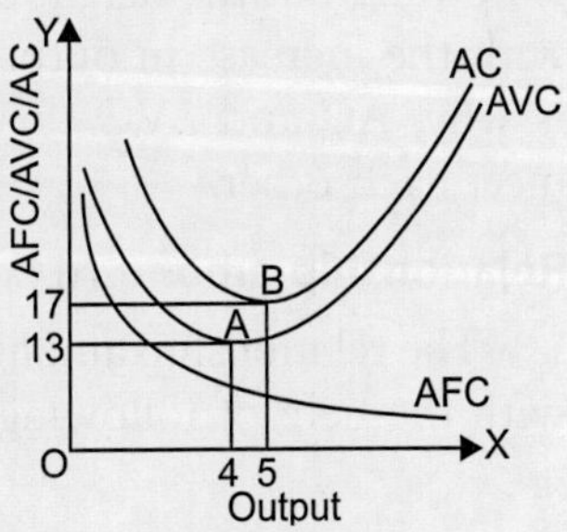

Fig. 8.6

right hand side of AC curve after its minimum point will be much steeper as much as the firm will go on production.

Diagrammatically, the vertical summation of AFC curve and AVC curve gives us the AC curve (AC = AFC + AVC). Thus the AC curve lies above the AVC curve at a distance which is equal to the height of AFC curve. It means that the vertical difference between AC curve and AVC curve gives AFC curve (AFC = AC – AVC). Again the vertical difference between AC and AFC curves gives the AVC curve (AVC = AC – AFC). It should be remembered that the minimum point of the AC occurs to the right of the minimum point of the AVC. So we can say that the AVC curve reaches first its minimum point at a lower rate of output before the AC curve does. 'B' is the minimum point of AC curve at the fifth unit of output corresponding to the cost of ₹ 17, whereas 'A' is the minimum point of AVC curve at the fourth unit of output corresponding to the cost of ₹ 13 as per our Table and Fig. 8.6 shown in the previous page.

The AC curve in the short run is U-shaped. Because it falls first, reaches the optimum point (B) and then rises to the expansion of output produced. Optimum point denotes the particular minimum point where unit cost of output is minimum. Optimum point is also called least cost combination of factors.

The AC and AVC curves after reaching their respective minimum points start to rise up and tend to come closer and closer to the expansion of output produced but never touch each other. The reason is that the gap between AC and AVC curves is nothing but the height of AFC curve which goes on declining with the increase in output but never touches the X-axis. That is why, AC and AVC curves come closer and closer but never meet each other.

Relationship among AFC, AVC, AC and MC

The relationship among AFC, AVC, AC and MC is illustrated with the help of following example and Fig. 8.7:

Output (Qnt.)	TFC (₹)	TVC (₹)	TC (₹) (2+3)	AFC (₹) (2÷1)	AVC (₹) (3÷1)	AC (₹) (4÷1) or, (5+6)	MC (₹)
1	2	3	4	5	6	7	8
1	20	18	38	20	18	38	–
2	20	30	50	10	15	25	12
3	20	40	60	6.66	13.33	20	(10)
4	20	52	72	5	(13)	18	12
5	20	65	85	4	13	(17)	13
6	20	84	104	3.33	14	17.3	19
7	20	105	125	2.86	15	18	21
8	20	144	164	2.5	18	20.5	39
9	20	189	209	2.22	21	23.2	45
10	20	260	280	2	26	28	71

From this example and Fig. 8.7 it is clear that initially AFC, AVC, AC and MC, all are falling as much as the output is going to be produced. But AFC is falling from the very beginning to the end of production and tends to touch but never touches the X-axis.

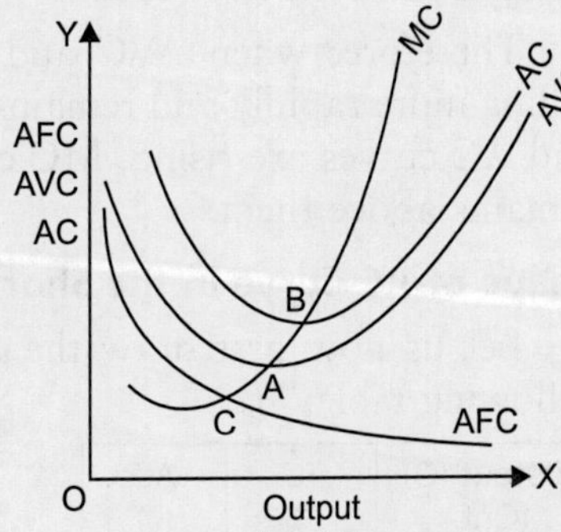

Fig. 8.7

AVC falls upto its minimum point A at the unit 4 of output produced after which it rises rapidly. AC is also falling upto its minimum point B at the unit 5 of output produced after which it also rises rapidly showing the same characteristics of AVC as AC is the sum total of AVC and AFC. But differences are that AC curve stands above the AVC curve. The AVC reaches first its minimum point at a lower rate of output than the AC does.

The AC and AVC curves after reaching their respective minimum points start to rise up and tend to come closer and closer to the expansion of output produced but never touch each other. The reason is that the gap between AC and AVC curves is nothing but the height of AFC curve which goes on declining with the increase in output but never touches the X-axis. That is why, AC and AVC curves come closer and closer but never meet each other.

Like AC and AVC, MC curve is also falling but more rapidly than AC and AVC fall. It reaches its minimum point C earlier corresponding to the unit 3 of output, i.e., at lower rate of output than AC and AVC do. From this minimum point MC starts to rise but it is below the AC and AVC curves. It cuts the minimum points of AVC first and then AC curves respectively from below and goes above AVC and AC curves. When MC is lower than AVC and AC, they all are falling but MC is falling more rapidly than AVC and AC do and MC remains below them. When MC is higher than AVC and AC, they all are rising but MC is rising more rapidly than the AVC and AC do and MC remains always above them.

Therefore, when AVC and AC curves are falling MC is falling more rapidly and remains below them. Again when AVC and AC curves are rising, MC curve is rising more rapidly and remains above them.

Shape of AC Curve in the Short Run

Let us now first draw the AC curve with the help of the following table:

Output (Q) (Qnt.)	TC (₹)	AC (₹)
1	38	38
2	50	25
3	60	20
4	72	18
(5)	85	(17)
6	104	17.3
7	125	18
8	164	20.5
9	209	23.2
10	280	28
11	440	40

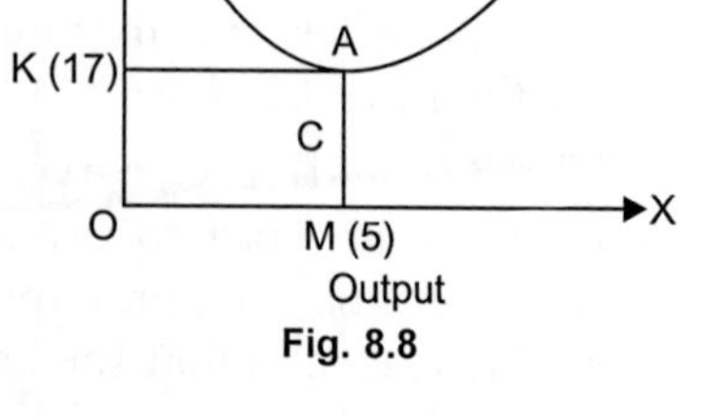

Fig. 8.8

The short run AC curve as shown above in Fig. 8.8 is U-shaped. In this figure, the AC curve falls in the initial stages when output is expanded from 'O' to 'M'. With further expansion in output beyond M, the AC curve starts rising upwards. 'A' is its optimum point and OM(5) units of output are its optimum output at the minimum cost of OK (₹ 17). It is 'U' shaped because of the operation of the law of variable proportion.

Now the question arises why AC curve is U-shaped or why does it first fall and then rises after having reached its minimum point? This can be explained in two ways:

(i) We know, AC is the sum total of the AFC and AVC. So, the shape of AC curve will depend on the shapes of the AFC and AVC curves. Since the AFC curve always slopes downward, it will tend to pull the AC curve at downward. Again AVC curve first falls downwards upto its optimum point, i.e., minimum point. Hence, it will try to pull AC curve in its own direction. So, in the beginning both AFC and AVC curves slope downwards, AC curve being the sum of AFC and AVC curves must fall likewise. AVC curve after crossing optimum point starts to rise but AFC curve continues to fall. In this situation the slope of AC curve will depend on the relative strength of slopes of AFC and AVC curves. When the upward sloping strength of the AVC curve becomes stronger than the downward sloping strength of the AFC curve, AC curve starts to rise upward after crossing its minimum point (optimum point). Thus, AC curve first falls and then rises like 'U'. That is why, AC curve is 'U'-shaped.

(ii) The AC curve is 'U'-shaped due to internal economies and diseconomies of the firm. In the beginning when output is increased, the law of increasing returns, i.e., law of decreasing cost condition operates. In this stage of increasing returns, firm gets the internal economies which reduces the average cost with the increase in output. That is why, the AC curve falls and falls with the increasing in output. But it is upto optimum point where the firm uses the factors in the 'optimum' proportions and get the optimum output at least possible cost. Thus, the AC curve falls upto its optimum point. After that the factor proportion becomes unfavourable and its economies turns into diseconomies which forces the AC curve to rise upward. This is the stage of diminishing returns, i.e., the stage of increasing cost condition.

Thus, AC curve first falls and after crossing minimum point it rises upward. As a result, the shape of AC curve is 'U'-shaped.

Marginal Cost (MC): Does Fixed Cost Affect Marginal Cost?

Marginal cost (MC) is the additional cost of producing an extra unit of output. That is, the extra cost to produce an extra unit of output is called marginal cost. Suppose ten units cost ₹ 100 and nine units cost ₹ 90. Then the extra cost for production of 10th unit is ₹ (100 – 90) = ₹ 10. This ₹ 10 is called marginal cost for 10th unit. Mathematically, we can write $MC_n = TC_n - TC_{n-1}$. It tells that by deducting the cost of producing (n – 1) units from that of n units, we get the marginal cost for n[th] unit (MC_n).

Thus, it is the increase in total cost resulting from raising the rate of production by one unit. In short, it may be called incremental cost. Since a change in total cost is caused only by a change in total variable cost, marginal cost may also be defined as the increase in total variable cost resulting from one unit increase in output. Thus, marginal cost is unaffected by fixed cost shown below:

Either, $MC = \dfrac{\Delta TC}{\Delta q}$ where ΔTC = change in total cost

ΔTVC = change in total variable cost

or, $MC = \dfrac{\Delta TVC}{\Delta q}$ Δq = change in quantity of output produced.

Output (Qnt.)	TFC (₹)	TVC (₹)	TC (₹)	MC (₹)
1	20	25	45	–
2	20	40	60	15
3	20	54	74	14
4	20	60	80	6
5	20	90	110	30
6	20	138	158	48
7	20	210	230	72
8	20	304	324	94
9	20	432	452	128
10	20	600	620	168

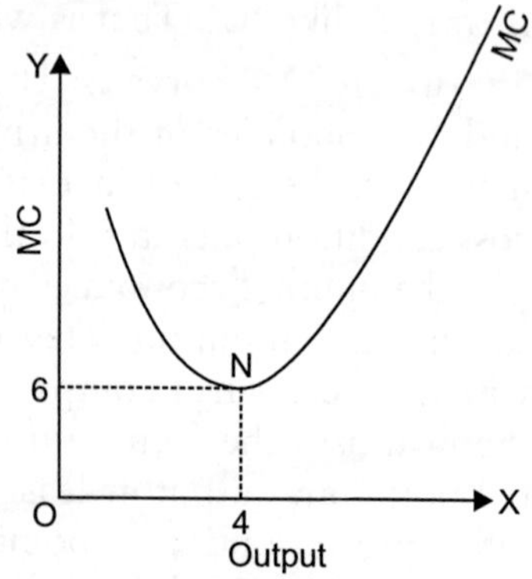

Fig. 8.9

From the above example and Fig. 8.9 it is clear that MC first decreases, reaches a minimum and then increases. That is why, MC curve first falls, reaches its minimum point, N and then rises upwards very sharply. The minimum point stands at the 4th unit of output corresponding to the cost of ₹ 6. It is U-shaped due to the operation of the law of variable proportion, i.e., due to the existence of different stages in the production process.

Now we shall see whether the fixed cost affects the marginal cost or not.

We know, TFC (₹ 20) is always fixed throughout the production process shown in the above Table. If MC were derived only from TFC, it would have been zero as ₹ 20 is deducted from ₹ 20 (20 – 20 = 0). So, the effect of TFC on MC is nil. It shows that MC derived either from TC or from TVC is same in the Table.

Again, if we assume TFC as constant term, say K, we have to add this K with TVC to get TC. That is,

$$TC = 25 + K, 40 + K, 54 + K \text{ and so on}$$

$$\text{Now, } MC_2 = 40 + K - (25 + K) = 40 + K - 25 - K = 15$$

$$MC_3 = 54 + K - (40 + K)$$

$$= 54 + K - 40 - K = 14 \text{ and so on.}$$

We get the same data of MC. It is clear that constant term is cancelled out in this way showing that TFC does not affect MC. Hence fixed cost does not affect marginal cost.

Relationship between Average Cost and Marginal Cost

The relationship between AC and MC is illustrated in the following example and Fig. 8.10:

Output (Qnt.)	TC (₹)	AC = (₹)	MC (₹)
1	38	38	–
2	50	25	12
3	60	20	10
4	72	18	12
5	85	17	13
6	102	17	17
7	126	18	24
8	160	20	34
9	225	25	65
10	320	32	95

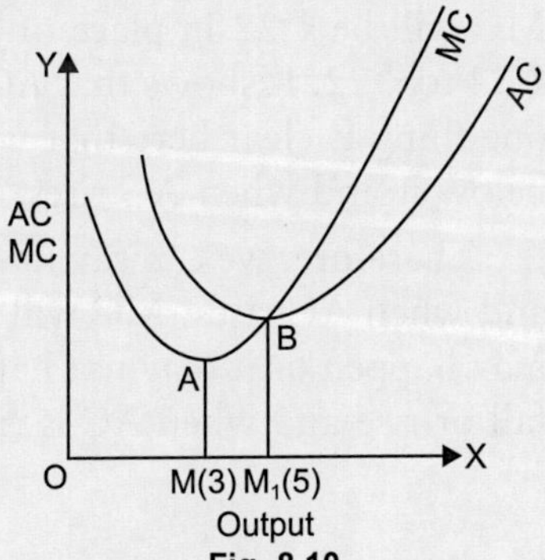

Fig. 8.10

From the example and figure, we can explain the following relationship.

(i) MC < AC ⇒ AC↓

It implies that when MC is less than AC (i.e., MC curve remains below AC curve), AC is falling but it is upto unit 5 in our example and upto OM_1 units of output in Fig. 8.10.

Both are falling but MC curve is falling more rapidly than that of AC curve. MC falls upto unit 3 at which MC reaches its minimum point A earlier than AC does. From unit 3 to unit 5 in our example and A to B in the figure, MC is rising though AC is falling, but MC is below the AC.

(ii) MC = AC ⇒ AC is parallel to X-axis.

It says that (a) when MC equals to AC, AC is constant and parallel to the X-axis from unit 5 to unit 6 in our example and AC reaches its minimum point B as shown in Fig. 8.10; (b) when MC cuts the minimum point of AC from below and goes above AC, AC starts to rise but MC is higher than AC. This situation is shown after unit 6 in our example and after point B in the figure.

(iii) MC > AC ⇒ AC↑

It shows that when MC is higher than AC, AC rises. Both MC and AC curves are rising, but MC is rising more rapidly than the AC curve. But it is not always true, AC is rising, MC must be rising, MC may fall. In our example, at unit 8, TC may be ₹ 148 instead of 160, then AC will be ₹ 18.5 in place of ₹ 20 and MC will be ₹ 22 in place of ₹ 34 showing that MC falls from ₹ 34 to ₹ 22. It shows that AC can rise when MC is falling. But one thing is clear here that when AC falls MC always remains below it and when AC rises, MC remains always above it.

Therefore, we can say that when AC falls, MC will also fall and when AC rises, MC will also rise. It is not fully correct. It may happen or it may not happen when AC is falling, MC may fall or rise and when AC is rising, MC may rise or fall.

LONG RUN COST

The long run is defined as a period of time during which a producer can bring changes in the scale of production through an adjustment of the quantity of the various factors employed. In the short run, total cost has two parts: total variable cost and total fixed cost. But in the long run, all costs are variable costs. There is no concept of fixed cost in the long run. In the technical language, the indivisible factors become divisible in the long run so that they can be used more economically. Plant size is changed according to the requirements of production. If the scale of production is to be expanded, new buildings can be hired, new machinery can be installed and the administrative or sale staff can be increased, new land can be purchased or hired. The long run cost function can be written as

$$C = f(Q, T, P_F)$$

where C is total cost of production, Q is the level of output, T is the technology used and P_F is the prices of factors used in production of a particular product. There are three types of cost curves seen in the long run. They are:

(i) long run total cost curve (LTC);

(ii) long run average cost curve (LAC); and

(iii) long run marginal cost curve (LMC).

Now, we shall discuss these one by one.

Long Run Total Cost Curve (LRTC or LTC)

(Long Run Total Cost Curve is the envelope of the Short Run Total Cost Curves)

In the long run, a firm can enlarge plants, equipments, etc., to produce more output in the most efficient way. In the short run, the firm is tied with a given plant. The long run cost of production is the least possible cost of production for producing any given level of output, when all inputs are variable including the size of the plant.

If we consider three consecutive time period of production where the firm is trying to enlarge its production by changing its plant size, we get three types of short run total cost curves

(SRTC). For a given output the producer calculates the total cost for each plant size and in the long run he selects that plant size for which total cost is minimum. The long run total cost curve (LRTC) and three short run total cost curves (SRTC) are illustrated in the Fig. 8.11 where we plot cost along the Y-axis and output along the X-axis.

In this figure, there are three short run total cost curves according to three plant sizes. Considering three short run total cost curves we can draw the long run total cost curves (LRTC). We see that the firm enlarges the plant sizes from $SRTC_1$ to $SRTC_2$ and to $SRTC_3$ in order to get higher output from time to time.

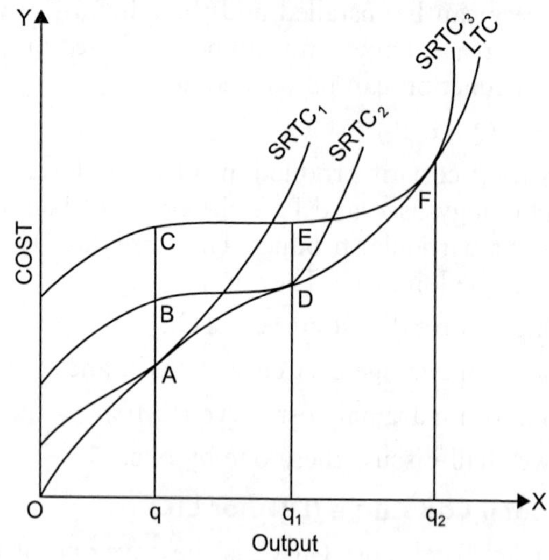

Fig. 8.11

We see that lower level of output like oq, $SRTC_1$ is fit for production. For oq level of output, $SRTC_2$ and $SRTC_3$ stand above $SRTC_1$. After certain output level both the curves come below the $SRTC_1$. For oq level of output, the plant sizes in the $SRTC_2$ and $SRTC_3$ are uneconomic having higher costs but $SRTC_1$ is economic and minimum at point A where the LRTC is tangent to $SRTC_1$. It is clear in the figure that oq level of output can be produced in the three different plants, where total cost is qA in $SRTC_1$. qB in $SRTC_2$ and qC in $SRTC_3$. qC is higher than qB and qB is higher than qA. Only qA is minimum for the production of output oq. But after oq level of output, to produce more in the plant of $SRTC_1$ will be uneconomic because, it goes up crossing the $SRTC_2$ and $SRTC_3$.

Again, if we consider to produce oq_1 level of output, $SRTC_2$ will be economic but $SRTC_3$ will be uneconomic because $SRTC_3$ stands above $SRTC_2$. The cost for oq_1 level of output is q_1D in the plant of $SRTC_2$ and q_1E in the plant of $SRTC_3$. So, for oq_1 level of output, the cost in the $SRTC_2$ at point D on it, where the LRTC is tangent to $SRTC_2$ is minimum.

Similarly, to produce oq_2 level of output, the plant in $SRTC_3$ will be economic and minimum at point F where the LRTC is tangent to it.

In every case, the long run total cost curve is a guide to the producer and it is an envelope of these three short run total cost curves, because it is tangent to all three short run total cost curves.

Thus, the long run total cost curve is the envelope of all short run total cost curves. This means, it is tangent to all short run total cost curves, but not intersects any one.

Long Run Average Cost Curve (LAC)

In the long run all factors are variable and there is nothing like fixed cost of production. In order to produce more output, the scale of production, i.e., the scale of operation is to be expanded, new buildings have to be acquired or hired, new machinery can be installed and the administrative and the sales staff have to be increased. But in the short run the plant size is taken as fixed, i.e., the production is subject to each plant size. Firm, in the short run, can change its output only by changing in the proportions of variable factors within the range of the existing capital equipment.

Long run average cost is the long run total cost divided by the level of output. It is the cumulative picture of short run average cost curves. That is, the long run average cost curve can be deduced from the short run average cost curves. The long run average cost curve is the envelope of the short run average cost curves just as the long run total cost curve is the envelope of the short run total cost curves. The long run average cost curve touches all the short run average cost curves but intersects none. This is illustrated in the Fig. 8.13.

In the short run, the firm is tied with a given plant. For each plant size or each scale of production, we get one short run average cost curve (SAC) of a firm. We assume that the plant size is varied continuously, according to which there will be any number of SAC curves.

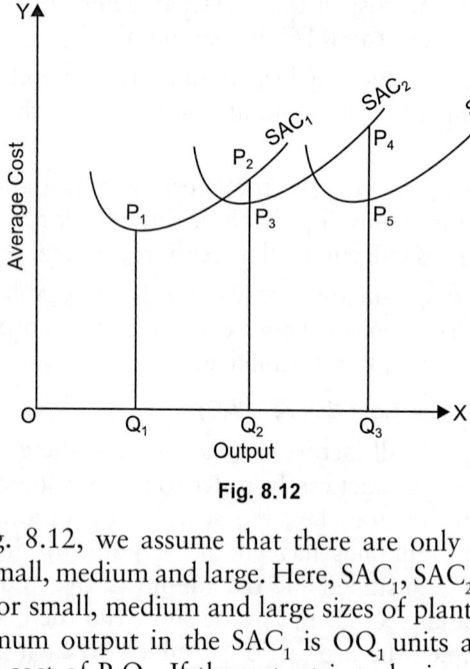

Fig. 8.12

In Fig. 8.12, we assume that there are only three sizes of plants—small, medium and large. Here, SAC_1, SAC_2 and SAC_3 are relevant for small, medium and large sizes of plants respectively. The optimum output in the SAC_1 is OQ_1 units at the average minimum cost of P_1Q_1. If the output is to be increased to OQ_2 in this short period, this would be possible only by increasing the average cost from P_1Q_1 to P_2Q_2. But in the long run when a second plant is adopted, the short run average cost curve shifts to a new position, SAC_2. Here the same output OQ_2 is produced at the lower cost of P_3Q_2. In this figure we see that the average cost in the long run has come down from P_2Q_2 to P_3Q_2. Again to fulfil the requirement of more output with the existing second plant, it would be possible, only at a higher cost. Suppose, to produce OQ_3, the average cost rises from P_3Q_2 to P_4Q_3. If in the long run third plant is added, the new short run average cost curve would be SAC_3. The same output OQ_3 can be produced at P_5Q_3 which is lower than P_4Q_3. Thus in the long run, the firm is able to adjust the scale of operation so as to produce the given output at the lowest average cost. For simplicity we have considered only three alternative scales of production. But in practice, there may be any number of alternative scales of production.

Therefore, we assume that (i) there are variable returns to scale and (ii) there are infinite number of short run average cost curves. The long run average cost curve (LAC) is shown in Fig. 8.13. In this figure, the successive short run average cost curves are at different heights. The long run average cost curve can be drawn in such a way that it would be tangent to all these short run curves and envelope them.

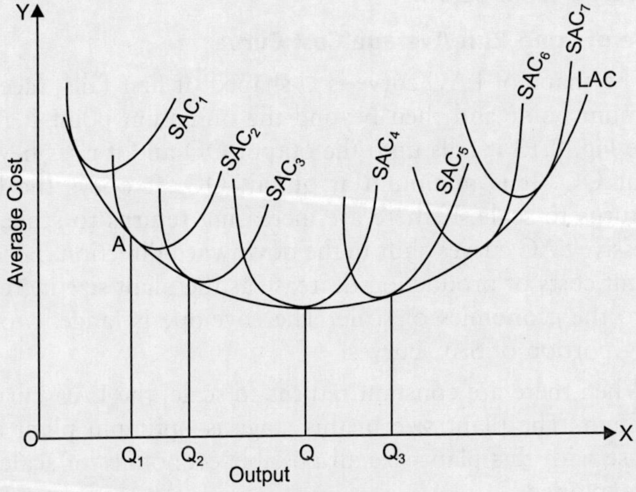

Fig. 8.13

That is, the long run average cost curve (LAC) is the locus of tangency points with short run average cost curves. This means that only one point of each short run average cost curve is a point on the long run average cost curve.

It indicates that for each level of output there is only one input combination for which short run cost is equal to long run cost. Each point of LAC curve shows the minimum (optimal) cost for producing the corresponding level of output. It is a planning curve because on the basis of this curve the firm decides what plant to set up in order to produce optimally the expected level of output. This means that if a firm desires to produce particular output in the long run, it will pick a point on the LAC curve corresponding to that output and then build up a relevant plant and operate on the corresponding SAC curve. Suppose, in Fig. 8.13 to produce OQ_1 the firm chooses the corresponding point A on LAC curve and at A the corresponding SAC_2 curve is tangent to LAC curve. The firm will construct a plant corresponding to SAC_2 and will operate on this curve at point A. Similarly, if the firm wants to increase the output to OQ_2, it will do accordingly. Thus, the long run average cost curve is called envelope curve, because it envelopes or supports a family of short run average cost curves from below.

Shape of Long Run Average Cost Curve

The shape of LAC curve is U-shaped. It first falls, faces its minimum point and then beyond the minimum point it rises. In the Fig. 8.13 it falls upto the output OQ and it rises beyond output OQ. It is minimum at output OQ. It obeys the laws of returns to scale. If there are increasing returns to scale, the successive SAC curves shift in the downward direction. Because the unit costs of production decrease as the plant size increases due to the economies of scale. The envelope is tangent to the falling portion of SAC curves.

When there are constant returns to scale, the LAC curve is minimum. The plant size in this stage is optimum plant size, because with this plant size all possible economies of scale are fully exploited.

If the plant size increases further than this optimum size, the economies of scale turn in to diseconomies of scale. In this stage the firm faces decreasing returns to scale, the successive SAC curves shift in the upward direction and the envelope is tangent to the SAC curves at their upward rising portion.

When all factors of production are perfectly divisible, the LAC curve is falling or rising depending on the nature of the returns to scale. Thus, the LAC is U-shaped for the normal production function in which the LAC curve is falling due to increasing returns to scale and then it is minimum due to constant returns to scale and then it is rising due to decreasing returns to scale.

Long Run Average Cost Curve under Constant Returns to Scale

When all factors of production are perfectly divisible and the prices of inputs remain constant, the long run average cost remains constant at all levels of output for a normal production function.

That is, the production function is linear and homogeneous of the first degree. Such type of production function obeys constant returns to scale. Constant returns to scale tells that when all inputs are increased in a certain proportion, output increases in the same proportion.

With constant returns to scale and fixed prices of inputs the unit cost of output remains the same. If we assume any number of short run average cost curves with different plants sizes, they have the same minimum average cost of production. When we join the minimum points of these SAC curves, we get a horizontal straight line as shown in Fig. 8.14. This horizontal straight line is nothing but an LAC curve. In this figure, we have taken three SAC curves such as SAC_1, SAC_2 and SAC_3. The minimum points of them are lying on the LAC line. Different plants are employed to get different output, such as OQ_1, OQ_2 and OQ_3 corresponding to SAC_1, SAC_2 and SAC_3 respectively.

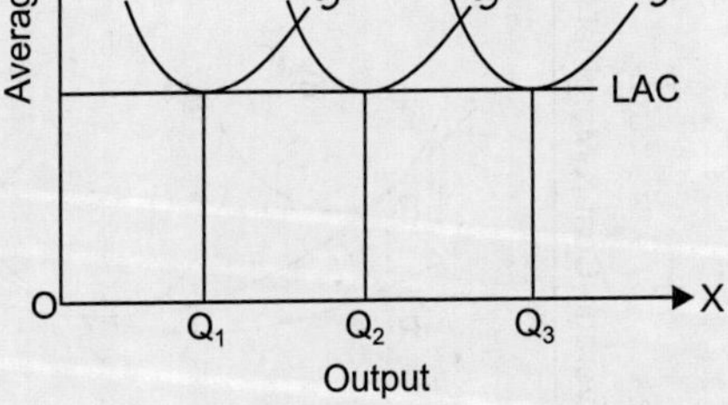

Fig. 8.14

Difference Between Short Run and Long Run Average Cost

1. The long run average cost curve is the locus of tangency points with the short run average cost curves.
2. The long run average cost curve cannot intersect any short run average cost curve. It can only touch the average cost curves.
3. The long run average cost cannot be higher than the short run average cost for any given output.
4. Both the curves are U-shaped but the U-shape of LAC curve is less pronounced than that of SAC curve.
5. The long run average cost curve envelopes a family of short run average cost curves from below.
6. Each point of LAC curve shows the minimum cost for producing a given output, but it is not seen in case of SAC curve.

LONG RUN MARGINAL COST CURVE

Long run marginal cost curve can be derived from the short run average cost curves, short run marginal cost curves and long run average cost curve. For the sake of simplicity, we consider here only three short run average cost curves, SAC_1, SAC_2 and SAC_3 as shown in Fig. 8.15.

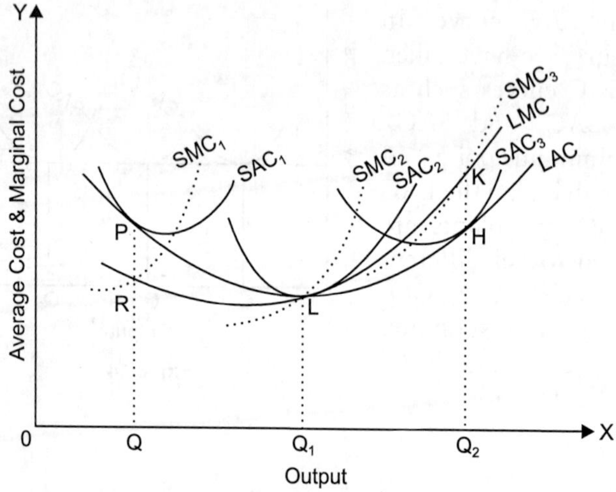

Fig. 8.15

Due to the operation of the laws of returns to scale, the long run average cost curve LAC is drawn in such a way that it is first tangent to the falling portion of SAC_1 and then passes through the minimum point of SAC_2 (where the minimum point of LAC is equal to the minimum point of SAC_2) and then becomes tangent to the rising portion of SAC_3.

It envelopes the three short run average cost curves. Corresponding to each short run average cost curve, we get one short run marginal cost curve. Thus, we get SMC_1 corresponding to SAC_1, SMC_2 corresponding to SAC_2, and SMC_3 corresponding to SAC_3. Every short run marginal cost curve passes through the minimum point of its corresponding average cost curve. Each short run average cost curve represents its own plant size. The points of tangency between the SAC and the LAC curves shows different output of different plant sizes.

Corresponding to tangency point P between the SAC_1 and the LAC, the firm wants to produce the output OQ in the long run, because only point P minimizes the cost for output OQ. Corresponding to the point P on SAC_1 and LAC, there is a point R on the short run marginal cost curve SMC_1. It shows that for output OQ, the average cost is QP and the marginal cost is QR. At tangency point P, SAC is equal to LAC for output OQ, similarly, the SMC must be equal to LMC for that output OQ. Therefore, LMC curve must pass through the point R corresponding to the output OQ.

If output OQ_1 is to be produced in the long run, it will be produced at point L which is a tangency point between the SAC_2 and the LAC. Again L is also the point on SMC_2 curve. It means that for output OQ_1, the short run average cost, long run average cost and short run marginal cost are the same. Therefore, the LMC curve will pass through the point L corresponding to the output OQ_1.

Finally, if the output OQ_2 is to be produced in long run, it will be produced at point H which is the point of tangency between SAC_3 and LAC curves. It shows that for output OQ_2, short run average cost and long run average cost are the same. Corresponding to point H on SAC_3 for output OQ_2, the relevant point on the SMC_3 is K. It indicates that the long run marginal cost for output OQ_2 is Q_2K. Therefore, K must lie on the long run marginal cost curve corresponding to the output OQ_2.

By joining points R, L and K, we get long run marginal cost curve LMC. The LMC cannot envelope the short run marginal cost curves. It should be noted that LMC also passes through the minimum point of LAC as SMC passes through the minimum point of SAC in the short run. The LMC curve, like the LAC curve, is U-shaped. But it is flatter than the SMC curves. Again it should be noted that as in the short run, when LAC is falling, LMC < LAC and when LAC is rising, LMC > LAC.

EXERCISES

1. Explain short run cost and long run cost.
2. Define total fixed cost (TFC) and total variable cost (TVC) with table and diagram.
3. What are the differences between fixed cost and variable cost?
4. How is total cost calculated in the short run? Explain the relationship among total cost, total fixed cost and total variable cost in the short run with an example and a diagram.
5. What do you understand by unit cost and unit cost curve in short run? Define average fixed cost (AFC) with an example and a diagram.
6. Explain the average variable cost (AVC) with an example and a diagram. Also explain its shape.
7. Explain the relationship among different short run unit cost curves with an example and a diagram. With the increase in output, AC and AVC curves come nearer but never meet, give reasons.
8. Explain the relationship among AFC, AVC, AC and MC with an example and a diagram.
9. Why is the AC curve U-shaped in the short run? Explain it with example and diagram.

10. Explain the concept of marginal cost (MC) with an example and a diagram. Does fixed cost affect marginal cost?
11. What is meant by average cost and marginal cost? Explain their relationship. Can the marginal cost rise when average cost is falling and can average cost rise when MC is falling? Explain all with an example and a diagram.
12. What do you mean by long run cost? Explain that long run total cost curve is the envelope of the short run total cost curves.
13. Derive long run average curve from short run average cost curves. How are they related to each other? Does the curve join the minimum points of the short run average cost curves to constitute long run average cost curve?

    Or

    The long run average cost curve is the envelope of the short run average cost curves. Explain.
14. Give reasons for the U-shape of long run average cost curve. Why is long run average cost curve usually called planning curve?
15. What would be the shape of long run average cost (LAC) curve when constant returns to scale occur?
16. Derive the long run marginal cost curve and explain the relationship between long run average cost curve and long run marginal cost curve.

Chapter 9

Market Forms: Perfect Competition

Some economists distinguish between pure competition and perfect competition, though for all practical purposes the two terms are used in the same sense. Pure competition exists when only some of the conditions of perfect competition are satisfied. Perfect competition prevails when certain additional conditions, viz. perfect knowledge, perfect mobility and absence of transport costs are also satisfied. Thus, basically the two terms refer to the same kind of market situation. While the concept of pure competition is more practical, that of perfect competition is more comprehensive. The definition of perfect competition is wider than that of pure competition. Perfect competition is a market situation in which there are many firms selling identical products with no firm large enough in relation to the entire market to be able to influence the market price. When no individual firm is in a position to influence the market price because of the smallness of its own size compared to the industry, it will have to sell its output at a price given to it by the market. Thus, under perfect competition every firm is a price taker, i.e., it sells at a price determined by the forces of demand and supply for the entire industry rather than fixing its own price for the product.

Assumptions

(i) **Many firms:** There are large number of firms in the industry so that an individual firm's output comprises an insignificant portion of total output.

(ii) **Homogeneity of products:** All firms produce more or less identical products.

(iii) **Freedom of entry and exit:** Any firm can enter or leave the industry at its will.

(iv) **Independence:** Individual consumer and producer are assumed to act independently. There is no collusion among buyers or sellers.

(v) **Independent decision-making:** Each firm is free to decide for itself how much it will produce.

(vi) **Profit maximisation:** The goal of every firm is to maximise its profit.

(vii) **No government regulation:** There is no government intervention in the market.

The market structure in which the above assumptions are fulfilled is called pure competition. It is different from perfect competition, which requires the fulfilment of the following additional assumptions.

(viii) **Perfect knowledge:** All buyers and sellers of a particular product have complete knowledge of the conditions under which the product is bought and sold. Both of them know the price at which the market demand is equal to market supply. This price is known as the market clearing price prevailing all over the market. At this price, there will be no unsatisfied buyers and sellers.

(ix) **Perfect mobility of factors of production:** The factors of production are free to move from one firm to another.

(x) **Absence of transport cost:** All firms work so close to each other that there is no transport cost for the mobility of factors of production.

So far equilibrium is concerned, there are two types of equilibrium: short run equilibrium and long run equilibrium.

SHORT RUN EQUILIBRIUM

Equilibrium of the firm in the short run: Short run can be defined as a period of time which is not sufficient to allow the firm to make an adjustment in the scale of operations, by changing the quantity of fixed factors engaged in production. It can, however, make any adjustment in the quantity of variable factors.

In the short run, an individual firm under perfect competition may make super normal profit, normal profit or subnormal profit. These three possibilities can be shown by the three short run equilibrium positions of a competitive firm. The equilibrium of a firm may be shown graphically in two ways either by using TR and TC curves, or the MR and MC curves.

Total Revenue (TR) – Total Cost (TC) approach for profit maximisation in the short run: The firm is in equilibrium when it produces the output that maximises its profits (π) defined as the difference between total cost and total revenue: $\pi = TR - TC$.

In Fig. 9.1, we see the equilibrium using the total revenue (TR) and total cost (TC) curves of a firm in a perfectly competitive market. The TR curve is a straight line through the origin showing that the unit price is constant at levels of output sold. The firm is a price taker and can sell any amount of output at the market price. The TR curve increases proportionately with its sales.

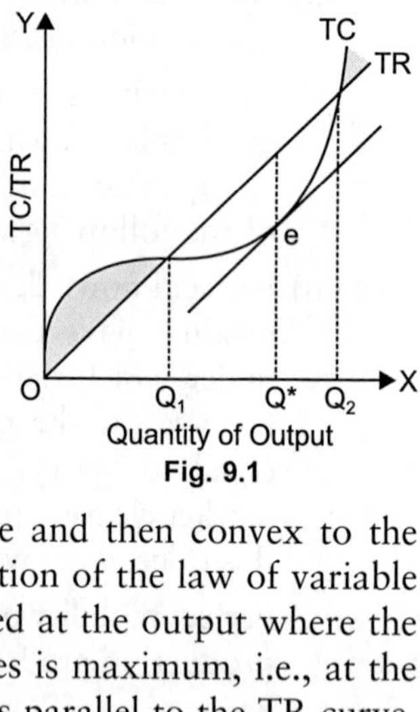

Fig. 9.1

The TC curve is at first concave and then convex to the horizontal axis. It is so due to operation of the law of variable proportions. Total profit is maximised at the output where the difference between TR and TC curves is maximum, i.e., at the point e on TC curve where tangent is parallel to the TR curve. OQ* is the profit maximising output level. At lower and higher levels of OQ* total profit is not maximised. At output levels smaller than OQ_1 and larger than OQ_2 where TC curve is higher than TR curve, the firm has losses. This is shown by the shaded region between TC and TR curves. Thus at OQ_1 and at OQ_2 the firm has normal profit. In between these there is super normal profit. Shaded region shows subnormal profit.

The total revenue–total cost approach is a useful one from some standpoints. However, it does not lead to an analytical interpretation of business behaviour. The alternative approach, which is based on marginal cost and marginal revenue, uses price as an explicit variable, and shows clearly the behavioural rule that leads to profit maximisation. The alternative approach is called marginal approach for profit maximisation in the short run.

Marginal Approach for Profit Maximisation in the Short Run Conditions for Equilibrium

We show the equilibrium using marginal cost (MC) and marginal revenue (MR) curves of a firm selling its output in a perfectly competitive market. Now we have to derive first the conditions for equilibrium of a firm.

We know, π = TR – TC. Taking derivative, we get

$$\frac{d\pi}{dQ} = \frac{d(TR)}{dQ} - \frac{d(TC)}{dQ}$$

$$\text{or, } \frac{d(TR)}{dQ} - \frac{d(TC)}{dQ} = 0 \left[\because \frac{d\pi}{dQ} = 0\right] \text{ or, MR – MC = 0}$$

$\therefore$ MR = MC ... (1) (Necessary condition)

$$\text{Again, } \frac{d^2\pi}{dQ^2} = \frac{d^2(TR)}{dQ^2} - \frac{d^2(TC)}{dQ^2} < 0 \qquad \left[\because \frac{d^2\pi}{dQ^2} < 0\right]$$

Slope of MR curve – Slope of MC curve < 0

$\therefore$ Slope of MR curve < Slope of MC curve ... (2)

(Sufficient condition)

Thus, the first condition for equilibrium of the firm is that marginal cost is equal to marginal revenue. However, this condition is not sufficient. Since it may be fulfilled yet the firm may not be in equilibrium. That is why, it is called necessary condition for equilibrium. The second condition for equilibrium is called sufficient condition which states that the slope of MR curve is less than the slope of MC curve, i.e., slope of MC > slope of MR. For equilibrium, the firm has to fulfil this second condition after fulfilment of first condition. That is why, it is called sufficient condition.

In Fig. 9.2, we see that the condition MC = MR is satisfied at point e′, yet clearly the firm is not in equilibrium, because the condition, slope of MC > slope of MR is not satisfied, rather slope of MC < slope of MR is obtained. But at point e, both the conditions are satisfied that (i) MC = MR and (ii) slope of MC > slope of MR. Thus, the second condition for equilibrium requires that the MC must be rising at the point of its intersection with the MR curve. This means that the MC must cut the MR curve from below, i.e., the slope of the MC must be steeper than the slope of the MR curve. At point e, the slope of MC is positive while the slope of MR is zero. Hence, the firm is in equilibrium at point e where it maximises its profit at the level of output defined by the intersection of the MC and the MR curves. To the left of e profit has not reached its maximum level though each unit of output to the left of X_e brings to the firm a revenue which is greater than its marginal cost. To the right of X_e each additional unit of output costs more than the revenue earned by its sale so that a loss is made and total profit is reduced.

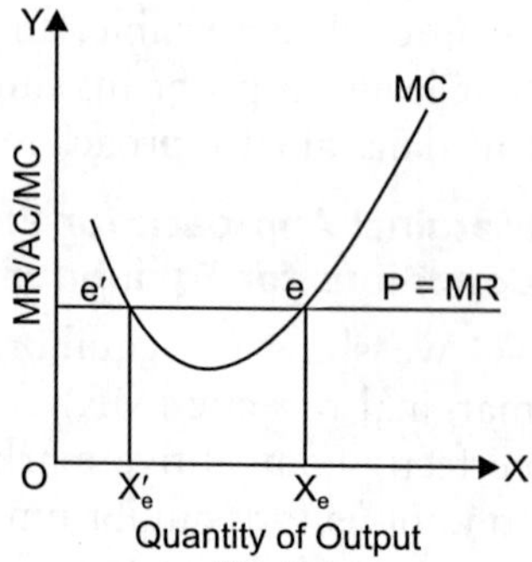

Fig. 9.2

CHARACTERISTICS OF SHORT RUN EQUILIBRIUM

A firm is in short run equilibrium does not necessarily mean that it makes excess profits. Whether the firm makes excess profit (super normal profit) or no profit no loss (normal profit) or losses (subnormal profit), it depends on the level (position) of the AC at the short run equilibrium. If the AC is below the price at equilibrium, the firm earns super normal profits. If the AC stands at equilibrium price, the firm earns normal profits. Again if the AC stands above the price of equilibrium, the firm earns subnormal profits. In Fig. 9.3, at point E both the necessary conditions, i.e., MC = MR and sufficient condition, i.e., slope of MC > slope of MR are fulfilled.

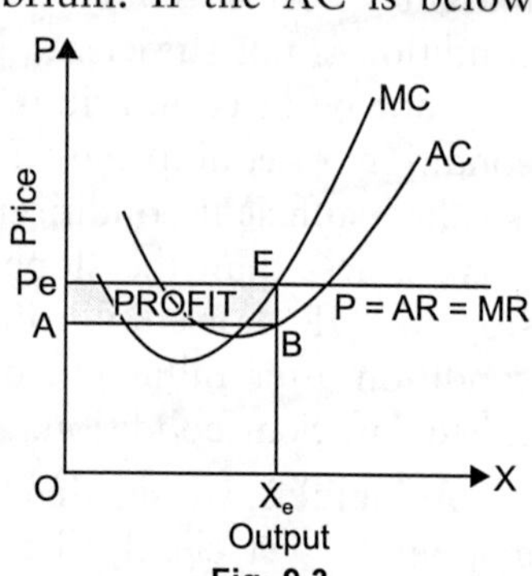

Fig. 9.3

So, E is the profit maximising equilibrium point where OPe is the equilibrium price and OXe is the profit maximising output.

Here TR = area of OPeEXe

and, TC = area of OABXe

So, Profit = TR – TC

= Area of OPeEXe – Area of OABXe

= Area of ABEPe ⇒ Super normal profit.

In Fig. 9.4, TR = TC = area of OXeEPe. That is, AC stands at the equilibrium point E.

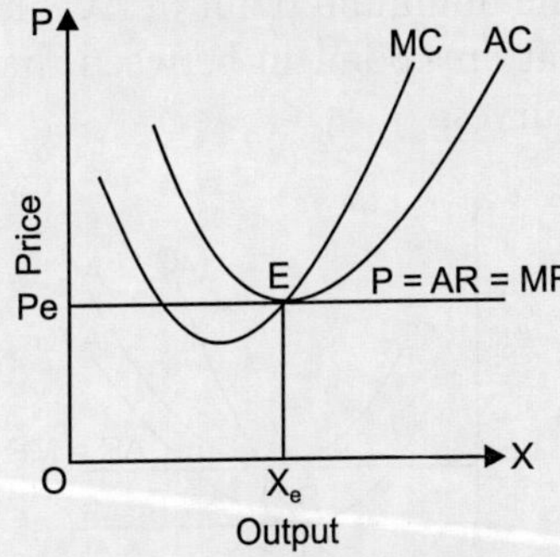

Fig. 9.4

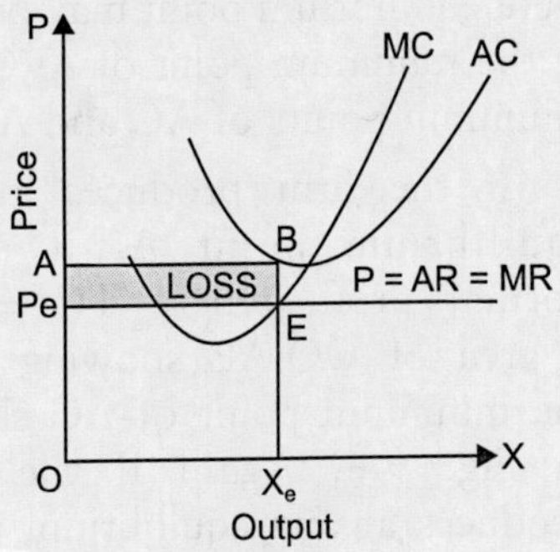

Fig. 9.5

Profit = TR – TC

= Area of OXeEPe – Area of OXeEPe

= 0 ⇒ Normal profit.

Hence, the firm earns normal profit

Again in Fig. 9.5, AC is above the equilibrium price.

TR = Area of OXeEPe

and TC = Area of OXeBA

Profit = TR – TC = Area of TR – Area of TC = Area of OXeEPe – Area of OXeBA = – Area of PeEBA = > Subnormal Profit, i.e., negative profit. That is, area of TC is greater than that of TR. Here the firm makes a loss.

Now question arises how long the firm will continue to produce when the firm is facing losses. [Q. What is meant by shut down point of a firm? Show the supply curve of a firm in short run.]

Since the firm is bound to pay fixed cost in short run even if it stops its production. So, it will produce so long as it has to pay a part of fixed cost or whole of fixed cost. Hence, the firm will continue to produce only if it covers its variable cost. Otherwise, it will close down (shut down) its production, since by discontinuing its operation, the firm is better off. It minimises its losses. The minimum point of AVC curve at which the firm covers its variable costs is called closing down point (or shut down point) or, the point at which the firm stops its production is called shut down point. This is shown in Fig. 9.6. Here equilibrium point may be at the minimum point of AC or, at the minimum point of AVC or, at any point in between the minimum points of AC and AVC curves.

If the firm produces at the equilibrium point A, it earns normal profit where TC = TR = area of OQ_1AP_1 showing A is the minimum point of AC shown in Fig. 9.6. Again if the firm produces at any equilibrium point in between A and B where B is the minimum point of AVC, it bears a part of fixed cost. If the firm produces at point B, then the firm has to bear the entire fixed cost. If the firm stops its production at point B, it will have to pay the entire fixed cost. But the firm will continue to produce to exist in the industry on the hope of future profit. However, if price falls below OP_2, the firm shuts down or closes down its production because it has to pay a part of its variable cost in addition to the entire fixed cost. So the firm never produces at the price below OP_2 corresponding to the minimum point of AVC. So B is called the shut down point or closing down point.

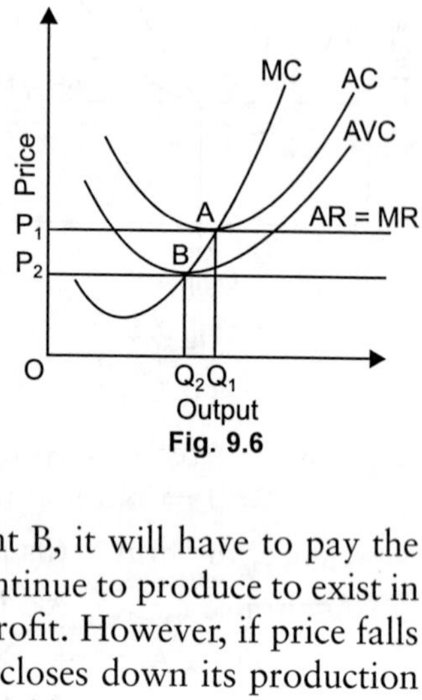

Fig. 9.6

By definition, shut down point is the minimum point of AVC curve corresponding to the price at which the firm produces its output facing the entire loss of fixed cost covering only its variable cost, below which the firm shuts down its production for facing a part of its variable cost in addition to the entire fixed cost.

SUPPLY CURVE OF THE FIRM IN THE SHORT RUN

The firm can produce at any point along the MC curve above the minimum point of AVC curve. The supply curve of the firm may be derived by joining the points of intersection of its MC curve with successive demand curves (P = AR = MR) assuming that the market price increases gradually. This causes an upward shift of the demand curve of the firm. Given the positive slope of the MC curve, each higher demand curve cuts the MC curve to a point which lies to the right of the previous intersection. This implies that the quantity supplied by the firm increases as price rises. The firm is not in a position to supply any quantity at the price below the minimum point B of AVC curve. Because at a price below the point B the firm does not cover its variable costs after facing the loss of the entire fixed cost. If we plot the successive points of intersections of MC curve above the minimum point of AVC curve on a separate graph paper corresponding to the prices we get the supply curve of the individual firm which is identical to its MC curve to the right of the shut down point B. Below B the quantity supplied by the firm is zero. As price rises above B the quantity supplied increases. Hence, the upper portion of MC curve above the minimum point of AVC curve is called the supply curve of the firm. The supply curve of the firm is shown in Fig. 9.8 corresponding to the Fig. 9.7.

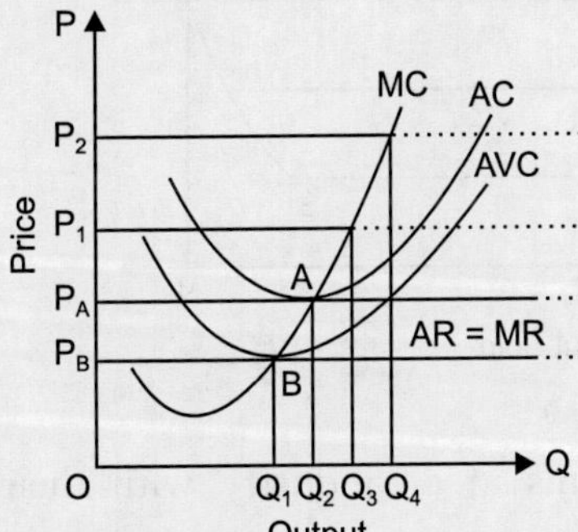

Fig. 9.7

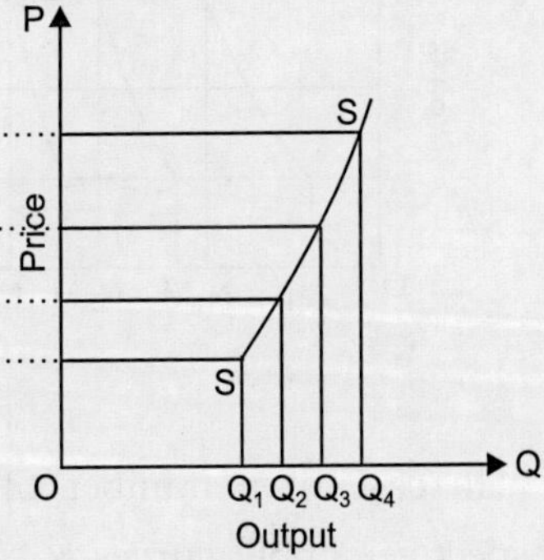

Fig. 9.8

SUPPLY CURVE OF THE INDUSTRY IN SHORT RUN

The short run industry supply curve is derived by the horizontal summation of all the supply curves of the individual firms consisting in the industry. It is assumed that (i) the factor prices and the technology are given and (ii) the number of firms is very large. Under these conditions the total quantity supplied in the market at each price is the sum of the quantities supplied by all firms at that price. Let us consider that an industry consists of four firms which have different supply curves denoted by S_1, S_2, S_3 and S_4 shown in Fig. 9.9. Now at the price OP_1, the first firm supplies OM_1, the second firm OM_2, the third OM_3 and the fourth nil. The total supply of the four firms at the price OP_1 would be equal to $OM_1 + OM_2 + OM_3$ which is equal to OM, i.e., $OM = OM_1 + OM_2 + OM_3$ in the figure. Similarly, at price OP_2, the respective supplies from the four firms would be ON_1, ON_2, ON_3 and ON_4, the total supply of the industry is being equal to ON as $ON_1 + ON_2 + ON_3 + ON_4 = ON$. Thus, the supply curve of the industry as a whole is shown by the curve SS being the horizontal summation of S_1, S_2, S_3 and S_4. All firms are not usually of the same size. The particular size of each firm in perfect competition depends on the entrepreneurial efficiency of the businessman.

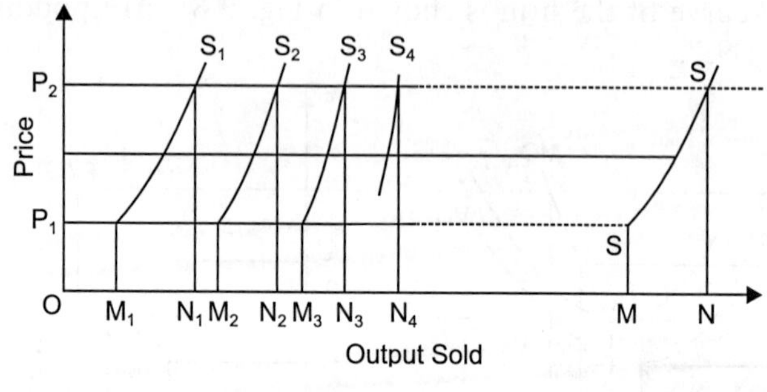

Fig. 9.9

In case of n number of firms in an industry with their respective supply curves S_1, S_2 ...., S_n, then the supply curve of the industry will be $\sum_{i=1}^{n} S_i$. Thus, we sum up the individual firms' supply curves to obtain the industry supply curve.

SHORT RUN EQUILIBRIUM OF THE INDUSTRY

Given the market demand and the market supply the industry is in equilibrium at that price which clears the market, that is, at the price at which the quantity demanded is equal to the quantity supplied. In Fig. 9.10 the industry is in equilibrium at price $\overline{P}$, at which the quantity demanded and supplied is $\overline{Q}$. However, this will be a short run equilibrium, if at the prevailing price firms are making excess profits shown by the area of $\overline{P}$ EBA in Fig. 9.11 or losses shown by the area of $\overline{P}$ ECF in Fig. 9.12. In the long run firms that make losses and cannot readjust their plant will close down. Those that make excess profits will expand their capacity, while excess profits will also attract new firms into the industry. Entry, exit and readjustment of the remaining firms in the industry will lead to a long run equilibrium in which firms will just be earning only normal profits.

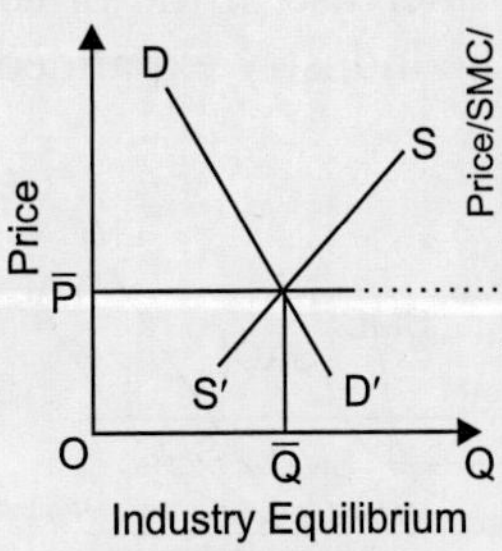

Fig. 9.10

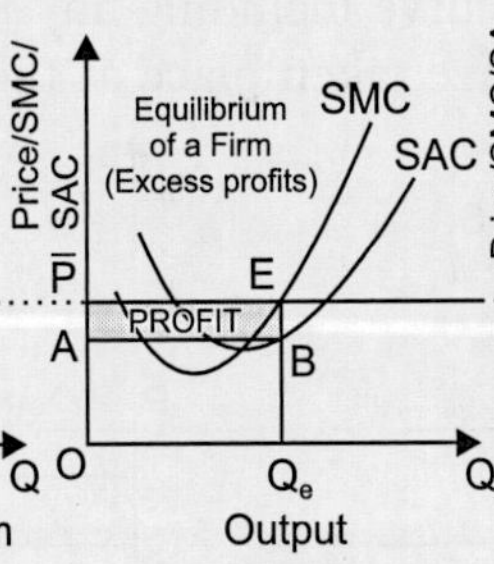

Fig. 9.11

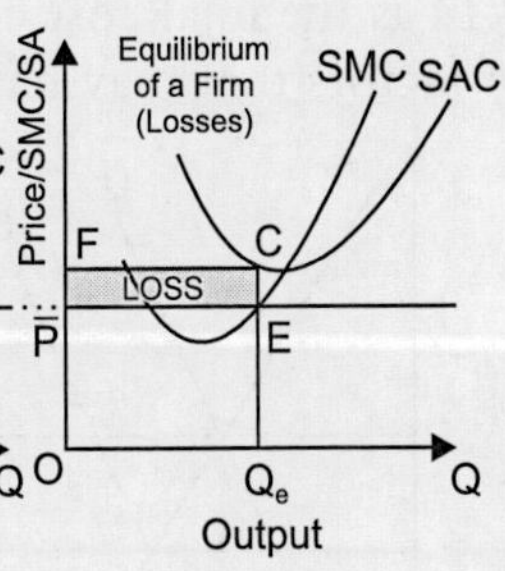

Fig. 9.12

LONG RUN EQUILIBRIUM

Equilibrium of the firm: In the long run firms are in equilibrium when they have adjusted their plant so as to produce at the minimum point of their long run AC curve, which is tangent at this point to the demand curve (P = AR = MR) defined by the market price earning just normal profits (no loss no profit just covering the cost). If they are making excess profits new firms will be attracted in the industry. This will lead to a fall in price due to excess supply in the market. This results a downward shift in the individual demand curves and an upward shift of the cost curves due to the increase of the prices of factors as the industry expands. These changes will continue until the LAC is tangent to the demand curve defined by the market price. If the firms make losses in the long run they will leave the industry, price will rise and costs may fall as the industry contracts, until the remaining firms in the industry cover their total costs.

In Fig. 9.14 we show how firms adjust to their long run equilibrium position. If the price is P, the firm is making excess profits working with the plant whose cost is denoted by SAC_1. It will, therefore, have an incentive to build new capacity and it will move along its LAC. At the same time new firms will be entering the industry attracted by the excess profits. As the quantity supplied in the market increases by the increased production of expanding old firms and by the newly established ones, the supply curve in the market will shift to the right and price will fall until it reaches the level of P_1 in Fig. 9.13 at which the firms and the industry are in long run equilibrium. The LAC in Fig. 9.14 is the final cost curve including any increase in the prices of factors that may have taken place as the industry expanded.

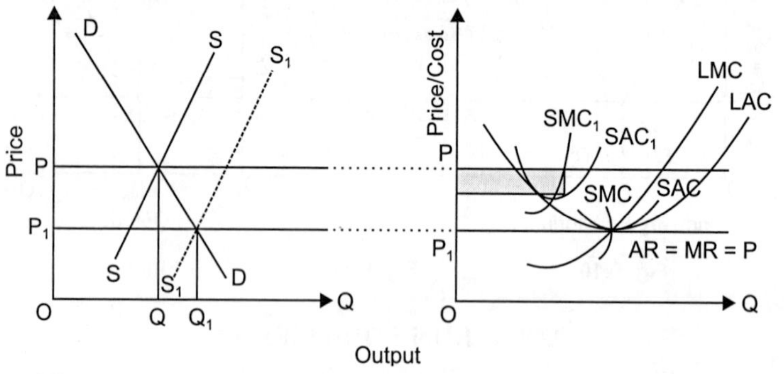

Fig. 9.13 Fig. 9.14

The condition for the long run equilibrium of the firm is that the long run marginal cost be equal to the price and to the long run average cost, i.e., LMC = P = LAC. The firm adjusts its plant size so as to produce that level of output at which the LAC is the minimum possible, given the technology and the prices of factors of production. At equilibrium the short run marginal cost is equal to the long run marginal cost and the short run average cost is equal to the long run average cost. Thus, given the above equilibrium condition, we have

SMC = LMC = SAC = LAC = P = MR

This implies that at the minimum point of the LAC the corresponding short run plant is worked at its optimal capacity, so that the minimum points of the LAC and the SAC coincide. On the other hand, the LMC cuts the LAC at its minimum point and the SMC cuts the SAC at its minimum point. Thus at the minimum point of the LAC the above equality between short run and long run costs is satisfied.

EQUILIBRIUM OF THE INDUSTRY IN THE LONG RUN

The industry is in long run equilibrium when a price is reached at which all firms are in equilibrium producing at the minimum point of their LAC curve and making just normal profits. The long run equilibrium of the industry is shown in Fig. 9.15(b). At the market price, the firms produce at their minimum cost earning just normal profits. The firm is in equilibrium because at the level of output Q, LMC = SMC = P = AR = MR. This equality ensures that the firm maximises its profit.

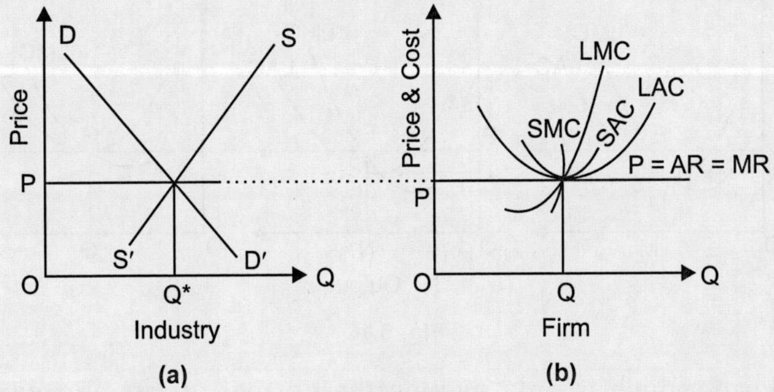

Fig. 9.15

At the price P the industry is in equilibrium because profits are normal and all costs are covered. As a result, there is no incentive for entry or exit of firm. The firms earn just normal profit is shown by the equality LAC = SAC = P which is observed at the minimum point of the LAC curve. With all firms in industry being in equilibrium and with no entry or exit, the industry supply remains stable. In Fig. 9.15(a), the price P is a long run equilibrium price and Q* or Q is long run equilibrium output which are determined by the interaction of market demand DD′ and market supply SS′ curves.

FIRM EARNS ONLY NORMAL OR SUPER NORMAL PROFIT BUT NOT SUBNORMAL PROFIT IN LONG RUN

The firms which have been incurring losses in the short run will try to exist in the industry on the hope of future profit but up to the point where the average revenue (price) equals to the average variable cost. In this situation, the firm has to give loss of entire fixed cost. But in the long run, the firm cannot continue to afford the losses. That is why, the firm leaves the industry. Only those firms which have been making either super normal profits or the normal profits remain in the industry. Thus, in the long run the firms earn only normal or super normal profits but not subnormal profit.

A firm makes normal profit when the price line (AR = P) is tangent to the U-shaped average cost curve of the firm, i.e., the market price just covers its average cost of production. This is shown in Fig. 9.16.

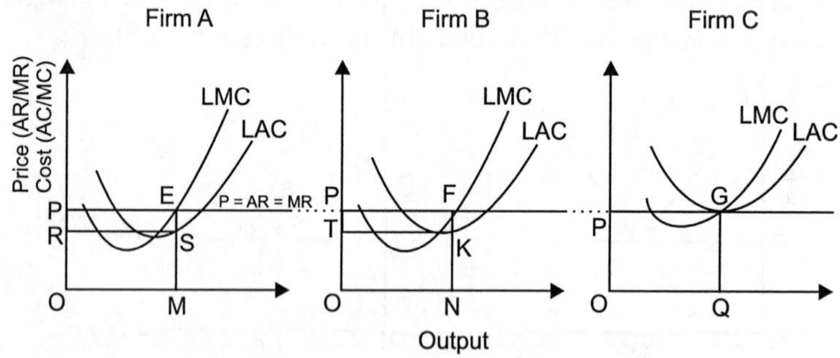

Fig. 9.16

Firm, which is only making the normal profits and would leave the industry, even with a small fall in price is called the 'marginal firm'. The average cost of the marginal firm is just equal to the market price (AR) at the point of equilibrium.

We know that for the firms under identical cost conditions long run equilibrium takes place where MR = MC = AR = AC. But in case of firm operating with different cost conditions, the long run equilibrium will be established when price (AR) is equal to the marginal cost of all the intramarginal firms and the average cost of the marginal firm. If price is higher than the average cost of the marginal firm, this firm would be earning super normal profits. This will attract new high cost firms whose entry would raise output supply of the industry and thus bring down price level (AR) which in turn will reduce the profits of the firms already working in the industry.

On the other hand, if the price becomes lower than the average cost of the marginal firms, such firms will incur losses and leave the market. With the exit of some firms from the industry, the market supply would be reduced and the price move up to a point where it would just be equal to the average cost of the marginal firm. Thus, the condition of long run equilibrium of firms with cost differentials is that

P(AR/MR) = MC of all the intramarginal firms
= AC of the marginal firm.

This can be explained with the help of Fig. 9.16 shown above, where in three firms A, B and C have been depicted, each of these firms is representative of the category to which they belong.

Among the three firms, price P (AR) equals marginal cost of the firm A at point E. This firm produces OM amount and gains super normal profits equal to RSEP, as the price is above the average cost of this firm. Similarly the firm B is in equilibrium at point F producing ON amount and makes a super normal profit of TKFP, as price is more than the average cost. But in the case of firm C, the equilibrium point G gives an output of OQ. At this point G, price being equal to the average cost, no super normal profits are earned. Thus the marginal firm earns only the normal profits while the intramarginal firms make super normal profits. If the market price goes down from OP to OT, firm C will leave the market and firm B would become marginal firm earning no abnormal profit is the only optimum firm operating in the industry. The intramarginal firms are of more than optimum size.

REVENUE CURVE OR PRICE LINE OF A FIRM

Two important features of perfect competition are (1) a very large number of sellers and buyers in the market and (2) the homogeneous product. First the number of firms being very large, no individual firm can influence the market price by its own action. In fact the firm is so insignificant a unit in the whole industry that even if it expands its output and sells more in the market, it will not make any difference to the price. Thus the firm can sell as much as it likes at the price determined in the market by the operation of the forces of total demand and total supply. Secondly, the homogeneous production implies that each firm is making exactly same goods. There is no natural or artificial difference in the products of different firms. If the quality of products is the same with all the firms, no firm would be in a position to charge higher or lower price than the price determined in the market. If a firm charges more, no one would purchase. Again no firm would charge lower than the market price, because it can sell as much as it likes at the given price. Thus under conditions of perfect competition, the price of commodity is given as fixed by the market demand and supply for the industry as a whole; it would remain same whether one firm sells more or less. Under such conditions, the total revenue of a firm would increase in the same proportion as the sale of output is increasing. And when the total revenue (TR) increases in direct proportion to the sale of output, the average revenue (AR) would remain constant. This is shown in example and Fig. 9.17.

No. of units sold	Price of the commodity (₹)	TR (₹)	AR (₹)	MR (₹)
1	5	5	5	5
2	5	10	5	5
3	5	15	5	5
4	5	20	5	5
5	5	25	5	5
6	5	30	5	5
7	5	35	5	5
8	5	40	5	5

Thus, under perfect competition average revenue (AR) and marginal revenue (MR) are constant and equal to its price. As price is fixed and given, MR is constant and is also equal to the

AR. In Fig. 9.17 the AR curve of the firm operating under competitive conditions coincides with MR curve and parallel to the X-axis at a distance which is equal to the price of ₹ 5 of the commodity in our example. The MR curve also lies at the same place at which AR is lying. Since AR is equal to MR under perfect competition, the same curve shows both the average revenue as well as the marginal revenue.

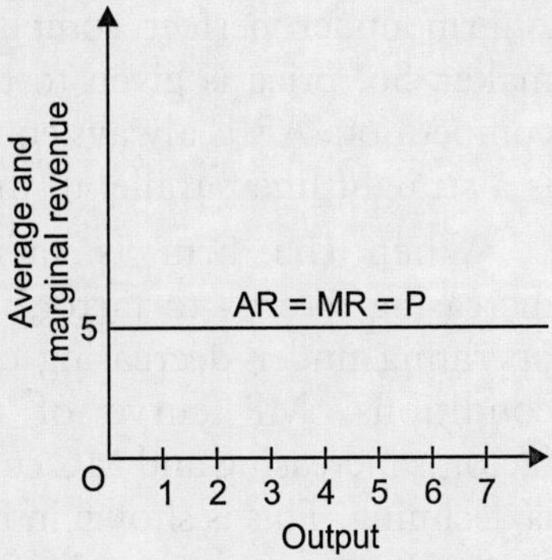

Fig. 9.17

LIMITATIONS OF MARKET UNDER PERFECT COMPETITION

There are so many limitations lying with its assumptions:

1. Every firm produces identical product. But practically it is not true because the product of a firm may be slightly different from that of another firm.
2. There is no government intervention in the market. But government can intervene in the market on special cases.
3. All buyers and sellers of a particular product have complete knowledge. But practically there may not have complete knowledge. Price of a product may be known to the seller and the buyer during the operation of the market. It may not be known at before hand.
4. The factor of production may or may not be free to move from one firm to another firm.
5. There is absence of transport cost. It is not true. For the mobility of factors of production there must be transport cost though all the firms operate so close to each other.

INCOMPATIBILITY OF INCREASING RETURNS AND CONSTANT RETURNS UNDER PERFECT COMPETITION

We know that the equilibrium of a firm under perfect competition requires the fulfilment of two conditions: (i) MC = MR and (ii) The slope of MC curve > the slope of MR curve.

A firm under perfect competition is a price-taker not price-maker. So, price is given to the firm. Therefore, under perfect competition, AR is always equal to MR and AR = MR = P curve is a straight line parallel to the horizontal axis.

When the firm is facing increasing returns to factor, i.e., operating under decreasing cost conditions, MP curve of the factor is increasing and MC curve is declining. This is shown in Fig. 9.18. Here e is the equilibrium point where we get MC = MR but the slope of MC > slope of MR is not fulfilled (but slope of MC < slope of MR). That is why, e will never be an equilibrium point.

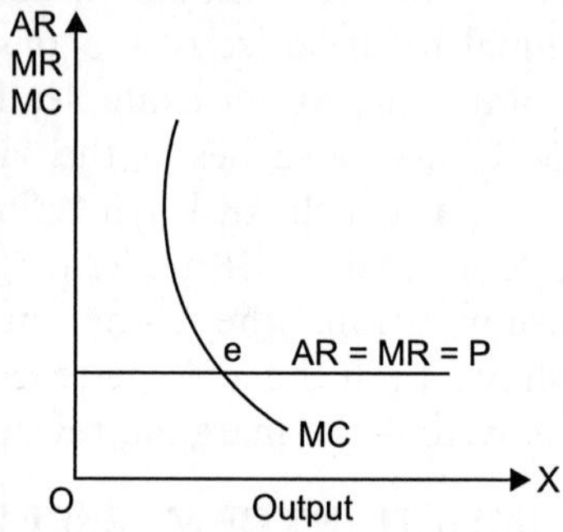

Fig. 9.18

Again, when the firm is operating under constant returns to factor, i.e., under constant cost conditions, its MP curve and its MC curve remain constant. If price, i.e., AR = MR = P in the market is either higher than MC or lower than MC, we never get equilibrium point.

Again if MR = AR = P curve coincides with MC curve, it is also not possible to get a unique equilibrium point. It is shown in Fig. 9.19. In this figure there may be three possibilities, i.e., (i) MC curve stands above MR = AR curve, (ii) MC curve stands below MR = AR curve or (iii) MC curve coincides with MR = AR curve. There is no equilibrium point where the two conditions for equilibrium (mentioned above) will be fulfilled.

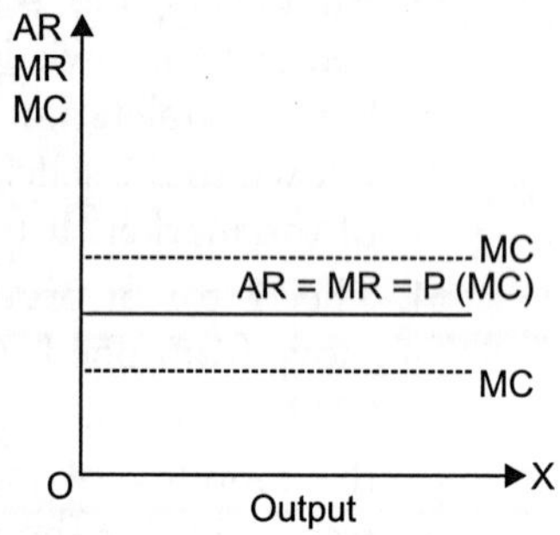

Fig. 9.19

Therefore, it is clear that increasing returns and constant returns are incompatible under perfect competition.

JUSTIFICATION OF PERFECT COMPETITION

The justification of perfect competition is supported to understand the market phenomena. In our real life we do not see the existence of perfect competition. Some conditions of perfect competition such as perfect knowledge, absence of transformation cost, etc. never be seen in anywhere. That is why, these conditions are absurd. Therefore, the absurd conditions reduce the usefulness of perfect competition. What we see in our surrounding area, it is not a market of perfect competition but a perfect competitive market. But some of the conditions of perfect competition are very much seen in our practical life.

However, perfect competition is really rare in the real world. But we still study it for the following reasons:

1. It furnishes us with a simple and logical starting point for economic analysis of the market.
2. It gives us a very useful knowledge about the structure of market.
3. It explains and predicts about many complicated economic phenomena of the market.
4. It gives us an overall idea about the mechanism of market.
5. If perfect competition is avoided from the market mechanism, the many practical market situations will be remained untouched.

EXERCISES

1. Define perfect competition with its assumptions. Show the equilibrium of a firm and an industry in short run and long run and also derive a supply curve.
2. Show that a firm in short run earns super normal, normal or subnormal profit or show equilibrium of a firm with having differential costs in short run.
3. Show that how does an industry achieve its equilibrium in the long run?
4. Show that in the long run firm earns only normal or super normal profit, but not subnormal profit.

Or

Show the operation of the firms having differential costs in the long run.

Or

Show the equilibrium of the firms under perfect competition having differential costs in the long run.

5. What do you mean by shut down point? Discuss with a diagram.

   Or

   How much loss can a firm bear? Discuss with a diagram.

   Or

   Where does a firm close down its production? Discuss with a diagram.
6. What are the differences between pure competition and perfect competition?
7. Discuss the revenue curve or price line of the firm operating under conditions of perfect competition with example and diagram.
8. Discuss the limitations of the perfect competitive market.
9. Discuss the incompatibility of increasing returns and constant returns under perfect competition, i.e., absence of equilibrium point in case of increasing returns and constant returns under perfect competition.
10. What is the justification of perfect competition in the market?

Chapter 10

Market Forms: Monopoly

The word 'monopoly' consists of two syllables: mono and poly, where mono means single and poly means selling. The literal meaning of the word 'monopoly' is that there is only single seller of a product in the market. But in Economics it bears a deep meaning on the basis of the degree of competition prevailing in the market. So, monopoly is a market situation where there is only one single seller of a product in the market. The monopolist sets a price whatever he wishes. Examples of pure monopoly are a single gas agency in a town, single water supply department, etc. It includes the following characteristics:

1. There is a single seller or producer who controls the entire market, but there are large number of buyers.
2. There is absence of close substitute of the product of the monopolist, i.e., cross elasticity of demand for the product is zero. It is one homogeneous product and completely under the control of the monopolist over the supply.
3. There is only one firm consisting industry.
4. There is artificial or real barrier to the entry of a new firm.
5. The aim of the firm is to maximise profit and hence, there may be existence of super normal profit.
6. The single firm is not price-taker like a firm in perfect competition but a price-maker. Being a sole supplier,

the monopolist is, thus in a position to fix up a price to his own advantage.

CONDITIONS OF EQUILIBRIUM IN MONOPOLY MARKET

We have to fulfil two conditions for equilibrium. Equilibrium means to maximise profit. We know, total profit (π) is the difference between total revenue (TR) and total cost (TC). That is, $\pi = TR - TC$. To maximise π the first order condition requires:

$$\frac{d\pi}{dq} = \frac{d(TR)}{dq} - \frac{d(TC)}{dq} \qquad \text{(where q = output)}$$

$$\text{or,} \quad \frac{d(TR)}{dq} - \frac{d(TC)}{dq} = 0 \qquad \left[\because \frac{d\pi}{dq} = 0\right]$$

or, $MR - MC = 0$, or, $MR = MC$.

This means that to maximise profit the first order condition requires that MR should be equal to MC. Second order condition of profit maximisation requires:

$$\frac{d^2(TR)}{dq^2} - \frac{d^2(TC)}{dq^2} < 0$$

or, Slope of MR – Slope of MC < 0

$\because$ Slope of MR < Slope of MC.

This means that the rate of change of MR should be less than that of MC. In other words, the slope of MR should be less than the slope of MC. In normal case when the MR curve is downward sloping and the MC curve is upward rising.

These two conditions are necessary for equilibrium of a producer in a monopoly market.

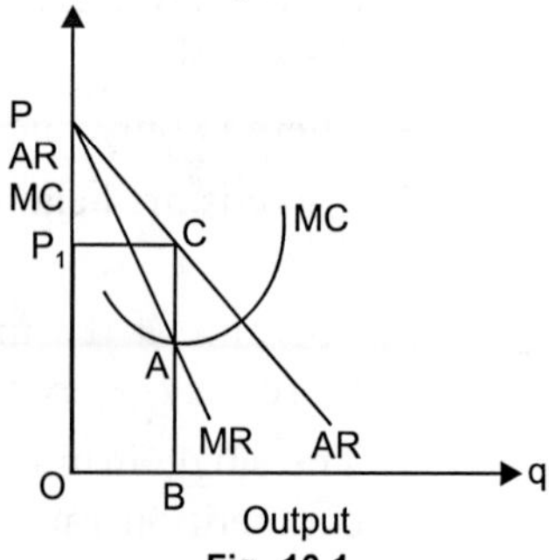

Fig. 10.1

The equilibrium of a monopolist can be represented with the help of Fig. 10.1. The first order condition, i.e., MR = MC is fulfilled at point A. The second order condition, i.e., the slope of MC > the slope of MR is also fulfilled at point A. So, 'A' is the equilibrium point of the firm in a monopoly market. The equilibrium output is OB and equilibrium price is OP_1. Profit of the monopolist depends on the position of AC curve.

EQUILIBRIUM UNDER MONOPOLY

Short Run Equilibrium

During short run the monopolist may enjoy super normal profit, normal profit or subnormal profit as shown in Fig. 10.2(a), (b) & (c) below:

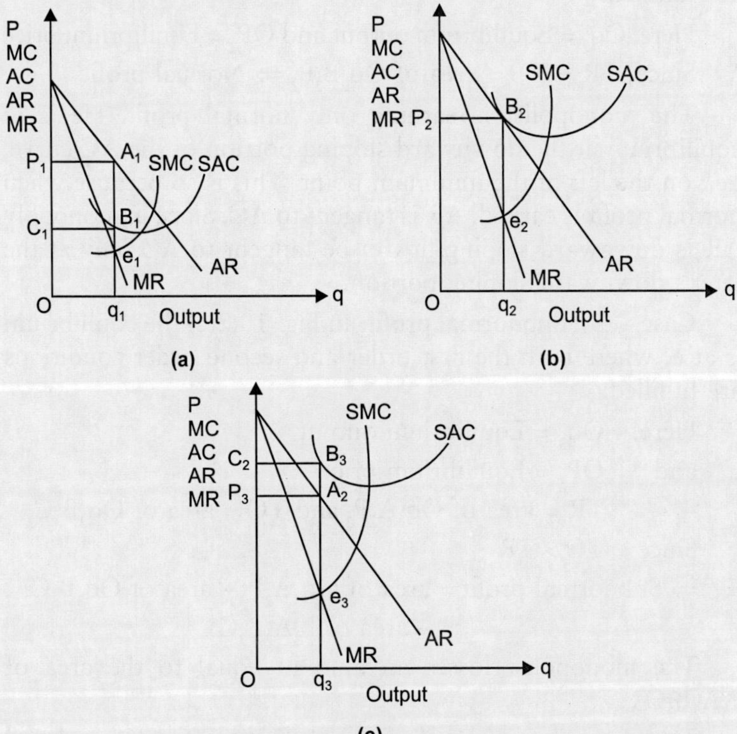

Fig. 10.2

Case – (1): Super normal profit: In Fig. 10.2(a) the monopolist is in equilibrium at point e_1 where both the first order and second order conditions are fulfilled. That is, MC = MR and slope of MC > slope of MR.

Here, Oq_1 = equilibrium output and Op_1 = equilibrium price

Total revenue (TR) = area of $Oq_1A_1P_1$

and Total cost (TC) = area of $Oq_1B_1C_1$

Since, TR > TC ⇒ Super normal profit

= area of $Oq_1A_1P_1$ – area of $Oq_1B_1C_1$

= area of $C_1B_1A_1P_1$

Case – (2): Normal profit: In Fig. 10.2(b) the equilibrium is at e_2 where both the first order and second order conditions are fulfilled.

Here, Oq_2 = Equilibrium output and OP_2 = Equilibrium price

Since, TR = TC = area of $Oq_2B_2P_2$ ⇒ Normal profit

The monopolist is earning only normal profit. He is in equilibrium at the downward sloping portion of the AC curve, i.e., on the left of the minimum point. This is so because when normal profit is earned, AR is tangent to AC. Since in monopoly AR is downward sloping, it can be tangent to AC only at the later's downward sloping portion.

Case – (3): Subnormal profit: In Fig. 10.2(c) the equilibrium is at e_3 where both the first order and second order conditions are fulfilled.

Here, Oq_3 = Equilibrium output

and OP_3 = Equilibrium price

TR = area of $Oq_3A_2P_3$ and TC = area of $Oq_3B_3C_2$

Since TC > TR

⇒ Subnormal profit = area of $Oq_3A_2P_3$ – area of $Oq_3B_3C_2$

= – area of $P_3A_2B_3C_2$

The monopolist losses an amount equal to the area of $P_3A_2B_3C_2$.

Therefore, the monopolist earns super normal, normal and subnormal profit in short run.

Long Run Equilibrium

In the long run, the monopolist has enough time to expand his plant or to use the existing plant at any level of output which maximises his total profit. Since entry of other firm is blocked, he earns either super normal or normal profit, but never subnormal profit in the long run. This is shown in the following Fig. 10.3:

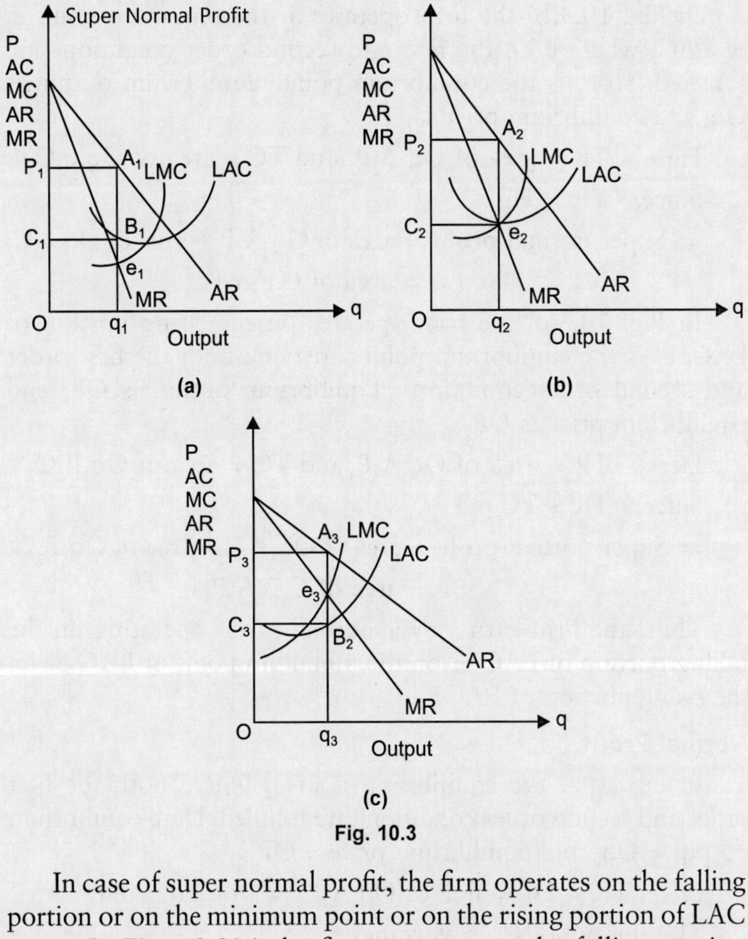

Fig. 10.3

In case of super normal profit, the firm operates on the falling portion or on the minimum point or on the rising portion of LAC curve. In Fig. 10.3(a) the firm operates on the falling portion of LAC curve at B_1 where e_1 is the equilibrium point satisfying both the first and second order conditions. Equilibrium output is Oq_1 and equilibrium price is OP_1.

Here, TR = area of $Oq_1A_1P_1$ and TC = area of $Oq_1B_1C_1$

Since, TR > TC

$\Rightarrow$ Super normal profit = area of $Oq_1A_1P_1$ – area of $Oq_1B_1C_1$

= area of $P_1A_1C_1B_1$

In Fig. 10.3(b) the firm operates at the minimum point e_2 of LAC, where both the first and second order conditions are satisfied. So e_2 is the equilibrium point. Equilibrium output is Oq_2 and equilibrium price is OP_2.

Here TR = area of $Oq_2A_2P_2$ and TC = area of $Oq_2e_2C_2$

Since, TR > TC

$\Rightarrow$ Super normal profit = area of $Oq_2A_2P_2$ – area of $Oq_2e_2C_2$

= area of $C_2e_2A_2P_2$

In Fig. 10.3(c) the firm operates on the rising portion of LAC. e_3 is the equilibrium point satisfying both the first order and second order conditions. Equilibrium output is Oq_3 and equilibrium price is OP_3.

Here, TR = area of $Oq_3A_3P_3$ and TC = area of $Oq_3B_2C_3$

Since, TR > TC

$\Rightarrow$ Super normal profit = area of $Oq_3A_3P_3$ – area of $Oq_3B_2C_3$

= area of $C_3B_2A_3P_3$

Thus, the firm earns super normal profit operating on the falling portion of LAC or on the minimum point of LAC or on the rising portion of LAC.

Normal Profit

In Fig. 10.4 the equilibrium is at e_4 where both the first order and second order conditions are fulfilled. Here equilibrium output = Oq_4 and equilibrium price = OP_4

Here, TR = TC = area of $Oq_4A_4P_4 \Rightarrow$ normal profit.

The monopolist is earning only normal profit. He is in equilibrium at the downward sloping portion of the LAC curve, i.e., on the left of its minimum point. This is so because when normal profit is earned, AR is tangent to LAC.

So, it is clear that in the long run a monopolist earns only normal or super normal profit.

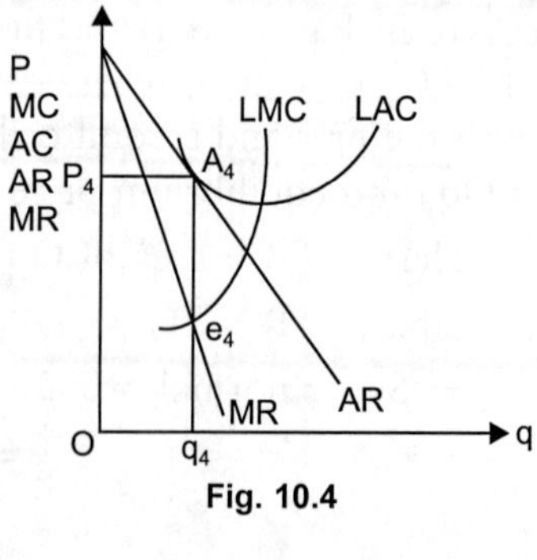

Fig. 10.4

ABSENCE OF SUPPLY CURVE IN MONOPOLY

Under conditions of perfect competition, the rising section of MC curve above the minimum point of SAVC curve represents the supply curve of a firm. There is one-to-one correspondence between price and quantity supplied in perfect competition. This means that corresponding to one price there is one and only one quantity of output that will be supplied and conversely corresponding to one quantity of output there is one and only one price at which this quantity of output will be supplied.

But under monopoly this unique relationship between price and quantity supplied is absent. There is no such one-to-one correspondence between price and quantity supplied. The monopolist can sell same output at different prices at different market demand conditions. Again he can charge same price for different quantities of output at different market conditions. So no unique relationship exists between supply and price. Therefore, we do not get any supply curve in monopoly. This can be proved by the following figures:

Case – (1): Same output at different prices: Suppose that AR_1 is the initial AR curve and MR_1 is the corresponding MR curve in Fig. 10.5. The initial equilibrium point is e_1 where the MR_1 curve intersects the MC curve. Oq_1 is the equilibrium level of output and OP_1 is the equilibrium price. If MR curve is rotated around the equilibrium point, e_1 then MR curve becomes MR_2 passing through the same equilibrium point e_1. Corresponding to MR_2, AR curve will be AR_2. When the position of the MR curve is MR_2, the equilibrium point remains the same. The equilibrium output level also remains the same. But when the AR curve is AR_2, the equilibrium price is changed and becomes OP_2 which is lower than OP_1 (previous price). Thus the same output level Oq_1 can be supplied at two different prices OP_1 and OP_2.

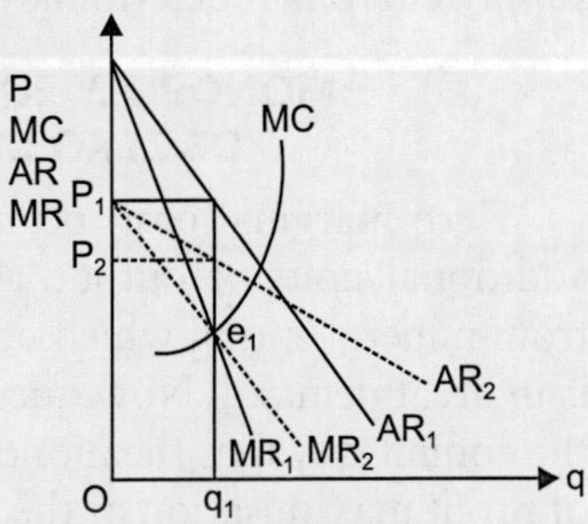

Fig. 10.5

Case – (2): Same price for different quantities of output: It can be seen that the monopolist can sell two different quantities of output at the same price. This is shown in Fig. 10.6. Initially the AR curve is AR_3 and MR curve is MR_3. The equilibrium point is e_2. The level of equilibrium output and equilibrium price are Oq_2 and OP_3 respectively. When AR curve and MR curve change their positions and become AR_4 and MR_4 respectively, the new equilibrium point is e_3. The new equilibrium output is Oq_3 but the price remains the same at OP_3. Hence, it is seen that two different output levels could be supplied at the same price OP_3.

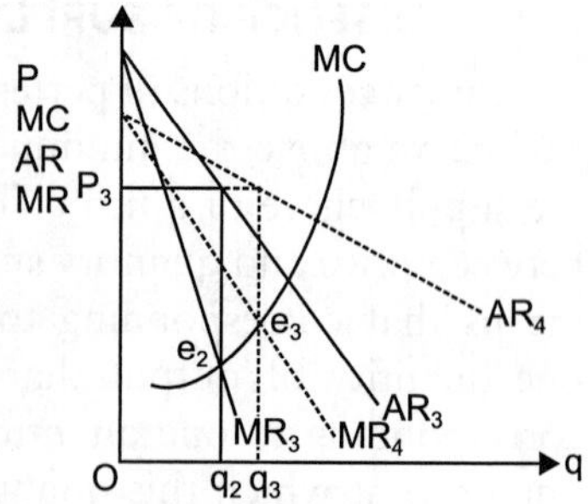

Fig. 10.6

Therefore, the above two cases show that due to absence of any unique relationship between price and output supplied, supply curve is indeterminate in monopoly.

MONOPOLY EQUILIBRIUM IN CASE OF ZERO MARGINAL COST

Zero marginal cost means that there is no cost to produce additional units of output. As an example we can take water from mineral spring which has no cost of production but which is in great demand. Now question arises: What is the amount of the commodity that the monopolist will sell so that the objective of profit maximisation of the monopolist is fulfilled? When total profit is maximised, the monopolist is said to be in equilibrium. Total profit will be equal to total revenue (TR) because total cost is zero. Total profit will be maximum where TR is maximum. The monopolist will sell the output up to the point where TR is maximum. TR is maximum when MR is zero. From the conditions of equilibrium, we know that

(i) MR = MC and (ii) Slope of MR < Slope of MC

In Fig. 10.7, both the conditions are fulfilled at point N where MR = MC = 0. X-axis itself is a MC curve as MC = 0.

So, N is equilibrium point. TR is maximum at ON level of output where MR is zero corresponding to the price OP_1. The price OP_1 is set by him in this situation where the price elasticity of demand on the AR curve is equal to one at point S (e = 1). Below the point S where we get e < 1, MR is negative. TR cannot be maximum. Above the point S we get e > 1 where MR > MC which cannot fulfil the conditions of equilibrium. We, therefore, conclude that when cost of production is zero, monopoly equilibrium will be established at a level of output where elasticity of demand is one with zero marginal revenue.

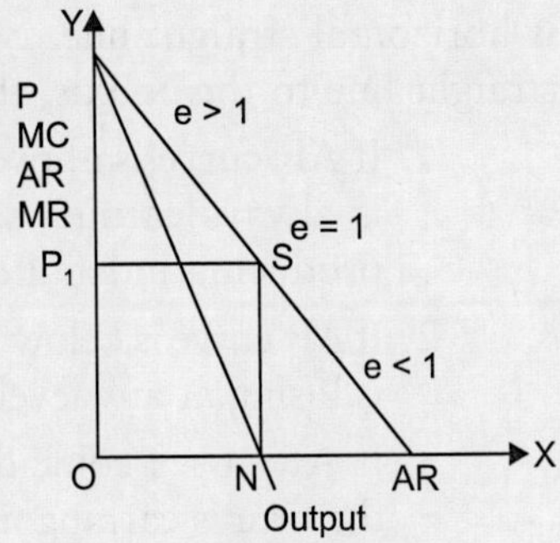

Fig. 10.7

EQUILIBRIUM OF A FIRM UNDER MONOPOLY WHEN ITS MC CURVE IS A HORIZONTAL STRAIGHT LINE

In the following Fig. 10.8, it is clear that we have get the equilibrium at point A, where both the first order and second order conditions are fulfilled. That is, (i) MC = MR and (ii) the slope of MC > the slope of MR are fulfilled. So, the equilibrium output is OB and the equilibrium price is BC (OP_1). In monopoly if the MC curve is horizontal, we get MC = AC. Here, price is greater than AC, the monopolist is earning super normal profit.

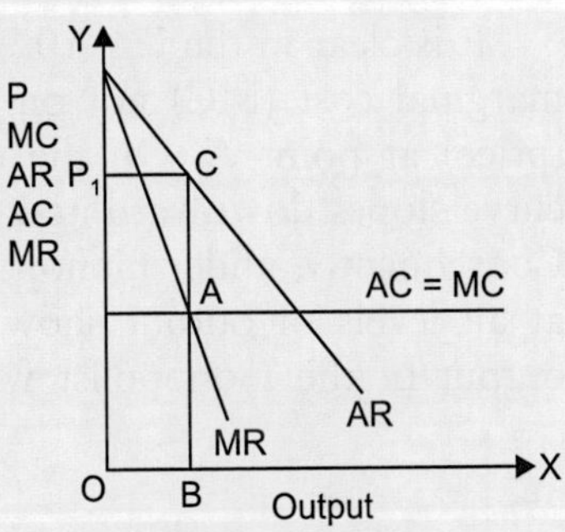

Fig. 10.8

Therefore, we get the equilibrium of a firm under monopoly when its MC curve is a horizontal straight line and output is determinate.

But let us see what will be happened under perfect competition? Under perfect competition, we get, P = AR = MR is horizontal straight line. Now if AC = MC is also horizontal straight line to the X-axis, there may be three possibilities:

1. If AR curve is above AC curve, i.e., AR > AC, the firm is always earning super normal profit and it goes on producing indefinitely.
2. If AR curve is below the AC curve, i.e., AR < AC, the firm is losing at any level of output and it stops production.
3. If AR curve coincides with AC curve, i.e., AR = AC, the firm is earning normal profit at any level of output.

We, therefore, conclude that when MC curve of a firm is a horizontal straight line under perfect competition, we cannot get its equilibrium point and hence its equilibrium output is indeterminate.

COMPETITIVE PRICE IS LOWER THAN MONOPOLY PRICE

Under perfect competition average revenue (AR = P) is a horizontal straight line and therefore, marginal revenue (MR) curve coincides with AR curve, as a result MR and AR are equal to each other at all levels of output shown in Fig. 10.9(a).

It is clear in the Fig. 10.9(a) that at the equilibrium output, marginal cost (MC) not only equals MR but also equals AR (price) at point A. On the other hand, under monopoly AR curve slopes downward and MR curve therefore, lies below it. Consequently, under monopoly, AR (price) is greater than MR at all levels of output shown in Fig. 10.9(b). At equilibrium output of the monopolist where MC equals MR at point B,

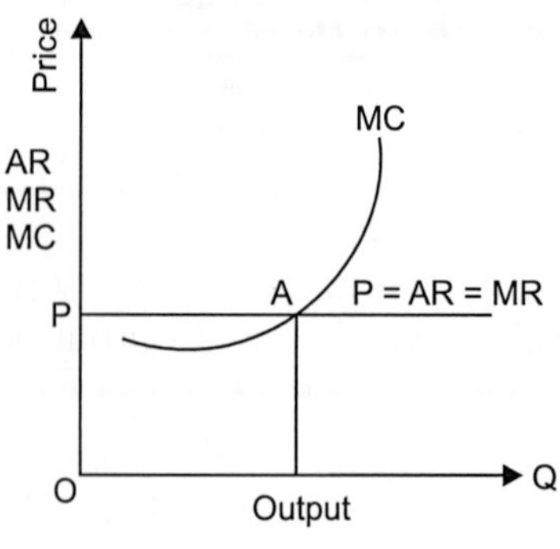

Fig. 10.9(a)

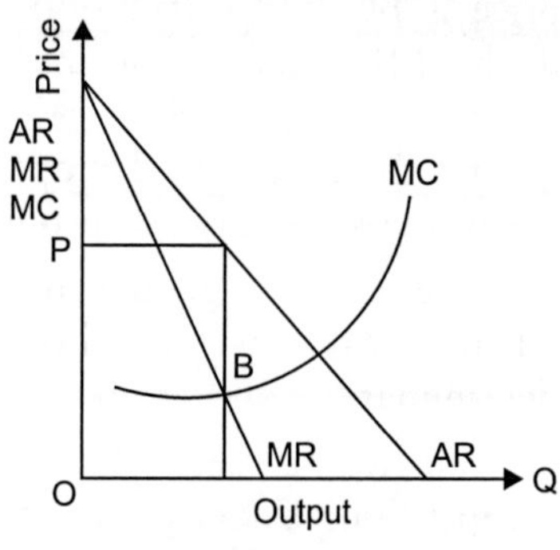

Fig. 10.9(b)

price stands higher than MC. Thus, in perfectly competitive equilibrium, price = MR = MC and in monopoly equilibrium, price > MC. Therefore, we conclude that a competitive firm will always operate at an output level where price equals MC. On the contrary, a monopoly firm will always operate at a level of output where price is higher than MC. In general, competitive price is lower than monopoly price.

So in this case, the firm earns normal profit under perfect competition and super normal profit under monopoly.

COMPARISON BETWEEN MONOPOLY EQUILIBRIUM AND PERFECTLY COMPETITIVE EQUILIBRIUM

We know that there are a large number of firms in perfect competitive market producing homogeneous products. Price and output are determined at the level where demand and supply curve intersect each other. No firm in perfect competition can affect either price or output in the market. Now, if we assume, all the firms constituting the competitive industry combine together so as to form a monopoly. We get same cost condition and same supply condition, i.e., cost or supply conditions remain unchanged. Now under monopoly the price and output are determined by the equality between marginal cost (MC) and marginal revenue (MR). Equilibrium under perfect competition and monopoly is shown in Fig. 10.10.

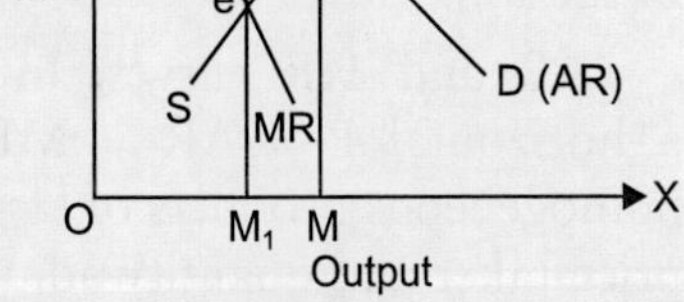

Fig. 10.10

Here DD and SS curves are respectively demand and supply curves of the perfectly competitive industry. The two curves intersect each other at point P_1. So, the equilibrium output is OM and equilibrium price is MP_1. Now the MR curve is drawn corresponding to the demand curve DD which is an AR curve also. The SS curve (supply curve) of perfectly competitive industry will be the MC curve of monopoly. The MR curve cuts the MC curve at point e. So, the equilibrium point of monopoly is e which corresponds the monopoly price M_1P_2 and monopoly output OM_1. Here, we get $M_1P_2 > MP_1$ and $OM_1 < OM$, i.e., monopoly price is greater than that under perfect competition and monopoly output is lower than that under perfect competition if cost conditions remain unchanged. Monopoly thus restricts output to raise price.

COMPARISON BETWEEN PERFECT COMPETITION AND MONOPOLY IN RESPECT OF PRICE, OUTPUT AND PROFIT

In both the models of perfect competition and monopoly there are some similarities and some dissimilarities. But dissimilarities are more vital than similarities. These are discussed below:

Goal: The firm in both the models has a single goal to maximise profit.

Manager: In both the models the owner of the firm is the manager. There is no separation of ownership from management.

Product: The product is homogeneous in both the models.

Number of sellers: In perfect competition there is a large number of sellers but in monopoly there is only one seller.

Entry and exit: There is free entry and exit in perfect competition but in monopoly entry is totally blockaded.

AC and MC curves: In both the models the AC and MC curves are assumed to be U-shaped both in the short run and in the long run.

AR and MR curves: In perfect competition a firm faces a horizontal P = AR = MR curve assuming that there are homogeneous products of large number of sellers. Each firm is a price-taker and quantity adjuster. But a monopolist firm faces a downward sloping AR and MR curves. It can change the price. It is not a price-taker.

Equilibrium: A firm both under perfect competition and monopoly is in equilibrium at the level of output at which MR equals MC. That is, in both markets, equilibrium is established by the equality of MR and MC.

Since in perfect competition the MR curve is a horizontal straight line, MC curve can cut the MR curve from below only when it (MC curve) is rising. We get the equilibrium point where MC curve cuts the MR curve fulfilling both the conditions of equilibrium, namely MC = MR and the slope of MC > the slope of MR. This is possible only when MC curve is rising.

But, under monopoly, MR curve is falling downward. MC curve can cut the MR curve from below whether it (MC curve) is rising or horizontal to establish the equilibrium point satisfying both the conditions of equilibrium.

Profit: In the short run equilibrium the firm either in perfectly competitive or in monopoly market may earn normal or super normal or subnormal profit. But in the long run a perfectly competitive firm only earns normal profit. It earns neither super normal nor subnormal profit, whereas the monopolist usually earns super normal profit both in the long run and in the short run.

Price: Price is always equal to marginal cost under perfect competition. Because in equilibrium under perfect competition we get price = MR = MC, i.e., price = MC. But in equilibrium under monopoly we also get MR = MC. AR(P) curve lies above MR curve, that is why P > MR = MC, i.e., price > MC. So, monopoly price is always higher than perfectly competitive price.

Output: Given the cost conditions monopoly output will be less than the competitive output and monopoly price will be higher than the competitive price.

Price discrimination: The monopolist can discriminate prices for his product. He can demand different prices in different markets for his same product depending on the elasticities of demand in different markets. But a perfectly competitive firm cannot discriminate the price of his product.

Supply curve: Under perfect competition the supply curve of the firm is uniquely determined. The rising portion of the MC curve above the minimum point of AVC curve is the supply curve. But the monopolist can sell his product (same amount) at different prices or can sell different amounts of his product at same price. Thus, there is no unique relationship between price and quantity supplied in monopoly market. So, there is absence of supply curve in monopoly.

EXERCISES

1. Define monopoly market with its characteristics.
2. Show the conditions of equilibrium in a monopoly market.
3. Show the equilibrium under monopoly in short run and long run.
4. Prove that there is absence of supply curve in monopoly.
5. Define monopoly equilibrium in case of zero marginal cost.
6. Do you get the equilibrium of a firm under monopoly when its MC curve is a horizontal straight line? And what will be happened under perfect competition?
7. Why is price always equal to marginal cost under perfect competition and higher than marginal cost under monopoly? Explain with the help of a diagram.

   Or

   Price under perfect competition, i.e., competitive price is lower than monopoly price. Discuss.
8. Make a comparison between monopoly equilibrium and perfectly competitive equilibrium and prove that under monopoly price is higher and output is smaller than under perfect competition, assuming cost conditions in both the cases to be the same.
9. Compare the results of perfect competition and monopoly in respect of price, output and profit.

   Or

   Make a comparison between monopoly equilibrium and perfectly competitive equilibrium.

   Or

   Compare the conditions of profit maximisation under perfect competition and monopoly.

   Or

   Describe the process of price and output determination under monopoly and compare it with that under perfect competition.

Chapter 11

Discriminating Monopoly and Monopolistic Competition

DISCRIMINATING MONOPOLY

Monopoly may be simple or a discriminating monopoly. Under simple monopoly, the producer restricts his output and sells it at a higher price, thereby making maximum possible profits. Under discriminating monopoly, the monopolist charges different prices from different customers for the same commodity. That is, the act of selling the same article, produced under single control, at different prices to different buyers is known as price discrimination. Two conditions must be fulfilled for price discrimination to be possible. Firstly, the market must be divided into submarkets with different price elasticities. Secondly, there must be effective separation of the submarkets, so that no reselling can take place from a low-price market to a high-price market. For example, the State Electricity Board charges different rates for electricity for different uses.

EQUILIBRIUM OF A DISCRIMINATING MONOPOLIST

Mathematical Expression

To get equilibrium, i.e., to maximize profit we have to fulfil the first order condition and the second order condition.

First order condition: Let us assume that the monopolist sells q_1 output at P_1 price in the first market and q_2 output at P_2 price in the second market. His total output is equal to $q = q_1 + q_2$. The revenue R_1 of the first market is a function of q_1, i.e., $R_1 = f(q_1)$ and similarly in case of the second marker,

$R_2 = f(q_2)$. Therefore, total revenue (TR) will be $R = R_1 + R_2 = R_1(q_1) + R_2(q_2)$. His total cost function will be $C = C(q) = C(q_1 + q_2)$. Now profit (π) will be difference between the total revenue and total cost.

That is, $\pi = TR - TC = R_1 + R_2 - TC$

$$= R_1(q_1) + R_2(q_2) - C(q_1 + q_2)$$

It is clear from this equation that π is a function of q_1 and q_2. So we maximize π with respect to q_1 and q_2. Thus, to maximize π, first order condition requires:

$$\frac{\delta\pi}{\delta q_1} = R_1'(q_1) - C'(q_1 + q_2) = 0$$

and
$$\frac{\delta\pi}{\delta q_2} = R_2'(q_2) - C'(q_1 + q_2) = 0$$

i.e., $R_1'(q_1) = C'(q_1 + q_2)$ and $R_2'(q_2) = C'(q_1 + q_2)$

$\therefore$ $R_1'(q_1) = R_2'(q_2) = C'(q_1 + q_2)$

Where $R_1'(q_1) = MR_1$ in the first market

$R_2'(q_2) = MR_2$ in the second market

and $C'(q_1 + q_2) = MC$

Thus, we get $MR_1 = MR_2 = MC$ which is the necessary condition usually referred as the first order condition. This condition implies that marginal revenue of each market is equal to the marginal cost. To maximize profit the monopolist will distribute his output level in the two markets in such a way that the MR is the same in both the markets and is also equal to MC. If $MR_1 > MR_2$, it will be profitable to shift the output from the second market to the first market so long as $MR_1 > MR_2$. Such shifting will be stopped when $MR_1 = MR_2$. The opposite will happen when $MR_1 < MR_2$.

Second order condition: The second order condition requires that the principal minors of the relevant Hessian determinant alternate in sign beginning with the negative sign and the value of the Hessian determinant will be greater than zero.

That is,

$$R_1'' - C'' < 0 \text{ and } \begin{vmatrix} R_1'' - C'' & -C'' \\ -C'' & R_2'' - C'' \end{vmatrix} > 0$$

i.e., $R_1'' - C'' < 0$ and $(R_1'' - C'')(R_2'' - C'') - (C'')^2 > 0$

$R_1'' - C'' < 0$ or $R_1'' < C''$ implies that the rate of change of marginal revenue in each market is less than that of marginal cost for the output as a whole.

That is, the slope of MR < the slope of MC.

Diagrammatical Expression

The equilibrium of a discriminating monopolist can be explained with the help of the following Fig. 11.1(a), (b) & (c):

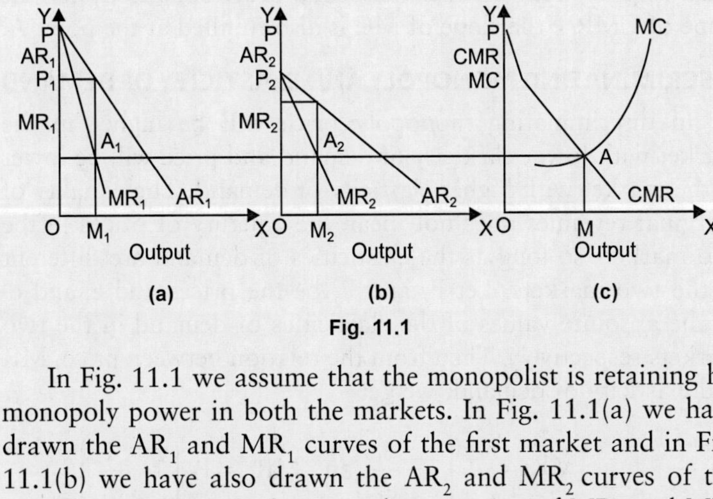

Fig. 11.1

In Fig. 11.1 we assume that the monopolist is retaining his monopoly power in both the markets. In Fig. 11.1(a) we have drawn the AR_1 and MR_1 curves of the first market and in Fig. 11.1(b) we have also drawn the AR_2 and MR_2 curves of the second market. By the horizontal summation of MR_1 and MR_2 curves we have obtained the combined MR curve (CMR) of Fig. 11.1(c). In Fig. 11.1(c) we have also plotted the MC curve of the monopolist. The CMR curve and the MC curve intersect at point A which determines the level of output OM. A is the equilibrium point where both the two conditions are fulfilled. Now this OM output is to be sold in two markets. How much of OM goes to each of these markets? To find this we draw from A, a line parallel to OX. This line, which shows marginal cost of the output produced, meet the marginal revenue curves MR_1

and MR_2 at point A_1 and A_2 respectively. So A_1 and A_2 represent the equality of marginal cost with the marginal revenue in the two respective markets, i.e., $MR_1 = MR_2 = MC$. Therefore, amount OM_1 would be sold in the first market and OM_2 in the second market, i.e., $OM = OM_1 + OM_2$. The respective price in two markets would, therefore, be OP_1 and OP_2. These two prices would be different because of the difference in the slope of the average revenue curves or because of the difference in the elasticities of demand of two markets. It is observed that the elasticity of demand of the first market is less than that of the second market and that is why, price in the first market is higher than that of the second market. So, the condition of equilibrium under discriminating monopoly is that $MR_1 = MR_2 = MC$ of total output is fulfilled and the second order condition, i.e., the slope of CMR < the slope of MC is also fulfilled at the point A.

DISCRIMINATING MONOPOLY AND ELASTICITY OF DEMAND

In discriminating monopoly price will be higher in the market with lower elasticity of demand and price will be lower in the market with higher elasticity of demand. The equality of marginal revenues does not mean the equality of prices in the two markets so long as the elasticities of demand are different in the two markets. Let P_1 and P_2 be the prices and e_1 and e_2 be the absolute values of the elasticities of demand in the two markets respectively. Then from the relation between price, MR and elasticity of demand, we get

$$MR_1 = P_1\left(1 - \frac{1}{e_1}\right) \text{and } MR_2 = P_2\left(1 - \frac{1}{e_2}\right)$$

If $MR_1 = MR_2$, then

$$P_1\left(1 - \frac{1}{e_1}\right) = P_2\left(1 - \frac{1}{e_2}\right)$$

or,

$$\frac{P_1}{P_2} = \frac{1 - \dfrac{1}{e_2}}{1 - \dfrac{1}{e_1}}$$

when $P_1 > P_2$

$$\text{i.e.,} \quad \frac{P_1}{P_2} > 1, \therefore \frac{1-\frac{1}{e_2}}{1-\frac{1}{e_1}} > 1 \text{ or, } 1-\frac{1}{e_2} > 1-\frac{1}{e_1}$$

$$\text{or,} \quad \frac{1}{e_2} < \frac{1}{e_1} \text{ or, } e_2 > e_1, \text{ i.e., } e_1 < e_2$$

We see that when $P_1 > P_2$ then $e_1 < e_2$. Therefore, price will be higher in the market with lower elasticity of demand and *vice versa*. Because of the lower elasticity of demand, the first market will not respond much to the changes in the price. Similarly, the second market having a higher elasticity would be very sensitive to price changes. That is why, the monopolists charges higher price in the first market and lower price in the second market. Therefore, price discrimination would be profitable if the monopolists were able to sub-divide the consumer into a large number of groups with different demand elasticities.

JUSTIFICATION OF PRICE DISCRIMINATION

Price discrimination is justified in some angles and is not justified in another angles. It depends on the position of the economic strength of the people. It is discussed as follows:

1. Economic welfare of the poor section: Price discrimination is practised and promoted by the government in case of public utility services such as telephones, railway, transport, etc. Price is charged more from those who can afford to pay and subsidised to those who are poor. So, this is done for the economic welfare of the poor section.

2. To remove inequalities: Price discrimination helps to reduce inequalities in the distribution of personal income in the society. People with higher incomes are made to pay higher price and people with lower incomes are made to pay lower price for the same commodity. Again higher income group people has to pay high percentage of income tax and lower income group people has to pay low percentage of income tax. People of low income upto certain limit has to pay no tax. Thus, the funds collected are used for subsidising the consumption of lower income groups.

3. To promote export: Sometimes a producer sells a part of his output at a high price in the home market and the remaining part of the output at a low price in the foreign market. It is called **Dumping** which is a special case of price-discrimination. Selling more in the foreign market means expansion in output, more employment and better use of domestic resources. It promotes export and brings more foreign currencies.

4. Mal-allocation of resources and their diversion from socially optimal uses: Price discrimination is not justified if it leads to mal-allocation of resources and their diversion from socially optimal uses. This neither maximises domestic output and employment nor results in the desirable pattern of resource allocations.

DUMPING

(Price Discrimination under Dumping)

Dumping is a special case of price discrimination where a producer sells a part of his output at a high price in the home market and the remaining part of the output at a low price in the foreign market. The monopolist producer having monopoly power in the domestic market may not have it in the world market where he has to face a lot of competition approximating to perfect competition. So, we have to discuss a situation how does the monopolist discriminate to sell his product between the home market and the world market and decide price-output equilibrium?

At a time the monopolist has to face two different types of demand curves. In the home market, where he is a monopolist, the demand curve (AR curve) and MR curve for his product are downward sloping. But in the foreign market where he is facing perfect competition the demand curve (AR curve) and MR curve both are represented by a single straight line, parallel to the X-axis. In the home market, demand is inelastic while in the world market, demand is elastic. The price-output equilibrium and price discrimination are shown in Fig. 11.2.

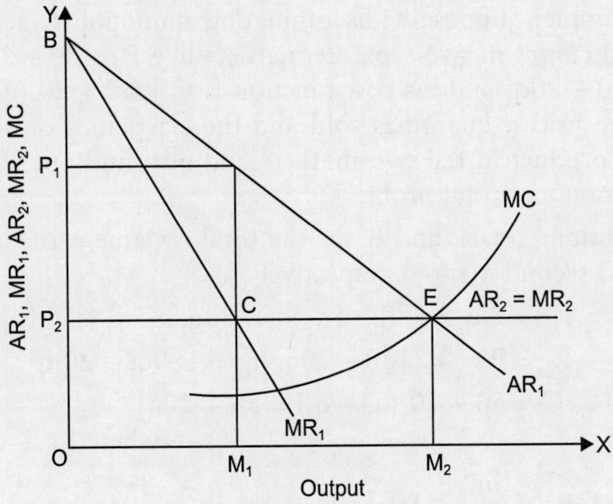

Fig. 11.2

In Fig. 11.2, AR_1 and MR_1 curves relate to the home market while AR_2 and MR_2 curve refer to the foreign market. The aggregate MR curve is the sum of MR_1 and MR_2 which is shown by a kinked curve BCE.

Now, we have to find out the equilibrium output where the MC curve cuts the aggregate MR curve BCE. The MC curve intersects with the BCE curve at point E which is the equilibrium position corresponding to the price OP_2 and output OM_2. Therefore, equilibrium price is OP_2 and equilibrium output is OM_2. Now, the total output OM_2 is distributed between the home market and the foreign market. The equilibrium position E, when extended to the MR_1, meets at C showing the equilibrium point for the home market. Corresponding to the C, the output for home market is OM_1 at price OP_1, which is indicated by the AR_1 curve. The remaining output M_1M_2 will be sold in the foreign market at price OP_2 which is indicated by the AR_2 curve.

Thus, the monopolist produces OM_2 level of output, out of which he sells OM_1 units in the monopoly market (home market) at the price OP_1 and M_1M_2 units in the competitive market (foreign market) at price OP_2. Since elasticity of demand in the monopoly market is less than that of the competitive market, the price in the home market is higher than that of the foreign market. This practice is called **Dumping**.

Example: Suppose a discriminating monopolist faces two demand curves in two separate markets like $P_1 = 80 - 5q_1$ and $P_2 = 180 - 20q_2$ and his cost function is $C = 50 + 20(q_1 + q_2)$. Find the prices, quantities sold and the elasticities of demand for his product in the two markets and also find out his total production and total profit.

Solution: Let R_1 and R_2 be the total revenue earned in the first and second markets respectively.

$$R_1 = P_1q_1 = (80 - 5q_1)q_1 = 80q_1 - 5q^2_1$$

$$R_2 = P_2q_2 = (180 - 20q_2)q_2 = 180q_2 - 20q^2_2$$

$$C = 50 + 20(q_1 + q_2) = 50 + 20q$$

where $[q_1 + q_2 = q]$

$$\therefore \quad MR_1 = \frac{\delta R_1}{\delta q_1} = 80 - 10q_1;$$

$$MR_2 = \frac{\delta R_2}{\delta q_2} = 180 - 40q_2;$$

$$\text{and } MC = \frac{\delta C}{\delta q} = 20$$

From the first order condition, we know that $MR_1 = MR_2 = MC$

Therefore, $80 - 10q_1 = 20$ or, $q_1 = 6$

And $180 - 40q_2 = 20$ or, $q_2 = 4$

Putting the values of q_1 and q_2 in demand equation, we get price.

Thus,

$$P_1 = 80 - 5q_1 = 80 - 5 \times 6 = 50$$

$$\text{and} \quad P_2 = 180 - 20q_2 = 180 - 20 \times 4 = 180 - 80 = 100$$

$$TC = 50 + 20(6 + 4) = 50 + 200 = 250$$

$$\pi = TR - TC = R_1 + R_2 - TC$$

$$= P_1q_1 + P_2q_2 - TC$$

$$= 50 \times 6 + 100 \times 4 - 250$$

$$= 300 + 400 - 250 = 450$$

Let e_1 and e_2 be the demand elasticities of his product in the first market and in the second market respectively.

We know from the relation of price, marginal revenue and demand elasticity,

$$MR_1 = P_1\left(1 - \frac{1}{e_1}\right) \text{ for the first market,}$$

and $$MR_2 = P_2\left(1 - \frac{1}{e_2}\right) \text{ for the second market.}$$

From the first order condition we know, $MR_1 = MR_2 = MC$. Here MC = 20

i.e., $MR_1 = 20$ and $MR_2 = 20$

and $P_1 = 50$ and $P_2 = 100$

Therefore,

$$20 = 50\left(1 - \frac{1}{e_1}\right) \text{ or, } 1 - \frac{1}{e_1} = \frac{2}{5}$$

$$\text{or, } \frac{1}{e_1} = 1 - \frac{2}{5} = \frac{3}{5} \text{ or, } e_1 = \frac{5}{3} = 1.67$$

$$\text{Again, } 20 = 100\left(1 - \frac{1}{e_2}\right)$$

$$1 - \frac{1}{e_2} = \frac{1}{5} \text{ or, } \frac{1}{e_2} = 1 - \frac{1}{5} = \frac{4}{5} \text{ or, } e_2 = \frac{5}{4} = 1.25$$

Here we see that $P_1 < P_2$ when $e_1 > e_2$. That is, price in the first market is lower with higher elasticity of demand and price in the second market is higher with lower elasticity demand.

Hence,

$P_1 = ₹ 50$ $q_1 = 6$ units $e_1 = 1.67$ $q = 10$ units

$P_2 = ₹ 100$ $q_2 = 4$ units $e_2 = 1.25$ $\pi = ₹ 450$

Again, we have to fulfil the second order condition.

$$\text{That is, } R_1'' - C'' < 0; \begin{vmatrix} R_1'' - C'' & -C'' \\ -C'' & R_2'' - C'' \end{vmatrix} > 0$$

$$\text{Here, } R_1'' - C'' = -10 < 0; \begin{vmatrix} -10 & 0 \\ 0 & -40 \end{vmatrix} = 400 > 0$$

Where,

$$R_1'' = \frac{\delta R_1^2}{\delta q_1^2} = -10; R_2'' = \frac{\delta R_2^2}{\delta q_2^2} = -40 \text{ and } C'' = \frac{\delta C^2}{\delta q^2} = 0$$

Thus, the second order condition is fulfilled.

MONOPOLISTIC COMPETITION
(Excess Capacity Remains under Monopolistic Competition)

The concept of monopolistic competition has been introduced by **Prof. E. Chamberlin** in his famous book *The Theory of Monopolistic Competition* in 1933. Monopolistic competition is one of the imperfect types of markets. It refers to that market situation intermediate between perfect competition and monopoly. Perfect competition and monopoly are two extreme types of market situations which are not likely found anywhere in the real world. What we find around us is a situation between these two extreme markets. A situation, where there is neither a complete monopoly nor a perfect competition, is known as imperfect competition or imperfect market. Therefore, it refers to a market situation in which there is neither homogeneous product as in the perfect competition nor remote substitute product as in the monopoly. So, in monopolistic market there are various monopolists competing with each other to sell their slightly differentiated products. Each firm informs the consumers about the distinctive features or the special characteristics of his own products. As a result, selling costs or advertising costs are necessary in monopolistic competition. But in perfect competition all firms are selling a homogeneous product, there is no need of selling cost. For example, the producers of toothpaste are working under conditions of monopolistic competition. Cibaca, Colgate, Forhans, Babool, Promise, etc., are all close substitutes of each other.

Now we consider the equilibrium of a firm and also of the group in short run and in long run. The term industry is used as a collection of firms when the firms are producing homogeneous products. But the term group is used here instead of industry because the group includes those firms which are producing slightly differentiated products.

Short Run Equilibrium of a Firm under Monopolistic Competition

Under monopolistic competition each firm behaves like a monopolist seller. He is producing a single product which is not produced exactly by others. The objective of the firm is to maximize profit. The profits are maximized where MR = MC. So the firm is in equilibrium where MR = MC and the MC curve cuts the MR curve from below. The downward sloping AR curve is its demand curve. Given the demand and cost conditions, a firm adjusts its price and output at the level in such a way that it can earn maximum total profits. This is illustrated in Fig. 11.3.

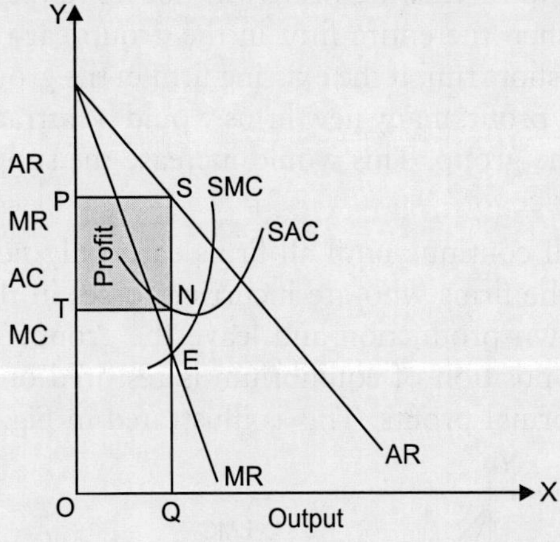

Fig. 11.3

In this figure the MR and the MC curves intersect each other at E. The MC curve also cuts the MR curve from below. So, E is the equilibrium point with OQ output and OP price. In this equilibrium position, the firm is earning super normal profits, equal to the area TNSP. This is maximum profit of the firm by fixing price at OP and output OQ.

In the short run, the firm may earn normal profit, supernormal profit or even subnormal profit. This depends on the shape and position of the AR and the AC curves. In our figure, if the AC curve touches the AR curve at S, then we get, price = AC. In this situation the firm earns only normal profit. Again if the AC curve lies above the AR curve, then the firm faces losses, i.e., subnormal profit. It should be noted that its loss cannot exceed its total fixed cost. Otherwise, it will close down its production. Thus, a firm under monopolistic competition, like monopoly and perfect competition may earn super normal profit, normal profit or even subnormal profit in the short run.

Group Equilibrium in the Long Run

We have explained the equilibrium of a firm under monopolistic competition. Now we analyze the case of group equilibrium of a number of firms taking them together at a time under monopolistic competition. We assume that no firm will enter the group or existing firms will not leave the group. This is possible when the entire firm in the group earn just normal profit. In the short run, if the existing firm in the group is making super normal profit, many new firms would be attracted to come in and join the group. This would increase the supply and thus reduce the price.

Entry will continue until all firms earn only normal profit. Similarly, if the firms who are incurring losses in the short run will close down production and leave the group. Thus, in the long run the position of equilibrium is restored only when the firms earn normal profits. This is illustrated in Fig. 11.4.

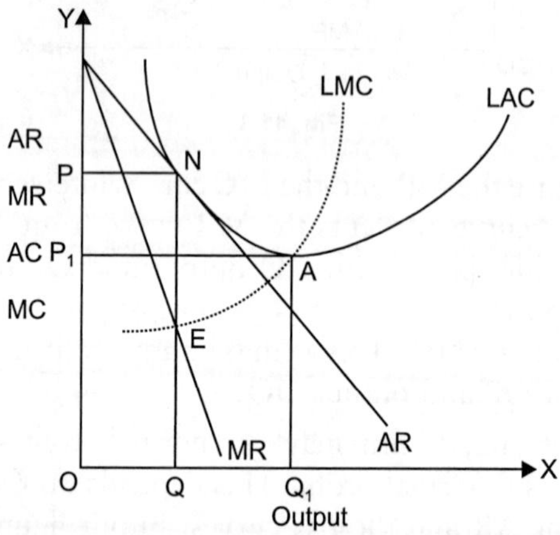

Fig. 11.4

The profits are normal when average revenue is equal to average cost. AR curve touches the LAC curve at N. That is, AR curve is tangent to LAC curve at point N. MC and MR curves intersect each other at point E, exact vertically below N. So, N is the long run equilibrium point where long run equilibrium price is OP and the output is OQ.

Excess Capacity

It should be noted that under monopolistic competition, the long run equilibrium takes place at the falling portion of the LAC curve, i.e., to the left of the minimum point A of LAC as shown in Fig. 11.4. Here equilibrium output is OQ. If the firm operates under perfect competition, equilibrium will be seen at the lowest point A of the LAC curve, where the equilibrium output will be OQ_1 it is clear that more output can be produced at the lowest cost, i.e., $OQ_1 > OQ$ and again cost for $OQ_1 <$ cost for OQ. This shows that excess capacity remains under monopolistic competition in each firm. But under perfect competition capacity is fully utilized and no excess capacity remains because long run equilibrium occurs at the minimum point of the LAC curve (point A). From the welfare viewpoint monopolistic competition is inferior to perfect competition. This property of equilibrium under monopolistic competition is known as the excess capacity theorem. So, excess capacity is defined as the difference between minimum cost output and the actual output produced in the long run equilibrium under monopolistic competition.

CHAMBERLIN'S MODEL
(An Alternative Approach of Monopolistic Competition)

The process of equilibrium under monopolistic competition may be better understood by an alternative approach explained by **Prof. E. Chamberlin.** He has taken the following assumptions. These assumptions are the same as in the case of pure competition except the assumption of homogeneous product.

(i) There are a large number of sellers and buyers in the group.

(ii) Products are differentiated. But they are close substitutes for each other.

(iii) There is free entry and exit of firms in the group.

(iv) The goal of the firm is profit maximization both in the short run and in the long run.

(v) The prices of inputs are given and technology is also given.

(vi) Demand and cost functions are known with certainty.

(vii) The demand and cost functions of all firms in the group are identical.

Equilibrium under Monopolistic Competition

Under monopolistic competition, we get two types of equilibrium levels: the equilibrium of an individual firm and the equilibrium of the group.

The Nature of Demand Curve under Monopolistic Competition

The demand curve for a firm under perfect competition is a horizontal line showing infinite price elasticity. The output of one firm is a perfect substitute for the output of the other firms. Under monopoly, on the other hand, the demand curve for the output of the firm is the demand curve for the industry and it is downward sloping showing low elasticity of demand as there are no substitutes available for the commodity. Under monopolistic competition, the demand curve for the firm will stand somewhere in between the demand curves of the two extreme situations. A firm under monopolistic competition faces two types of demand curves. One demand curve is based on the assumption that the firm's pricing decisions do not make any impact on its rivals' prices. This demand curve means a rise in quantity demanded of the product of a firm when it cut down its price assuming that others do not. Again, a fall in its quantity demanded is faced when it raises its price with an assumption that others do not raise their prices. This type of demand curve is known as anticipated or perceived or subjective demand curve, because this is based on the individual firm's anticipation. It is shown by the curve dd_1 in Fig. 11.5.

The other type of demand curve is known as market demand curve or proportional demand curve consisting of a large number of firms. It shows the demand or sales of the products of the whole group. Each firm in a group is so small relative to the whole group as there is a large number of firms in the group. The price changed by a firm will have negligible impact upon its competitive firms in the group. As a result the market demand curve of a firm will be less elastic than its anticipated demand curve. The market demand for each firm varies with the number of firms in the product group. The greater the number of firms in a product group, the smaller will be the share of an individual firm. Thus, market demand curve facing an individual firm shifts to the left of the individual anticipated (expected or perceived) demand curve as more and more firms enter the group. The market demand traced as DD_1 is shown in the following Fig. 11.5:

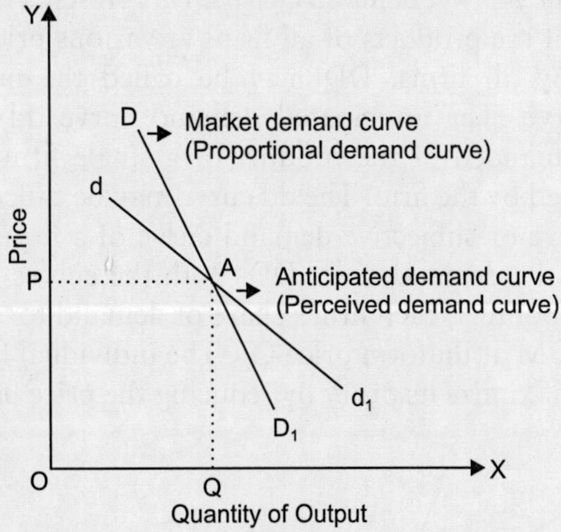

Fig. 11.5

The two demand curves intersect each other at point A corresponding to the price OP and quantity demanded OQ. The proportional share of each firm in the group at the price OP is OQ. So, DD_1 is also called proportional demand curve. All firms are assumed to produce and to sell individually OQ quantity of output at price OP. An individual firm anticipates that its quantity demanded is elastic and it can increase its sales by reducing its price. The reduction of price will attract the customers of other firms. This firm believes that if it makes small reduction in price, it will have inappreciable effect on each of its many competitors. They will not readjust their prices. As the price reduction has negligible effect upon each of its competitors, the actual movement would not be along the anticipated demand curve dd_1 but along the market demand curve DD_I when the prices of all change equally.

Equilibrium of a Firm in Short Run under Monopolistic Competition

The short run equilibrium of a firm in terms of two demand curves (market demand curve and anticipated demand curve) is illustrated in Fig. 11.6. It is assumed that all firms (i) have identical costs, (ii) charge uniform price of their products and (iii) get a proportional share of the total market demand for the products. The market demand curve DD represents the quantity demanded of the products of all firms at various prices charged uniformly by all firms. DD may be called the proportional demand curve. The anticipated demand curve dd shows the quantity demanded of the product of a single firm at various prices charged by the firm. The dd curve may be called perceived demand curve or subjective demand curve of a firm. It is more elastic than the demand curve DD. Both the curves intersect at point A. At point A, each firm's share of demand for its product is equal to OM at uniform price OP. The individual firm notices that it can maximize its profit by reducing the price below OP to

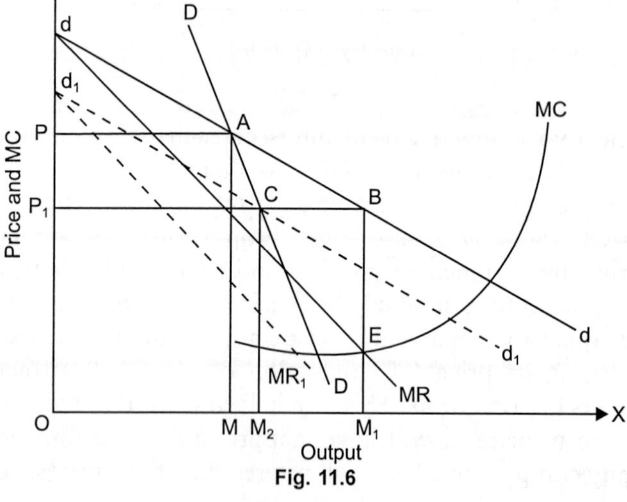

Fig. 11.6

sell more output. In this figure in order to maximize profit, the firm reduces price to OP_1 and sells OM_1 output assuming that other firms would keep their price at OP. We have also drawn MR curve corresponding dd curve. Further we have drawn MC curve also. It is assumed that MR and MC curves intersect at the output level OM_1 where the price is OP_1.

But each firm in monopolistically competitive market is free to perceive that they can lower the price to attract the customers from others assuming that others would keep their prices as constant. Ultimately each firm will not be in equilibrium at point B to produce OM_1 output. Instead, they will be at point C on the DD curve getting the proportionate share of the increase in market demand at lower price OP_1 and producing OM_2 output. It is clear that due to reducing price, the perceived demand curve dd of each firm slides down along the proportional demand curve DD from A to C and dd becomes d_1d_1. This process will continue until the firm will have no incentive to change its price when the perceived marginal revenue curve corresponding to the perceived demand curve falls below the marginal cost curve. If marginal revenue curve falls below the marginal cost curve, it means loss. A firm under monopolistic competition like a perfectly competitive firm can earn super normal profit, normal profit or subnormal profit in the short run depending upon the position of average cost curve.

Long Run Equilibrium of Firm and Group under Monopolistic Competition

The long run equilibrium is illustrated in Fig. 11.7. Like perfectly competitive market, there is free entry and free exit in the monopolistic markets. If there is super normal profit earned by all firms, new firms will enter the group. As new firms enter, the market demand is shared by more firms. As a result, the proportional demand curve DD shifts to the left. Along with the shift of the proportional demand curve DD, the perceived demand curve will also shift to the left. The process of entry continues until all economic profit becomes zero. All economic profits will be zero when the perceived demand curve dd becomes tangent to the long run average cost curve LAC at point A. In

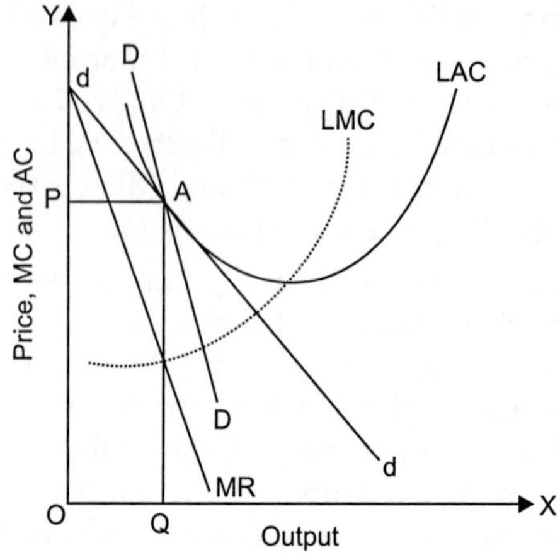

Fig. 11.7

this situation, each firm earns only normal profit and there is no tendency of the firms to enter or to leave the group. The market demand curve DD intersects the dd and LAC at their point of tendency. The long run equilibrium restores at point A where equilibrium price is OP and equilibrium output is OQ.

Again if too many firms have entered the group, the dd curve will fall to the position below the point of tangency. In this situation, the firms will make loss. As a result, some firms will be leaving the group until the entire loss will disappear and the DD curve along with dd curve will shift to the right. In the long run equilibrium two conditions must be fulfilled: (i) the perceived demand curve dd must be tangent to the LAC curve and (ii) the proportional demand curve DD must intersect both the dd and the LAC curve at their point of tangency.

Chamberlin's Measure of Excess Capacity

The difference between the output produced at the minimum point of the LAC curve and the output actually attained in the long run equilibrium is measured as the excess capacity under monopolistic competition. It indicates that productive efficiency is not achieved under monopolistic competition in the sense that resources are not being used fully to reach the minimum average costs. But Chamberlin does not accept the above difference as the excess capacity. According to him, consumers desire a variety of products and they are ready to pay higher price to get choice among the differentiated products in the monopolistic market. Consequently, higher cost faced by the firms is socially accepted and production is done to the left of the minimum average cost of LAC. According to him, excess capacity arises under monopolistic competition when here is free entry of firms and price competition is absent. This is illustrated in Fig. 11.8.

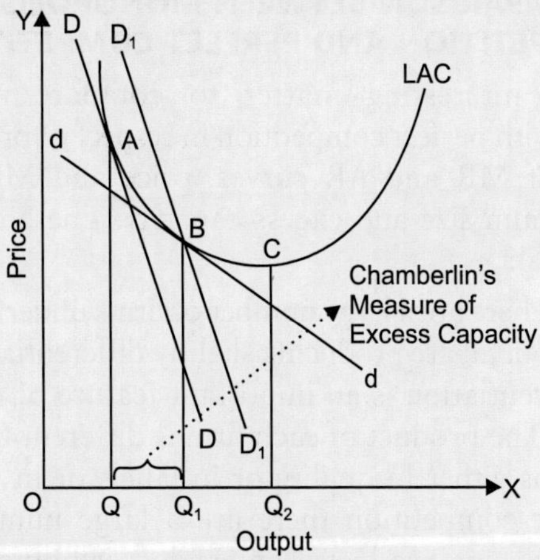

Fig. 11.8

In this figure, with free entry of firms and active price competition long run equilibrium under monopolistic competition is attained at B where the perceived demand curve dd is tangent to the LAC curve with output OQ_1. Chamberlin argues that OQ_1 is the output under monopolistic competition and where there is no excess capacity with free entry and active price competition. If price competition is absent but free entry of firms is allowed, there is no regard for the existence of perceived demand curve dd. The proportional demand curve DD is only main concerned with general rise or decline in price. Due to free entry of firms but absence of price competition, the DD curve is tangent with LAC curve at A. Long run equilibrium is attained at point A with output OQ. Chamberlin opines that the difference between Q and Q_1 is the excess capacity. It should be noted that the minimum point C of the LAC is the competitive equilibrium point with output OQ_2 in the perfectly competitive market. Both the points A and B must lie to the left of C.

Therefore, the difference between B and C is the excess capacity under monopolistic competition with free entry of firms and presence of price competition. But in Chamberlin's view, the difference between B and A represents the excess capacity under monopolistic competition with free entry of firms and absence of price competition.

COMPARISON BETWEEN MONOPOLISTIC COMPETITION AND PERFECT COMPETITION

It is an interesting matter to compare monopolistic competition with perfect competition in respect of product, selling cost, shape of MR and AR curves, price and MC, price and output, optimum size and excess capacity. These are discussed below in detail:

Product: There are a large number of firms under monopolistic competition, but all are producing slightly differentiated products. Product differentiation is an important feature of monopolistic competition. The product of each firm is different from those of the other firms either in quality or in labels or in trade marks. Under perfect competition there are a large number of firms producing the same product. The product is homogeneous.

Selling cost: The producers of differentiated products under monopolistic competition are competing with one another to sell their differentiated products. Each firm informs the customers about the distinctive features of his own product. As a result, selling costs or advertising costs are necessary to attract the customers in monopolistic competition. But under perfect competition all firms are producing a homogeneous product. There is no need of selling costs.

Shape of AR and MR curves: Under monopolistic competition the demand curve (AR) is downward sloping representing different output levels sold at different prices. A firm has some control over the price of its product. As a result, MR curve lies below AR curve. It is shown in Fig. 11.9. But

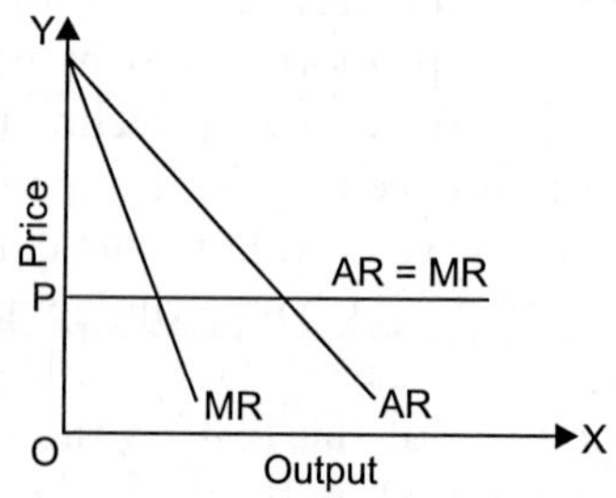

Fig. 11.9

under perfect competition, a firm has no control over its product and accepts the price as given and constant in the market. As a result AR curve is a horizontal straight line and MR is equal to AR (price). It is depicted in Fig. 11.9.

Price and MC: In equilibrium under monopolistic competition when a firm equates upward rising MC curve with downward sloping MR curve, corresponding to their intersection point, price stands on AR curve vertically above the MC curve. This is depicted in Fig. 11.10. Here equilibrium point is E corresponding to which price is QT (= OP). But under perfect competition in equilibrium, price is equal to MC since AR = MR is a horizontal straight line, i.e., P_1 = AR = MR = MC. Therefore, in equilibrium under monopolistic competition, price is greater than MC, but in equilibrium under perfect competition, price is equal to MC.

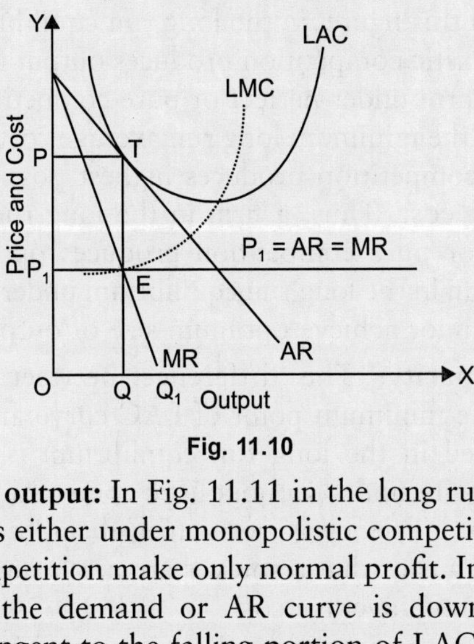

Fig. 11.10

Price and output: In Fig. 11.11 in the long run equilibrium, both the firms either under monopolistic competition or perfect (or pure) competition make only normal profit. In monopolistic competition, the demand or AR curve is downward sloping curve. It is tangent to the falling portion of LAC curve only to the left of its minimum point. Equilibrium is restored at point A with price OP_1 and output OQ_1. But in perfect competition AR = MR curve is a horizontal straight line. It is tangent to the minimum point of LAC curve. Equilibrium is obtained at point B with price OP_2 and output OQ_2. So it is clear that the price under monopolistic competition is higher than the price under perfect competition but the corresponding output at that price under monopolistic market is lower than that under perfect competitive market, i.e., $OP_1 > OP_2$ and $OQ_1 < OQ_2$.

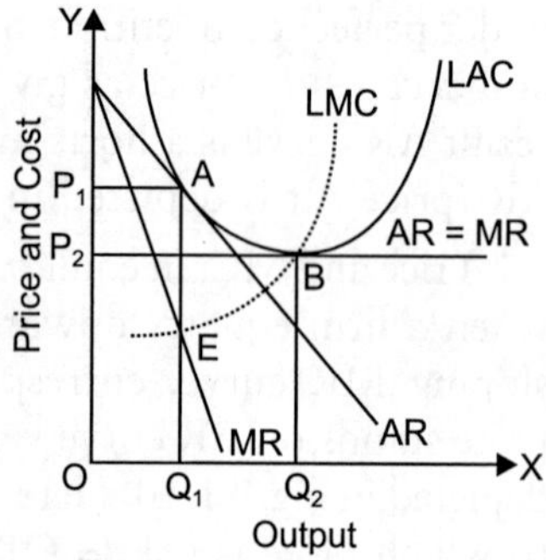

Fig. 11.11

Optimum size: In Fig. 11.11 we see that in the long run under monopolistic competition, equilibrium of a firm is restored at the falling portion of LAC curve only to the left of its minimum point. It means that less output is produced at higher cost. It produces less than its optimum size of output. But a firm under perfect or pure competition produces the output at the minimum point of the LAC curve in the long run equilibrium. In this figure, in the long run equilibrium, the firm under monopolistic competition produces output OQ_1 at higher cost while the firm under perfect or pure competition produces output OQ_2 at the minimum long run average cost, i.e., the firm under perfect competition produces highest possible output at lowest possible cost. Thus, a firm in the long run equilibrium under perfect or pure competition produces optimum size of output but a firm in the long run equilibrium under monopolistic competition cannot achieve optimum size of output.

Excess capacity: The difference between the output produced at the minimum point of LAC curve and the output actually attained in the long run equilibrium is measured as the excess capacity under monopolistic competition. It signifies that productive efficiency is not achieved under monopolistic competition. It means that resources are not being used fully to reach the minimum average cost.

In the Fig. 11.11 a firm in the long run equilibrium under perfect or pure competition produces at the minimum point of LAC curve with output OQ_2. But a firm in the long run equilibrium under monopolistic competition produces at point A on the falling portion of LAC curve only to the left of the minimum point B of LAC curve. This indicates that maximum economic efficiency is not achieved under monopolistic competition. It implies waste of resources. So the difference between Q_1 and Q_2 are regarded as excess capacity which remains under monopolistic competition. But Chamberlin does not accept this difference as the excess capacity. He opines that consumers desire a variety of products and they are ready to pay higher price to get choice among the differentiated products under monopolistic competition. Consequently less output at higher cost is socially accepted.

He tells that a lot of excess capacity arises under monopolistic competition as a result of free entry of a large number of firms when price competition is absent. But with free entry of firms under monopolistic competition excess capacity is less in the long run, when active price competition is present.

EXERCISES

1. What is price discrimination and under what conditions is it possible and profitable?
2. Under what conditions and on what basis will a monopolist seeking maximum profits divide sales among a number of different markets and charge different prices in each market?
3. Discriminating monopolist maximizes profits after charging different prices in different markets. Explain. [RGU 2004]
4. Discuss the equilibrium of a discriminating monopolist. [RGU 2003]
5. A monopolist firm supplies his product in two markets, demand being more elastic in one market than the other. Show how the price and output in each market are determined.
6. Explain the equilibrium of a discriminating monopolist when he is discriminating prices in the two markets. Show that he will charge higher price in the market where price elasticity of demand is lower as compared to the one where demand is relatively more elastic.
7. What is monopolistic competition? Explain the important features of monopolistic competition.
8. What is product differentiations? What role does it play in the determination of price and output under monopolistic competition?

9. What do you understand by selling costs? How do these costs influence the conditions of monopolistic competition?
10. Analyze the short run and long run equilibrium of a firm working under monopolistic competition.
11. What is group equilibrium? Explain how group equilibrium is achieved under monopolistic competition.
12. What is meant by excess capacity? Show that how a firm working under monopolistic competition works with excess capacity in the long run.
13. Explain Chamberlin's concept of proportional and perceived demand curves of firms operating under monopolistic competition and also show the equilibrium of a firm and the group in short run and long run in Chamberlin's view.
14. Explain Chamberlin's concept of excess capacity. What, according to him, is responsible for the existing of excess capacity under monopolistic competition?
15. Distinguish between monopolistic competition and perfect competition.
16. Do you consider monopolistically competition market is better than pure monopoly and perfect competitive market? Give your assessment of this from the viewpoint of attaining economic efficiency.
17. Construct the average revenue and marginal revenue curve of a firm under monopoly and monopolistic competitions.

Chapter 12

Oligopoly

NATURE AND CHARACTERISTICS OF OLIGOPOLY

The word 'oligopoly' is derived from the Greek word 'oligois' which means 'few' and the Latin word 'polis' which means 'sellers'. Oligopoly is that form of imperfect competition where there are a few firms (sellers) in the market, producing either a homogeneous product or a differentiated product. A few firms means the strong interdependence among the firms. Each firm takes into account the possible reactions of his rival producers before taking decision about his price and output policy. The actions of any one firm will have a noticeable impact on the demand for product of each of the other firms. A few firms' product are difficult to quantify. Generally it is said that when the number of firms of a product are two to ten in a market, oligopoly situation exists. If there are only two firms of a product in a market, it is called duopoly. Duopoly is a simplest case of oligopoly. Simply, it is said that a market with two firms of a product is a duopoly, and a market with a small number, but greater than two is an oligopoly. The manufacture of motor cars by Hindustan Motors (Ambassador Car), Premier Automobiles (Fiat Cars) and Standard Motor Company (Standard Cars) may be the examples of oligopoly.

Classification of Oligopoly

Oligopoly may be divided into following classes:

1. Oligopoly is classified as perfect and imperfect oligopoly on the basis of product differentiation. It is perfect when

the products are homogeneous and imperfect when the products are close but not perfect substitutes, i.e., differentiated.

2. Oligopoly may be classified as open and closed oligopoly on the basis of freedom to enter the industry. An open oligopoly tells that market situation where the new firms are free to enter the industry while a closed oligopoly is that market situation where the new firms are not free to enter the industry.
3. Oligopoly may be classified into collusive and non-collusive oligopoly on the basis of agreement among the firms. A collusive oligopoly is that market situation where the firms combine together to fix the prices and their outputs. Again, collusive may be divided into (a) Explicit collusion where the oligopolists collude to fix price in a legal manner involving no violation with signing an agreement and (b) Tacit collusion where the oligopolist collude together to fix price in a secretive manner without signing any agreement. Non-collusive oligopoly tells where there is no agreement among the firms to fix the prices and their outputs.

Characteristics of Oligopoly Market

There are some characteristics of oligopoly market. These are discussed below:

1. Interdependence among the firms: An oligopoly market is characterized by interdependence among the firms in an industry. As there are a few number of firms or sellers, the actions of any one of firm will have a noticeable impact on the demand of a product of the other firms. Hence, each seller, while deciding about his price and output policy, will take into account the effect of his policy on his rival and in turn will take into account also the effect of the reaction of his rival on his own policy.

2. Indeterminateness of demand curve: As there exists interdependence among the firms, a firm itself cannot determine his output definitely at different market prices. Because the quantities of output will be different depending on different reaction patterns of the rivals. When any firm changes its own price, rivals will also change their prices and as a result we do not get a definiteness of the demand curve. Hence, price-output determination in oligopoly is indeterminate.

3. Group behaviour: We see a group of interdependent firms under oligopoly. The group behaviour depends on the behaviour of the members of the group. There may be a competition among the members of the group or the members may come to an agreement to promote their common interests.

4. Profit maximisation: The main objective of a firm under any form of markets is to maximise its profit. But this objective has been challenged by some economists in oligopolistic market. **W.J. Baumol** says that the objective of the oligopolistic firm is to maximise sales rather than profits. The view of the most of the economists is not in favour of profit maximisation of an oligopolist firm. There is a controversy among the economists about the objective of the firm in the oligopolistic market.

5. Management: An oligopolistic firm faces a problem how to manage the account of its competitors' reaction patterns. The firms' attempts to outguess one another is likely to lead to an interplay of anticipated strategies and counter-strategies which is tangled beyond the hope of direct analysis.

6. Uncertainty: There is considerable uncertainty in this type of market, where there is a variety of different behaviour patterns. Rivals may join hands and cooperate in the pursuit of their objectives or may try to fight each other. Again cooperation agreements may break down sooner or later.

7. Presence of monopoly power: The number of firms in oligopoly market is very small. Hence, collusion among the sellers is possible. The firms in a oligopoly market may act likely as firm in a monopoly market. They may charge higher prices for their products.

8. Excessive expenditure on advertisement: The firms under oligopoly produce close substitutes. But they are interdependent. To sell more depends upon advertisement only. Hence, each firm spends a lot of money on advertisement to attract the customers in favour of its product.

COURNOT'S MODEL OF DUOPOLY

The simplest case of oligopoly is duopoly. Duopoly is a special case of oligopoly where there are only two sellers of either a homogeneous product or a slightly differentiated product. Both the sellers are completely independent and neither price nor output agreement exists between them. The number of sellers being only two, each one of them is quite influential in the sense that a price changed by one of them is bound to have its effect on the sale and the price policy of the other. Therefore, each seller, while deciding about his price and output policy will take into account the effect of his policy on his rival and in turn will take into account also the effect of the reaction of his rival on his own policy. Thus, each seller in seeking to maximise his profits has to look into total consequences of his move. He must consider not only what the rival is doing now but also what he will be forced to do in the wake of changes which he himself is contemplating. **Augustin Cournot**, a French economist, published this theory of duopoly in 1838.

Cournot's model is based upon the following assumptions:

(i) There are two independent producers (sellers) producing identical products.

(ii) There are large number of buyers of these products in the market.

(iii) Both the producers have identical costs. For simplicity Cournot assumes that cost of production is zero.

(iv) Each duopolist makes an output plan during a period to maximise his total profit in each period.

(v) Each duopolist is not a price-maker for his product, but accepts the market price at which the total output can be sold.

(vi) Each producer decides his own profit maximising level of output assuming that his competitor will not change his own level of output in each plan period. That each duopolist is ignorant about his rival's plan about output.

Diagrammatic Representation

Here there are two producers: Producer I and Producer II. We plot I's output q_1 along the X-axis and II's output q_2 along the Y-axis. MN of producer I and RS of producer II are the reaction curves. OM is the monopoly output which I produces in the initial stage when II produces nothing. Here producer I were sole producer and seller. In reverse, we can say that OR is monopoly output which II produces in the initial stage when I produces nothing and hence II were sole producer and seller. Since I and II are identical in all respects, OM = OR (OS = ON).

The main proposition is established by the fact that the two curves intersect and the intersection point makes stable equilibrium. The path by which equilibrium is reached is shown in Fig. 12.1. In the initial stage, I is a monopolist and producing OM units of his output q_1 to maximise his profit assuming that II is producing nothing. In this period, II will produce OR_1 units of his output q_2 assuming that I will continue to produce OM units of his output q_1. So in this stage, total output is denoted at point A on the reaction curve RS of II where total output is OM units of I and OR_1 units of II.

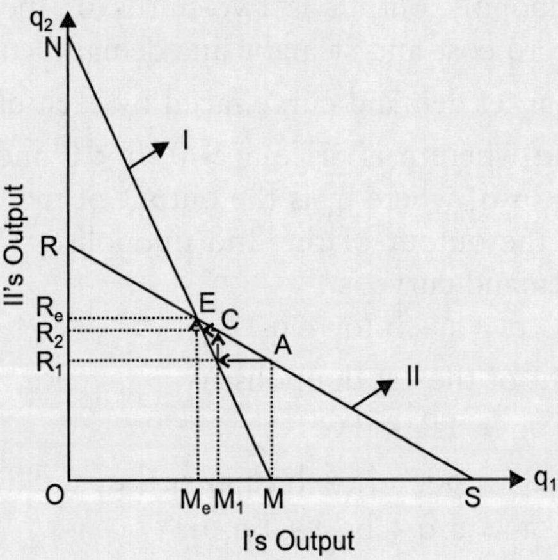

Fig. 12.1

In the second stage, I assuming that II will continue to produce OR_1 of his output q_2 will produce OM_1 of his output q_1 to maximise his profit. But II will take into account of the production produced by I and will produce OR_2 units of his output to maximise his profit. So total output at point C on the reaction curve RS of II is OM_1 units of I and OR_2 of II.

In the third stage, I assuming II to produce OR_2 will produce OM_e units of q_1 to maximise his profit. But II will take it in his notice and produce OR_e to maximise his profit. Total output is represented at E where E is the equilibrium point lying on both the reaction curves. Ultimately, in this way they come to this equilibrium point. This process will continue untill the equilibrium point is reached. At equilibrium point E, I produces OM_e units of his output and II produces OR_e units of his output. We shall get same thing if we start from the point R on the Y-axis.

The characteristic feature of Cournot Model is that each duopolist believes that his rival will go on producing a definite quantity of output irrespective of the quantity he produces. Ultimately they will prove that they will be wrong during the approach towards the equilibrium.

Mathematical Version of Cournot's Model

(Prove that the monopoly output is half of the competitive output and duopoly output is two-thirds of the competitive output with zero cost and straight line demand curve.)

Let the market demand curve faced by each duopolist be

$p = a + bq$ where p is price, $a > 0$, $b < 0$ and q is output and $q = q_1 + q_2$ where q_1 is the output of the 1st duopolist and q_2 is the output of the 2nd duopolist. Therefore, the market demand curve is

$$p = a + b\,(q_1 + q_2)$$

Total profit of the 1st duopolist is

$$\pi_1 = TR_1 - TC$$

where $TR_1 = pq_1 = [a + b\,(q_1 + q_2)]\,q_1$ and $TC = 0$

$$\therefore \quad \pi_1 = a\,q_1 + bq_1^2 + bq_1\,q_2$$

The objective of each duopolist is to maximise his profit in variation of his output assuming that the output produced by the other is constant. Now to maximise π_1 for variation in q_1,

we get $$\frac{d\pi_1}{dq_1} = 0$$

$\therefore \quad a + 2bq_1 + bq_2 = 0$ ... (1)

It can be written as $q_2 = -2q_1 - \frac{a}{b}$.

This is an equation of a straight line whose slope is –1/2 and intercept is $-\frac{a}{b}$. This straight line is called the reaction function of the first duopolist.

Similarly, total profit of the 2nd duopolist is

$$\pi_2 = [a + b(q_1 + q_2)]q_2$$

i.e., $$\pi_2 = aq_2 + bq_1q_2 + bq_2^2$$

For profit maximisation, the 2nd duopolist will vary q_2 assuming q_1 as constant. That is,

$$\frac{d\pi_2}{dq_2} = 0$$

i.e., $a + bq_1 + 2bq_2 = 0$ ... (2)

Again, it can also be written as

$q_2 = -\frac{1}{2} q_1 - \frac{a}{2b}$ which is a equation of a straight line whose slope is $-\frac{1}{2}$ and intercept is $-\frac{a}{2b}$. This is the reaction function of the second duopolist. Both the straight lines are downward sloping with different values and different positive intercepts. They will intersect each other, since the absolute value of the slope of the 1st equation is greater than that of the 2nd equation (2 > 1/2). At the intersection point both the duopolists will maximise their profits corresponding to the level of their output.

Solving (1) and (2), we get the values of q_1 and q_2.

Here, $q_1 = -\frac{1}{3}\frac{a}{b}$ and $q_2 = -\frac{1}{3}\frac{a}{b}$

Thus, total output in duopoly market

$$q = q_1 + q_2 = -\frac{1}{3}\frac{a}{b} - \frac{1}{3}\frac{a}{b} = -\frac{2}{3}\frac{a}{b}$$

Therefore, $q = -\frac{2}{3}\frac{a}{b}$. If we put the value of q in the market demand equation, we get $p = a + bq = a - b\frac{2}{3}\frac{a}{b} = a - \frac{2}{3}a = \frac{1}{3}a$.

Here, $p = \frac{1}{3}a$, which shows that the price in the duopoly market is $\frac{1}{3}a$. Again, if there is a perfectly competitive market with the demand curve p = a + bq where cost of production is zero. Equilibrium will be established where P = MR = MC = 0, i.e., a + bq = 0;

$$\text{or,} \quad a + bq = 0;$$

$$\text{or,} \quad bq = -a$$

$$\text{or,} \quad q = -\frac{a}{b}.$$

It tells that output in perfectly competitive market is $-\frac{a}{b}$.

Again, in monopoly market with zero cost of production and same demand function p = a + bq, equilibrium will be established, where

$$MR = MC = 0$$

$$\text{Therefore,} \quad TR = pq = (a + bq)\, q = aq + bq^2$$

$$\therefore \quad MR = a + 2bq = 0$$

$$\text{or,} \quad a + 2bq = 0$$

$$\text{or,} \quad q = -\frac{1}{2}\frac{a}{b}$$

Thus, output in monopoly market is $-\frac{1}{2}\frac{a}{b}$.

Hence, with zero cost and straight line demand curve the monopoly output is half of the competitive output and duopoly output is two-third of the competitive output.

Criticisms

1. This is a model of two firms, where there is no possibility of entry of new firms. Hence this is a closed model.
2. It does not tell that how much time will be required for adjustment between the two sellers to reach the equilibrium point.
3. In this model it is assumed that there is no cost of production. It is practically absurd in most of the cases. That is why, this model is applicable in rare cases.

4. In the Cournot Model the firms do not learn from the past experience, each firm works independently.

KINKED DEMAND CURVE

Kinked demand curve is a case of non-collusive oligopoly. Non-collusive oligopoly exists when the oligopolistic firms, instead of joining hands and pursuing a common output or price policy, compete with each other to gain more profits. In such a market, it is not so easy to draw a demand curve for an individual producer's product. Because, any change in price or output done by him will cause unpredictable reaction in the price and output policies of his rivals which, in turn, will have further repercussions on his own price and output policy. **Paul Sweezy** in an article, "Demand under Conditions of Oligopoly," *Journal of Political Economy* in 1939 used the concept of kinked demand curve. He wanted to explain the rigidity of price in a non-collusive oligopoly market. The oligopolistic prices, which have come to prevail in the market over a period of time, generally remain fixed or rigid.

This model anticipates the following competitive reaction pattern to a change in price:

1. Price increases: When a single seller increases the price of his product in order to face of rising cost of production, other sellers will not increase their prices. They will welcome the new customers whom they will gain from the price-raising firm. They have no motivation to match the price rise.

As a result, the price-raising seller will lose his customers to his rivals and his sales will be reduced considerably. This means that the demand curve of his product is more elastic for a rise in price.

2. Price decreases: When a single seller reduces the price of his product to raise his sales, other sellers will also reduce the price of their product very quickly so that they will not lose their customers to the price-reducing seller. As a result the volume of sales of his product will not increase very much. This means that the demand curve for his product is less elastic for a fall in price.

This type of a market situation gives rise to what is called a **'Kinked Demand Curve'**. It is shown in the Fig. 12.2.

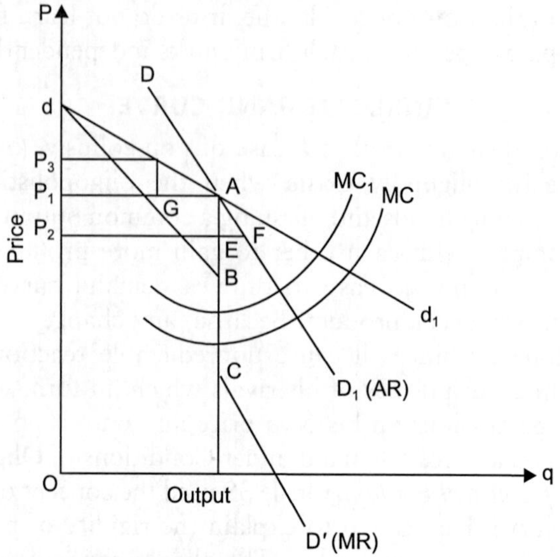

Fig. 12.2

Considering such type of market situation we have drawn two demand curves dd_1 and DD_1. They intersect at point A which represents the current price-output combination. In the kinked demand curve analysis, it is assumed that the fall in price will be matched while the rise in price will be unmatched. Thus, the demand curve (AR) is dAD_1 having kinked at point A. When the price is reduced from OP_1 to OP_2, the quantity demanded increases by EF as other sellers reduces the prices of their product. Similarly, when price is increased from OP_1 to OP_3, the quantity demanded will be reduced by GA if other sellers do not increase their prices. Hence, the demand (or average revenue) curve in the range dA above OP_1 price is more elastic viz., a small rise in price may cause a large fall in demand. Again, between A and D_1, the demand curve below OP_1, demand is less elastic, i.e., a large fall in price may cause a small rise in demand. Thus, we have a kinked demand curve dAD_1.

If the demand curve (AR) is kinked, the corresponding MR curve will be discontinuous. The MR curve in this case is broken line like dBCD′. This fact is also indicated by the discontinuity of the MR curve between B and C. The length of this gap is determined by the difference between two elasticities of demand. The greater the differences in these two elasticities of demand the greater will be the length of the discontinuity of the MR curve.

If the marginal cost curve happens to pass anywhere through the gap BC in the MR curve, the profit maximising firm (seller) will have no motivation to leave the market at the current price, P_1. Even if there is, for example, a sharp rise in costs, so long as the MC curve does not rise above point B, it will not lead to change price. There is a rigidity about this price. Any one firm will neither raise its price for the fear of losing its sales, nor reduce the price for the fear of others who will follow the same and thus the firm will not gain anything out of it.

So, the equilibrium of the firm is defined by the kink point A where total profit is maximised though the profit maximising condition (MR = MC) which is not fulfilled at the kink point A. The discontinuity between B and C of the MR curve implies that there is a range within which costs may change without affecting the equilibrium price and output of the firm.

Limitations: There are some vital limitations of kinked demand curve theory developed by **Paul Sweezy**. These are discussed below:

(a) This theory does not tell us how and at what height the kink is established.

(b) There is no one point where MC = MR, it can happen on any point of the gap BC. Hence, the position of maximum profit equilibrium is indeterminate as there can be many such points between the gap B and C.

COLLUSIVE OLIGOPOLY

The feature of an oligopolistic market is uncertainty arising from oligopolistic interdependence. In order to avoid this uncertainty resulting from price war and cut-throat competition, firms under oligopolistic market join hands and agree to enter into collusive agreements to follow a uniform price-output policy. The agreement among them may be either formal or tacit (informal/secret). Formal agreements are discussed under the heading of cartel while tacit agreements are discussed under the heading of price leadership. Hence, there may be two main types of collusion: cartel and price leadership. So collusive oligopoly is a market situation where a few firms come in contact with agreement regarding price and output.

Most of the agreements are tacit as in most of the countries any such formal agreement is banned under Monopolies and Restrictive Trade Practices Laws and Anti-Monopoly or Anti-Trust Legislations.

CARTEL

Cartel implies direct agreements among the competing oligopolists. Originally, the word cartel is used to describe a type of an association among the various firms under which they form a common sales agency. Thus, production is done under an individual firm's decision, but sales are done through a common agency at a uniform price. It is based on the following assumptions:

1. For simplicity we are assuming that there are only two firms in the cartel.
2. Producers produce homogeneous product.
3. These firms have different sets of cost curves.
4. The prices of the products of both the firms are same.
5. Joint profit maximisation is their aim.
6. The firms appoint a central agency to which they delegate the authority:
   (i) to determine the total output to be produced by the participating members of the cartel;
   (ii) to determine the price to be set;
   (iii) to allocate the production to be produced among the members of the cartel;
   (iv) to allocate the joint profits among the participating members.

So, the central agency determines the price and output in such a way that the joint profits are maximised.

Let us now first analyse the equilibrium situation mathematically.

Let q_1 and q_2 represent the output of two firms and P be the price determined by the central agency.

$C_1 = C_1 (q_1)$ and $C_2 = C_2 (q_2)$ are the cost functions of the two firms.

Now, $\pi_1 = R_1 - C_1 = pq_1 - C_1,$

and $\pi_2 = R_2 - C_2 = pq_2 - C_2$

(where π_1 and π_2 = profits of the two firms and R_1 and R_2 = revenues of the two firms)

We have, $\pi = \pi_1 + \pi_2$

$= R_1 + R_2 - C_1 - C_2$

or, $= pq_1 - C_1 + pq_2 - C_2$

(where π = joint profit and $pq = R$ = joint revenue $= R_1 + R_2$)

$= p(q_1 + q_2) - (C_1 + C_2)$

$= pq - [C_1 (q_1) + C_2 (q_2)]$

$= pq - C (q)$

$= R - C (q)$ [where $q = q_1 + q_2$ and combined cost $= C (q) = C_1 (q_1) + C_2 (q_2)$]

Here, π, π_1 and π_2 are functions of q, q_1 and q_2. To maximise π, π_1 and π_2, the first order condition requires $\frac{\delta \pi}{\delta q} = \frac{\delta \pi_1}{\delta q_1} = \frac{\delta \pi_2}{\delta q_2} = 0$

$$\text{Therefore,} \quad \frac{\delta \pi}{\delta q} = p + q \frac{\delta p}{\delta q} - C'(q) = 0 \qquad \dots (1)$$

$$\text{and} \quad \frac{\delta \pi_1}{\delta q_1} = p + q_1 \frac{\delta p}{\delta q_1} - C_1'(q_1) = 0 \qquad \dots (2)$$

$$\text{and} \quad \frac{\delta \pi_2}{\delta q_2} = p + q_2 \frac{\delta p}{\delta q_2} - C_2'(q_2) = 0 \qquad \dots (3)$$

That is, MR = CMC; $MR_1 = MC_1$ and $MR_2 = MC_2$ where $P + q \frac{\delta p}{\delta q} = MR$ and so on. From (1), (2) and (3), we get, MR $= MR_1 = MR_2$ since a uniform price is determined by the central authority. $\therefore$ $MR = MR_1 = MR_2 = CMC = MC_1 = MC_2$ where

CMC = combined marginal cost and MC_1 and MC_2 = marginal costs of the two firms respectively.

Again, the second order condition for profit maximisation requires:

$$\frac{\delta^2 \pi}{\delta q^2} < 0; \frac{\delta^2 \pi_1}{\delta q_1^2} < 0 \text{ and } \frac{\delta^2 \pi_2}{\delta q_2^2} < 0$$

When, $\frac{\delta^2 \pi}{\delta q^2} < 0$, we get $\frac{\delta^2 R}{\delta q^2} - \frac{\delta^2 C}{\delta q^2} < 0$;

when, $\frac{\delta^2 \pi_1}{\delta q_1^2} < 0$, we get $\frac{\delta^2 R_1}{\delta q_1^2} - \frac{\delta^2 C_1}{\delta q_1^2} < 0$;

and when, $\frac{\delta^2 \pi_2}{\delta q_2^2} < 0$, we get $\frac{\delta^2 R_2}{\delta q_2^2} - \frac{\delta^2 C_2}{\delta q_2^2} < 0$

Therefore, the slope of the MR curve of the central agency < the slope of the CMC curve; the slope of the MR_1 curve < the slope of the MC_1; and the slope of the MR_2 curve < the slope of the MC_2.

The decision regarding the level of output by the central agency, the price at which this output will be sold, the allocation of output among various firms to be produced and also the allocation of profit can be explained with the help of the following Fig. 12.3(a), (b) & (c):

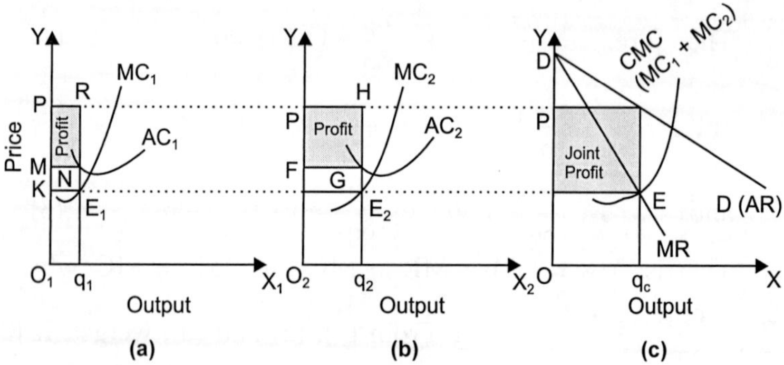

Fig. 12.3

The central agency has to estimate first the total market demand of the product which the firms under this cartel are to produce. In Fig. 12.3(c) the market demand curve is DD which is downward sloping curve.

Fig. 12.3(a) shows AC_1 and MC_1 of the first firm while Fig. 12.3(b) shows AC_2 and MC_2 of the second firm. By adding horizontally the marginal cost curves of the two firms we get the combined marginal cost curve ($CMC = MC_1 + MC_2$) of the cartel in the third Fig. 12.3(c). In order to maximise the joint profit, the central agency determines the equilibrium price and output at the intersection point E of the MR and the CMC curves. The equilibrium output and equilibrium price corresponding to the equilibrium point E are Oq_c and OP respectively. That is, this output is sold at OP price per unit. Having decided the total output Oq_c, the cartel allocates output quota to be produced by the two firms. Now, we draw a horizontal straight line EK from the equilibrium point E parallel to the X-axis which intersects the MC_1 at E_1 in Fig. 12.3(a) and the MC_2 at E_2 in Fig. 12.3(b). The first firm produces O_1Q_1 and the second firm produces O_2q_2 corresponding to the points E_1 and E_2 respectively. In this way, we get, total output $Oq_c = O_1q_1 + O_2q_2$. The distribution of profit of the first firm is equal to the area MNRP while the profit of the second firm is equal to the area FGHP. The distribution of profits is decided by the central agency of the cartel according to the prior agreements. The firms with lower costs produces a larger amount of output and takes the larger share of the total joint profit and *vice versa*.

Limitations

Though theoretically the cartel can maximise joint profit, in practice this is not possible for several reasons:

1. Mistakes may arise in the estimation of market demand and in the estimation of the MC curves.
2. Agreement among the firms takes a long time to negotiate due to differences in sizes, costs and markets of the firms.
3. The existence of high cost firms sets an obstacle towards joint profit maximisation. If the cost curve of a firm lies

fully above the equilibrium price, profit maximisation requires that the high cost firm should close down. Practically it is not possible. Hence the cartel will have to be satisfied at less than maximum profits.

4. Sometimes to keep a good public image the cartel may not maximise profit.
5. The cartel may not also maximise total profit for the fear of government intervention or for the fear of new entry.
6. Sometimes, some members may reduce the price to sell more of their product to achieve a large market share. This attitude leads to non-maximising situation.
7. Again, the attitude regarding freedom of selling activities leads to increase cost and hence to reduce profits.

PRICE LEADERSHIP MODEL

Independent price setting is rare in oligopolistic markets. Generally, there exists some forms of understanding among the oligopolists in a particular industry. One form of collusion (understanding) is price leadership. In this form one firm sets the price and the others follow it to avoid uncertainty about their competitors' reactions. More often price leadership is tacit (secret/informal) since open collusive agreements are illegal in most of the countries.

There are various forms of price leadership. The most common types of price leadership are: (i) Price leadership by a low cost firm, (ii) Price leadership by a large (dominant) firm and (iii) Barometric price leadership.

The price leader sets the market price according to the MR = MC equilibrium principle and the other firms are simply adopt the price set by the leader. Thus, the other firms are price-takers who will not normally maximise their profits. Let us now discuss these three categories of price leadership.

PRICE LEADERSHIP BY A LOW COST FIRM

A low cost firm is the firm whose per unit cost (AC) is the lowest among all the firms. This firm has more competitive power and can drive out the other firms from the market. The other firms realising this fact accept the price set by it.

Assumptions

(i) For simplicity we assume only two firms viz., firm I and firm II and firm II has lower cost of production than firm I.

(ii) Products are homogeneous.

(iii) Two firms have their share in the market.

This situation of the market is explained in Fig. 12.4. In this figure, DD is the total market demand curve. Dd is the demand curve facing each individual firm I and firm II. It is just half of the total market demand curve DD. MR is the marginal revenue curve of both the firm I and firm II, where we get $MR_1 = MR_2$. AC_1 and MC_1 are the respective average cost and marginal cost of firm I. AC_2 and MC_2 are the respective average cost and marginal cost of firm II. Here AC_1 and MC_1 of firm I is higher than AC_2 and MC_2 of firm II showing that firm II has lower cost of production than firm I. So, the firm II will play the role of the price leader.

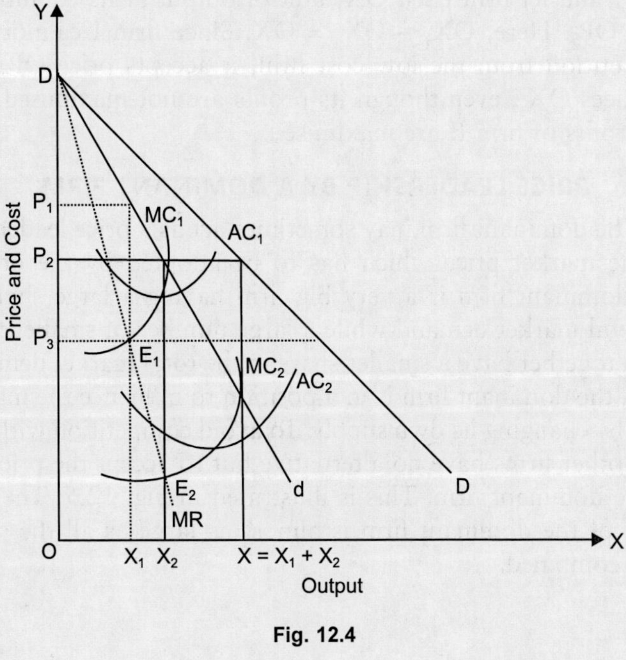

Fig. 12.4

Firm II is in equilibrium at output OX_2 corresponding to equilibrium point E_2, where MR intersects MC_2. It sells its output at a price OP_2.

But the equilibrium of firm I is at E_1 giving output OX_1 at price OP_1. Here, OP_1 is greater than OP_2. Since firm II sells at a lower price OP_2 and products are homogeneous, none will buy the products of firm I at the higher price OP_1. So, firm I has to sell at the price OP_2 set by the low cost firm II. If firm I is not willing to do so, its sales will be zero and it will be driven out from the market. Thus, firm I prefers to follow the leader, sacrificing some of its profits in order to avoid price war with firm II.

If firm II wants to drive firm I out of the market, firm II can do easily by setting price OP_3 which is below the AC_1 of firm I. But firm II has to face anti-monopoly law like MRTPA in India. So, a better solution from the viewpoint of the lower cost firm II is to tolerate a competitor like firm I. So, firm II splits the market evenly and let firm I sell OX_1 unit of output at its equilibrium price OP_2. Here, $OX_1 + OX_2 = OX$. Since firm I cannot face competition from the low cost firm, it accepts price OP_2 and produces OX_1, even though its profits are not maximised. But the profits of firm II are maximised.

PRICE LEADERSHIP BY A DOMINANT FIRM

The dominant firm may sometimes act as a price leader and fix the market price which has to be adopted by the others. The dominant firm is a very big firm having a large share of the total market demand while a large number of smaller firms taken together have a smaller share in the total market demand. Thus, the dominant firm is in a position to influence the market price by changing its own supply. To avoid competition with this firm, other firms have no alternative but to accept the price set by the dominant firm. This is illustrated in Fig. 12.5. The MC curve of the dominant firm is almost as large as all the small firms combined.

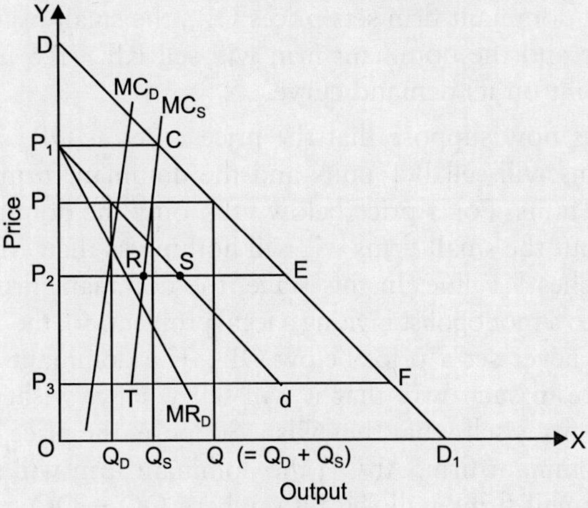

Fig. 12.5

The dominant firm could possibly eliminate all its rivals by a price-war. But this would establish a monopoly which will invite legal problems. The desirable course of action for the dominant firm will be to establish the market price and let the small firms sell all, they wish at that price. These small firms recognising their position will behave just as perfectly competitive firm. That is, they will regard their demand curve as a horizontal line at the prevailing price and sell that amount for which MC equals price. But this does not mean long run zero profit solution because price may be set far above the minimum AC.

The dominant firm will fix price in such a way as to maximise its profit while allowing the small firms to sell all they wish at that price. For this it is necessary to find the demand curve for the dominant firm. Let us suppose DD_1 is the market demand curve and MC_S is the horizontal summation of the marginal cost curves of all small firms. Since, the small firms equate MC and price, MC_S is also the collective supply curve of the small firms. MC_D and MR_D are the marginal cost and marginal revenue curves of dominant firm and P_1D is its AR curve.

Let us suppose that the dominant firm sets the price OP_1, the small firm would sell P_1C units. But the dominant firm sells nothing at this price as C is a point on the demand curve where MC_S intersects.

If the dominant firm sets prices OP_2, the small firm will sell P_2R units and the dominant firm will sell RE = P_2S units, S is also a point on its demand curve.

Let us now suppose that the price is set at OP_3. Then the small firms will sell P_3T units and the dominant firm will sell TF = P_3d units. For a price below OP_3, only the dominant firm will sell but the small firms will sell nothing as their MCs curve only touches P_3F line. In this stage, the dominant firm will be turned into a monopolist inviting a legal problem. So, the dominant firm will never set a price below OP_3. The dominant firm will set a price in such way that it will sell what it wishes and let the small firms sell what they wish. Suppose, the price OP is set by the dominant firm. At OP, the dominant firm will sell OQ_D and the small firms will sell OQ_S where $OQ = OQ_D + OQ_S$ is the total quantity sold.

Many variations of the basic price leadership model can be constructed by changing the assumption. We may allow for two or more dominant firms, for product differentiation, for geographically separated seller and transportation cost and so on. Nevertheless the basic results are the same.

BAROMETRIC PRICE LEADERSHIP

It is not necessary that under the price leadership model of oligopoly, the price leader must either be a low cost firm or a dominant firm. There may be a case of a price leader which is neither the low cost firm nor the dominant firm. There may be a firm which has achieved reputation because it is very old in the market and hence most experienced and widely respected. Such a firm may assume the role of a custodian for protecting the interest of all the firms in an industry and, therefore, works as a price leader. This firm assesses the changed market conditions with regard to the demand for the product of that industry, competition from the related products, changes in cost of production, likely entry of other firms etc., and makes price changes accordingly. This firm chosen as the leader is considered as a barometer, reflecting these changes in economic environment. This firm is believed to be the custodian of all the firms in the industry and it makes price changes which are supposed to serve the interest of all the firms. All the firms follow it and accept its leadership willingly.

Difference between Perfect Competition and Imperfect Competition

Perfect Competition	Imperfect Competition
1. There are unlimited number of buyers and sellers.	1. There are limited number of buyers and sellers.
2. Every seller charges only one price.	2. All the sellers charge different prices.
3. All the sellers sell only one commodity.	3. All the sellers sell close substitutes of a commodity.
4. Buyers have complete knowledge of the prevailing market prices of commodities.	4. Buyers have not got up-to-date knowledge of prices of commodities.
5. There is no transport cost for bringing the commodities from one place to another place.	5. Transport costs take place for bringing the commodities from one place to another place.

CHART FOR CLASSIFICATION OF MARKET FORMS

The following chart shows the different types of market forms on the basis of degree and nature of competition.

Types of Markets	Number of firms	Nature of the commodity
Perfect or pure competition	Infinite number of buyers and sellers	Homogeneous
Monopoly	One seller but many buyers	Homogeneous
Imperfect Competition		
(a) Monopolistic Competition	Many sellers and many buyers	Differentiated
(b) Perfect Oligopoly	A few sellers but many buyers	Homogeneous
(c) Imperfect Oligopoly	A few sellers but many buyers	Differentiated
(d) Duopoly	Two sellers but many buyers	Homogeneous
(e) Bilateral Monopoly	One seller and one buyer	Homogeneous
(f) Monopsony	One buyer but many sellers	Homogeneous
(g) Duopsony	Two buyers but many sellers	Homogeneous
(h) Oligopsony	A few buyers but many sellers	Homogeneous or differentiated

EXERCISES

1. Define oligopoly with its nature and characteristics.
2. What do you mean by duopoly? Define Cournot's model of duopoly problem with its characteristic features.
3. Why is there a kinked in the demand curve of an oligopoly firm? How do you draw the marginal revenue curve of the oligopoly firm where there is a kinked demand curve?
4. What are the main characteristics of oligopoly? Is it correct to say that price under oligopoly is interdependent?
5. Explain the kinked demand curve solution under independent action.
6. What are the main types of collusion? Explain briefly the pricing problem of oligopoly under the centralised cartel and under market sharing cartel.
7. What is price leadership? Explain the pricing process under price leadership by a low cost firm and by a dominant firm.
8. Does the kinked demand curve solution offer a satisfactory explanation of price-output decision under oligopoly?
9. Distinguish between perfect competition and imperfect competition.
10. Prove that the monopoly output is half of the competitive output and duopoly output is two-third of the competitive output with zero cost and straight line demand curve.

Chapter 13

Theory of Distribution

MARGINAL PRODUCTIVITY THEORY OF DISTRIBUTION

Marginal Productivity Theory was first an attempt to explain the determination of wages, i.e., reward for labour but later on, prices of other factors of production such as land, capital, etc., also explained with marginal productivity theory. It is the work of many economists each improving, amending and modifying the ideas of the other. The origin of the concept of marginal productivity theory can be traced to **Ricardo.** But it is re-discovered by economists like **J.B. Clark, Jevons, Wicksteed, Walras, Marshall** and **J.R. Hicks.** According to **J.B. Clark,** "Under static conditions, every factor including the entrepreneur would get a remuneration equal to marginal product."

Assumptions: The theory stands on the following assumptions:

1. All factors of production are variable and continuously divisible. Moreover, all factors of production are assumed to be homogeneous in character.
2. The marginal productivity of each factor is positive and diminishing.
3. Factor proportions of production are changeable.
4. There is perfect competition both in the factor market and in the commodity market.
5. There is perfect mobility of each factor.
6. Factors are versatile and substitutable.
7. The technique of production is assumed to remain the same.
8. The motive of the entrepreneur is to maximise his profit.

The basic propositions of this theory are: (a) each input is paid according to its marginal productivity and (b) total product is exhausted when each factor is paid according to its marginal productivity. It should be noted that when we say, that each factor is paid according to its marginal productivity, it does not mean that each unit of the factor receives its marginal productivity. From the assumption of diminishing marginal productivity, we know that as more and more units of a factor are employed, its marginal productivity diminishes. The marginal productivity theory states that all units of a factor receive a reward equal to the marginal productivity of its last unit. Thus if ten units of labour are employed in the production process, each unit of labour will receive a wage rate which is equal to the marginal productivity of the tenth unit of labour, by virtue of perfect competition. The marginal productivity theory of distribution can be better understood with the help of the Fig. 13.1.

In Fig. 13.1, unit of labour is measured along the X-axis and marginal revenue product of labour along the Y-axis. The marginal revenue productivity curve of labour (MRP) is a downward sloping curve due to the operation of law of diminishing returns. This means that the marginal productivity of labour falls downward as more and more of labour is employed.

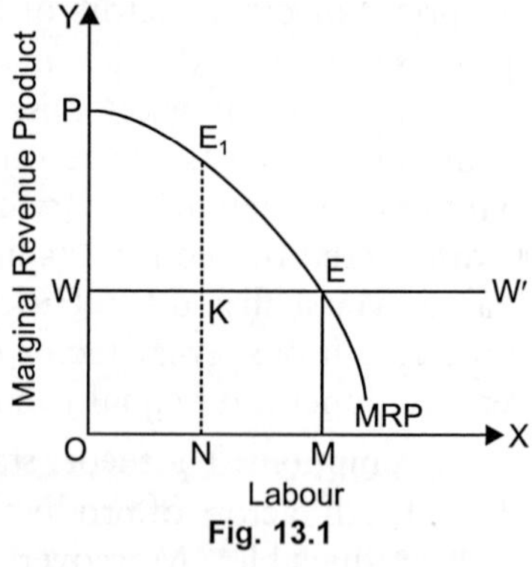

Fig. 13.1

As there is perfect competition in factor market, the wage rate curve is WW′ which is a straight line parallel to the X-axis. A profit maximising firm can employ any number of labour at prevailing wage rate OW. Suppose the firm employs OM units of labour. At this level of employment, MRP curve intersects WW′ curve at point E where the marginal productivity of labour is equal to wage rate. At any extra unit of employment of labour after the point E the firm will face loss, because the MRP curve lies below the WW′ line after the point E. After E, wage rate of the labour is greater than its marginal revenue product. So, the firm never employs labour after the point E.

If the firm employs OM units of labour, the total product will be OMEP and total wage cost will be OMEW. So profits will be WEP (area of OMEP – area of OMEW). If the firm employs less than OM, say ON units of labour, the total product will be ONE_1P and total wage cost will be ONKW. So the profits will be WKE_1P (area of ONE_1P – ONKW) which is lower than the previous profits, WEP by E_1KE. Thus, employment of less than OM number of workers will mean that the firm is not maximising its profits and beyond OM, the firm is facing loss. Hence, OM is the level of employment which gives maximum profits and this corresponds to point E where marginal productivity of labour is just equal to wage rate. Thus, according to the marginal productivity theory, an employer will employ that quantity of a factor where its marginal productivity is equal to the payment made to the factor of production.

Now let us see when the wage changes in Fig. 13.2. Suppose, the wage rises from OW to OW_1, the new equilibrium point is shifted from E to E_1 where the MRP curve intersects the higher wage rate W_1W_1'. The firm will be employing ON of labour where the marginal product is equal to wage rate. Profits will be lower than before by an amount equal to WEE_1W_1. Again if the firm continues to employ OM units of labour at the wage rate OW_1, it will make an extra loss in range E_1E of the MRP curve by an amount equal to E_1KE. Hence, the firm will never employ more than ON units of labour at wage rate OW_1.

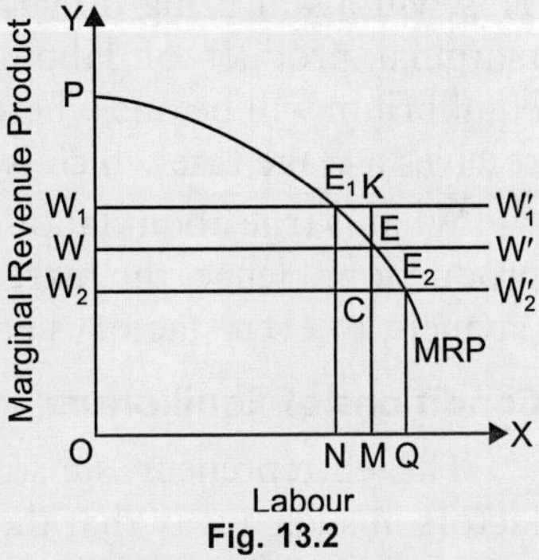

Fig. 13.2

Again if the wage rate line shifts from WW′ to a lower $W_2W'_2$ due to fall in wage rate from OW to OW_2, the equilibrium will also be shifted from E to E_2 where the MRP curve intersects the lower wage rate line $W_2W'_2$. Corresponding to the new equilibrium E_2, the firm will employ OQ units of labour. The employment of MQ number of additional units of labour will bring extra profits to the firm by an amount equal to EE_2C to maximise its gain. It can be noted again that marginal product of labour is equalised with the wage rate at its margin as shown by the point E_2 and employment is extended to OQ number of labour. So it will be profitable for the firm to extend employment from OM to OQ number of workers by giving the wage rate at the margin.

Thus, in equilibrium, every firm will employ that much amount of labour where its marginal product is equal to the wage rate. The unit of labour at the margin will be paid wage which is equal to its product. Since all units of labour have been assumed to be homogeneous, everyone will be paid the same wages. If a worker is being paid less than the marginal product, he can leave this job and shift to some other where he gets wages equal to his marginal product. No one will come and take job with this firm till it raises its wage rate to become equal to the marginal product of labour as there is perfect competition in the labour market.

Again wage rate is higher than the marginal product of labour, the firm will soon realise that it would be more profitable to reduce employment of labour. Some labourers become unemployed. These unemployed workers will secure employment. This will again bring down wage rate to become equal to the marginal product of labour. Thus, the ultimate position of equilibrium will be one where the employers pay and the labour receives a wage rate which is equal to its marginal productivity.

What is true about labour, is also true about other factors of production. Hence, the marginal productivity theory states that payment to every factor is equal to its marginal productivity.

Conditions of Equilibrium

The entrepreneur substitutes and combines the different factors in such a way that the increase in the product due to the employment of an additional unit of any factor is equal to the price that he has to pay for it. The equilibrium position where there is no inducement for the producer to affect any further change in the proportions of the different factors is as follows:

$$\frac{\text{Marginal Productivity of Factor A}}{\text{Price of Factor A}} = \frac{\text{Marginal Productivity of Factor B}}{\text{Price of Factor B}}$$

If the marginal productivity of factor A is greater than its price while that of factor B is lower than its price, it is not the optimum combination of the different factors and the entrepreneur is obviously losing on factor B. He must employ more of A and less of B. As he employs less of factor B, its marginal productivity will rise and as he employs more of factor A, its marginal productivity will fall. This process must continue so long as the relation between marginal productivity and price for each of the two factors becomes equal and thus the point of equilibrium will reach, because there will be no further inducement to substitute one factor for another.

Criticism

The marginal productivity theory is a general theory of distribution since it can serve as the principle of payment to any factor of production. But it is based on some unrealistic assumptions.

1. Assumption of divisibility is unjustified: It is assumed that it is possible to make infinitesimally small changes in the amounts of factors employed. But divisibility beyond a limit is not possible. Factor indivisibility restricts the free choice of factor proportions in production.

2. Assumption of variability of factor proportions is unrealistic: Factor proportions can be changed at least in the long-run. The assumption has been challenged on technological grounds. Modern technology does not allow any such variation. In most cases, factor proportions are rigidly fixed under the engineering data. Any attempt to violate these proportions results in complete wastage of one factor for the other.

3. Factor heterogeneity is ignored: The theory assumes that all the units of a factor are homogeneous and perfect substitutes for each other. The reality is that land, labour and entrepreneurial talents are heterogeneous.

4. Marginal productivity is not calculable in practice: Marginal productivity is not calculable in many cases. It has questioned the practical utility of the theory itself. With regard to entrepreneurship at least it is not possible to find out the marginal productivity at all. This has led many economists to build up alternative theories.

5. It explains the demand side of factors only: The theory does not tell us how factor prices are determined; it merely states how an employer will hire a factor with given its marginal productivity. This is because of the fact that it makes into consideration only the demand side of a factor and assumes the supply side as constant. A complete theory of factor prices must analyse in detail the force working on the demand side as well as on the supply side.

6. It ignores the powerful influence of selling cost: The theory simply ignores the influence of selling cost. It was based on the highly abstract assumption of perfect competition. It is neither theoretically complete nor practically helpful.

7. It is mainly applicable in the long-run: The theory is set within the framework of the long-run. It has limited validity for the short-run.

8. It ignores the relationship between rewards and factor productivities: The most fundamental objection to the marginal productivity theory is that it ignores the interrelations between rewards and productivities of factors of production.

9. It is a static theory: Marginal productivity theory neglects the problem of technical change altogether. It is a static theory. Modern economists have tried to correct the theory considering the peculiar characteristics of the supply side of each factor and the influence of monetary factors.

EULER'S THEOREM – ADDING-UP PROBLEM (The Product Exhaustion Problem)

Leonhard Euler was a Swiss mathematician. Some of his propositions have been found by economists to be usefully applicable to problems in economic theory. Euler's theorem has been applied to the analysis of production and distribution. The application of this theorem disposed of the 'adding-up problem' which troubled early marginal productivity theorists who had been unable to demonstrate conclusively that the sum of factor rewards determined by the marginal productivity of the different factors added up to the total product, neither more nor less.

According to marginal productivity theory, every input is paid the value of its marginal product. This means that the entire product will always be distributed to those who work on it. That is, the sum of the marginal products will add up exactly to the total output having neither a surplus nor a deficit.

This proposition can be proved by using Euler's theorem. Euler's theorem holds that if a production function involves constant returns to scale (i.e., production function is linearly homogeneous), the sum of the marginal products will exactly be equal to the total product.

The Euler's theorem is based on the following assumptions:

1. The production function is homogeneous of degree one indicating constant returns to scale.
2. The factors of production are perfectly divisible.
3. The relative shares of factors of production are constant and independent of the level of output.
4. There is perfect competition in the economy.
5. This is long-run phenomenon.
6. There is no scope of abnormal profits.

Let a production function with constant returns to scale be

$$Q = f(L, K)$$

According to the Euler's theorem, we get

$$Q = \frac{dQ}{dL} \cdot L + \frac{dQ}{dk} \cdot K \quad \left[\text{where } \frac{dQ}{dL} = MPP_L \text{ and } \frac{dQ}{dk} = MPP_K \right]$$

Therefore, $Q = MPP_L \cdot L + MPP_K \cdot K$

The theorem can be extended to cover any number of inputs. The equation states that the MP of labour multiplied by the number of labourers plus MP of capital multiplied by the amount of capital is exactly equal to the total product.

The marginal productivity theory satisfies the adding-up condition for the special case of constant returns to scale. It shows that the sum of factor shares is equal to one.

That is, share of labour + share of capital = 1.

Proof of Euler's Theorem

A production function,

$$Q = f(L, K), \text{ is homogeneous of degree v if}$$
$$f(g^v L, g^v k) = g^v f(L, K)$$

Differentiating with respect to g, we get

$$L \cdot \frac{df}{dL} + K \cdot \frac{df}{dk} = vg^{v-1} f(L, k)$$

If it is constant returns to scale, v = 1 and we get

$$L \cdot MPP_L + K \cdot MPP_K = f(L, K)$$

or, $$Q = L(MPP_L) + K(MPP_K)$$

Total physical payments to factors would exhaust the total physical output. Multiplying through by P, (the price of output), we get

$$PQ = L \cdot (MPP_L \times P) + K(MPP_K \times P)$$

Or, value of product = L × value of the MP of labour + K × value of the MP of capital.

i.e., value of product = cost of labour + cost of capital.

Again, if

$$1 = \frac{\text{cost of labour}}{\text{value of product}} + \frac{\text{cost of capital}}{\text{value of product}}$$

i.e., 1 = share of labour + share of capital

Thus, payment of factors according to their value of marginal product exhausts the value of output and share of factors adds up to unity. Hence, Euler's theorem is an identity. It holds true for all values of the variables. It plays a major role in the development of the marginal productivity theory of distribution.

Diagrammatic Representation of Euler's Theorem

Euler's Theorem can be shown diagrammatically where we measure labour along the X-axis and total product along the Y-axis. In the Fig. 13.3, the curve OP represents the total product which shows production function Q = f (L, K). The straight line AB is tangent on the OP curve at point E representing constant returns to scale.

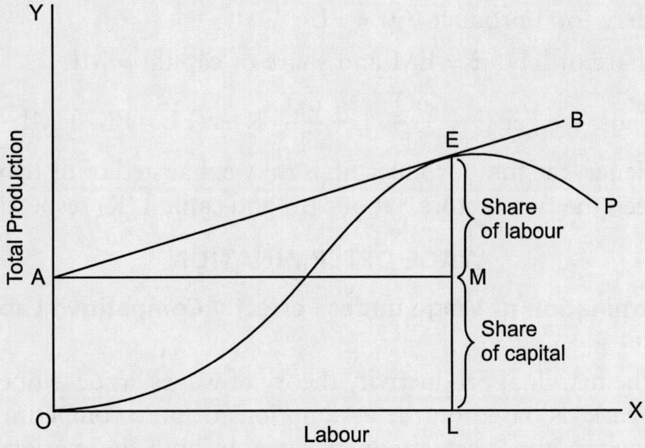

Fig. 13.3

The slope at E = $\frac{EM}{AM} = \frac{EM}{OL}$ $\qquad (\because AM = OL)$

Now, the equation of Euler's theorem is

$$Q = \frac{\delta Q}{\delta L} \cdot L + \frac{\delta Q}{\delta K} \cdot K \qquad \text{... (1)}$$

At point E, we get

$$\frac{\delta Q}{\delta L} \cdot L = \frac{EM}{OL} \cdot OL = EM$$

where $\frac{\delta Q}{\delta L}$ = marginal product of labour which is the slope of production function and equal to $\frac{EM}{OL}$. Again the quantity of labour (L) at point E is OL. Therefore, the share of labour $\left(\frac{\delta Q}{\delta L} \cdot L\right)$ in the total product is EM.

Now to find out the share of capital we consider the equation 1.

Here, $$\frac{\delta Q}{\delta K} \cdot K = Q - \frac{\delta Q}{\delta L} \cdot L$$
$$= EL - EM$$

$\therefore$ The share of capital, $\frac{\delta Q}{\delta K} \cdot K = ML$

Here total product (Q) = EL

Share of labour = EM and share of capital = ML

Thus, we get $Q = \frac{\delta Q}{\delta L} \cdot L + \frac{\delta Q}{\delta K} \cdot K \quad \therefore EL = EM + ML$

Hence, the total product EL is fully exhausted or distributed between the two factors, labour (L) and capital (K) respectively.

WAGE DETERMINATION

Determination of Wage under Perfectly Competitive Labour Market

The marginal productivity theory of wages, as developed by **J.B. Clark**, is based on the assumptions of pure competition in both commodity and labour markets. In both the markets the buyers and sellers are supposed to be price-takers.

The determination of the wage rate will be different in different market structures. Here we consider how the wage rate is determined in a perfectly competitive labour market.

Assumptions

1. There are a large number of labourers selling labour and large number of firms buying labour.
2. There is an agreement between the employer and the labourers that they are employed for a fixed number of hours in a week.
3. The labourers are employed on the basis of wages or salaries.
4. They have full knowledge of prevailing wage.
5. All units of labour are homogeneous in character.
6. Wage discrimination among the workers is ruled out.

In the perfectly competitive market no firm has the power to influence the wage rate. Each firm takes the wage rate determined by the interaction of demand for labour and supply of labour. Similarly no labourer has also the power to influence this wage rate. The firm can engage a number of workers at a given wage rate. Given the wage rate the firms try to maximise their profit and from this profit maximisation process we get the demand curve of labour. Similarly at any given wage rate the labourers try to maximise utility and from this process of maximisation of utility we get the individual labour supply curve. An increase in demand for labour, with the given supply, will cause the wage rate to rise and similarly an increase in supply of labour, with a given demand, will cause the wage to fall. The demand curve for labour will be downward sloping and its supply curve will be upward rising. By adding the demand curves of different firms we can get the market demand curve. Likewise, by adding the supply curves of different individuals we get the market supply curve of labour.

What will be the market wage rate and how much labour a firm will employ are discussed with the help of Fig. 13.4.

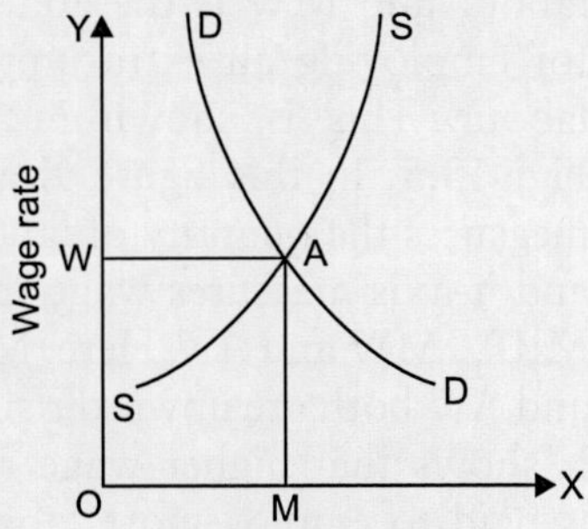

Fig. 13.4

In this figure X-axis measures demand for labour and supply of labour and Y-axis measures wage rate. DD is the demand curve of the labourers and SS is the supply curve of the labourers. Both the curves intersect at point A. Point A is the equilibrium point. At point A, the equilibrium wage rate is OW and equilibrium demand for labour and equilibrium supply of labour are OM. Both are equal at this wage rate. They are not equal at any other wage rate except at the equilibrium wage rate OW. If wage rate is greater than OW, the supply of labour is greater than demand. In this situation there is a competition among the labourers to get work. As a result, the wage rate falls and falls until the wage rate OW is reached. Again if the wage rate is smaller than OW, the demand for labour is greater than the supply of labour. The employer wants more labourers to give them work. Higher demand for labour raises the wage rate up to OW. In this way equilibrium wage rate OW is established.

DETERMINATION OF WAGE UNDER IMPERFECTLY COMPETITIVE LABOUR MARKET

In a perfectly competitive labour market all the workers are willing to work at the fixed wage rate. That is why average wage (AW) is equal to the marginal wage (MW). But in case of imperfectly competitive labour market the labour supply curve is upward rising. As a result MW increases but we have MW > AW. It implies that MW curve lies above the AW curve. The motive of the employer is always to maximise his profit and he employs labour upto the point where MW = MRP_L (MRP_L = marginal revenue productivity of labour). MW < MRP_L implies that to employ additional labour is profitable and MW > MRP_L implies that to employ additional labour is unprofitable. The MRP_L is the additional revenue obtained by employing an extra unit of labour and MW is the additional wage paid by the employer for employing an extra unit of labour. This is shown in the Fig. 13.5. In this figure X-axis measures the quantity of labour and Y-axis measures wage rate, MRP_L, MW and AW. Here, MW and AW both are upward rising. It shows that higher wage rate is paid to employ more labour. When AW increases, MW increases more than AW. MRP_L curve is downward sloping and concave to the origin.

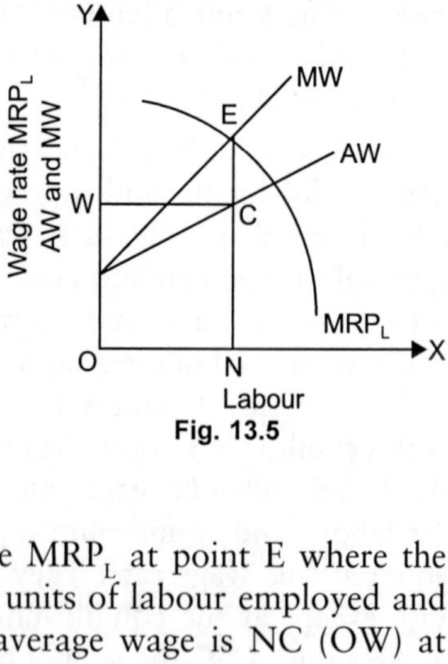

Fig. 13.5

The MW curve intersects the MRP_L at point E where the MRP_L equals to the MW at ON units of labour employed and total profit is maximum. Here average wage is NC (OW) at ON units of labour employed. So, the equilibrium wage rate in the labour market is OW and the equilibrium amount of labour employed is ON. But the equilibrium wage rate is not determined at point E where EN is the marginal wage and CN is the average wage. The employer will give only average wage. So, the average wage CN is the equilibrium wage. CN is less than the MRP_L by EC which is difference between the MRP_L and the average wage. This difference is called exploitation of labour as their wage rate is less than their MRP_L. That is why, in an imperfectly competitive labour market the wage rate is lower than in the perfectly competitive labour market.

DETERMINATION OF WAGES UNDER COLLECTIVE BARGAINING

Collective bargaining shows a situation where workers form trade unions (associations) bargain collectively with the employer (or the union of the employers) to achieve higher wage rates, more non-wage benefits and improving general conditions of work. Non-wage benefits mean provident fund, gratuity, pension, medical, reduction in hours of work, better conditions of work, security, regular payment of wages, etc. Collective bargaining takes the situation is like that of a bilateral monopoly where one buyer faces one seller.

Now question arises: Can the trade unions achieve higher wages and more non-wage benefits without adversely affecting volume of employment of labour? Let us see how they can.

We know that a firm employs labour upto the point where its marginal revenue productivity (MRP) is equal to its marginal wage rate (MW). Since wage rate is determined by the demand for and supply of labour in the market, an individual employer accepts this wage rate and seeks to equal MRP of labour with the marginal wage rate. As in the perfect competition in the labour market, the wage rate having been decided by the industry, the employing firm faces a horizontal labour supply curve which shows both the average and the marginal wage rate (i.e., AW = MW). Again, since there is a monopoly in the product market, firm's MR is less than AR (price) and hence the marginal revenue product (MRP) of labour is less than the average revenue product (ARP) of labour and both the curves are downward sloping.

In Fig. 13.6 demand curve for and supply curve of labour are DD and SS respectively. They intersect at point A and determine the wage rate OW. Corresponding to this wage rate, the firm faces the equilibrium at point E where the MRP of labour is equal to MW of labour and employs OM level of labour.

Now, if the trade union restricts the supply of labour in the market, the supply curve of labour will shift upward resulting to rise in wage rate. As a result the supply curve shifts from SS to S_1S_1 and the wage rate rises from OW to OW_1. Corresponding to OW_1 the new equilibrium of the firm will be established at E_1 where the firm will employ only OM_1 level of labour. Thus

M_1M level of labour will be unemployed in the firm and N_1N level of labour will be unemployed in the industry as a whole.

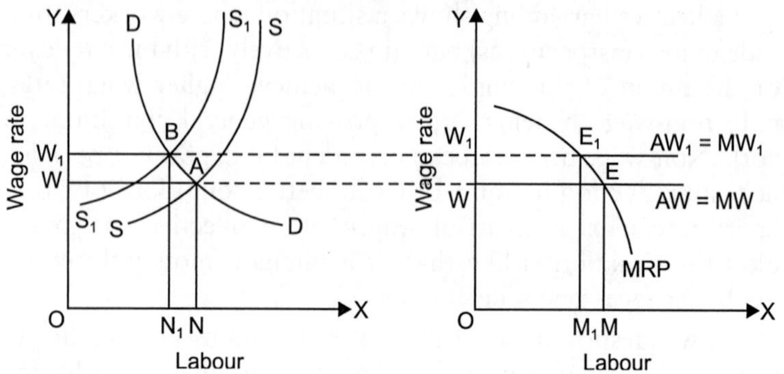

Fig. 13.6

In Fig. 13.6 we assume that while the unions secure a rise in wage rate, the MRP of labour and the demand for labour remain the same. But if we drop the assumption of static marginal productivity of labour and assume that due to impact of higher wage the work capacity of labour rises, i.e., marginal physical productivity of labour rises. Then MRP of labour rises and the MRP curve of labour shifts upwards. Now MRP of labour is the demand curve for labour of a firm and the sum total of firms' demand curves is the market demand curve for labour. The demand curve for labour of the whole industry shifts upward when the MRP curves of the firms shift upward. Thus labour will be fully employed instead of being unemployed or employment of labour may even increase. This is explained in Fig. 13.7 given below:

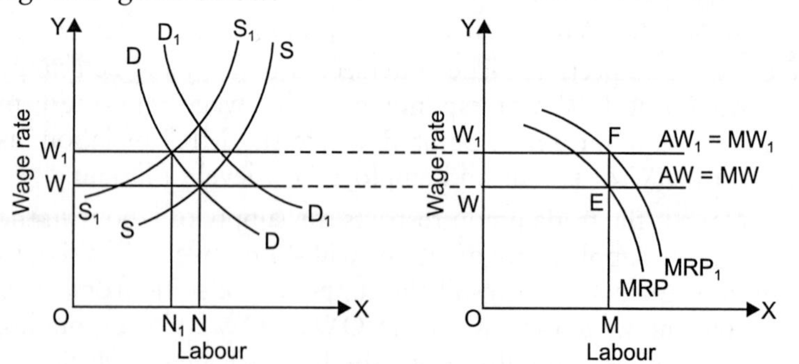

Fig. 13.7

The efficiency of labour increases with the increase in wage rate from OW to OW_1 and MRP of labour also increases from MRP to MRP_1. Hence, the total demand for labour in the market goes up from DD to D_1D_1. Consequently, the industry employs the same old ON level of labour causing no unemployment. The individual firm, which employed OM of labour earlier at wage rate OW and wanted to employ less labour when wage rate rose from OW to OW_1, is now willing to employ initial level of labour OM as the MRP of labour has increased to MRP_1. To employ OM of labour is profitable at the wage rate OW_1. It is so even at the higher wage rate than OW_1. Thus, trade unions by their collective bargaining can attain higher wage rate for their workers and can maintain these higher wages if the workers improve their efficiency and marginal productivity.

When labour is facing with a monopsony, i.e., a single buyer of labour or any other imperfection in the labour market, the firm does not face a horizontal demand curve for labour. A monopsony firm can buy more labour by offering higher wages and less labour by offering lower wages. Because, it is the single biggest buyer of labour. Hence, the monopsonist is facing a rising average and marginal wage curve. He will equate MRP of labour with the marginal wage rate (MW) and make maximum profits. This is shown in Fig. 13.8. The monopsonist is in equilibrium at point E where MRP = MW_2. But corresponding to this equilibrium he is paying average wage rate OW employing OM level of labour. Here his total production = OMSR and total wage paid by him = OMKW. Total profit earned by him = OMSR – OMKW = WKSR. Labour is getting a wage rate MK below its marginal revenue product ME.

The difference = ME – MK = KE is the monopsonistic exploitation of labour.

Now, the trade unions through collective bargaining can secure wage at a higher rate which removes the exploitation of labour and as well as maintain or even increase the employment of labour. If the union can attain a wage rate OW_1 and supply of labour as much as demanded by the firm at this wage rate but supply is nothing below this rate. The supply curve of labour will become W_1W_1 parallel to the X-axis with $AW_1 = MW_1$. The new position of equilibrium would be E_1 where we get MRP = MW_1 corresponding to the wage rate OW_1 and level of employment OM_1. Here the exploitation of labour somehow only eliminated but more employment of labour is also obtained.

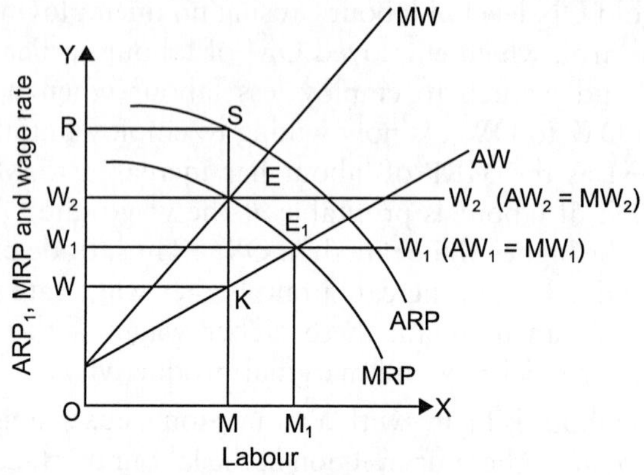

Fig. 13.8

Again, if a trade union is very much powerful, it can even secure a still higher wage rate equal to OW_2 with a supply curve of labour W_2W_2. The firm will establish its equilibrium point at its old point E where MW_2 = MRP and the employment level will be maintained at OM. Thus, without causing any unemployment trade union can succeed in securing higher wage rate for labour.

LOANABLE FUNDS THEORY OF INTEREST
(The Neo-Classical Theory of Interest)

According to the classical theory, rate of interest is determined by the interaction of the forces of demand for savings and the supply of savings. Demand for savings comes from the firms who want to undertake investment.

The loanable funds theory also known as neoclassical theory of rate of interest was first formulated by **Wicksell.** A group of Swedish economists like **Bertil Ohlin, Myrdal, Bent Hansen** further improved this theory.

According to this theory, rate of interest is determined by the equilibrium between demand for and supply of loanable funds in the money market.

Supply of Loanable Funds

The supply of loanable funds is derived from four basic sources, namely, (1) savings, (2) dishoarding, (3) Bank money and (4) disinvestment. The further details of these various sources of loanable funds are given below:

1. Savings: One of the most important sources of the supply of loanable funds is the savings. Savings may be personal or corporate.

Personal savings: Savings by individuals or households may be looked in two ways—exante and expost. Exante savings is the intended savings which the people plan at the beginning of the period. Expost savings on the other hand is the savings which is actually realised at the end of the period. This is equal to the difference between the income of the preceding period and the consumption of the present period.

Corporate savings: Like individuals, corporate businessmen save from the undistributed profits.

Savings are high at high rate of interest and *vice versa*. Therefore, supply of savings curve slopes upwards to the right shown in Fig. 13.9.

2. Dishoarding: Dishoarding of past accumulated savings constitutes another source of supply of loanable funds. Individuals may dishoard money from the hoarded stock of the previous period. Thus, the idle cash balances in a previous period become active cash balances in the present period and add to the supply for loanable funds. It is evident that dishoarding is interest elastic and the curve of dishoarding slopes upward to the right shown in Fig. 13.9.

3. Bank money: Now-a-days, the banking system is the most important source of supply of loanable funds. It was totally disregarded by the classical economists. **Wicksell** believed that the expansion or contraction of bank money was not affected by changes in the rate of interest. In his opinion, the banking system offers the amount of credit which depends upon the liquidity position of the banks. But subsequently it is felt that it is not correct. The banks will lend more money at higher rate of interest and *vice versa*. Again banks also purchase and sell securities and thereby affect the supply of loanable funds. Thus, the supply curve of bank money is reasonably interest elastic and slopes upward to the right shown in Fig. 13.9.

4. Disinvestment: Disinvestment is another source of the supply of loanable funds. It is opposite to investment. It takes place due to structural changes, i.e., either machines and equipments are allowed to wear out without replacement or when the inventories are drawn below the level of previous period. The firm may decide to let this capital run down and to put the depreciation funds into the market for loanable funds. Thus, the process by which disinvestment is made is (a) running down of inventories and not replacing them and (b) non-replacement of the machinery worn out during the process of production. So, disinvestment adds to the supply of loanable funds. Disinvestment may be higher when the rate of interest is very high and *vice versa*. So, the slope of disinvestment curve is upward rising to the right shown in Fig. 13.9.

By the lateral summation of the four curves, savings (S), dishoarding (DH), bank money (BM) and disinvestment (DI), we get the total supply curve (SL) of loanable funds which slopes upwards to the right. Upwards sloping means that a greater amount of loanable funds will be available at higher rates of interest and *vice versa*. It is shown in Fig. 13.9.

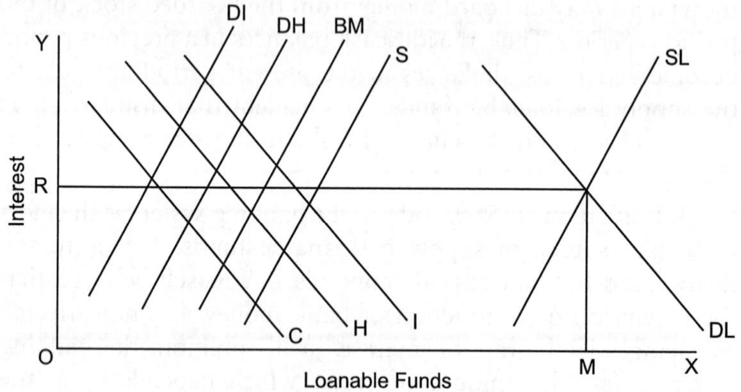

Fig. 13.9

Demand for Loanable Funds

The demand for loanable funds comes mainly from three fields: (i) Investment, (ii) Consumption and (iii) Hoarding.

(i) **Investment:** The primary demand for loanable funds is the investment demand of business firms. The business people are constantly comparing the cost of borrowing of loanable funds (rate of interest) with the expected rate of profit by investment of it. They would keep on borrowing up to that extent where the rate of interest is equal to the expected rate of profit. When the rate of interest falls, businessmen will find it profitable to increase investment in capital goods as a result their demand for loanable funds will rise. Thus, it is clear that demand for loanable funds for investment is interest elastic. At a low rate of interest there will be greater investment demand and *vice versa*. Thus, the curve of investment demand for loanable funds slopes downwards to the right as shown in Fig. 13.9.

(ii) **Consumption:** Another major source of demand for loanable funds comes from the consumer who wants to borrow more funds when they want to spend more than their current income. Generally, the consumer needs more loans to purchase durable goods like cars, automobiles, refrigerators, television sets, air conditioners, furnitures, etc. A lower rate of interest will naturally stimulate the demand for loanable funds to purchase more of such goods and *vice versa*. Thus, the slope of consumption demand for loanable funds is downward sloping to the right as shown in Fig. 13.9.

(iii) **Hoarding:** The third source of demand for loanable funds comes from those who want to hold idle cash balances for the purpose of hoarding in order to satisfy their desire for liquidity. At higher rate of interest, people will hold less on account of higher loss. So, the demand for hoarding money is interest elastic and slopes downwards to the right shown in Fig. 13.9.

The total demand for loanable funds is the sum of these three, viz. investment demand (I), consumption demand (C) and demand for hoarding (H). These three curves are shown in Fig. 13.9. By lateral summation of these three curves, we get total demand curve for loanable funds as shown in Fig. 13.9.

Equilibrium Rate of Interest

In the economy, there are lender of loanable funds and there are borrowers of loanable funds. The rate of interest is determined by the equilibrium between the total demand for loanable funds and the total supply of loanable funds.

The curve DL of total demand for loanable funds obtained by lateral summation of C, H and I curves and curve SL of the total supply of loanable funds also obtained by lateral summation of DI, DH, BM and S curves intersect each other at the rate of interest OR. At this rate of interest OR both demand for and supply of loanable funds are equal to OM. Below OR, the demand for loanable funds is higher than the supply of loanable funds. Again above OR, the supply of loanable funds is higher than the demand for loanable funds. Thus, at any other interest rate either the demand for loanable funds will exceed the supply of loanable funds or the supply of loanable funds will exceed the demand for loanable funds. They will be equal only at the rate of interest OR. Hence, OR is the equilibrium rate of interest.

Criticisms

The neo-classical loanable funds theory is an improvement over the classical theory. The classical theory explains the phenomenon of rate of interest depending only on real factors. On the other hand, loanable funds theory considers both the monetary and non-monetary factors in the determination of rate of interest. But it is not free from criticisms.

(i) Though loanable funds theory considers the real as well as monetary variables, it cannot succeed in integrating the two types of variables simply for the reason that real variables are flow variables and the monetary variables are stock variables.

(ii) The loanable theory states that the SL can be increased by releasing cash balances of savings and decreased by observing cash balances into savings. But this is not correct.

(iii) This theory is based on the assumption of full employment of resources which does not hold in the real world. In this view, **Keynes** theory is superior since it is based upon the assumption of less than full employment.

(iv) The equilibrium rate of interest cannot say the equilibrium level of income. If the level of income is not in equilibrium, the rate of interest changes with the change in the level of income. So, the equilibrium rate of interest becomes indeterminate.

(v) Lastly, the loanable funds theory is a synthesis between the classical theory and the Keynesian 'liquidity preference theory'. Because it takes into account the savings and investment from the classical theory and liquidity preference theory from the Keynes' theory.

INNOVATION THEORY OF PROFIT

Prof. Joseph Schumpeter developed the idea of the innovation theory. According to Schumpeter, the main function of the entrepreneur is to incorporate innovations into production and thus the profits are the reward of the entrepreneur for successfully introducing innovations. Innovations are mainly two types: (a) those which change the production function and reduce the cost of production, and (b) those innovations which stimulate the demand for the product. The first type involves a new technique of production, introduction of new machinery, finding a new cheap source of raw materials, a new and better organisational pattern for the firm, etc. Second type includes evolving a new variety of product, finding a new market to sell, methods of persuading customers to buy more of product through publicity and propaganda, discovery of new markets etc.

Any entrepreneur who successfully incorporate these innovations makes more profits. But such profits are temporary in nature and tend to be competed away as others imitate and also adopt that. When an entrepreneur introduces a new innovation, he is first in a monopoly position. Because the new innovation is confined to him only. When after some time others also adopt it, his profits will disappear. But in this dynamic world and progressive economy, the superior entrepreneurs continue to make innovations and enjoy the profits thereof. This is the process through which development takes place.

Profit is a necessary incentive for the entrepreneur to detect and introduce innovations. Innovations are the important source of profits.

Schumpeter's innovation theory is not satisfactory on the following grounds:

(i) **Schumpeter** ignores uncertainty as a source of profit. He does not give any importance on uncertainty in explaining of his theory.

(ii) He also neglects any role of risk-bearing theory in the explanation of his theory. This is far from the reality.

(iii) This theory attributes profits only to innovations and ignores the other factors which are responsible for the profit of the entrepreneur.

EXERCISES

1. Define marginal productivity theory of distribution. What are its assumptions and criticisms?
2. How would you explain the factor pricing in terms of the marginal productivity theory of distribution under the conditions of perfect competition?
3. Explain Euler's Theory, adding up problem and product-exhaustion theorem.
4. "In equilibrium all factors of production receive a payment just equal to the value of their marginal product." Explain.
5. Explain Euler's Theory diagrammatically.
6. How is the problem of distribution solved with the help of Euler's Theorem? Explain.
7. How do you determine wage in perfectly competitive market?

   Or

   Explain the equilibrium of a firm in the labour market under perfect competition.
8. Explain how to determine wage in an imperfectly competitive labour market.

9. How do you determine wages under collective bargaining? Discuss.
10. Explain how the rate of interest is determined.
11. "Interest balances the supply of capital savings and capital investment." Discuss.
12. What do you understand by loanable funds? Show that the rate of interest is determined by the supply of and demand for loanable funds.
13. Critically examine the loanable funds theory of interest.
14. Explain the innovation theory of profit.

Chapter 14

General Equilibrium Theory

Equilibrium: The word 'equilibrium' is derived from the Latin word 'aequilibrium' which means equal balance. In the words of **Prof. Mehto,** "Equilibrium denotes in economics absence of changes in movement." Again **Scitovsky** says, "A market, or an economy, or any other group of persons and firms is in equilibrium when none of its members feels impelled to change his behaviour."

It refers to a state of balance, i.e., a position from which there is no tendency to move showing a situation in which any force for change within a system affect each other to the point, that there is no internal tendency for the system to change. So, in ordinary sense, equilibrium means balancing of the opposing or the interacting forces.

Equilibrium positions may be stable or unstable. Equilibrium will be stable if it tends to restore itself in the face of disturbances. On the other hand, it is unstable if it does not tend to do so in the same circumstances.

Equilibrium in a market for commodities is attained when the supply coming into the market at any given price is equal to the demand at that price. Since the number of units bought at a price must necessarily be equal to the number sold at that price, supply and demand in this sense must be equal. But there is only one price at which there is equilibrium in the sense that at that price the amount that suppliers wish to supply is just equal to the amount that consumers wish to buy. To show it in a simple way, let us take a supply curve and a demand curve.

Supply: $X_s = a + bp$ [where b and d are slopes and a and c are the intercepts]

Demand: $X_d = c + dp$

At equilibrium, supply = demand

$$a + bp = c + dp$$

or, $$p_e = \frac{c - a}{b - d}$$ [where p_e is equilibrium price]

So, equilibrium quantity $X_e = a + bp_e$

$$= \frac{ad - bc}{d - b}$$

Graphical Representation

Demand curve DD and supply curve SS intersect at point E. E is the equilibrium point where equilibrium price is OP_e and equilibrium quantity demanded and supplied is OX_e.

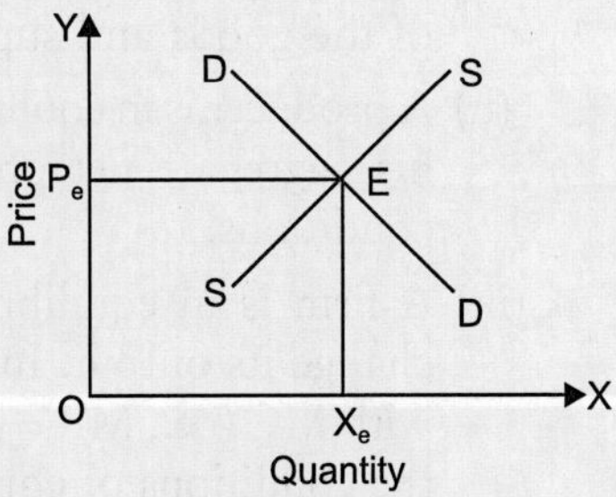

Fig. 14.1

Equilibrium may also refer to either partial (particular) or general equilibrium. Partial equilibrium assumes that all other prices and quantities in the economy are constant while the equilibrium conditions relating to one commodity or sector are examined. General equilibrium is concerned with the conditions under which there will be a simultaneous equilibrium of prices and outputs in all the different markets of the whole economic system.

PARTIAL EQUILIBRIUM

Partial equilibrium analysis is the study of the equilibrium position of an individual or a firm or an industry or a group of industries. It determines the prices in which one or two variables are discussed, keeping all other as constant. In the words of **Prof. Stigler,** "A partial equilibrium is one which is based on only a restricted range of data, a standard example is price of a single product, the prices of all other products being held fixed during the analysis." Partial analysis has at least three advantages: (i) We can broadly classify the causes of a change in the behaviour of any individual household or firm, or of a change in the price of any individual commodity in partial analysis. (ii) This analysis enables us to predict the more immediate consequences of any general revision in the plans of the consumers and the sellers. (iii) In partial analysis we concentrate on one or a small number of economic subjects and thus reduce the number of variables whose value must be examined.

Applications: Partial equilibrium has following applications:

(i) Consumer's equilibrium is achieved when he is getting maximum aggregate satisfaction from a given expenditure subject to a given set of conditions relating to his tastes and preferences, money income, the prices of the goods and supply of the commodity.

(ii) A producer is in equilibrium when he is able to maximize his aggregate net profit subject to a set of economic conditions.

(iii) A firm is in equilibrium when it has no tendency to change its output. In the short run it equalizes its MR with MC (i.e., MR = MC) and in the long run it satisfies the conditions of equilibrium, MC = MR = LAC at its minimum. Thus, it earns only normal profits and has no tendency to leave the industry.

(iv) Equilibrium of an industry shows that there is no incentive for firms to enter it or for the existing firms to leave it. This will happen when the marginal firm in the industry is making only normal profit.

(v) A factor of production is in equilibrium when it is paid in the highest so that its income is maximized. It is a position where its price equals its marginal revenue product. It has no willingness to be employed else where.

Thus, the partial equilibrium analysis renders the study of economic problems simply and understandably.

Significance: The partial equilibrium analysis is, in fact, the threshold to the general equilibrium analysis.

(i) It helps us in analyzing the causes of a change in the price of a product or in the behaviour of an individual, a firm or an industry.

(ii) It can predict the behaviours and the plans of the market participants and also the effects of changes of it.

(iii) It is an indispensable tool of analysis for the solution of practical problems.

(iv) It helps to understand the interdependence of economic variables and general equilibrium analysis also.

Limitations: Partial equilibrium analysis suffers from serious drawbacks. It takes the most unrealistic assumptions to study a market or an entity in isolation from the rest of the economy. In the real world, the totality of all the economic dispositions and plans in an exchange economy forms one great interdependent system. The result is that economic disturbance in one market generates a chain of causation travelling from one market to another and ultimately engulfs the entire economy. Hence, the genuine course of an economic process as a whole can be visualized by means of general analysis and not by partial one. Partial equilibrium may be regarded as a worm's eye-view, whereas the general equilibrium is a bird's eye-view.

GENERAL EQUILIBRIUM

We have seen that the partial equilibrium analysis enables us to study the relationship between only selected few variables, keeping others as unchanged. But general equilibrium analysis is an extensive study of a number of economic variables, their interrelations and interdependences as a whole in the economy. It brings together the cause and effect sequences of changes in the prices and quantities of commodities and services in relations to the entire economy. An economy can be in general equilibrium only if all consumers, all firms, all industries and all factor-services are in equilibrium simultaneously and they are interlinked. As **Stigler** has said, "The theory of general equilibrium is the theory of interrelationship among all parts of the economy."

General equilibrium analysis has two variants: (1) **Walrasian** Model developed by **Walras** and (2) the input-output analysis developed by **Prof. Leontief.**

THE WALRASIAN MODEL OF GENERAL EQUILIBRIUM

Leon Walras, a French economist was the first to develop a general equilibrium model in the economy as a whole. In his book, *Elements of Pure Economics* in 1874, **Walras** argued that all prices and quantities in all markets are determined simultaneously through their interactions with one another. He used a system of simultaneous equations to describe the interaction of all buyers and all sellers in all markets. His model is static in which all prices are in equilibrium. His model is based on the following assumptions:

(i) Each consumer spends his given income to maximize his satisfaction.

(ii) All firms in industry are in equilibrium at all prices and outputs.

(iii) Supply and demand for productive resources is equal at equilibrium prices.

(iv) Tastes and incomes are given and known.

(v) There is perfect competition both in commodity and factor markets.

(vi) Factors of production are perfectly mobile.

(vii) There are constant returns to scale.

(viii) All firms operate under identical cost conditions.

(ix) All units of a productive service are homogeneous.

(x) There is no change in the technique of production.

(xi) There is full employment of labour and other resources.

The Model: Under these assumptions the economy is in a state of general equilibrium where the demand for every commodity and every service is equal to their supply. The decisions of consumers for the purchase of each commodity must be perfect in accordance with the decisions of producers for the production and sale of each commodity.

Price: The quantity of each commodity demanded depends not only on its own price but also on the prices of other commodities available in the market. Thus, marginal utility depends not only upon the quantity and price of the respective commodity but also on the quantities and prices of other commodities.

Income: Each consumer is assumed to spend his entire income on consumption so that his expenditure is equal to his income. His income depends on the prices at which he is selling his productive services.

Market Demand: To obtain the market demand for each commodity we add together the demand of the entire consumer for that commodity in the economy.

Market Supply: Assuming constant returns to scale and identical cost conditions for all firms, each producer will produce and sell that quantity of output at which the demand price for the commodity is equal to both the minimum average cost and the marginal cost. Thus, the total supply of commodities in the market depends on the costs of the firms and the prices and quantities of the various services used by them.

The equality of demand and supply of productive services is essential for the **Walrasian** general equilibrium system. The demand for productive services comes from the producers and the supply of the productive services comes from the consumers. Since there is full employment in the economy, the markets for productive services must be in equilibrium. It implies the equalities of the total quantities of productive services offered with the total quantities employed. Thus, the economy is in a state of general equilibrium when commodity prices make each demand equal to its supply; service prices make the demand for each productive services equal to its supply so that all commodity markets and service markets are in equilibrium. It also implies that all consumers and all producers in the economy are in equilibrium.

But how are the equalities between the demand and the supply of commodities and services brought about?

Walras solved this problem with the theory of **'tatonnement'** or **'grouping'**. Suppose that all buyers and sellers announce the quantities they wish to buy and sell at stated prices. If there is negative excess demand, sellers offer low prices and when there is excess demand, buyers offer high prices. They continue to make such announcements till they hit upon a price that brings equilibrium in the general market. It is only when the contracted prices happen to be such where demands and supplies for services are equal, the equilibrium prices for the whole system will be reached. Thus, the **Walrasian** model shows the determinacy as well as the stability of the general market equilibrium.

Criticisms: This model is criticised on the grounds mentioned below:

(i) It is based on a number of unrealistic assumptions.

(ii) It is a static model. All consumers and producers in the model consume and produce the same products without any time lag, which is unrealistic in real world.

(iii) Producers and consumers never act and think alike.

(iv) It assumes the existence of a unique consistent real set of prices which will simultaneously equalize the demand and the supply of all goods and factors. The critics point out that the solution obtained by solving the simultaneous equations may give answers which lie in the domain of imaginary numbers.

Uses: The general equilibrium analysis has many theoretical and practical applications:

(i) It helps to get an overall picture of the economy and to study the problems arised in the economy as a whole.

(ii) It represents the maximization of satisfaction which implies the maximization of welfare.

(iii) It solves the fundamental problems of a free market economy, viz. what to produce, how to produce, how much to produce, etc.

(iv) It gives us the clue to predict the consequences of an economic event.

(v) The great importance of it is to provide the conceptual basis for the input-output analysis developed by **Prof. Leontief.**

(vi) It is more realistic in the fields of economic study regarding monetary and welfare economics.

Problems for General Equilibrium Solution

Three problems may arise to get general equilibrium solution. They are: the existence problem, the uniqueness problem and the stability problem.

The Existence Problem

The existence problem is concerned whether an equilibrium exists or not. Competitive market equilibrium will exist if there is one price at which the demand and the supply is equal. At such a price there is neither excess demand nor excess supply. In terms of conventional diagram, equilibrium will exist if the demand and the supply curves have at least one point in common in the non-negative quadrant.

Three situations in which the demand and the supply curves have no common point in the non-negative quadrant are pictured in the following Fig. 14.2:

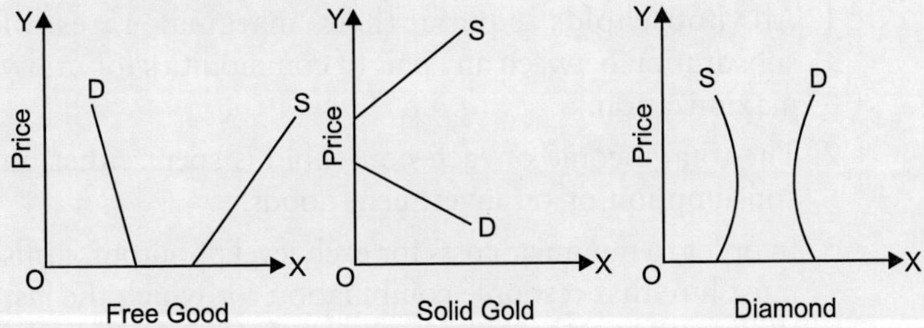

(a) (b) (c)

Fig. 14.2

In Fig. 14.2(a) the supply is always more than the demand. It may be the case of free good because the supply of free good always exceeds the demand at any price. In Fig. 14.2(b), the demand price is less than the supply price. This case may be seen in case of solid gold. Again in Fig. 14.2(c) the demand exceeds at any price than the supply. It is also observed in case of diamond. In the above three cases, there is no existence of equilibrium.

Walras considered the existence problem by the equality of the number of unknowns and the number of equations. But it is neither a sufficient nor a necessary condition for the existence of equilibrium. **Walras** was never able to solve this problem.

Arrow and **Debreau** solved the existence problem of a general equilibrium in a perfectly competitive market in which there are no externalities and no increasing returns to scale. If the number of unknowns is greater than the number of independent equations, the values of all the unknowns cannot be determined.

To solve this problem they took one commodity as numeraire and prices of other commodities are expressed in terms of this numeraire commodity. In this way the prices obtained from this system will be relative prices. Thus, the absolute prices are indeterminate in the Walrasian general equilibrium system.

But practically, the equality of the number of equations and the number of unknowns is neither necessary nor sufficient to give guarantee for the existence of solution. The equations must be independent and consistent for the existence of equilibrium. However, there are some necessary conditions for the existence of general equilibrium. These are given below:

1. All households equate their marginal rates of substitution between any pair of commodities for utility maximization.
2. The total income of each household is spent either on consumption or on investment goods.
3. In order to minimize costs for each level of output, firms must hire that resource combination for which the last shilling (British coin) spent on each factor yields the same marginal product.
4. For joint-product firms, the rate of technical transformation between the products must be exactly equal to the ratio of their prices.
5. In order to maximize profits or minimize losses each firm must produce that output for which its marginal revenue is equal to its marginal cost.
6. All income derived from sales revenue represents factor payments plus profits (or losses).
7. All factors are paid according to the value of their marginal products.
8. All markets must be in equilibrium such that there exists no excess demand for products or factors.

The Uniqueness Problem

The uniqueness problem arises when a unique solution is not achieved. Equilibrium is unique when the point of intersection of the opposing market forces is one and only one. Here market forces mean the demand and the supply in the market. If the demand and the supply are functions of price, we get D = D(P) and S = S(P). The slope of the demand function is $\frac{dD}{dP} = D_1(P)$ and that of the supply function is $\frac{dS}{dP} = S_1(P)$.

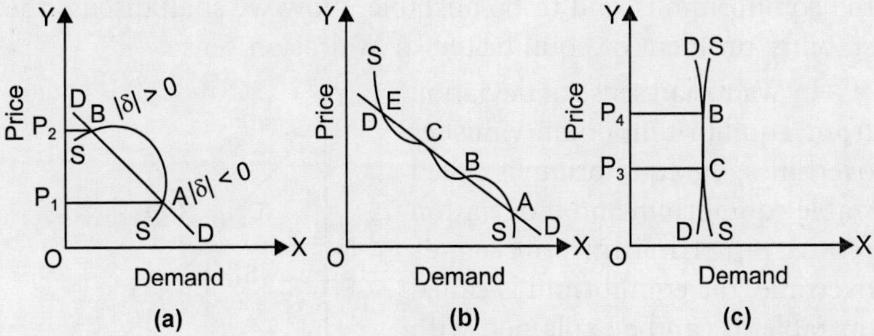

Fig. 14.3

Here δ be the difference between the slopes of the demand and the supply curves, $\delta = D_1(P) - S_1(P)$. If the demand curve is negatively sloped throughout and the supply curve is positively sloped throughout, δ will be less than zero, i.e., δ < 0 for all prices. Under these conditions there cannot be more than one equilibrium point. In the following figures different types of equilibrium and its uniqueness problems are discussed.

In Fig. 14.3(a), the demand curve cuts the supply curve at point A and at point B. At point A, we get δ < 0. So, the equilibrium point is A. Again as long as δ < 0 the demand curve will remain to the left of the supply curve. It is in between the point A and B, corresponding to the prices P_1 and P_2. At point B, there is second equilibrium point, where |δ| > 0. There cannot be more than one equilibrium point. Again in Fig. 14.3(b), the snake like supply curve cuts the downward sloping demand curves at different points and in Fig. 14.3(c) the demand and the supply curves between the points C and B corresponding to the prices P_3 and P_4 show a broad common area. Thus, problems arise due to lack of single equilibrium point. It is difficult to locate the exact unique equilibrium point in the above three cases.

The Stability Problem

Stability of market equilibrium means that for any reason if the equilibrium is disturbed, i.e., quantity demanded and price are deviated from their equilibrium values, this equilibrium again will restore over a period of time, i.e., deviation will vanish overtime. If this deviation will grow in magnitude overtime, then the equilibrium is said to be unstable. Now we shall discuss the stability problem of equilibrium in Walrasian sense.

In **Walrasian** sense, if deviation from equilibrium point vanishes overtimes, the equilibrium is called stable equilibrium and if deviation from equilibrium increases overtime, the equilibrium is called unstable. It can be explained with the help of following Fig. 14.4.

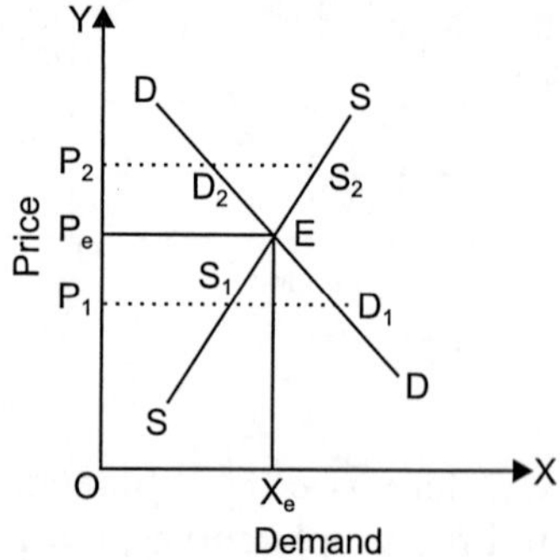

Fig. 14.4

In this figure OP_e and OX_e are the equilibrium price and quantity demanded respectively. If for any reason, price is deviated from OP_e to OP_1 at which the quantity supplied is less than the quantity demanded ($P_1S_1 < P_1D_1$). Overtime price deviation would be decreasing and OP_1 would tend to reach equilibrium price OP_e. Thus, equilibrium is restored. Hence the equilibrium is stable. Similarly, price may deviate upward direction. Suppose price rises from OP_e to OP_2 where the quantity supplied is higher than quantity demanded ($P_2S_2 > P_2D_2$), equilibrium would again be restored.

But this may not be so in the cases where the demand and the supply curves are of irregular shapes. These are explained in Figs. 14.5(a), (b) & (c):

In Fig. 14.5(a), the demand curve, DD is positively sloped while the supply curve, SS is negatively sloped. It shows that demand increases with rise in price and decreases with fall in price while supply increases with fall in price and decreases with rise in price. So it is unstable equilibrium.

In Fig. 14.5(b) and 14.5(c) the demand curves are of usual shape but the supply curves are not of usual shape.

In Fig. 14.5(b): | the slope of the supply curve | > | the slope of the demand curve |.

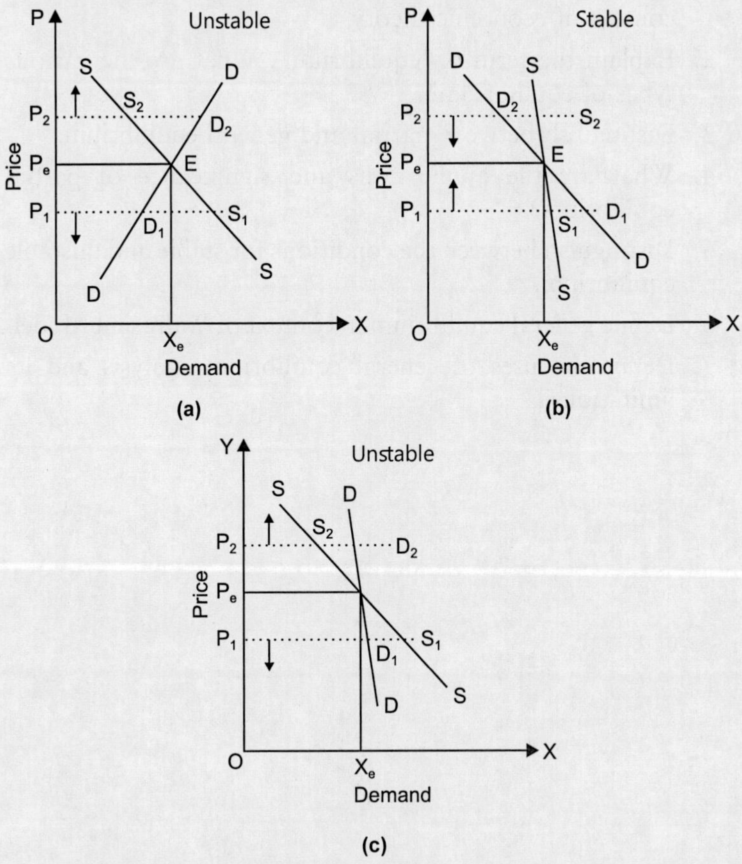

Fig. 14.5

In Fig. 14.5(c): | the slope of the supply curve | < | the slope of the demand curve |.

In the **Walrasian sense,** if | the slope of the supply curve | > | the slope of the demand curve |, the equilibrium would be stable. Otherwise the equilibrium would be unstable.

When both the demand and the supply curves are positively sloped, but the slope of the supply curve is greater than that of the demand curve, then the equilibrium would be unstable in the **Walrasian sense** and *vice versa*.

EXERCISES

1. Discuss the significance and the concept of equilibrium in context of economic theory.
2. Explain the term of 'equilibrium'. What are the various types of equilibrium?
3. Distinguish between partial and general equilibrium.
4. What are the applications and significance of partial equilibrium?
5. Distinguish between the conditions for stable and unstable equilibrium.
6. Define general equilibrium in context of Walrasian Model.
7. Define the uses of general equilibrium analysis and its limitations.

Chapter 15

Linear Programming and Input-Output Analysis

LINEAR PROGRAMMING

Introduction

Resources are limited and used in different alternative uses. The central problem of economics is how to achieve maximum possible satisfaction through proper allocation of limited resources. In view of these points the technique of linear programming was developed by an American mathematician **George Dantzig** in 1947 for planning the diversified activities of the U.S. Air Force related with the problem of supplies to the forces. A Russian mathematician **L.V. Kantorovich** was first to formulate independently the technique of linear programming. It was further developed in its application to the economic theory of the firm, managerial economics, welfare economics and finally to the development planning.

Meaning

The term 'Linear Programming' implies only the linear relationship between two or more variables. Again the linear relationship shows the relation between the variables which can be represented by a straight line. It is a mathematical technique for solving maximization and minimization problems subject to certain constraints in the form of linear inequalities. It is also used to finalize a technique out of several alternatives so as to produce maximum output at the minimum cost. That is, it deals with the optimum allocation of limited resources to achieve the desired objectives.

Therefore, linear programming is a mathematical tool for the analysis of optimum decision subject to some constraints in the form of linear inequalities.

CONDITIONS FOR THE APPLICATION OF LINEAR PROGRAMMING TECHNIQUE

The linear programming (LP) technique is applied under certain conditions. These are discussed below:

1. Objective functions: The application of LP technique must have a definite objective. It may be the maximization of profits, income, output, sales, etc. or the minimization of costs. Suppose $z = 6x + 7y$ where x and y are the inputs and z is total output which is to be maximized.

2. The concept of process: There are alternative production processes to achieve the objective. The LP technique helps the planning authorities to select the most efficient process to achieve the objective of planning.

3. Constraints: There are certain limitations or restrictions within which a firm or a planning authority has to operate in achieving the objective. For example, there may be quantity limitations on particular inputs used by a firm which aims to maximize its output. Or, the income of a consumer is constraint for the maximization of his satisfaction. Constraints are generally expressed in the form of inequalities. For example, 100 million or less rupees are available for the project (i.e., ≤ 100 million) and 50 million or more rupees are needed to purchase a plant for the project (i.e., ≥ 50 million).

Another constraints are also known as non-negativity constraints. Suppose, the inputs, x and y, used by a firm can be either zero or positive but never be negative, i.e., $x \geq 0$, $y \geq 0$.

4. Choice of variables: There are certain choices of variables among which the particular choice of variables is to be selected so as to maximize or minimize the objective function satisfying all the constraints.

5. Feasible and optimal solution: There may be a number of feasible solutions. Every feasible solution satisfies all the constraints. Among all feasible solutions the optimal solution is the best one which can maximize or minimize the objective function. Suppose, all possible combinations of the goods are purchased feasibly by a consumer with his given income and the prices of goods. Feasible solutions are those possible combinations which satisfy all the constraints.

But the best one of the feasible solutions is the optimal solution which maximizes or minimizes the objective function.

Assumptions

The linear programming technique is based on the following assumptions:

1. The authority for using this technique faces certain constraints. The constraints may be raw material, space, nature, capital, labour, etc.
2. It assumes a limited number of alternative processes of production.
3. It assumes linear relations with different variables. This relation shows a constant proportionate relation between inputs and outputs within the process.
4. Coefficients and input-output prices are given and constant. It implies that there is perfectly competitive market in the factor market as well as in the product market.
5. It underlies the assumption of additivity. It implies that the total resources used by all firms must be equal to the sum of resources used by each individual firm.
6. It assumes that there is continuity and divisibility in products and factors.
7. The institutional factors are constraint.
8. It needs a certain period for programming.

Problem and Solution—Maximization of Revenue

Example 1: A firm produces two products X and Y. Each of these products is processed through two different machines. One machine can run 12 hours and another machine can run 8 hours at a stretch. Each unit of product X requires 2 hours of time on both the machines. Each unit of product Y requires

3 hours of time on the first machine and 1 hour on the second machine. Profit per unit of product X is ₹ 6 and profit per unit product Y is ₹ 7. The firm can sell as many units of each product as it can produce. The objective of the firm is to maximize profits. The problem is to determine how many units of X and Y should be produced by the firm within the limits available of machine capacities.

Solution

Formulation: The input-output data for this problem is presented in the following Table:

Input-Output Data

	Hours needed by the products to be processed		Total hours available of the machines
Machine	X	Y	Units
1st	2	3	12
2nd	2	1	8
Profit per unit of product	₹ 6	₹ 7	

Let x and y represent the units of product X and product Y and let z represents total profits.

Objective Function: The objective function of the firm is:

Maximize $z = 6x + 7y$

Constraints: Now each unit of product X needs 2 hours on the both machines and each unit of product Y needs 3 hours on the first machine and 1 hour of the second machine. Hence, total hours of the first machine to be needed is $2x + 3y$. So, we must have $2x + 3y \leq 12$.

Similarly, total hours of the second machine to be needed is $2x + y$. So, we can write $2x + y \leq 8$.

Non-negativity constraint: The units of X and Y cannot be negative. So obviously, we have, $x \geq 0$ and $y \geq 0$.

Therefore, the formulation of the linear programming problem in mathematical form is to:

Maximize $z = 6x + 7y$

Subject to: (i) $2x + 3y \leq 12$ ... (1)

$2x + y \leq 8$ ... (2)

(ii) $x \geq 0, y \geq 0$.

Solution

The linear programming problem can be solved in two different methods—graphical method and simplex method. The graphical solution is simple with two variables when the problem can be presented on two dimensional diagrams. When there are more than two variables the graphical method becomes extremely complicated. If there are three variables we get a three-dimensional figure. Since, it is difficult to deal with a three dimensional figure, we shall confine our analysis to two variables.

Simplex method is the best procedure for the optimal solution of the linear programming problem in a numerical way with two or more than two variables.

Graphical Solution: Now we discuss graphical method. The graphical solution involves two steps:

(i) The graphical determination of the region of feasible solution and

(ii) The graphical presentation of the objective function.

A solution is called feasible when it satisfies all the constraints. The non-negativity constraints in our example are shown graphically by the area of the positive quadrant of the usual orthogonal coordinate system. Points on the horizontal axis denote that the production of y is zero while the production of x is positive. That is, on the X-axis , $x \geq 0$ and $y = 0$. Similarly, points on the Y-axis denote that there is no production of x while the production of y is positive. That is, on the Y-axis, $x = 0$ and $y \geq 0$. Clearly points lying inside the two axes imply some production of both commodities ($x > 0$ and $y > 0$).

Graphical Solution of the Maximization Problem

Maximize $z = 6x + 7y$

Subject to (i) $2x + 3y \leq 12$

$2x + y \leq 8$

(ii) $x \geq 0, y \geq 0$.

Let us now consider the first constraint $2x + 3y \leq 12$. If the equality sign holds then we have $2x + 3y = 12$. It represents the equation of a straight line. If we put $x = 0$, then $y = 4$, i.e., the point = (0, 4). Again if we put y = 0, then x = 6, i.e., the point = (6, 0). Now we put this two points, (0, 4) and (6, 0) on graph paper and join them by a line AB. So, this equation is represented by the straight line AB shown in Fig. 15.1. Any point on AB or to the left of AB represents this constraint. So, the area AOB fulfils the first constraint.

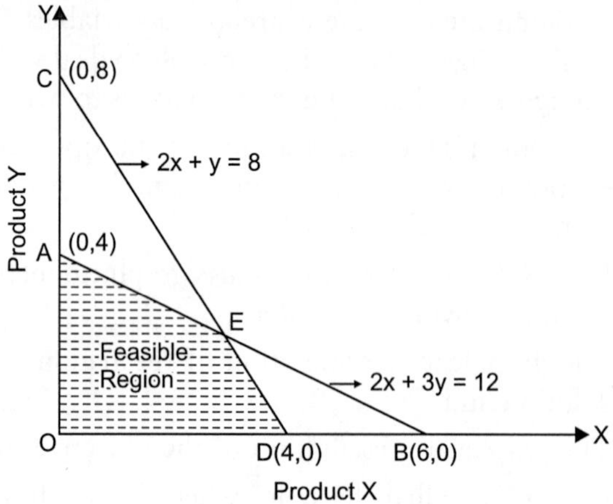

Fig. 15.1

Similarly, in case of second constraint, we can consider 2x + y = 8. If we put x = 0, then y = 8, the point = (0, 8) and if we put y = 0, then x = 4, the point = (4, 0). In Fig. 15.1, this equation is represented by the line CD. Now this inequality is satisfied at any point on CD or to the left of CD. So, the COD area fulfils the second constraint. The two straight lines intersect at point E. Hence, OAED is the common area satisfying both the constraints. The common area OAED is shaded in this figure. It is called feasible region. Any point within this area satisfies all constraints. Within the feasible region there are a large number of combinations of x and y. We get a corresponding value for each combination. Now we have to find out that particular combination of x and y for which the value of z is maximum. But we need not consider all points in the feasible region. We should consider only the corner points of the feasible region because the value of the objective function is maximum at any one of the corner points. We have coordinates of points A, O and D but not have of E.

Now we have to find out the coordinates of the point E by solving the two equations:

$$2x + 3y = 12$$

and $2x + y = 8.$

Suppose,

$$2x + 3y = 12 \quad \text{... (1)}$$

and $2x + y = 8$ ... (2)

(1) – (2) gives $y = 2$

Putting the value of $y = 2$ in equation (1), we get $x = 3$. Hence, the coordinates of E are (3, 2).

Let us now find out the values of the objective function, $z = 6x + 7y$ at corner points, A (0, 4), D (4, 0) and E (3, 2).

At point A (0, 4): $z = 6 \times 0 + 7 \times 4 =$ ₹ 28

At point D (4, 0): $z = 6 \times 4 + 7 \times 0 =$ ₹ 24

At point E (3, 2): $z = 6 \times 3 + 7 \times 2 =$ ₹ 32

It is clear from the above calculations that the value of z is maximum at point E. Hence, the required solution is $x = 3$ and $y = 2$ and the corresponding maximum value of $z =$ ₹ 32. So the producer will produce at point E where his revenue is maximized subject to the given constraints. Hence, E is the optimal point where he produces 3 units of product X and 2 units of product Y.

Example 2: A firm can produce two goods X, Y and sells at given prices of ₹ 12 and ₹ 15 respectively for each unit. For the production of X, the firm needs 12 units of input A, 6 units of input B and 14 units of input C and for Y it requires 4 units of input A, 12 units of input B and 12 units of input C. Total available inputs are 48 units of A, 72 units of B and 84 units of C. Calculate the maximum revenue earned by the firm and also show the maximum amount of two goods X and Y to be produced.

Solution

The input-output data is shown in the following Table:

Input-Output Data

	Amount of inputs required to produce one unit of output		Total inputs available in each case
Input	X	Y	Units
A	12	4	48
B	6	12	72
C	14	12	84
Price per unit of good	₹ 12	₹ 15	

Let x and y represent the units of goods X and Y and Z represents total profits.

Objective Function: The objective function of the firm is:

Maximize $z = 12x + 15y$

Constraints: Each unit of X needs 12 units of A and each unit of Y needs 4 units of A. The maximum availability of input A is 48 units that cannot be greater than 48 units. That is, $12x + 4y \leq 48$.

Similarly in case of B and C inputs, we get

$6x + 12y \leq 72$

and $14x + 12y \leq 84$

Therefore, the constraints are:

$$12x + 4y \leq 48 \quad \text{... (1)}$$

$$6x + 12y \leq 72 \quad \text{... (2)}$$

$$14x + 12y \leq 84 \quad \text{... (3)}$$

Non-negativity constraints: The goods X and Y can be zero or positive, but it cannot be negative, i.e., $x \geq 0$ and $y \geq 0$.

Therefore, the formulation of the linear programming problem in mathematical form is:

Maximize: $z = 12x + 15y$

Subject to (i) $12x + 4y \leq 48$ ... (1)

$6x + 12y \leq 72$ ... (2)

$14x + 12y \leq 84$ ... (3)

(ii) $x \geq 0$ and $y \geq 0$

Graphical Solution

To show each inequality graphically, we replace the inequality sign (≤) by the equality sign (=). We can write (1) as

$$12x + 4y = 48$$

If we put x = 0, then y = 12, i.e, the point = (0, 12)

Again, if we put y = 0, then x = 4, i.e., the point = (4, 0)

Now, if we put these two points (0, 12) and (4, 0) in a graph paper and join them by a straight line AB, then the equation 12x + 4y = 48 is represented by this line AB. Any point on AB or to the left of AB satisfies the inequality 12x + 4y ≤ 48. It is shown in Fig. 15.2:

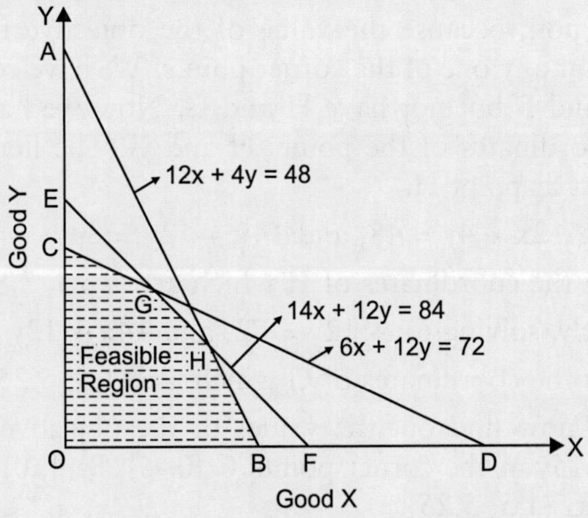

Fig. 15.2

Similarly, we can write (2) as 6x + 12y = 72.

Putting x = 0, we have y = 6; the point = (0, 6). Again putting y = 0, we have x = 12; the point (12, 0). Substituting the two points (0, 6) and (12, 0) in a graph paper and joining them by a straight line CD we get the straight line representing 6x + 12y = 72 as shown in Fig. 15.2. Any point on CD or to the left of CD satisfies the inequality 6x + 12y ≤ 72. It is shown in Fig. 15.2.

Similarly, considering (3) as 14x + 12y = 84 when x = 0, y = 7; the point = (0, 7), when y = 0, x = 6; the point = (6, 0).

Putting these two points (0, 7) and (6, 0) and joining them by a line EF, we get a straight line representing 14x + 12y =

84. Any point on EF or to the left of EF satisfies the inequality $14x + 12y \leq 84$. It is shown in Fig. 15.2.

Feasible Region: The lines EF and AB intersect at point H and the lines EF and CD intersect at point G. So, the shaded region COBHG is feasible region of production because any point within the region or on the boundary of the region satisfies the three inequalities (constraints).

Optimum Solution: To get optimum solution we have to locate the optimum point within the feasible region which maximizes the revenue of the firm. There are a large number of points within the feasible region. We need not consider all the points. We should consider only the corner points of the feasible region, because the value of the objective function is maximum at any one of the corner points. We have coordinates of C, O, and B but not have H and G. Now we have to find out the coordinates of the points H and G. The lines AB and EF intersect at point H.

Solving $12x + 4y = 48$, and $14x + 12y = 84$

We get the coordinates of H which are (2.73, 3.81).

Similarly, solving $6x + 12y = 72$, and $14x + 12y = 84$

We get the coordinates of G which are (1.5, 5.25).

Let us now find out the values of the objective function, $z = 12x + 15y$ at the corner points C (0, 6), B (4, 0), H (2.73, 3.81) and G (1.5, 5.25).

At point C (0, 6): $z = 12 \times 0 + 15 \times 6 =$ ₹ 90

At point B (4, 0): $z = 12 \times 4 + 15 \times 0 =$ ₹ 48

At point H (2.73, 3.81): $z = 12 \times 2.73 + 15 \times 3.81$

$=$ ₹ 89.91

At point G (1.5, 5.25): $z = 12 \times 1.5 + 15 \times 5.25 =$ ₹ 96.75

From the above calculations, it is clear that the value of z is maximum at point G. At point G, the firm earns maximum revenue of ₹ 96.75 subject to the given constraints. Hence, G is the optimal point where he produces 1.5 units of good X and 5.25 units of good Y.

Problem and Solution — Minimization of Cost

Example 1: A group of patients require a diet that contains at least 2000 calories and at least 600 units of Vitamin D per person per day. The dietician recommends that the requirement of calories and Vitamin D may be fulfilled from two foods X_1 and X_2. Each unit of X_1 supplies 40 calories and 8 units of Vitamin D and each unit of X_2 supplies 20 calories and 12 units of Vitamin D. The cost of 1 unit of X_1 ₹ 4 and the cost of 1 unit of X_2 is ₹ 5. Find the mix of X_1 and X_2 that minimizes the cost while meeting the dietary requirements.

Solution

Formulation: The data is summarized in the following Table:

Data for the Diet

Content of calory and Vitamin D			
Content	Food X_1	Food X_2	Total Requirement
Calory	40	20	2000
Vitamin D	8	12	600
Cost per unit of food	₹ 4	₹ 5	₹ ?

Let x_1 and x_2 represent the units of diet X_1 and X_2 and z represent the total cost.

Objective Function: The objective function of the patient is to:

Minimize $z = 4x_1 + 5x_2$

Constraints: Each unit of X_1 and X_2 supplies 40 calories and 20 calories respectively. Total requirement of calories per patient is at least 2000 calories. It means that a minimum daily requirement of calories must be either greater than or equal to 2000 calories.

Mathematically, it can be written as

$$40x_1 + 20x_2 \geq 2000 \quad \text{... (1)}$$

Similarly, a minimum daily requirement of Vitamin D can be expressed by the inequality

$$8x_1 + 12x_2 \geq 600 \quad \text{... (2)}$$

Non-negativity Constraint: The quantity consumed of X_1 and X_2 may be zero, but never be negative, i.e., $x_1 \geq 0$ and $x_2 \geq 0$.

Therefore, the linear programming problem can be formulated in the following way:

Minimize $z = 4x_1 + 5x_2$

Subject to (i) $40x_1 + 20x_2 \geq 2000$ ... (1)

$8x_1 + 12x_2 \geq 600$ ... (2)

(ii) $x_1 \geq 0, x_2 \geq 0$

Graphical Solution

To express each inequality in a graph paper we convert the inequality sign (≥) into equality sign (=). That is, (1) can be written as

$$40x_1 + 20x_2 = 2000$$

If we put $x_1 = 0$, then $x_2 = 100$, therefore, the point will be (0, 100).

Again if we take $x_2 = 0$, then $x_1 = 50$, therefore, the point will be (50, 0).

Putting these two points in a graph paper and joining them by a line AB, we get a straight line representing $40x_1 + 20x_2 = 2000$. Any point lying on this straight line shows the combination of two foods yielding exactly 2000 calories. Again any point to the right of AB shows the combination yielding more than 2000 calories. Thus, $40x_1 + 20x_2 \geq 2000$ is satisfied. It is shown in Fig. 15.3.

Similarly, (2) can be written as

$$8x_1 + 12x_2 = 600.$$

If we put $x_1 = 0$, then $x_2 = 50$, therefore, the point will be (0, 50).

Again, if we put $x_2 = 0$, then $x_1 = 75$, therefore, the point will be (75, 0).

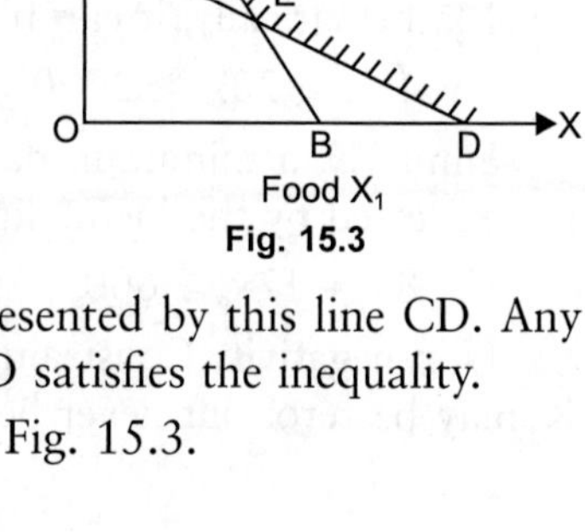

Fig. 15.3

Now, if we substitute these two points (0, 50) and (75, 0) in the graph paper and join them by a straight line CD, then the equation $8x_1 + 12x_2 = 600$ is represented by this line CD. Any point on CD or to the right of CD satisfies the inequality.

$8x_1 + 12x_2 = 600$ as shown in Fig. 15.3.

But the common area which is to the right of both AB and CD satisfies both the constraints simultaneously.

Feasible Region

The lines AB and CD intersect at point E. So the shaded region AED is feasible region of prescribed diet. Any point in the region or on the boundary of the region satisfies the two inequalities (constraints).

Optimal Solution

The objective function will be minimized at one of the three corner points A, E and D. The coordinates A and D are known but the coordinates of E are not known. It will be known by solving the two equations $40x_1 + 20x_2 = 2000$, and $8x_1 + 12x_2 = 600$.

Solving the equations, we get the coordinates of E which are (37.5, 25).

Let us now find out the values of the objective function, $z = 4x_1 + 5x_2$ at the corner points A (0, 100), E (37.5, 25) and D (75, 0).

At point A (0, 100): $z = 4 \times 0 + 5 \times 100 =$ ₹ 500

At point E (37.5, 25): $z = 4 \times 37.5 + 5 \times 25 =$ ₹ 275

At point D (75, 0): $z = 4 \times 75 + 5 \times 0 =$ ₹ 300

From the above calculations, we find that the value of the objective function is minimum at point E where the patient has purchased 37.5 units of food x_1 and 25 units of food x_2 at the total cost of ₹ 275.

Hence, the required solution is $x_1 = 37.5$ units and $x_2 = 25$ units and the corresponding value of $z =$ ₹ 275.

Uses of Linear Programming

The main uses of the linear programming are discussed below:

1. Selection of definite technique: Linear programming technique selects a definite technique among all possible techniques to maximize production or minimize costs.

2. Formulation of five-year plan: The country's Five-Year Plans are being formulated on the basis of linear programming technique and other econometric models in the areas of foodgrain storage, transportation, multi-level planning.

3. **Indian railways:** This technique is being applied in various areas by Indian Railways.

4. **Commercial institution:** The commercial institutions and also the individual traders are applying linear programming technique for cost minimization and profit maximization.

5. **Agricultural sector:** It is used in agricultural sector on a limited scale for determining the optimum alternatives of crops.

6. **National airlines:** It is being applied by the national airlines in the selection of routes. The officials have found it most suitable and appropriate tool.

7. **Hindustan Lever Limited:** Linear programming technique is used by the organization like the Hindustan Lever Limited for the distribution of consumers' goods throughout the country.

8. **Steel plants:** The Steel plants are applying linear programming techniques for finding the combination of the final product like billets, rounds, bars, plates and sheets.

9. **Paint industry:** The paint industry uses linear programming technique to select the product mix. Telco uses it to decide what casting and forgings to be made in their own shops.

10. **Solution of different problems:** Linear programming technique in underdeveloped countries helps to solve the different problems regarding purchasing, production and marketing in order to minimize costs and maximize profits with given the various constraints in each case.

11. **Solution of diet problem:** Linear programming technique is being applied for the minimization of costs of diet when the values of minimum nutrients of the diet and the prices of foods are given.

12. **Assignment of jobs:** This technique helps to assign jobs to the work force for maximum effectiveness and optimum results with given wages and other costs.

13. **Planning:** The application of this technique is very much useful for development planning. The developing countries have to depend largely upon trained personnel to apply this technique

successfully for development planning in every sector of the economy.

Thus linear programming technique helps us to solve many economic problems in our practical life. It helps us to select one project from a number of different projects.

Limitations of Linear Programming

Linear programming technique has proved to be very efficient tool for the analysis of development in different sectors. But it suffers from the following limitations:

1. Objectives: It is not so easy to define a specific objective function. It is difficult to identify the various social, institutional and financial factors which may affect the given objectives.

2. Constraint: Constraints may not be directly expressed as linear inequalities.

3. Linearity: Linear programming technique is based on the assumption of linear relations between input and output, output and output or input and input. But in practice, most of such relations are non-linear. So, this technique can be used for a limited number of cases.

4. Relevant value of constraint coefficient: One problem is how to estimate the relevant value of the various constant coefficients in the linear programming approach such as population, prices, etc.

5. Perfect competition: This technique assumes that there is perfect competition in both markets—the product market and the factor market. But in the real world, the situation of perfect competition cannot be seen.

6. Constant returns: This technique assumes that there are constant returns in the economy. But it is somehow unrealistic. So these models are based on trial-and-error solutions. In this way it is difficult to find out real optimal solutions to the various economic problems.

7. Prediction: Linear programming cannot predict but other technique like marginal analysis of conventional theory can somehow predict regarding production function.

8. **Assumption of product prices:** Linear programming assumes that product prices in perfectly competitive market can reflect the marginal valuation of the society. But it is a questionable assumption. Very often product markets are imperfect markets where prices are higher than their marginal cost.

INPUT-OUTPUT ANALYSIS

Introduction

The concept of input-output analysis was first introduced by the famous French economist **Quesnay** in the 18th Century in the name of Tableau Economique. Later an American economist of Harvard University, **Professor Wassily W. Leontief** developed this technique to give a practical shape to the theoretical framework of general equilibrium analysis of **Walras** in his famous work *Structure of the American Economy* in 1951. For his contribution in the field of economics he was honoured with the 1973 Nobel Prize.

Meaning: Input-output analysis is a method of analyzing how an industry undertakes its production by using the output of other industry. In the modern economic system all industries have interrelationship and interdependencies to a large extent. Output of one industry is an input of other industries and *vice versa*. Such inter-relationships lead to equilibrium between supply and demand in the entire economy. Since input-output analysis explains the interdependence and interrelationship among the various industries, it is also known as inter-industry analysis. The input-output analysis helps us to analyze the economic equilibrium between the supply of intermediate goods and the demand of final products, i.e., the money value of total output of the whole economy must be equal to the sum of the money values of inter-industry inputs and the sum of the money values of inter-industry outputs. Thus, the input-output analysis explains the interdependence of inputs and outputs of various industries in the economy.

Main features: There are three main features of input-output analysis which are discussed below:

1. This analysis deals almost with production. Given the available resources and the techniques of production,

it is concerned with the use of various inputs in the industries and output derived from them.

2. This analysis is based upon empirical facts. The estimation of the quantities of various inputs and outputs of various industries have to be obtained from empirical investigations.
3. The input-output analysis tries to give a practical shape of general equilibrium analysis of **Walras**.

Thus, it is based on the concept of general equilibrium. It takes account of the interdependence of the various industries in the economy. The interdependence among the industries arises due to the fact that each industry employs the outputs of other industries as its raw materials. For example, steel is used as an input for coal industry and coal is an input for steel industry, though both are outputs of the respective industries.

Assumptions: The input-output analysis is an attempt to show the mutual dependence of planned production of various industries in the economy. It is based on the following assumptions:

1. The whole economy is divided into two sectors—"inter-industry sector" and "final demand sector".
2. Constant returns to scale are assumed.
3. Each industry produces only one homogeneous product and there is no scope for joint products.
4. The total output of any inter-industry sector is used as an input by other inter-industry sectors, by itself and by final demand sectors.
5. There are no external economies and diseconomies of production.
6. There are fixed input coefficients of production. That is, different factors of production can be used in fixed proportion. In case of two factors, this tells that the isoquant is L-shaped.
7. It is assumed that prices, consumer demands and factor supplies are given.
8. There are n-industries producing n-commodities.
9. Production technology is static.
10. Production relations are linear.

Construction of input-output table: An input-output table consists of several rows and columns. Every row shows the output distribution of a particular sector among the different sectors and every column implies the inputs of this particular sector receiving from itself and other sectors in the economy.

Let us take an example of an economy where there are only 4 producing sectors. The product of each sector is used as an input by all sectors and is also used for final consumption.

Let, (i) X_1, X_2, X_3 and X_4 are total outputs of the 4 sectors;

(ii) C_1, C_2, C_3 and C_4 are the amounts of final consumption; and

(iii) X_{11}, X_{12}, X_{13} and X_{14} are the amounts of product of 1st sector used as an input by the 1st, 2nd, 3rd and 4th sectors respectively.

Similarly, X_{21}, X_{22}, X_{23} and X_{24} are the amounts of product of 2nd sector used as an input by the 1st, 2nd 3rd and 4th sectors respectively.

Similarly, we get same thing in case of 3rd and 4th sectors.

Input-Output Transaction Table

	Selling Sector	Purchasing Sector				
	Total output of the sectors	Input requirements of producing sectors				Final demand for consumptions
		X_1	X_2	X_3	X_4	C
	1	2	3	4	5	6
	X_1	X_{11}	X_{12}	X_{13}	X_{14}	C_1
	X_2	X_{21}	X_{22}	X_{23}	X_{24}	C_2
	X_3	X_{31}	X_{32}	X_{33}	X_{34}	C_3
	X_4	X_{41}	X_{42}	X_{43}	X_{44}	C_4
Primary input (Labour)	Total primary input = L →	L_1	L_2	L_3	L_4	0

From the above table we can derive two types of equations. In this table we have zero figure in the 6th column and 5th row which tells that labour is simply a spending (consuming) sector which does not sell anything to itself.

(i) Columns 2, 3, 4 and 5 of the above table represents total inputs utilized by the 1st, 2nd, 3rd and 4th sectors respectively taking from all sectors including itself in the form of production function, which we can write for each sector by taking column-wise:

$$X_1 = F_1(X_{11}, X_{21}, X_{31}, X_{41}, L_1)$$
$$X_2 = F_2(X_{12}, X_{22}, X_{32}, X_{42}, L_2)$$
$$X_3 = F_3(X_{13}, X_{23}, X_{33}, X_{43}, L_3)$$
$$X_4 = F_4(X_{14}, X_{24}, X_{34}, X_{44}, L_4)$$

If we consider **n** number of producing sectors, the production function upto **n** number can be written as:

....

....

$$X_n = f_n(X_{1n}, X_{2n}, \ldots\ldots\ldots, X_{nn}, L_n)$$

(ii) Again, row-wise, we get that total output of each sector is used partly by itself and partly by other 3 sectors and the rest is finally consumed. Thus, each row of the table gives us the equality between the supply and the demand of each product of each sector.

Thus, we have

$$X_1 = X_{11} + X_{12} + X_{13} + X_{14} + C_1$$
$$X_2 = X_{21} + X_{22} + X_{23} + X_{24} + C_2$$
$$X_3 = X_{31} + X_{32} + X_{33} + X_{34} + C_3$$
$$X_4 = X_{41} + X_{42} + X_{43} + X_{44} + C_4$$

In general terms, if there are n producing sectors, we have

$$X_1 = X_{11} + X_{12} + X_{13} + X_{14} + \ldots + X_{1n} + C_1$$
$$X_2 = X_{21} + X_{22} + X_{23} + X_{24} + \ldots + X_{2n} + C_2$$
$$X_3 = X_{31} + X_{32} + X_{33} + X_{34} + \ldots + X_{3n} + C_3$$
$$X_4 = X_{41} + X_{42} + X_{43} + X_{44} + \ldots + X_{4n} + C_4$$

....

....

$$X_n = X_{n1} + X_{n2} + \ldots\ldots\ldots + X_{nn} + C_n$$

Leontief calls these equations as balance equations. It implies how the output of each sector is used in various sectors as input and also used to meet final demand for consumption.

We can convert the above input-output transaction table in terms of input coefficients. An input coefficient means the amount of an input required to produce one unit of the output of a sector, i.e., $a_{i j} = \frac{{}_{ij}}{}$ $(a_{ij} \geq 0)$ or $x_{ij} = a_{ij}xj$, where x_j = total output of jth sector, x_{ij} = output of i th sector used as input in jth sector and a_{ij} = input used of i th commodity to produce one unit of jth commodity.

We can show the input-output transaction table in terms of input coefficients neglecting primary input (labour).

Input-Output Coefficients Table

Selling Sector	Purchasing Sectors				
Total output of the sector	Input requirements of producing sectors				Requirements for final consumption
	X_1	X_2	X_3	X_4	C
X_1	$a_{11}x_1$	$a_{12}x_2$	$a_{13}x_3$	$a_{14}x_4$	C_1
X_2	$a_{21}x_1$	$a_{22}x_2$	$a_{23}x_3$	$a_{24}x_4$	C_2
X_3	$a_{31}x_1$	$a_{32}x_2$	$a_{33}x_3$	$a_{34}x_4$	C_3
X_4	$a_{41}x_1$	$a_{42}x_2$	$a_{43}x_3$	$a_{44}x_4$	C_4

The above table gives us the total output of each sector along the row in terms of input coefficients and final consumption. We have

$$X_1 = a_{11}x_1 + a_{12}x_2 + a_{13}x_3 + a_{14}x_4 + C_1$$
$$X_2 = a_{21}x_1 + a_{22}x_2 + a_{23}x_3 + a_{24}x_4 + C_2$$
$$X_3 = a_{31}x_1 + a_{32}x_2 + a_{33}x_3 + a_{34}x_4 + C_3$$
$$X_4 = a_{41}x_1 + a_{42}x_2 + a_{43}x_3 + a_{44}x_4 + C_4$$

If there are n number of producing sectors, we have

$$X_1 = a_{11}x_1 + a_{12}x_2 + \dots\dots + a_{1n}x_n + C_1$$
$$X_2 = a_{21}x_1 + a_{22}x_2 + \dots\dots + a_{2n}x_n + C_2$$
$$\dots\dots\dots\dots\dots\dots\dots\dots$$
$$\dots\dots\dots\dots\dots\dots\dots\dots$$
$$X_n = a_{n1}x_n + a_{n2}x_2 + \dots\dots\dots + a_{nn}x_n + C_n$$

The equation may be represented in matrix form.

$$\begin{bmatrix} x_1 \\ x_2 \\ \cdots \\ \cdots \\ x_n \end{bmatrix} = \begin{bmatrix} a_{11} & a_{12} \ldots\ldots\ldots\ldots a_{1n} \\ a_{21} & a_{22} \ldots\ldots\ldots\ldots a_{2n} \\ \ldots\ldots & \ldots\ldots\ldots\ldots\ldots\ldots\ldots \\ \ldots\ldots & \ldots\ldots\ldots\ldots\ldots\ldots\ldots \\ a_{n1} & a_{n2} \ldots\ldots\ldots\ldots a_{nn} \end{bmatrix} \begin{bmatrix} x_1 \\ x_2 \\ \cdots \\ \cdots \\ x_n \end{bmatrix} + \begin{bmatrix} C_1 \\ C_2 \\ \cdots \\ \cdots \\ C_n \end{bmatrix}$$

Or, $X = AX + C$

Or, $X - AX = C$

Or, $[I - A]\, X = C$

Or, $X = [I - A]^{-1} C$, where A is the coefficient matrix of input coefficients, while X and C are the column vectors of output and final demand of each producing sector. If $|I - A| \neq 0$ we can solve and determine the value of output of each sector with given value of input coefficients and final demand for consumption. Or we can determine the final demand for consumptions if outputs are given.

A TWO-SECTOR INPUT-OUTPUT MODEL
(Numerical example)

Input-Output Table

(in crores)

Selling Sectors	Purchasing Sectors			
	Agriculture	Manufacturing	Final demand for consumption	Total demand
Agriculture	75	125	100	300
Manufacturing	100	150	250	500
Labour	125	225	—	350
Total Output	300	500	350	1150

Input Coefficients or Technology Matrix

In the above input-output table we have taken absolute values of various outputs and inputs hypothetically. Now we can find out input coefficients by applying following formula:

$$a_{ij} = \frac{x_{ij}}{x_j}$$

where, a_{ij} = the amount of output of ith sector required to produce one unit of output of jth sector.

x_{ij} = output of ith sector used in the production of jth sector.

x_j = the total output of jth sector.

Now we construct an input coefficients or technology matrix.

Input Coefficient or Technology Matrix

	A	M		A	M
Agriculture (A)	$\frac{75}{300}$	$\frac{125}{500}$		0.25	0.25
Manufacturing (M)	$\frac{100}{300}$	$\frac{150}{500}$	=	0.33	0.30
Labour (L)	$\frac{125}{300}$	$\frac{225}{500}$		0.42	0.45

The above table indicates that to produce output of Re. 1 in agriculture we need 0.25 rupee worth of its own products, 0.33 rupee worth of manufacturing output and 0.42 rupee worth of labour. Similarly, 0.25 rupee worth of agricultural output, 0.30 rupee worth of industrial output and 0.45 rupee worth of labour are required to produce output of Re. 1 in industry.

Uses of Input-Output Analysis

The basic concept of input-output analysis is utilized for different purposes. Its main uses and applications are discussed below:

1. Integration of economic process: The idea of inter-relationships between various sectors helps both the socialist and the communist countries to integrate the whole economic process into a well coordinated unified system to be managed under the central guidance of national planning body.

2. Precised picture of economic activities: With the help of input-output matrix the statisticians can form a precised picture of the input-output relationship of the whole economic activities. They can maintain in a much smoother flow of products through the various stages of manufacture and distribution to the consumers and to the manufacturers without shortages and surpluses.

3. Consistency in plans: The input-output analysis helps the planner to achieve consistency in plans. If there is any inconsistency in plans, production process and overall growth activity in the country will be hampered. The inter-industry transaction matrix informs the planner of the quantities of various commodities to be needed in future.

4. Usefulness in context of developed and underdeveloped countries: In developed countries the production processes are inter-linked and inter-dependent among various productive units. The idea of input-output relationships is very much helpful in exercising growth and planning.

But in case of underdeveloped countries, a large part of output is either directly consumed or exported. There is very much lack of considerable backward and forward linkages between different sectors. If the planners uses this technique, he will find that so many rooms in the inter-industry transaction matrix are empty. Hence, this technique serves little purpose in case of underdeveloped economy.

5. Simulation purpose: Input-output analysis is used for searching what is economically feasible. This is called simulation purpose. A planner first identifies the input-output technique for simulation purpose. He uses the inter-industry transactions matrix to see the impact of changes of different factors on the various aspects of the economy and also to solve the different problems evolved from this changing. It also helps us to know the repercussions of newly setting up basic industries or the repercussions of the adoption of some protective measures.

6. Information and planning: This model gives us the information about the inter-relationships among various sectors. On the basis of this information, the authority can identify the impact of a change in one sector on all other sectors and make planning accordingly.

7. National economic planning: This input-output analysis is also utilized to make national economic planning. It gives the necessary information to make a framework of planning for economic development.

8. Forecasting: According to **Professor J.K. Mehta**, "Input-output analysis plays an important part in preparing an economic policy for economic forecasting in developed countries and for economic planning (programming) in developing countries."

9. Input-output table in Kerala: P.P. Pillai has prepared an input-output table of industries of Kerala for the year 1964. He identified 24 production sectors. 24 × 24 input-output matrix requires a larger volume of data among which many of these data are not readily available. He concludes that the economy of Kerala is an open economy. It trades with the rest of India and with other countries. The transaction matrix indicates that the main intersectoral forward linkage sectors are paper and paper products, wood and cork, chemicals, basic metal and metal products and electric light and power.

10. Indian Statistical Institute and Central Statistical Organization: The Indian Statistical Institute started some works on all India level in 1950-51. They studied only a limited number of big sectors and prepared a 36 × 36 Transaction matrix in the initial year of the First Five-Year Plan, 1951-52. In 1952, Planning Commission started working on input-output analysis through the Central Statistical Organization (C.S.O.) agency.

Hence, input-output analysis plays a very important role in the economy because of its uses in different fields.

Limitations of Input-Output Analysis

The input-output analysis is very much used in development planning. Despite its obvious advantages, it suffers from the following limitations which restrict its usefulness for development planning:

1. The usefulness of the input-output analysis depends very much on the reliability of input coefficients. The input coefficients are assumed to be constant which restricts the change of technology, the possibility of factor substitution, industry outputs reaching capacity, changing prices and input proportions for the possibilities of increasing output. Again the input coefficients are derived from inter-industry transaction data which are always a few years old. Thus, it has less relevance for further planning.

2. The unit of measurement of different commodities is different. It is difficult to form input coefficients. To avoid this difficulty, money values of different commodities are considered but money values are influenced by the price level in the market. Hence, the fixed input-output coefficients cannot give us the true picture of the economy.
3. This analysis has great importance in industrially advanced countries where inter-industry transactions practices are very rich. But in case of agrarian economies, large part of output is either used to meet final demand or exported. Since inter-industry transactions of these economies are very poor, this analysis is of little use to them.
4. The assumption of constant returns to scale will not be in operation for a long period of time due to change in different factors.
5. The assumption of linear equations makes the ratio of output of one industry to inputs of others. Factors are not always divisible. To increase in output does not always show proportionate increase in inputs. Thus, input coefficients will not remain constant. Hence, this assumption is unrealistic.
6. The input-output analysis fails to consider a note of gestation lag of investment. But it is an essential element in the dynamic process of production.
7. The labour scarcity assumption of this model is quite unrealistic for those countries where labour force is growing very fast.
8. The use of this model is inapplicable for those industries which are producing joint products at a time.
9. The assumptions of fixed prices and fixed consumer demands are not valid in imperfect market.
10. Sectoral division is limited for many practical purposes. Such a sectorisation is not fine enough in the point of view of forecasting.
11. There is no scope for mechanism of price adjustment in this model. It makes this model unrealistic.

EXERCISES

1. What do you mean by linear programming? Explain its important assumptions.
2. Explain how to implement the technique of linear programming approach in the field of production.
3. What are the uses of linear programming? Discuss briefly the limitations of linear programming.
4. Solve the following by graphical method:

(i) Maximize : $z = x_1 - x_2$

Subject to : (i) $-2x_1 + x_2 \leq 0$

$x_1 - 2x_2 \leq 2$

$x_1 + x_2 \leq 5$

(ii) x_1 and $x_2 \geq 0$

Show that $x_1 = 4$ and $x_2 = 1$ is an optimal solution.

(ii) Maximize : $z = 2x + 5y$

Subject to : (i) $x + 4y \leq 24$

$3x + 4y \leq 21$

$x + y \leq 9$

(ii) x and $y \geq 0$

(iii) Minimize : $C = 5x + 4y$

Subject to : (i) $2x + y \geq 1$

$x + 3y \geq 2$

$-x + y \geq 2$

(ii) $x, y \geq 0$

5. A firm can produce two products X and Y. The profits per unit of X and Y are ₹ 5 and ₹ 3 respectively. Production of one unit of X requires 4 Kg of a raw material and one unit of Y requires 3 Kg of that raw material. The supply of raw material is limited to 36,000 Kg. Production of one unit of X takes 4 hours of machining time and 2 hours of assembly-line time while production of one unit of Y takes 10 hours of machining time and 2.5 hours of assembly-line time. 60,000 hours of machine time and

20,000 hours of assembly-line time are available to the firm. Find the number of units at X and Y which the firm can produce within the given limited resources in order to maximize the profit.

6. What do you understand by input-output analysis? Explain its main features and its assumptions.
7. Bring out Leontief's technique of input-output analysis with its limitations.
8. How do you construct the input-output tables? Explain briefly the use of input-output analysis.

References

Agarwal, H.S. (1998), *Advanced Economic Theory*, 9th ed., Konark Pub. Pvt. Ltd., Delhi.

Ahuja, H.L. (2004), *Advanced Economic Theory*, 5th ed., S. Chand & Company Ltd.

Allen, R.G.D. (1967), *Macroeconomic Theory: A Mathematical Treatment*, Macmillan.

Barthwal, R.R. (1991), *Microeconomic Analysis*, Wiley Eastern Ltd., New Delhi.

Bhaduri, S. (2004), *Microeconomics*, 2nd ed., New Central Book Agency (P) Ltd., Kolkata.

Bhargava, B.K. (1994), *Economics*, Sudha Pub. Pvt. Ltd., New Delhi.

Bhatia, H.L. (1976), *Public Finance*, 19th ed., Vikas Pub. House Pvt. Ltd., New Delhi.

Bhattacharyya, H. and Sarkhel, J. (2001), *An Introduction to Managerial Economics*, 3rd ed., Book Syndicate Pvt. Ltd., Kolkata.

Baumol, W.J. (1966), *Economic Theory and Operations Analysis*, 2nd ed., Prentice-Hall of India Pvt. Ltd., New Delhi.

Chiang, A.C. (1984), *Fundamental Methods of Mathematical Economics*, 3rd ed., Megran-Hill Book Company, Auckland.

Dewett, K.K. (1999), *Modern Economic Theory*, 21st ed., Shyamlal Charitable Trust, New Delhi.

Ferguson and Gould (1983), *Microeconomics Theory*, AITBS.

Gould, J.P. and Lazear, E.P. (1996), *Microeconomic Theory*, Richard D. Irwin, INC, Homewood, Illinois.

Hanson, J.L. (1976), *A Textbook of Economics*, 6th ed., The English Language Book Society and Macdonald and Evans Ltd., London.

Henderson, J.M. and Quandt, R.E. (1980), *Micro Economic Theory: A Mathematical Approach*, 3rd ed., McGraw-Hill, Hongkong.

Koutsoyiannis, A. (1979), *Modern Microeconomics*, 2nd ed., Macmillan.

Lipsey, R.G. (1983), *An Introduction to Positive Economics*, ELBS.

Lipsey, R.G. (1989), *An Introduction to Positive Economics*, 7th ed., ELBS, Frome and London.

Mehta, B.C. and Madnani, G.M.K. (2004), *Mathematics for Economists*, 8th ed., Sultan Chand & Sons, New Delhi.

Mukherjee, S. (1996), *Modern Economic Theory*, 3rd ed., Wishwa Prakashan, New Delhi.

Mukherjee, S. (2004), *Economic Principles and Problems*, 3rd ed., New Central Book Agency (P) Ltd., Kolkata.

Rao, S.R.K., *Economics*, Cosmos Bookhive (P) Ltd., New Delhi.

Samuelson, P.A. & Nordhaus (1985), *Economics*, McGraw Hill.

Sankaran, S. (2000), *Micro Economics*, 7th ed., Margham Pub., Chennai.

Sarkhel, J. (2001), *Microeconomic Theory*, Book Syndicate Pvt. Ltd., Kolkata.

Sarkhil, J. and Salim, S. (2003), *Introductory Economics*, 1st ed., Bengal Book Syndicate (P) Ltd., Kolkata.

Varian, H.R. (1987), *Intermediate Microeconomics: A Modern Approach*, 4th ed., EWP.

Yamane, T. (1998), *Mathematics for Economics*, 2nd ed., Prentice-Hall of India, New Delhi.

Index